Quiltmaking
in America
Beyond the Myths

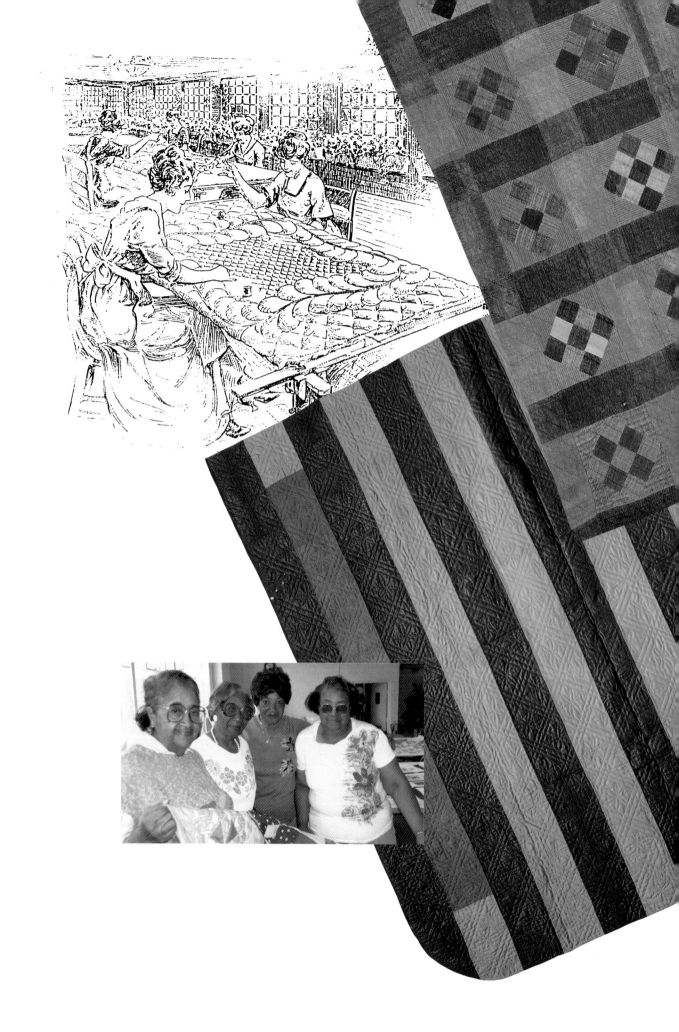

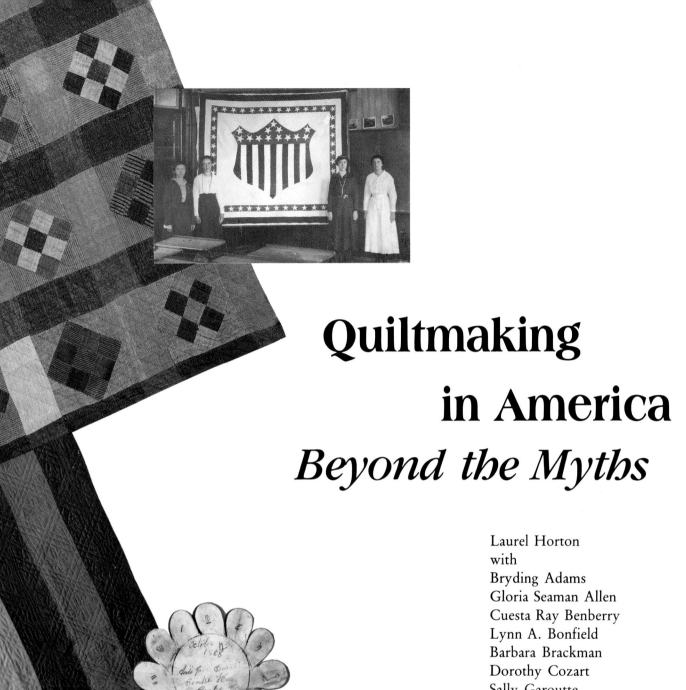

Quiltmaking
in America
Beyond the Myths

Laurel Horton
with
Bryding Adams
Gloria Seaman Allen
Cuesta Ray Benberry
Lynn A. Bonfield
Barbara Brackman
Dorothy Cozart
Sally Garoutte
Joyce Gross
Virginia Gunn
Tandy Hersh
Erma H. Kirkpatrick
Suellen Meyer
Joyce B. Peaden
Bets Ramsey
Wilene Smith
Merikay Waldvogel

Foreword by Jean Ray Laury

Rutledge Hill Press
Nashville, Tennessee

Published in Nashville, Tennessee, by Rutledge Hill Press, Inc. 211 Seventh Avenue North, Nashville, Tennessee 37219. Distributed in Canada by H. B. Fenn and Company, Ltd., 1090 Lorimar Drive, Mississauga, Ontario L5S 1R7.

Editing: Laurel Horton
Design: Karelis & Timm and Jeannette Lasansky
Typography: D&T/Bailey, Inc., Nashville, TN
Printed in Hong Kong through Palace Press International

Gratis materials have been provided by Barbara Brackman, Cuesta Ray Benberry, Dorothy Cozart, Virginia Gunn, Tandy Hersh, Laurel Horton, Erma H. Kirkpatrick, Suellen Meyer, Joyce B. Peaden, Bets Ramsey, Wilene Smith, Kathy Sullivan, and Merikay Waldvogel as well as from the Birmingham Museum of Art, the Bolton Museum and Art Gallery, Cabin Creek Quilters, the Goschenhoppen Historians, the Heritage Quilt Project of New Jersey, Inc., MAFCE, the Maryland Historical Society, the Ohio Quilt Research Group, the Oral Traditions Project, the North Carolina Quilt Project, Quilts of Tennessee, the Shelburne Museum, and the Wichita-Sedgwick County Historical Society.

Institutions that have waived their publication fee or given the American Quilt Study Group a reduced rate are the Chester County Historical Society, the Mercer Museum of the Bucks County Historical Society, the Philadelphia Museum of Art, and Joel and Kate Kopp at America Hurrah, New York.

Title Page (clockwise from upper left): Illustration from the *Wilkinson Art Quilt*, published by the Wilkinson Sisters, Ligonier, Indiana, 1921, Mildred Dickerson Collection owned by Merikay Waldvogel; Linsey quilt, maker unknown, 79″ x 63¼″. Collection of Jerry Ledbetter. Courtesy of Quilts of Tennessee; real-photo postcard circa 1910, collection of the Oral Traditions Project; "1868" paper quilt template from Centre County, Pennsylvania, collection of Louise Reish; Bar quilt of Brush family glazed wool counterpane from, Jericho, Vermont. Thirteen strips each 7″ wide, 98½″ x 96¾″ wool plain weave back in three panels 27¼″–35″ wide. Filled with thin layer of wool and quilted with 9–10 stitches per inch. Collection of the Shelburne Museum (#10-714). Courtesy of the Shelburne Museum; from left to right: Mattie Porter, Idell Townsend, Ann Fisher, and Ethel Daniel admire Mattie's Star Quilt at the Senior Neighbors in Chattanooga, Tennessee, 1993. Courtesy of Bets Ramsey.

Quoted material found in the text contains original grammar, punctuation, and spelling.

Library of Congress Cataloging-in-Publication Data

Quiltmaking in America : beyond the myths : selected writings from the American Quilt Study Group / [edited by] Laurel Horton with Bryding Adams . . . [et. al.] ; foreword by Jean Ray Laury.
    p.   cm.
    Includes index.
    ISBN 1-55853-319-2
    1. Quilts—United States.   2. Quilting—United States.
  I. Horton, Laurel. II. Uncoverings. III. American Quilt Study Group.
NK9112.Q53 1994
746.46′0973—dc20
                                            94-22315
                                            CIP

To Winifred Sharp Reddall (1919–94), a charter member of American Quilt Study Group, whose generous support made this volume possible.

Her husband, Henry, tells us during her last days she loved to have him read to her, and he assures us, "When this book is published, it will be read to her every last page. She will be thrilled."

Contents

Textiles And Tools

Among the important influences on the ways women made quilts were the availability and cost of fabric and major shifts in textile technology. These chapters examine the quilts that were influenced by these changes.

Many Hands: Group Quilting

Quilters of the nineteenth and early twentieth centuries discovered the means for economic empowerment through the use of their needles, whether to support themselves or to raise money for a cause.

Shifting Functions: Quiltmakers in the Twentieth Century

The twentieth century has witnessed the recognition of individual quilters as artists, the expansion of quilting events from a local to a larger audience, and the shift from making quilts solely as bedcovers to a greater emphasis on the reflection of personal achievement.

Foreword

Jean Ray Laury

When making my first quilt in the 1950s, I was told by a somewhat haughty department store clerk that there was no such thing as quilting thread. I decided then I'd better find a quilter who could guide me. I was in graduate school, which was not a hotbed of quilting, and those I asked seemed totally mystified. After a dozen dead ends, I was ultimately referred to a woman who quilted for her church. What excitement! I'd found another quilter. I needed guidance on how to actually quilt the piece I was doing as part of my master's project.

That contact marked, for me, the beginning of networking—the opportunity to exchange with another quilter information of mutual interest. It offered access to information not available through known sources, and included observations, opinions, and intuitive responses that crisscrossed with one's own. It continued the tradition of sharing among quilters. Today, the tradition of networking is a vital part of the American Quilt Study Group (AQSG).

The decade of research represented by this book is a highly significant

one. Changes within any ten-year period may be great, but for quilt research, the years 1980 to 1989 were particularly spectacular and impressive. The changes included not only a great surge in the numbers of research projects undertaken, but an escalation of standards and scholarship. Evidence found in documents, commentary, and records was under careful scrutiny, along with the re-examination of quilts, fabrics, and patterns. The narratives and portrayals that emerged were more compelling than the myths they sometimes replaced. Much of the intense and spirited interchange of information and ideas was made possible through the AQSG, which provided both a nucleus and a structure for this exchange.

Parallel to this change in emphasis has been the great proliferation of quilting books. While this reflects widespread interest in quiltmaking, the books themselves may pose difficulties if inaccurate or incomplete information is given. AQSG, through its networking, publications, and conferences, has set new standards of excellence that influence and stimulate all areas of quilt interest and publications.

AQSG has also significantly expanded the contextual base of quilt studies. The chapters in this book, for example, represent a full spectrum of quilting interests: quilting cooperatives, fundraising quilts, research on individual quiltmakers, African-

American quilters, quilts related to national conflicts, information from primary sources, as well as studies of cotton mills and sewing machines. As a collection, they clarify the degree to which quiltmaking permeates almost every aspect of daily life.

Writing and research now are in many ways easier than ten years ago. There are more sources available, worldwide, in books, catalogs, and collections. But in other ways, both are more difficult. There was a time when *any* information was welcomed openly. Now the material must be authentic and accurate, knowledgeable and critical, with sources or corroboration to separate verifiable information from stories. The resources have expanded and the responsibility is greater.

The cumulative efforts of quilt research are exemplified by the variety and richness of this publication. The evidence of meticulous investigation in each article strengthens and enriches the solid base upon which further research is dependent. Each area of inquiry adds a new facet, expanding and enhancing our view in the same way that quilt patterns change from varying perspectives. We look at a tiny bit of the quilt puzzle and we have a Tumbling Block. With more pieces, a star emerges. Each piece that is added contributes to our seeing the whole field of stars. The small, seemingly insignificant details of research mesh in this same way to offer a fuller context and a more complete picture.

The American Quilt Study Group extends to us the ultimate publication, an unparalleled collection of ideas, observations, wisdom, scholarship, and lore. We will all find our views profoundly affected and expanded by this remarkable publication.

Preface

Laurel Horton

In November 1980, fifty people gathered at the Ralston-White Center in Mill Valley, California, for the first American Quilt Study Group (AQSG) Seminar. Brought together by a shared interest in an accurate history of quilts, quiltmakers, and textiles, these participants recognized the need for an organization that would foster and promote original research on American quiltmaking.

The gathering included pattern collectors, quilt collectors, authors, design artists, museum curators, and quiltmakers. But the one person responsible for channelling the interest and enthusiasm into a workable organization was Sally Garoutte.

For the first eight years following the initial seminar, Sally Garoutte ran the organization from her home in Mill Valley. Requisitioning the family dining room for an office and library, Sally maintained membership records (in that nearly forgotten era before the personal computer), collected quilt-related publications, planned the annual seminar, and provided personalized responses to members and others. Because there was no other published forum through which quilt research was available to the public, Sally taught herself book publication and *Uncoverings* was born.

The first volumes, modest in appearance with plain covers and black-and-white illustrations, could hardly compete visually with the colorful how-to quilt books that appeared in response to the swell of interest in quilts in the early 1980s. However, a growing number of readers had begun to question the validity of much of the historical background presented in the majority of quilt publications. Once a critical number of these discerning readers discovered *Uncoverings*, the course of quilt research was changed forever.

The foremost quality that Sally brought to her work as editor was an insistence on accuracy rather than a reliance on the erroneous assumptions proposed by early writers and repeatedly quoted as fact by later authors. Additionally, she served as a mentor for a generation of quilt researchers. During her tenure she encouraged and supported the work of both academically trained and self-trained scholars.

Sally Garoutte died of cancer in 1989. She did not live to see the second decade of the organization that she fostered. The volumes of *Uncoverings* that Sally edited are a testament to her commitment to excellence and her belief in the significance of quiltmaking as a key to understanding the history of American women. All future generations of quilt scholars owe a debt to Sally's vision, although many will never realize to what extent. As one of those who benefitted from my association with Sally, I was pleased to succeed her as editor of *Uncoverings* for volumes 1987–93.

Quiltmaking in America: Beyond the Myths celebrates the first decade of the publication of *Uncoverings*, 1980–89. This volume contains a selection of research papers from those years, which remain vital and important today. Some have been revised or updated, and all appear with new illustrations.

The world of quilt research in the 1990s is different from the one in which Sally carved out a niche for the American Quilt Study Group. Quilt documentation projects, most of them conducted with guidance from AQSG members, have collected and published volumes of region-specific quilt research. Universities increasingly support quilt-related topics for graduate research degrees. And AQSG supports its growing membership from a professionally staffed office in San Francisco. *Uncoverings*, still the most vital reference for current research in its field, is now housed in libraries internationally and is included in a half-dozen or more scholarly indexes.

Uncoverings remains a comparatively modest annual volume in visual terms, but its contents continue to be on the cutting edge. *Quiltmaking in America: Beyond the Myths* contains a sampling of the research articles found in the annual volumes, but in a visually enhanced format that will delight all who love quilts and the stories behind them. We hope you enjoy this book, and we invite you to join us in the American Quilt Study Group as we continue our efforts in the twenty-first century.

The 1842 Primitive Hall Pieced Quilt Top

The Art of Transforming Printed Fabric Designs through Geometry

Tandy Hersh

Primitive Hall quilt top, pieced cotton, linen, and silk with paper templates, 66" square, 1842–43. Collection of the Chester County Historical Society, West Chester, Pennsylvania. Courtesy of Winterthur Museum.

Quilt block 3c. This ink drawing documents the quilt geographically by illustrating the Pennock house in West Marlborough Township, Chester County. It is inscribed "1738," which is when Joseph Pennock built the house. By 1842, when the quilt top was made, the original pent roof had been removed and replaced by a porch over the front door and an adjacent window. The signature of the artist, Isabella P. Lukens, is in the tree trunk to the right. Courtesy of Tandy Hersh.

Primitive Hall, a house in Chester County, Pennsylvania, is the ancestral home of the Pennock family. In 1842 and 1843, women in this Quaker family made a quilt top now referred to as the Primitive Hall quilt top or the Pennock Album quilt top. The word "primitive" usually calls to mind artifacts that are archaic, naive, or made without the benefit of sophisticated skills. These associations are not appropriate for this pieced album quilt top made for Sarah Wistar Pennock because it shows inventive artistry through three unusual aspects: documentation, geometry, and planned use of fabric.

Similarly, the house built by Joseph Pennock in 1738 should not be considered primitive. Joseph Pennock was born in Clonmel, Ireland, and lived in Killhouse, his affluent maternal grandfather's home, until he came to Philadelphia in 1700. In contrast to that Irish estate his American house was, perhaps to him, a primitive residence. By American standards, though, the brick house was a fine colonial home for Pennock, the prominent local justice and representative to the Pennsylvania Assembly. Examples of the quality of the house include the Flemish bond brick pattern, the pent roof, panelled wainscot over the mantel and up the stairs, chair rails, and ornamented ceilings. A pen-and-ink drawing of Primitive Hall is the center block of the quilt top. The house is in rural West Marlborough Township, very near the London Grove Quaker Meeting House where Joseph Pennock attended meetings.

Tandy Hersh is a textile researcher. In addition to several scholarly articles on quilting, she co-authored Samplers of the Pennsylvania Germans *and published articles on their embroidered aprons, handkerchiefs, and quilted pillowcases. 1860 Walnut Bottom Road, Carlisle, PA 17013.*

Documentation

The quilt top contains the type of documentation that every quilt researcher would like to find. The names of a married couple, Caspar Wistar Pennock and Caroline Morris Pennock, and those of their grandparents, parents, brothers, and sisters are given in one block. Also in this genealogical block (1c) are the date the quilt top was made, 1842, and the information that Caspar Wistar Pennock gave the quilt top to his two-year-old daughter Sarah Wistar Pennock. All of this family history is in freehand calligraphy in indelible ink and is drawn to appear as pages of an open book and as the spine of a second book. The Pennocks' marriage date is written below the books.

The ink drawing of Primitive Hall includes its location, the date it was built, the builder's name, and the signature of the artist. A third block (5c) contains the Pennock coat of arms and the name of Caspar's father George, who died in 1799, the year Caspar was born.[1]

Names found in the pieced signature blocks are of the Pennock side of the family, either with that last name or the married names of Caspar's female relatives. One block (2c) contains his mother's name, S. Pennock, for Sarah Wistar Pennock, and also gives her age, seventy-two, and her political preference. A log cabin and hard cider barrel are drawn above her name indicating she was a Whig, a supporter of William Henry Harrison and John Tyler in the 1842 presidential campaign.[2] None of Caroline Morris Pennock's family provided signature blocks for the quilt. The makers of the quilt had a special interest in Primitive Hall through their family connections, and must have wanted Caspar's baby daughter, who lived then with her parents in Philadelphia, to have the same special interest in her father's family home.

Geometry

When the Pennocks designed this album quilt top, sixty-six inches square, with twenty-five blocks, a wide variety of published quilt block patterns probably was not available, according to Virginia Gunn's study of American periodicals.[3] However, if one begins with a twelve-inch square of paper representing the block size in the quilt top, and has a straightedge, ruler, compass, and pencil, one can draw all of the geometric designs found in this top. The concept and drawing techniques essential to the designs were taught in the Society of Friends' Westtown School near Primitive Hall.

One design (1a) is based on a small central square that is surrounded by larger squares, each having sides of a standard additional width until a twelve-by-twelve-inch block is achieved by these "concentric" squares. Another way of using the central square is to construct a larger square on its diagonals (4e). This process is continued to complete a pattern of "rotated" squares. Some four-pointed stars (1d, 2c, 2d) are constructed with their points at the midpoints of the sides of the twelve-by-twelve-inch square and others (1b, 2c, 2d, 4d, 5c, 5e) with their points on the diagonals of the block. These stars are combined to form one eight-pointed star (1e) having four short and four long points in one of the design blocks. When combining these stars with squares and circles, added variations are obtained by deciding which figure should be on top or be dominant.

Stars with points of the same length are also constructed, one with six (3a), one with eight (2b), and one with ten points (2c). The ultimate in combining stars with squares appears in a block (2d) that has five "rotated" squares with four four-pointed "rotated" stars.

Circles provide the central figure in five of the blocks, none alike. One (3b) begins with a central circle and adds three concentric circles, each with a radius of a standard increase over the first. Another (3d) is made in the same fashion, but is segmented eight times and pieced to produce an

a   *b*   *c*   *d*   *e*

1   *2*   *3*   *4*   *5*

Diagram of the quilt top. Horizontal rows are numbered; vertical rows are lettered. The empty block, 2e, is a single piece of chintz. Courtesy of Tandy Hersh.

effect somewhat like Japanese Imari patterns found in porcelain. A sixteen-sided figure (4c), about the same size as the circles, although not a circle, is pieced concentrically and has a circular effect. Intersecting circles (3e) are used in one block to form a well-balanced and intriguing pattern.

Octagonal figures are used as background in five blocks (1d, 2c, 4b, 4d, 5b). Another block (5a) almost defies description. The designer must have established a grid system with one-inch blocks and drawn in most of the diagonals of these blocks. Then, by deciding which squares or triangles to combine in a piece, a pattern of intersecting ribbons and contrasting squares was produced. A similar method was probably used to design other blocks (4a, 5d). The design in another block (4b) is an arrangement of irregular shapes laid out in a cir-

cular form. All pieces radiate from the central point of the square, and three different four- and five-sided shapes ring the central ink design.

Planned Use of Fabric
The precise placement of fabric designs on each part of the geometric design is the third outstanding feature of this quilt top. This systematic use of fabric repeats of flowers, stripes, and other figures from calico or chintz creates new designs that enhance the geometric shapes. Throughout the twenty-two geometric blocks, nineteen are ornamented by skillful cutting to use pattern repeats. For example, the regular, eight-pointed star (2b) has been ornamented by cutting the fabric to center an identical floral pattern in each point of the star.[4] This, with the ribbon-like outline or border for each point, completes the design and adds

The block with Caspar Pennock's mother's name and age, "S. Pennock Aged 72," is the most complex block because of its ten-sided center. The striped fabric was cut using a paper template with four irregular sides. Two of these pieces were needed on each of the ten sides. Although the effect is of a swirling circle, the geometric shape is a twenty-sided figure.

The front of the block shows in detail the precision achieved with the English piecing method. Courtesy of Tandy Hersh.

The back of the block shows the seams and permits one to count the 70 pieces required for this twelve-inch block. The paper templates, all still in place, help the viewer understand the block's construction. Courtesy of Winterthur Museum.

interest to the shape and color. A more complicated problem was to take a printed ornamental chain (3b), possibly arranged in a large circle or ellipse in the original print, and cut thirteen pieces to produce a circular band of a different, smaller circumference. The artist succeeded in creating the appearance of a continuous, unbroken chain. Patches of varying sizes were cut to obtain this effect. At their intersections very slight discrepancies in the form of the links show how intricate a solution was required.

Perhaps the finest example is the block signed "S. Pennock Aged 72" (2c). Seven different printed fabrics are used in this block. The inner decagon border is an overall small dark print. Attached to it is a ten-pointed star with an identical small paisley motif centered in each point. Triangles cut from a floral fabric surround this star. The block's twenty-sided circular figure took the most skill because its fabric is a stripe turned to create a feeling of motion. Two irregular-sided pieces were cut to make the stripe fit each facet of the outer decagon. The two four-pointed stars of this block are ornamented with a larger paisley motif on one and a tiny floral motif on the other. The octagon joining these stars is made from a small floral print in a receding color, which provides a background for the dominant stars. This use of receding and dominant colors to accent particular geometric forms is a characteristic of this quilt top.

Assembly and Ink Work

The precision involved in the geometry and fabric design placement was achieved through the use of paper templates.[5] This technique of piecing provides a means of creating and controlling designs for each block limited only by the ability to draw the design on paper. As we see in this quilt top, it also provides the opportunity to arrange the printed cloth on the paper template in such a way that these fabric designs may be employed in the

total composition. As with all methods there are some "costs." This English method of piecing uses more cloth; the cutting and basting are more time-consuming; and the whipping requires more closely spaced stitches.

In an album quilt each signer can make a block or a block can be made by several people; for instance, a designer, a piecer, and the person who does the calligraphy. A study of the back of this quilt top with the paper templates still in place reveals clues to the number of makers of the Primitive Hall quilt top.

First, the paper is not all the same quality or color. Most is heavy, supple, and cream colored. Two blocks are made on different textured, caramel-colored paper, and one block has two pieces of thin, lined paper in it.

Second, there is no uniformity in the information written on the paper. Some blocks have no markings of any kind. Some have penciled numbers and some inked numbers to assist in the assembly. Others have the word "white" or "buff" on certain pieces. One has the penciled words "white," "dark," and "light" in appropriate places. One has "R W" (right white) and "L Wh" (left white). Several have the word "white" and the words "Mark the donor's name in durable ink" centered on the back of the signature area. For these blocks it is possible that the donor did not participate in the construction. Blocks with this marking are among the most difficult to execute, yet other difficult blocks, for instance the one by Sarah Wistar Pennock (age seventy-two) and the block with interlocking circles, have no writing on the back.

The third observation concerns the stitching. The method of making basting stitches varies widely among blocks, from one stitch per inch up to six. The basting threads most often are cotton but occasionally are silk. The whipping or overcasting is done with closely placed stitches and is carefully sewn throughout, but there

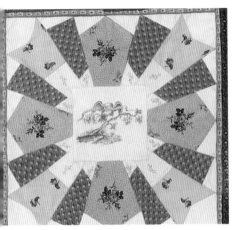

The English method of piecing facilitates the location of identical motifs from the printed fabric on each like piece. The fabric is not cut to maximize the number of pieces, rather, many pattern repeats are necessary to cut identical motifs. The Primitive Hall quiltmakers combined this use of fabric motifs with their knowledge of geometry to create their blocks.

1d. The piecing materials for the five rotated squares set in a four-pointed star surrounded by an octagon in this block give the illusion of a three-dimensional object.

2d. Four rotated squares alternate with four rotated four-pointed stars in this block. Its red, yellow, and gray colors balance with 4b.

4b. It is more difficult to see the geometric forms from which this block was constructed because the quilt pieces do not follow completely any one of the geometric forms. From the center were drawn: a square, a four-pointed star, two rotated octagons, and a four-pointed star that extends beyond the block. Quilt pieces were shaped by selecting intersections of the sides of these figures.

5a. There are 101 pieces in this block, and some of the brown fabric in the ribbon star motif is pieced in order to have a uniform concentration of flowers in the ribbon. Different size squares, rectangles, and triangles—some rotated—are used to form these pieces. The overall appearance follows the star and diamond pattern of early Pennsylvania-German woven coverlets. *Courtesy of Tandy Hersh.*

are differences in execution. Some stitches are evenly spaced, while others are so closely spaced that the threads pile up on each other.

Fourth, the seam allowance varies from block to block, and fifth, one block has a white signature area where double the amount of fabric needed was cut but never trimmed.

Although this quilt top does not contain any block made by a beginning piecer, the expertly constructed blocks reflect differing abilities. These differences from block to block support a conclusion that several different expert needleworkers sewed the blocks.

The freehand ink work also shows different levels of skill, though all the ink work is done on tightly woven, unwashed linen. The genealogical listings are contoured artistically to fit the curved pages of an open book. The penmanship in this block has the characteristics of engraving, that is, every letter is given measured spacing. Some block signatures are made with

the same measured spacing and are by the same hand. The rendering of the house, the legend below the house, and the artist's signature, Isabella P. Lukens, are less precise than the engraving style. The drawing is made of many light ink strokes that make a sepia-colored picture. That sepia quality is found in other drawings, for example, a dog retrieving a stick. There is a bolder, more assertive hand that achieves a stronger line and develops a deeper density of ink with fewer strokes illustrated in a cornucopia, a log cabin with a cider barrel, and a flag topped with a liberty cap. An amateurish hand drew small ornamentations: oak leaves, acorns, birds, and pennants.

Quaker Schools

Quaker schools for girls and boys were organized in Pennsylvania in the late eighteenth century. Early nineteenth-century records of the Westtown School, established in 1799 in Chester County, contain informa-

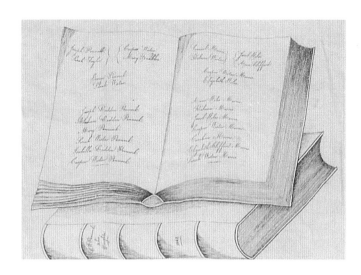

tion on the subjects offered and scheduling of classes. The materials in the Chester County Historical Society Library include: names of students; their workbooks (penmanship, essay or "piece" books, mathematics or "cipher" books, geometric measurement or "mensuration" books); and other materials such as autograph or album books, teachers' diaries, and student letters to parents and friends.[6]

Girls attended the same classes as boys but their schedules were arranged to provide two weeks of sewing classes in every six-week period. Sewing classes included instruction in plain sewing, care and mending of clothes, darning, and making samplers.[7] In addition to these sewing skills, the girls learned to make silk terrestrial globes. Carefully cut segments of silk were fashioned into solid spheres, a task in itself, but to make the effort more valuable, latitude and longitude lines were embroidered on the spheres and the geographic features were inked in by hand to become the earth. Creating

these globes provided practical work in drawing geometric forms.

In calligraphy and penmanship classes girls worked with ink on cloth. Ink block lettering and elaborate writing taught in class were used to copy quotations from classical scholars in the album books exchanged at year's end. In every course an attempt was made to apply principles to everyday problems and to integrate learning across the courses.

With this education many Quaker girls would have developed the skills necessary to design and sew intricate blocks in a quilt and do the ink art work and penmanship found on the quilt under study. At school, boys had training in surveying, trigonometry, and astronomy.[8] Therefore, within the Quaker families there was technical help available to free quilt designers from dependence on copying.

Design History
Quilters have a series of artistic decisions to make when designing a quilt.

These decisions are similar to those a painter must make when designing a painting. For example, the painter must decide what size and shape the canvas will be. The size and shape of the quilter's "canvas" are determined by the dimensions of the bed, plus the necessary side and end allowances. Considerations of traditional versus innovative design, choice of medium, geometric proportions, dominant and recessive areas through strong contrasts or subtle color harmony, and framing control the finished painting or quilt. Of course the painter and quilt designer are influenced by time and place, and the product becomes a part of the material culture of the society in which it is created and used.

In historical sequence, wholecloth, chintz appliqué, and early block quilts preceded the 1842 Primitive Hall quilt top. In a wholecloth quilt the canvas is two or three lengths of the same solid or printed fabric sewn together to make one overall quilt top. The ornamentation is the large-scale quilted design that produces contrasts in the quilted texture. Geometric considerations are limited to the shape of the bed itself and to the type and placement of quilting designs.

In a chintz appliqué quilt the canvas is a neutral background cloth ornamented with appliqué. Decorative motifs are cut from a variety of printed fabrics and sewn onto the background in a new creative placement. Borders, central medallion, color contrasts, and design contrasts are added to the quilted ornamentation found in wholecloth quilts. Geometry is variously involved in this process to center some designs, outline or separate others, to form borders, or to balance the composition.

Subdividing the quilter's "canvas" into a network of squares, diamonds, hexagons, or other grid systems introduces additional possibilities for natural and geometric ornamentation in pieced and appliqué quilts. If the units of the grid are quite small, the overall effect is directed to how they ornament the whole bed. However, as in the Primitive Hall quilt top, if a small number of larger grid blocks is used, especially with sashing, the eye is directed to the contents of each block and then to the way they fit into the general composition. The Primitive Hall quilt top "canvas" contains twenty-five different blocks, each twelve inches square and framed by rather narrow sashing. The blocks with genealogy, house drawing, and family coat of arms are centered vertically but are separated by two large circular blocks. Plain and geometrically complex blocks are placed to balance the overall design. The viewer's interest within these blocks centers on the "message" conveyed by the geometric figures, the chintz motifs, the ink designs, and the donors' names.

Examples of Technique

The innovative and patient twentieth-century quilt artist, the late Averil Colby, has taken us a step beyond the Primitive Hall quilt top technique. She borrowed the concept of free-form design from chintz appliqué quilting and applied it to create free-form designs using a piecing technique that relied on careful selection of pieces from printed fabrics. An interesting illustration is the way Colby created a large floral wreath for the center of a quilt.[9] If she had found a large wreath printed on fabric she could have cut it out as one large motif for appliquéing, but instead she drew a free-form wreath on paper, then laid a grid of three-quarter-inch paper hexagon templates over the drawing to guide the piecing. She composed the wreath from forms and colors cut from many floral printed fabrics. She covered each small hexagon template with its carefully selected fragment of the whole design. One rose might be made of several hexagons with parts of the petals on each. She built her flowers as though working in chintz appliqué technique but was constantly restricted by the geometric piecing templates. Colby's

Opposite: 1c. The names of the paternal and maternal grandparents, parents, and children in Caspar Wistar Pennock's family are written on the left page of an open book. The relatives of his wife, Caroline Morris, are written on the right page. The words are contoured to fit the perspective of an open book. Information that the quilt top was given to Caspar Pennock for his two-year-old daughter Sarah Wistar Pennock is on the spine of a second book. The marriage date of Caspar and Caroline is written below the two books: "December 17th, 1833."

2b. The liberty cap and flag were symbols of freedom in the American Revolution. At the time this quilt top was made, the liberty cap could have been a symbol of freedom for slaves, a cause of members of the Society of Friends in the abolitionist Liberty Party.

2c. "Log Cabin and Hard Cider" was the Whig Party slogan in the 1840 Harrison-Tyler presidential campaign and victory. We can assume that this was the political preference of Caspar Wistar Pennock's mother, Sarah Wistar Pennock, who was born in 1770.

3b. The ink drawing of Christ calming the wind and waves is very small, under two inches square. Comparison of free-hand script letters and pen strokes used in the drawings indicates the hand of more than one artist. Ink work was done in "durable" (indelible) ink, a term found on paper templates on the back of the quilt top, "White with the donor's name in durable ink." Courtesy of Tandy Hersh.

way of working with chintz motifs to enhance her quilts is extraordinary. She bought bolts of material and cut out tiny hexagon-shaped designs throughout the entire bolt.[10] The ideas expressed and the methods used in the Primitive Hall quilt top need not be taken to that exquisite extreme to be useful to today's quilters.

Eighteenth- and nineteenth-century chintz appliqué, the nineteenth-century Primitive Hall quilt top, and Colby's twentieth-century designs are related in technique. Chintz appliqué is completely free-form in the sense that any printed fabric motif or part of a motif can be cut out and applied to a background cloth to create an original design. The Primitive Hall quilt top's paper templates form a controlled geometric shape, but there is freedom in choosing what printed fabric motif to place within each template to create further designs. Averil Colby's work sets up two constraints: (1) the choice of a geometric template controls the shape of each piece, and (2) the artist's free-form drawing determines what fabric motifs will be cut and placed on the templates. All three methods deal with selecting printed fabric motifs as an additional way to ornament a quilt.

Other quilters have used these techniques. An eighteenth-century English quilt illustrates that Colby's technique was used very early in England and that some of the earliest work was the most exquisite.[11] This quilt has the appearance of the complex marquetry from which it was copied, because the maker's husband was a cabinetmaker dealing in ornate inlaid woodwork. Each quilt piece is formed from plain or printed fabric just right for each paper template of the design. The overall effect is one of geometric perfection. Similar piecing was used elsewhere in Europe. In the early nineteenth century a Netherlands quilt employed hexagons with centered floral designs using pieces cut from floral chintz patterns.[12] In each of these quilts, separated in time and place from Primitive Hall, the

quilt's design impact was heightened by the planned use of fabric motifs.

Caspar Wistar Pennock's Quaker family members had the opportunity to study under English sewing teachers and respected mathematics and calligraphy instructors in the Society of Friends' Pennsylvania schools.

The Pennock coat of arms has three wren heads, three scallops, and at the crest a clothed arm with a hand holding a wren. At the lower left of this ink drawing is the name "G. Pennock," for Caspar's father George Pennock. Courtesy of Tandy Hersh.

Their social status gave them access to fine chintz household furnishing fabric and dress material. Their interest in commemorating their family heritage, which centered on the Pennock house, led them to a group project. Combining their skills, they created an imaginative quilt top. As they planned how to enhance the geometric shapes, careful selection and placement of motifs transformed the printed fabric motifs into new relationships.

Notes and References

[1] George Valentine Massey II, *The Pennocks of Primitive Hall* (West Chester, PA: Chester County Historical Society, 1951).

[2] Joseph B. Hudson, Jr., "Banks, Politics, Hard Cider, and Paint," *The Metropolitan Museum Journal* 10 (New York: Metropolitan Museum, 1975), 107–18.

[3] Virginia Gunn, "Victorian Silk Template Patchwork in American Periodicals 1850–1875," *Uncoverings 1983*, ed. Sally Garoutte. (Mill Valley, CA: American Quilt Study Group, 1984), 9–25.

[4] Locate square in diagram and then examine same square in photograph.

[5] Averil Colby, *Patchwork* (New York: Scribner's, 1982), 164–75; Beth Gutcheon, *The Perfect Patchwork Primer* (New York: Penguin, 1974), 159–60.

[6] Chester County Pennsylvania Historical Society, Manuscript and Vault Files for Westtown School: Student workbooks, e.g., Alice Hallowell's "Copy and Ciphering Book," George Sharpless's "Mensuration Book 1824," "Samuel M. Painter's Book 1823," and Ann Elisabeth Pennock's "Autograph Album."

[7] Watson W. and Sarah B. Dewees, *History of Westtown Boarding School 1799–1899* (Philadelphia: Sherman, 1899), 45, 65–69.

[8] Helen G. Hole, *Westtown Through the Years* (Westtown, PA: Westtown Alumni Assoc., 1942), 75–77.

[9] Colby, 155.

[10] Interview and correspondence with Shiela Betterton, textile and needlework specialist, the American Museum in Britain, Bath, England.

[11] Averil Colby, *Patchwork Quilts* (New York: Scribner's, 1965), 34–35.

[12] An Moonen, *Quilts, the Dutch Tradition* (Arnhem: the Netherlands Open Air Museum, 1992), 64.

Primitive Hall as it appears today. In contrast to the drawing in block 3c, the restored Flemish bond brick house has its original pent roof between the first and second levels. Its external colonial architectural features are consistent with the restored interior panelling, chair rails, and ornamented ceilings. Courtesy of Tandy Hersh.

Signature Quilts

Nineteenth-Century Trends

Barbara Brackman

Over the past twenty-five years, researchers in the fields of folklore, anthropology, and cultural geography have studied pattern in surviving nineteenth-century artifacts to determine the history and origins of American culture. By tracing the diffusion of innovations such as the banjo, gravestone motifs, and agricultural practices, inferences can be drawn about cultural influences. Backtracking along paths of diffusion has pinpointed four major points of origin for American cultural traditions: the New England area (New York/Boston), the Midland Zone (the valleys of the Susquehanna and Delaware rivers in eastern Pennsylvania and western New Jersey), the Chesapeake Bay region (near Baltimore), and the Southern Coast (from North Carolina to Georgia).[1]

Domestic architecture has been a popular subject for analysis since Fred B. Kniffen advocated using folk housing to reconstruct diffusion routes of material culture in 1965. He proposed that scholars identify and classify artifacts according to type and plot the types through time and space, geographical methods that allow interpretation of origins, dissemination routes, and the diffusion of a culture.[2] Using Kniffen's methods, Terry G. Jordan and Matti Kaups mapped dogtrot or open-passage folk housing throughout the United States and Europe, finding Finnish origins for this backwoods house rather than the purely British influence that had been suggested in the past.[3]

Folk housing, such as the dogtrot cabin, the shotgun house, or the Colonial Revival house, has several advantages for study. Buildings are diverse yet classifiable according to form. They are durable, and they usually remain where they were built, giving later observers the opportunity to map their occurrence and draw conclusions about settlement patterns and changes in style.

Barbara Brackman *writes about quilts for popular and scholarly publications. She is a former board member of the American Quilt Study Group. Her books include* Encyclopedia of Pieced Quilt Patterns *and* Clues in the Calico: A Guide to Identifying and Dating Antique Quilts. *621 West Galer St., Apt. 105, Seattle WA 98119.*

Sampler album quilt of pieced and appliqué print and white cottons, made in Swedesboro, Glouster County, New Jersey. Stamps, signatures, and dates from 1842–43 in ink. Bound with Trenton tape and quilted in tan thread. Collection of Marjorie R. Brooks. Courtesy of the Heritage Quilt Project of New Jersey.

Quilts are similar in that they are diverse yet classifiable. They are durable. Despite their apparent fragility thousands of nineteenth-century examples remain. But unlike buildings, quilts do not often endure in the spot where they were made. Their portability and practicality made quilts and bedding among the few household items that nineteenth-century migrants were encouraged to take with them on the road west.[4] The difficulty in determining exactly where an emigrant's quilt was made renders many of them useless for studying regional differences in quilt design or for studying patterns of migration and culture.

Signature quilts, however, are one type of quilt that can be analyzed using the methods Kniffen advocated for the study of folk housing. Signature quilts are group projects in which each block is sewn or signed by a different person. The finished quilt might be presented as a gift or kept by the organizer as a tangible reminder of friends and relatives.

The makers of signature quilts often recorded not only their names but also their homes and the dates on the piece, so no matter where their current locations, the quilts reveal their origins in inked or embroidered inscriptions. Many of those without inscribed place names are accompanied by reliable family histories passed down with the quilt. Because a signature quilt contains records of several people, rather than of an individual, origins can often be corroborated using written records, such as censuses and church membership lists, which can pinpoint where and when the individuals lived as a community.

In this chapter I examine the national distribution of the signature quilt style in the nineteenth century. Most researchers have focused on signature quilts from specific regions, primarily Baltimore, Maryland, and the Delaware River Valley. As a Kansan, I was interested in a wider view of the signature quilt. When I see an

1861 friendship quilt thought to have been made in Lecompton, Kansas, or a Peabody, Kansas, sampler album that looks to have been made in the 1850s, I want to know how accurate the Kansas attribution might be. Were Kansas settlers making signature quilts in the 1850s? How fast and how far did the signature quilt fashion spread?

While examining date-inscribed quilts as a means of developing guidelines for dating unsigned quilts,[5] I also analyzed signature quilts by plotting them across time and space to determine the source and transmission of the style. I collected data on quilts made anywhere in the United States. I used quilts I found pictured in current quilt literature and that of the recent past. I also used quilts I saw on exhibition and in museums and private collections. I relied on museum catalog cards when I could not see the quilts themselves, and I read some of the forms from three statewide quilt surveys (Quilts of Tennessee, the North Carolina Quilt Project, and the Kansas Quilt Project). At this point I have information on more than 1,000 date-inscribed American quilts in a computerized file. Of these, 227 were nineteenth-century signature quilts, upon which I have based this study.

I defined a signature quilt as a block-style quilt with more than one signature on its face. (Some had only two signatures.) I studied two types, the album in which each block is different, and the friendship quilt in which all the blocks are identical (early examples often included a second design in the corners or center square). As the terms "friendship quilt" and "album quilt" can be confusing, I will be more descriptive, calling the first a *sampler album*, the second a *single-pattern friendship* quilt. The designs in either may be piecework, embroidery, or appliqué. I omitted from the database fundraiser quilts, which also have more than one signature per block, and crazy quilts, as these styles were most popular after 1880 when magazines and other forms

of popular culture began influencing what previously had been folk culture. In my database I included 121 sampler albums and 106 single-pattern friendship quilts.

Dates of Popularity

Those who have studied signature quilts are in general agreement about the dates of origin and peaks of fashion along the East Coast. William Rush Dunton, the first to note the many signature quilts made in Baltimore, determined their heyday to be the years 1842 to 1853.[6] Dena Katzenberg, who studied Baltimore sampler albums, narrowed the dates of popularity in that city to 1846 to 1852.[7] Jessica Nicoll looked at signature quilts made in the Delaware River Valley areas of Delaware, Pennsylvania, and New Jersey and suggested a span of 1841 to 1855.[8] Jane Bentley Kolter described signature quilts made throughout the United States and concluded that 1840 was the starting point and 1870 the end of the style.[9] Linda Otto Lipsett characterized the span of signature quilts as 1840 to 1875 with the 1840s and 1850s as the peak.[10]

The earliest signature quilt in the literature with a reliable date actually inscribed on it is a single-pattern friendship quilt dated 1839 to 1843.[11] There are three signature quilts in my database with blocks dated 1841, and twelve with blocks dated 1842, indicating that the idea of signing blocks for a group quilt caught on in the early 1840s. As the early examples usually contain blocks that span several years, it is difficult to determine if one type predates the other. However, four of the five quilts with blocks dated before 1842 are single-pattern friendship quilts, an indication that this style was initially more popular than the sampler album style.[12]

The fad (and it does appear to be a fad with a sudden emergence and a sharp immediate rise followed by a trailing off of popularity) hit its peak in the mid-1840s and faded in the late 1850s. I found more dated examples

Double X, a single-pattern friendship quilt pieced of cottons, 108" x 106", made by Mary Brown Batten (1814–?), Swedesboro, Gloucester County, New Jersey, with inked stamping, signatures, and dates 1841–45. Collection of the great-great-granddaughter, Eleanor Shoemaker Spencer. Courtesy of the Heritage Quilt Project of New Jersey, Inc.

Album Patch, single-pattern friendship quilt of pieced cottons, 102½" x 111½", 6–7 stitches per inch, made by Quaker women from Montgomery County, Pennsylvania. Signatures and dates from 1843–45 in ink. Courtesy of the Mercer Museum (#26698), gift of Mr. and Mrs. Albert C. Watson.

of the sampler album than of the single-pattern friendship type; the sampler album type also maintained its initial popularity a few years longer. There were few examples of either type dated in the 1860s. The Civil War may have disrupted the practice during that decade, but a decline in both types is evident in 1853, eight years before the war began.

Kolter and Lipsett, who looked at quilts from the widest areas, indicated dates of 1870 and 1875, respectively, as the end of the album tradition.[13] However, a national overview of dated examples conflicts with this view. Rather than dying out, signature quilts enjoyed a revival in the 1880s and 1890s with a few changes. The single-pattern friendship quilt succeeded the sampler album as the more popular type in the last decades of the nineteenth century and into the twentieth. Sampler albums revived at the end of the century, but appliqué was no longer the most common technique. Album quiltmakers began to favor outline-embroidered blocks, a trend that continued into the twentieth century. The typical sampler album of 1930 might be a collection of floral blocks, embroidered on pre-

stamped squares sold by the Rainbow Quilt Company or Home Art Company.

I limited my study of signature blocks to the nineteenth century as I felt I lacked a national view of twentieth-century signature quilts. Few are pictured in books, collected by museums, or exhibited in galleries due to their visual qualities (currently unpopular with decorators and collectors), sources as kits and commercial patterns, and their relatively recent origins. My experience with twentieth-century signature quilts is limited to those I see in Kansas, primarily through the Kansas Quilt Project. That observation indicates that embroidered sampler albums and pieced single-pattern friendship quilts were quite popular in Kansas in the 1920s and 1930s, and this may also

be true throughout the rest of the country.

In summary, examination of dated nineteenth-century examples corroborates information in the recent literature ascribing the origins of the signature quilt to the early 1840s, followed by a sudden surge of popularity through the early 1850s, and a general decline in the 1860s and 1870s. It offers new evidence that the style revived in the 1880s and 1890s.

Geographic Patterns of Popularity
Kolter speculated that the fashion for signature quilts originated in Pennsylvania and Maryland and spread first to New York and Ohio, then to Virginia and North Carolina.[14] Nicoll described the source as the Delaware River Valley, which runs along the Pennsylvania-New Jersey border.[15] A

look at the earliest quilts (six quilts with blocks dated 1842) indicates that both are correct; the fashion seems to have originated in a wide area, from Morristown, New Jersey, south to Baltimore, generally along a line between the two largest cities of the era—New York and Baltimore. When the entire group of quilts dated before 1845 is mapped, the same area from northern New Jersey along the Delaware River to the Chesapeake Bay is highlighted, with additional indications that the fashion had spread to western Maryland and central Virginia. Some geographic preference for type appears in the early years, as most of the single-pattern friendship quilts are grouped along the Delaware River, and the early sampler albums range over a wider area from central Virginia north to Staten Island with the highest concentration in the Baltimore area.

During the next five-year period, 1845–49, the signature style spread north to Maine, south to coastal South Carolina, and west to Ohio's Western Reserve. There is even one quilt in this period attributed to New Braunfels, Texas. However, most of the blocks made between 1845 and 1849 continued to spring from the Baltimore, Philadelphia, and New Jersey areas.

In the next five-year period, 1850–54, the only significant geographical change is that Pennsylvania is no longer as well-represented; the fad seems to have faded there first. By the period 1855–59, the fashion had also waned in New Jersey and Baltimore. Apparently, the urban trendsetters tired of the style while their rural sisters continued to organize signature quilts.

During the 1860s and 1870s, the few quilts made ranged over a wider area, as far west as Salt Lake City where the women of the Female Relief Society made an appliqué album in 1870, fifteen years after the style had become passé in Baltimore.[16]

In the 1880s and 1890s, the single-pattern friendship quilt began to increase in numbers, but little geographic clustering is evident. Quiltmakers from the Great Plains eastward made signature quilts. One area not represented, however, is the area where it all began. From New York City south to Baltimore I found no dated examples in these decades.

Geographic clustering over the years indicates a continuing regional preference for type. The sampler albums were most popular early in the Baltimore and Philadelphia areas, while the single-pattern friendship quilts were preferred by quilters in the Delaware Valley of eastern Pennsylvania and western New Jersey. Sampler album quilts tended to cluster along the Baltimore-New York axis, while single-pattern friendship quilts were made in more scattered areas,

especially central New York and New England, where few sampler albums were made.

Trends are also apparent in the distribution of the sampler album quilt. The fashion for signing quilt blocks was initially popular in and near Philadelphia. Three of the six sampler albums dated 1842 came from that city and its environs, and only one from Baltimore. They do not focus on the complex appliqué patterns that we consider the hallmark of the sampler album. One of the six (from Philadelphia) is entirely pieced and another (from New Lisbon, New Jersey) is all cut-out chintz appliqué (or *broderie perse*). The rest are a combination of intricately pieced blocks, cut-out chintz, and rather simple appliqué, with piecework the predominant technique. We do not begin to see the classic appliqué sampler we call a Baltimore Album quilt until 1845 or 1846. I surmise that the idea of a sampler began in the Philadelphia area and spread rapidly to Baltimore where seamstresses developed the distinctive appliqué sampler that eclipsed the earlier sampler of elaborate pieced blocks, which might be referred to as the Philadelphia Album.

Most of us are familiar with the appliqué Baltimore Album look. It is important to note that these elaborate appliqué samplers were not exclusively from Baltimore, even in the early years, but also were made in Pennsylvania, Connecticut, Virginia, and other Eastern Seaboard states.

In summary, the style began in the Midland and Chesapeake Bay zones and rather quickly diffused north and south along the Atlantic coast, and as far west as Ohio. As the fashion for signature quilts faded in the East after the Civil War, it appeared in the newly settled Western states.

Because mid-century signature quilts are found all over the United States today, one is inclined to believe they were made throughout the country. The data indicate that during the first twenty years of the style, a na-

Opposite: Sampler album friendship quilt of pieced and appliqué block- and roller-printed cottons, and silk with silk thread embroidery, 97" x 126", made by Quaker Charlotte Gillingham of Philadelphia. Drawings, inscriptions, signatures, and dates of 1842–43 in ink. Courtesy of the Philadelphia Museum of Art (#45-35-1), gift of Mrs. Levis Lloyd Mann, Mrs. H. Maxwell Langdon, Mrs. George K. Helbert, Mrs. Nelson D. Warwick, and Mrs. Granville B. Hopkins.

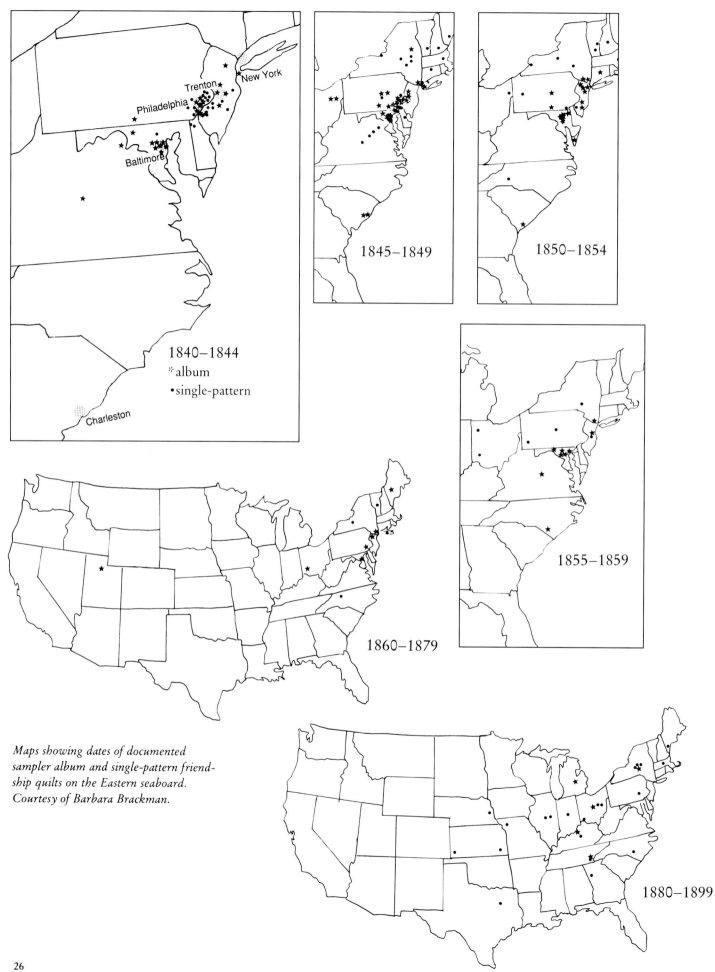

1840–1844
∗ album
• single-pattern

1845–1849

1850–1854

1855–1859

1860–1879

1880–1899

Maps showing dates of documented sampler album and single-pattern friendship quilts on the Eastern seaboard. Courtesy of Barbara Brackman.

tional view of the signature style is actually a regional view. Although there were twenty-eight states in the Union in 1847 when the style was at its peak, signature quilts were most likely to be made in only half of them. The women who settled the Western states in the 1840s and 1850s may have brought their signature quilts with them, but the idea of making the quilts did not diffuse so rapidly.

The pattern of migration demonstrated by these figures should encourage a sense of skepticism in ascribing Midwestern origins for mid-century signature quilts. A personal example: After looking at the data, I checked the 1860 and 1865 censuses for names of the alleged Lecompton settlers who made the quilt dated 1861 (the year of Kansas statehood) and found none of them. It was most likely made in the eastern United States and brought to Kansas at a later date.

Construction Trends
As Clues to Date

The patterns of origin and diffusion can assist quilt historians in assigning geographical locations to signature quilts. Some details of construction can also be useful clues to date. Most sampler albums in the database had blocks of identical size, but some quiltmakers persisted with an older concept, a central design focus obtained by including one large block in the center of a field of equally sized blocks. Thirty percent of the sampler albums dated between 1840 and 1844 included this central design focus, a format that faded over the years. Between 1845 and 1849 only 11% featured larger blocks in the center. Not one sampler album dated in the 1850s had a central focus, an indicator that a large block in the center of the quilt is a clue to a sampler album from the 1840s.

Observation also indicated that sampler album quilts and samplers made by individuals in the 1840s and 1850s can be characterized as orderly.

After the Civil War we begin to see a hodgepodge of different block sizes arranged rather haphazardly. Thus a chaotic arrangement of different-sized blocks is an indication of a date after 1865.

Trends in Appliqué Patterns

I had projected that studying signature quilts would give me some insight into pattern development, especially the origins and diffusion of the traditional appliqué designs that developed at the same time as the sampler album. To track trends, I cut up photocopies of ninety-two sampler albums dated from 1840 to 1876 and organized the hundreds of appliqué blocks into groups of similar patterns, such as fleurs-de-lis, bouquets, closed wreaths, and open wreaths. I sought to create an index useful in identifying the source of undated quilts, for example an unsigned appliqué sampler found in Peabody, Kansas, by the Kansas Quilt Project.[17] I knew it was unlikely to be Kansas-made, but was it a Baltimore quilt? I could not match the eighteen blocks to the hundreds in the index. Although there are similar baskets or wreaths, an identical design or even a near match is rare. I am not optimistic that this sort of pattern index could help date or place a quilt beyond a general attribution of "1840–1860, probably East Coast of the United States."

Through the pattern index I also attempted to support my thesis that the popularity of the sampler album style generated the appliqué designs that became popular for single-pattern quilts made by individuals. I did find that most of the standard appliqué designs appeared concurrently as single-maker, single-pattern quilts and as blocks in sampler albums. The Mexican Rose appears in single-pattern quilts dated 1849 and 1853 (two examples), and in sampler albums dated 1847, 1853, 1855 (two examples), and 1863. The fleurs-de-lis appears in dozens of sampler albums made after 1844 and in single-pattern quilts dated 1846–48, 1856, and 1859. However, I

Sampler album friendship quilt of appliqué block- and roller-printed chintz, 91½″ x 92″, made by Sarah Flickwir of Philadelphia. Drawings, stamping, inscriptions, signatures, and dates of 1840–46 in ink. Courtesy of the Philadelphia Museum of Art (#52-63-1), gift of Mrs. F Willard Wood in memory of Mrs. Frank W. Wood, née Rebecca Williamson.

have too few dated examples of most patterns and the dates are too close to determine whether the design originated as a sampler album pattern or as a single-maker, single-pattern quilt. One exception is the Oak Leaf and Reel design, which was quite common in both types of signature quilts. There are single-pattern, single-maker quilts in this design dated 1818, 1829, and 1830. It is one of the few appliqué patterns that predates the signature style.[18]

Most of the standard appliqué designs that appeared after 1840 seem to have originated in the Baltimore/ Chesapeake Bay area. One exception is a symmetrical arrangement of hearts that seems to have developed in the New York-New Jersey region.[19] A few patterns that were very popular for single-pattern quilts by an individual, such as the Princess Feather and the Whig Rose, rarely appear in album quilts. The complexity of these designs often dictates a large block (eighteen inches or more), which may have deterred quiltmakers from using them in the smaller blocks that generally made up signature quilts. However, equally complex designs were popular for album quilts, so some other factors may have influenced the categorization of some designs as more appropriate for single-pattern quilts by individual makers. The reverse is more commonly true. Many designs popular in the album quilts never became standard patterns. The broad range of appliqué patterns in the sampler albums of the mid-nineteenth century indicates that the makers were exploring the design possibilities of a new technique. Certain patterns caught on and spread around the country; others disappeared after a few years or after a single block. These signature quilts were design workbooks as well as expressions of friendship.

Conclusion

This study indicates a definite regional origin for the signature quilt style, an origin in the Midland and Chesapeake regions that have generated many of the vernacular arts we define as America's folk culture. My work represents an adaptation of geographical methodology using quilts as artifacts. As state and regional surveys of quilts add to the database, we will have more opportunities to study quilts in their geographical contexts. Signature quilts from the Philadelphia region in the early 1840s may offer interesting contrast to the Baltimore/Chesapeake Bay quilts of the same years, and signature quilts from the South Carolina coast may show regional variations in the 1850s and 1860s. More information on quilts from the South (Northern quilts are currently collected and pictured far more often than Southern quilts) may give us additional insight into the diffusion of the signature style.

State and regional quilt projects acquiring information about quilts that are reliably attributed to specific geographical origins can also use these methods with quilts other than signature quilts. By comparing types across regions we may soon be able to draw many new conclusions about the origins and diffusion of mid-nineteenth-century pattern and style.

Notes and References

[1]Wilbur Zelinsky, *The Cultural Geography of the United States* (Englewood Cliffs, NJ: Prentice Hall, 1973), 83; Henry Glassie, *Pattern in the Material Folk Culture of the Eastern United States* (Philadelphia: University of Pennsylvania Press, 1968), 35–36. Zelinsky lists three nuclear modes for cultural dissemination: Southern New England, the Midlands, and the Chesapeake Bay region. Glassie lists four.

[2]Fred B. Kniffen, "Folk Housing: Key to Diffusion," *Annals of the Association of American Geographers* 58 (1965): 549–77.

[3]Terry G. Jordan and Matti Kaups, "Folk Architecture in Cultural and Ecological Context," *The Geographical Review* 77, No. 1 (January 1987): 52–75.

[4]Among the guidebooks that listed bedding as a top priority for pioneers are Randolph B. Marcy, *The Prairie Traveler: A Hand-Book for Overland Expeditions* (New York: Harper and Brothers, 1859), 40; and James Redpath and Richard Hinton, *Hand-book to Kansas Territory and the Rocky Mountains Gold Region* (New York: Colton, 1859), 30. Marcy suggested, "The bedding for each person should consist of two blankets, a comforter, and a pillow, and a gutta percha or painted canvas cloth to spread beneath the bed upon the ground and to contain it when rolled up for transportation."

[5]Barbara Brackman, *Clues in the Calico: A Guide to Identifying and Dating Antique Quilts* (McLean, VA: EPM, 1989).

[6]William Rush Dunton, *Old Quilts* (Catonsville, MD: privately printed, 1946), 175.

[7]Dena S. Katzenberg, *Baltimore Album Quilts* (Baltimore, MD: Baltimore Museum of Art, 1981), 14, 65.

[8]Jessica F. Nicoll, *Quilted for Friends: Delaware Valley Signature Quilts, 1840–1855* (Winterthur, DE: Winterthur Museum, 1986), 5.

[9]Jane Bentley Kolter, *Forget Me Not: A Gallery of Friendship and Album Quilts* (Pittstown, NJ: Main Street Press, 1985), 9, 52.

[10]Linda Otto Lipsett, *Remember Me: Women and Their Friendship Quilts* (San Francisco: Quilt Digest Press, 1985), 19.

[11]The example inscribed 1839–43 is pictured in Kolter, plate 93. There are a few signature quilts in the literature with earlier dates that appear to have been altered.

Other early dates are of a commemorative nature, rather than the date the quilt was made. See the ELI quilt dated 1817 in Myron Orlofsky and Patsy Orlofsky, *Quilts in America* (New York: McGraw Hill, 1974), 235; and a quilt dated 1828–91 in Mary Merriam and Suzanne C. Flynt, *Quilts* (Deerfield, CT: Pocumtuck Valley Memorial Association, 1985), 21. The fabrics, patterns, and style in both appear to be far later than the inscribed dates.

Since the research for this article was completed in 1988, signature quilts with dates of 1840 have been published. For example, the Heritage Quilt Project of New Jersey pictures a Nine Patch from Burlington County in Rachel Cochran, Rita Erickson, Natalie Hart, and Barbara Schaffer, *New Jersey Quilts: 1777 to 1950* (Paducah, KY: American Quilter's Society, 1992), 99. Nancy and Donald Roan note one from Montgomery County, northwest of Philadelphia, in *Lest I Shall Be Forgotten* (Green Lane, PA: Goschenhoppen Historians, 1993), 16.

[12]New evidence in the form of quilts dated 1840–45 may prove this assumption to be wrong.

[13]Kolter, 52; Lipsett, 19.

[14]Kolter, 10.

[15]Nicoll, 7.

[16]Quilt is pictured in Kate B. Carter, *Pioneer Quilts* (Salt Lake City: Daughters of Utah Pioneers, 1979), 71.

[17]Kansas Quilt Project #Fa125.

[18]Barbara Brackman, *Encyclopedia of Appliqué* (McLean, VA: EPM, 1993).

[19]An example of a single-pattern quilt in a variation of this design is pictured in Marguerite Ickis, *The Standard Book of Quilt Making and Collecting* (New York: Greystone Press, 1949; reprinted by Dover, 1959), 47. She calls it "traditional geometric design."

Quilt Blocks—
Or Quilt Patterns?

Wilene Smith

Little has been written about how nineteenth- and early twentieth-century quiltmakers collected, recorded, and exchanged patterns. Several authors have touched on the subject, but Dolores Hinson, writing for *The Antiques Journal* in 1970, delved deeper, referring to collections of quilt blocks as "Quilters' Catalogs." She stated that these "were made by quilters as reference files of patterns. Paper was scarce and books of quilt patterns were totally unknown."[1]

Other writers have observed that "many of the quilt blocks we find today were sample pattern blocks never meant to be incorporated into a quilt top."[2] "It was customary to make a block of a pattern to keep for reference, and some quilters had a collection of blocks, occasionally with the name of the pattern pinned to [them]."[3] "A new design would be held in memory and the block pieced when the seamstress was back in her house to be stored as a 'sketch' for future reproduction."[4] "These . . . frequently included single blocks of both pieced and patched designs."[5]

"There was always a neighbourly and friendly interest taken in such collections, as popular designs were exchanged and copied many times."[6] "Some collections . . . were extensive and were handed down in families from generation to generation."[7] These statements from Dolores Hinson, Patsy and Myron Orlofsky, Ruth McKendry, Jonathan Holstein, and Marie Webster illustrate that the idea of quilt block collections is not a new one, but a plausible one that I will attempt to explore.

Wilene Smith *is an independent researcher whose interests focus on quilt patterns, especially those circulated by late nineteenth-century periodicals and by twentieth-century companies. She maintains a database of early print references to pattern names. 815 West 61st North, Wichita, KS 67204.*

Pattern quilt, pieced and appliqué, print and solid-color cottons, 79" x 65".

The blocks were made by Sally Vira Cox Hadley (1830–98), Hendricks County, Indiana, and represent the entire period during which she lived. They were stitched together and quilted in 1938 by her granddaughter, Flora Hadley Pickering, and great-granddaughter, Clarise Pickering Epley. Collection of great-great-granddaughter, Karen Dolanc. Collection of the Wichita-Sedgwick County Historical Museum. Courtesy of Wilene Smith.

The earliest reference to quilt block pattern collections that is presently known appears in the January 1911 issue of *Woman's Home Companion*, in which Charlotte F. Boldtmann writes that

one of the greatest pleasures derived by women from patchwork was in the memories it recalled. Each woman had her own box of patterns and they furnished many an evening's entertainment. The box would be brought out, each pattern displayed, the name of the block and also of its giver stated, usually with some pleasant reminiscences or exciting bits of history. These boxes were, in fact, veritable memory boxes.[8]

Mary E. Bradford, *Hearth and Home*'s needlework editor, indirectly referred to pattern collections in September 1914 when she suggested to her readers that "a nice way to keep sample blocks" is to make "a 'variety' or 'oddity' quilt."[9]

Pattern collections were apparently so well known in some families or communities that Gertrude West incorporated one into a 1924 short story about an old man (a widower) who, as he explains to a neighbor lady, pieces quilts "'to make my last days go a little faster.'" The neighbor explains that she has "'a lot of patterns'" and invites him inside to see them. As he sits down, she hands him "a huge box of 'pattern' blocks" to look through.[10]

It has been my personal experience to purchase eight collections of quilt block patterns. Ranging from a few examples to more than seventy-five blocks, the fabrics generally span a century in time (often as early as the 1840s and continuing into the 1930s). The blocks are often badly stained, their fabrics softened by much handling through the years. Usually, when a collection contains two or more blocks of the same design, each example proves to be a different size or is made up in different color combinations from various time periods, often with the light and dark contrasts reversed.

The larger collections seem to demonstrate the expertise (or the lack thereof) of more than one maker. However, I recently learned of one explanation for the less exacting blocks. During a conversation with Kansas quiltmaker Lillie Webb, she related that these do not necessarily indicate a lack of sewing skills. When recording or sharing a pattern, even the most skilled seamstress would sometimes quickly "throw together" a block without regard to colors, contrasts, or workmanship to simply "give the idea of the pattern." (In Lillie's words, "roughly together.") Paper pattern pieces were often included with the block so the recipient could see their relationship. Lillie went on to explain that her mother was "a beautiful hand seamstress. She could make the nicest, tiniest little stitches, and *so* fast! I never could master the way she did it."[11]

Sometimes, a collection will include one or more blocks with missing pieces that had been there at one time indicating, perhaps, at some point more fabric of a certain color or print style had been needed and the quiltmaker resorted to her pattern collection for the needed piece. Or it's possible that she may have used them as pattern pieces.

One also finds unfinished blocks. Did the quiltmaker not like the design or did she just tire of its making? Had she gone far enough to remember the rest of the design or to know that she liked it well enough to make a complete quilt? One also discovers designs in these pattern collections that cannot be identified in published reference sources. Are these original designs, or examples of memory and time playing tricks? Without accompanying written notes, we cannot know the true answers and are left, instead, to contemplate the possibilities.

Two classic collections have been illustrated in recent books. Twenty-four blocks attributed to Mrs. Mary Ellen Wood, a nineteenth-century Canadian resident, are pictured in *Traditional Quilts and Bed Coverings* by Ruth McKendry.[12] Twenty-nine Pennsylvania examples from Jane Brosius Rothermel (1877–1936) are included in the 1985 book by Jeannette Lasansky, *In the Heart of Pennsylvania*.[13]

Is it possible that further research might show regional differences in forming these collections? The three quiltmakers interviewed for this chap-

ter have roots in several states: Kentucky, Illinois, Missouri, Kansas, and California; yet two of them remember mothers, grandmothers, or great-grandmothers having quilt block pattern collections. Considering the many thousands of quiltmakers across America, three interviews are not definitive, but the response to these collections in central Pennsylvania research is less enlightening. Conversations with seventeen quiltmakers, most born during the first decade of the twentieth century, revealed that "most of their patterns were obtained through trading with family or neighbor ladies" but "few of [them] remembered seeing a collection of 'sample' patches." The Oral Traditions Project, apparently aware of their existence, located only three such collections within a seven-county area during its initial research.[14]

Pattern block collections have also been found in Southern states. Quilt historians Bets Ramsey and Sandra Todaro report that blocks have been found strung onto threads in the same fashion as a group of buttons (a button string) or groups of fabric pieces cut in preparation for quiltmaking. They tend to be loosely strung and the blocks turn like pages of a book.[15]

The most unusual collection that has been described to me was acquired from an estate auction in southeast Kansas some years ago by an antiques dealer interested in quilts. Among her purchases that day was a bushel basket full of little bundles of old fabric, each tied neatly with string. As each one was untied and opened, a quilt block and its cardboard pattern pieces were revealed.[16]

One occasionally sees a quilt made up of these mismatched blocks, though I suspect that some were put together by a later generation and not by the original maker of the blocks. Unfortunately, when a later generation comes into the possession of a collection, the new owner is often inclined to "finish the unfinished," sewing the blocks together into a quilt not realizing that this had not been the purpose for their creation.

Pattern Sources

As recently as sixty years ago, rural women found themselves isolated for periods of time. In a letter dated February 12, 1932, from near Jewell, Kansas, Gertrude relates to Gladys:

We . . . didn't get any mail for two days and then we didn't expect any to-day but he went. The roads froze last night so he could go. Last night Ruth & Robert had to walk & lead their horse from north of Abrams on home. The wheels would ball up till they wouldn't turn. Bob got behind the buggy & pushed. They broke the harness & had a terrible time. Mrs. Maud Mitchell said there were fourteen cars stuck yesterday past their place. The roads are worse than we ever saw them. Of course the highways are some better but the sand has sunk into the mud till one hardly knows they are graveled. . . . Ray is going to town while roads are frozen. 24°.

Overleaf: Page from a scrapbook of Hearth and Home *quilt patterns, 1880s–1910s. Collection of Barbara W. Halgowich.*

Collection of pieced and appliqué pattern blocks, print and solid-color cottons, made by Jane Brosius Rothermel (1877–1936), Washington Township, Northumberland County, Pennsylvania. Collection of Laura E. Latsha. Courtesy of Oral Traditions Project. Photo by Terry Wild Studio.

She goes on to tell about the basket quilt for which she plans to finish the blocks later in the day using scraps left from her children's clothes, and how her husband "has taken more interest in this quilt than any other one I have made."[17]

Letters have been a convenient method of exchanging patterns for many generations.[18] Before ending her letter, Gertrude tells Gladys that "I am going to send you the pattern [of the basket quilt] so you can make a quilt . . . if you care too."

We have read many times about the popularity of and the circumstances surrounding quilting bees throughout the past 200 years. New patterns were carried away from these communal affairs, either in memory or "in the cloth."[19] County and state fairs, with their displays of everything imaginable that could be produced by loving and talented hands, were another source of patterns for the rural quiltmaker as well as the urban quiltmaker.[20] Miss Ethel Vanderwilt of Solomon, Kansas, made five sketches, hand-drawn in pencil and hand-colored with watercolors, of quilts she had seen at state fairs in 1921 and 1925. She faithfully reproduced one of these, a Broken Star, which sold at her estate auction in 1985.[21]

The country peddler, sometimes referred to as an itinerant peddler or kitchen merchant,[22] undoubtedly was another source of patterns for the quiltmaker. Tinsmiths of the time, many of whom were itinerant peddlers, produced both quilt and quilting patterns of cut tin.[23] Edward Sands Frost, a Maine tinsmith and peddler of the 1860s and 1870s, created metal stencils and stamped these designs on burlap to be sold door-to-door for hooking rugs.[24] While not *quilt* patterns, his ingenuity illustrates that an alert and talented merchant observed the world around him in an attempt to better the life of his customers while also increasing his sales of merchandise.

Florence Peto describes a quilt design said to have been created by a Pennsylvania peddler with scissors and a piece of folded paper.[25] Three quilts with folded paper designs, two accompanied by family stories attributing the designs to peddlers, were documented in 1986 by the Tennessee Quilt Project.[26] The existence of these four quilts and their stories tends to indicate that creative original designs were passed out by the peddlers rather than traditional quilt designs.

Publications such as *Godey's Lady's Book*, *Peterson's*, *Arthur's*, and *Frank Leslie's* magazines, as well as several needlework books, occasionally included patchwork patterns during the mid-nineteenth century,[27] but most of these patterns had an English provenance and were generally not the ones near and dear to American quiltmakers. By 1883, however, familiar patterns with familiar names were beginning to appear in American farm magazines such as *Farm and Fireside*. When four designs were offered in the December 1, 1886, issue, there was no commentary about them other than the brief statement: "We present, this time, four new quilt patterns and several most excellent patterns of laces."[28] In June 1890, the magazine published a two-part article on patchwork but the author reverted to the habits of earlier magazines by including designs and names similar to those that had previously been published in *Godey's* and others.[29] But the article offered one important thing this time that the earlier publications had not done—full-size diagrams of the pieces needed for each design.

Three events during the last decades of the nineteenth century eventually led to new pattern sources for the quiltmaker. The first of these was the discovery of an inexpensive method of making paper from wood pulp. For many centuries paper was made by hand from cotton or linen, a slow and expensive process making it neither easily available nor affordable. Consequently the demand for it was

minimal, and it was used primarily by early printers. A series of discoveries and inventions stretching from 1750 until after the Civil War led to more effective methods of mass-producing paper and of making paper from wood. By the mid-1880s, wood pulp paper was cheap and abundant.[30] The second event occurred during the same decade—the creation of the first early form of the linotype machine, revolutionizing the printing industry and making efficient the previously time-consuming process of hand-setting type.[31] Combined, these two events led to the availability of more books, newspapers, and magazines than had ever been known. Of these, magazines soon became a popular source by which quiltmakers exchanged patterns through needlework columns and reader exchange columns.

The third event began in 1872 when Aaron Montgomery Ward and George R. Thorne started a mail-order business in a Chicago livery stable loft by distributing their first "catalog," a single sheet of paper listing a small variety of dry goods items. Fourteen years later, Sears, Roebuck and Company experienced its humble beginnings in Minnesota.[32] The convenience of shopping at home quickly caught on, particularly in rural areas, and many other entrepreneurs seized upon the new idea, among them the Ladies' Art Company in St. Louis.

Founded in 1889, Ladies' Art became an innovator in the field of quilt patterns by using mail order as its distribution tool.[33] Along with art needlework and gadgets, the company advertised 272 different quilt patterns in 1895, gradually increasing to 500 by February 1922. The 1928 catalog, which experienced one revision and several printings, eventually listed 530 designs.[34] Paper pattern pieces for these were all available to the quiltmaker: one pattern for 10 cents, three for 25 cents, or seven for 50 cents. The ambitious woman could order fifteen for $1.00. For a price consider-

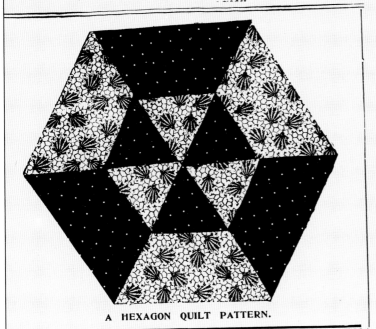

A HEXAGON QUILT PATTERN.

A NEW QUILT PATTERN.

One more design for bed-quilt blocks, pattern for which will be furnished by the publishers of FARM AND HOME, is shown herewith. No 3 is known as the "lost ship." The illustration shows one-quarter of the design, and is several sizes smaller than the pattern offered for sale.

NO 3. LOST SHIP PATTERN.

The whole block is made by sewing together four pieces cut according to this design, the four pieces all occupying a similar position; that is, the large white space being in the upper right-hand corner. The material may be blue on a white back-

CHIMNEY SWALLOW.

PATCHWORK FOR SOFA-CUSHION.

This design is of old-gold and maroon colored satin. The pieces must be lined with paper muslin before they are embroidered.

Use light blue real Scotch linen floss and red on the maroon blocks, and on the old-gold ones use darkest shade of olive-green. This design will also be pretty for bedspreads.

FANTASTIC PATCHWORK.

Our Quilt Blocks.

"Charlie's Choice" has a romantic history, being the pattern which "Charlie" selected for his mother to make a quilt to send his bride by. The corner half squares and the pieces joining, which meet in the center, were of a golden brown sateen, with a tiny dot of a lighter color in it. The center half diamonds were a lovely shade of blue, and the light pieces cream with an orange figure. All were of a very

Charlie's Choice Quilt Block.

fine sateen. Every one who saw that quilt praised its beauty and, no doubt, it won the bride's love for her clever mother-in-law. It might be made of four colors, having the corner half squares different from that adjoining, which, when set solidly, would make a square.

Mosaic quilt blocks are always odd and striking if a pretty combination of colors is used. They are certainly cheerful, for bright colors seem to be called for in them, the only thing

Mosaic Quilt Block.

being to have those which will contrast well and avoid those which "fight." It should be set solidly, as sashwork will utterly destroy the effect, and each square must be exactly like every other square in the quilt.   J. S. A.

* * *

JEWEL PATCHWORK.

This is sewed on to a cloth foundation, and is made of two shades only. It may be easily worked from the design.

LINCOLN'S CABIN.

This very interesting quilt block is called Lincoln's cabin. A full-size pattern by

LINCOLN'S CABIN.

which to cut this design, which is No 5 in the F & H series, will be furnished on receipt of 10c and the coupon which accompanies this article, properly filled out. The shaded portions indicate material of a colored or figured pattern, the other pieces white. Directions accompany the pattern.

Examples from a set of sixteen Carolina Lily blocks in various stages of completion made about 1880, accompanied by their pattern block that dates about forty years earlier. Collection of Wilene Smith. Photo by Terry Wild Studio.

The blocks were found in north-central Kansas in the early 1980s along with an uncompleted quilt top of a different design containing a large variety of early 1840s Turkey red calicos similar to the red print in the pattern block.

ably higher than the paper pattern, she could order a finished block of calico ($.20–1.00) or silk ($.35–3.00). There were also numerous Ladies' Art catalogs of appliqué and quilting designs, some containing even more pieced designs.

In 1891, the Modern Art Company (New Haven, CT) advertised "Three Beautiful Quilt Patterns. Diagrams Full Size, new and elegant designs, all different. Sent by return mail, with catalog of specialties, for only 10c."[35]

An enterprising South Carolina woman placed an advertisement in the *Home Magazine* in 1902 for

Quilt Patterns. Cut paper patterns with diagrams of square will be supplied for 5 cents or 3 for 10 cents. Pieced square with cut paper pattern 12 cents. 400 styles from which to choose. Address MISS MAMIE PEARSON, Clinton, South Carolina.[36]

The magazines themselves seemed slow to recognize the economic advantages of supplying mail-order quilt patterns although patterns for dresses and other clothing had existed for some years.[37] *Ladies' Home Journal* in July 1909 offered a transfer pattern

that included one pieced and two appliqué designs and yet another one in the January 1912 issue for two appliqué designs by Marie Webster.[38] *Farmer's Wife* magazine (St. Paul, MN) offered quilt patterns by mail in its December 1912 issue.[39]

Apparent resistance (possibly a holdover from the attitude that patchwork was so simple as not to need instruction[40]) can be seen within the pages of *Farm and Fireside* (Springfield, OH). Toward the end of 1911,[41] the magazine published another article illustrating quilt designs that included, this time, very small diagrams of the pieces (not full size as they had done in 1890). At the end of the text was an editor's note: "We do not furnish the patterns for these quilt designs."[42] This leads one to believe the magazine had been receiving requests from its readers for patterns published in previous issues. Apparently, even with this notation, requests continued. When seven more designs were published four months later, the editor's note read somewhat differently: "So many of our subscribers have written to us, asking for quilt-block patterns, that we have decided to furnish them. Tissue-paper patterns and directions for making these quilt-blocks will be forwarded to anyone on receipt of ten cents in coin or stamps."[43]

In the January 4, 1913, issue, six more designs were offered, along with the comment that "Makers of quilts have been besieging us with requests for new patterns. In response to these requests the Fancy-Work Editor has selected six of the very prettiest quilt-blocks that have been submitted to us for this department."[44]

Ordering quilt patterns by mail through magazines was now firmly established, but old habits and familiar ways are difficult to change. Seeing a quilt, or top, or even a block, in front of you—"in the cloth," in color—has always been and will continue to be more striking and more memorable than any black-and-white illustration or sketch. Even though paper patterns and illustrations were everywhere around them (and these *were* collected) as the twentieth century progressed, quiltmakers continued to gain ideas from their neighbors' and relatives' quilts as their mothers and grandmothers had done before them.

Oma Haines, another Kansas quiltmaker, remembered her grandmother's box of quilt block patterns in detail: "It was in a great big shirt box like they used to pack shirts six in a box. I wouldn't even begin to guess how many there were, but they were pieced blocks and she had the patterns basted to each block with several stitches of thread." These pattern pieces were also cloth. When she wanted to make one of the designs, she removed them to use in making her cardboard patterns. She also used buckram, a very stiff fabric. The designs had been gathered from friends and relatives because "people were more dependent on one another in those kind of days than they are now." This was her "pattern box" and whatever happened to it, Oma doesn't know. It was kept on top of the chiffonier in her grandmother's bedroom out of the reach of an inquisitive young girl but was brought down often. Many pleasant and memorable hours were spent by grandmother and granddaughter poring over the pretty patterns and colors. Oma remembers the time period as about 1920 to 1930.[45]

Lillie Webb has similar memories. "When somebody would go to a friend's house and see a quilt that they liked, usually that person made a block, [sometimes] just out of anything, just so they had the pattern and they'd make it up and send it to them or give it to them." Lillie still has some of these pattern blocks. As a child, she accompanied her mother and grandmother to quilting bees but doesn't recall going to fairs.[46]

Pansy Smith has "always just loved to sew." Her grandmother lived with them throughout the fall and winter months during Pansy's formative years. Three generations of women spent many winter evenings sitting before the fireplace in their farmhouse about sixty miles east of Springfield, Missouri, cutting pieces for quilts and sewing them together while Pansy's father often popped corn. Although her mother was more tolerant about her young daughter's seams ("You can do better next time."), her grandmother wasn't. "'Honey, that won't do. You got to do it all over again.' And that's what she meant. I'd have to

Pattern block, 6½" x 6½", with numbers handwritten in pencil, circa 1885–1900. Collection of Wilene Smith. Photo by Terry Wild Studio.

The unknown quiltmaker noted the requirements needed to complete a quilt made in this design right on her pattern block. All the numbers are correct except one—it's not known what "84" signifies. Her design was called Wandering Lover when it was published in the October 1895 issue of Hearth and Home *(Augusta, ME).*

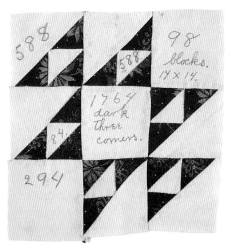

do it over several times. It got to looking kind of rugged time I got it done." Neighbors helped neighbors and occasionally two or three ladies would come for an afternoon to help Pansy's mother and grandmother quilt. They exchanged patterns by making sample blocks for each other. *Capper's Weekly* (Topeka, KS) and the *Weekly Kansas City Star* were clipped, saved, and used, but Pansy's family never bought patterns nor did they send away for them. Attending the county fair was an annual family outing. One year, young Pansy dressed "a huge, big doll," entered it in competition, and won ribbons for it.

When a new quilt was completed, household members competed to determine who would be the first to sleep under it because whatever was dreamed that night would come true.[47]

So it seems that wherever quilts have been a part of daily life, so has the custom of collecting and exchanging patterns in the form of fabric blocks. Now, when you find a box of assorted quilt blocks at an auction, flea market, or antique shop, you'll know that you have probably stumbled upon a quiltmaker's pattern collection. "Treat it with respect as a textbook of American life."[48]

Notes and References

[1]Dolores A. Hinson, "Quilters' Catalogs," *The Antiques Journal* 25, No. 9 (September 1970): 12–14.

[2]Patsy Orlofsky and Myron Orlofsky, *Quilts in America* (New York: McGraw-Hill, 1974), 49, 248.

[3]Ruth McKendry, *Traditional Quilts and Bed Coverings* (New York: Van Nostrand Reinhold, 1979), 103.

[4]Jonathan Holstein, *The Pieced Quilt: An American Design Tradition* (Boston: New York Graphic Society; Little, Brown, 1973), 85.

[5]Marie D. Webster, *Quilts: Their Story and How to Make Them* (Garden City, NY: Doubleday, 1915; 1926), 136.

[6]Ibid.

[7]Orlofsky, 248.

[8]Charlotte F. Boldtmann, "Patchwork Quilts of A Hundred Years Ago," *Woman's Home Companion* (January 1911).

[9]Mary E. Bradford, "Useful and Fancy Work," *Hearth and Home* (September 1914).

[10]Gertrude West, "A Block For Friendship," *The Farmer's Wife* (June 1924).

[11]Lillie Webb, taped interview with author, Wichita, KS, Sept. 20, 1986.

[12]McKendry, 100–02.

[13]Jeannette Lasansky, *In the Heart of Pennsylvania* (Lewisburg, PA: Oral Traditions Project, 1985), 26–27.

[14]Ibid., 26.

[15]Bets Ramsey, conversation with author, October 1986; Sandra Todaro, conversation with author, October 1986.

[16]Joan Willis, conversation with author, Iola, KS, 1987.

[17]Correspondence from Gertrude (possibly Mrs. S. N. Frank) and family to Gladys (Mrs. George Browning Dalrymple) and family, Feb. 12, 1932, Jewell, KS. Collection of the author.

[18]Holstein, 85; Linda Otto Lipsett, "A Piece of Ellen's Dress," *Remember Me: Women & Their Friendship Quilts* (San Francisco: Quilt Digest Press, 1985), 80.

[19]Ruth E. Finley, *Old Patchwork Quilts and the Women Who Made Them* (1929; reprint, Newton Centre, MA: Charles T. Branford, 1970), 37.

[20]Webster, 136–39; Orlofsky, 248; Holstein, 85; Mary Antoine de Julio, "A Record of a Woman's Work—The Betsey Reynolds Voorhees Collection," *Uncoverings 1982*, ed. Sally Garoutte (Mill Valley, CA: American Quilt Study Group, 1983), 77, 81.

[21]Miss Vanderwilt's extensive collection of quilt patterns (newspaper clippings, etc.), including the sketches, was purchased by

the author, June 13, 1985, Abilene, KS. The Vanderwilt family owned a general store in nearby Solomon, KS, for many years.

22Unpublished research relating to the ancestry of Phillip Gene Smith, collection of the author. 1870 Federal Population Census, Ozark County, MO, Bridges Township, Gainesville. Martin Robert Smith, known to have had a general store, was listed in 1870 as a kitchen merchant with real estate valued at $1,050 and personal property valued at $1,317. Ozark County, in the heart of the Ozark Mountains in south-central Missouri, is sparsely populated because of its mountainous terrain.

23Elmer L. Smith, *Tinware: Yesterday and Today* (Lebanon, PA: Applied Arts Publishers, 1974; 1976), 18–19; Jeannette Lasansky, "Form and Decoration in Unpainted Pennsylvania Tinware," Part One, *Spinning Wheel* 38, No. 5 (September-October 1982): 20–25.

24Robert Bishop, William Secord, and Judith Reiter Weissman, *Quilts, Coverlets, Rugs, & Samplers* (New York: Knopf, 1982), Plate 266; Joel and Kate Kopp, *American Hooked and Sewn Rugs: Folk Art Underfoot* (New York: Dutton, 1985), 80.

25Florence Peto, *American Quilts and Coverlets* (New York: Chanticleer Press, 1949), 40.

26Bets Ramsey and Merikay Waldvogel, *The Quilts of Tennessee* (Nashville, TN: Rutledge Hill Press, 1986), 52–55; photograph, 53.

27Virginia Gunn, "Victorian Silk Template Patchwork in American Periodicals 1850–1875," *Uncoverings 1983*, ed. Sally Garoutte (Mill Valley, CA: American Quilt Study Group, 1984), 9–25.

28Our Household, *Farm and Fireside* (Dec. 1, 1886): 88.

29Eva M. Niles, Our Household; "Patchwork," Parts 1–2, *Farm and Fireside* (June 1, 1890): 292; (June 15, 1890): 308–09.

30*World Book Encyclopedia*, s.v. "paper"; Robert Bray Wingate, "Restoring Old Books," *Early American Life* (December 1977): 36–39.

31Joseph Gustaitis, "Ottmar Mergenthaler's Wonderful Machine," *American History Illustrated* 21, No. 4 (June 1986): 28–29.

32*World Book Encyclopedia*, s.v. "mail-order business"; *World Book Encyclopedia*, s.v. "Aaron Montgomery Ward"; Brian McGinty, "Mr. Sears & Mr. Roebuck," *American History Illustrated* 21, No. 4 (June 1986): 34–37, 48–49.

33Wilene Smith, "Quilt History in Old Periodicals: A New Interpretation," *Uncoverings 1990*, ed. Laurel Horton (San Francisco: American Quilt Study Group, 1991), 192–94.

34Actually 519; nine designs were discontinued and two numbers were skipped.

35*Farm and Fireside* (Nov. 1, 1891); Smith, "Quilt History," 194.

36*Home Magazine* (July 1902).

37Margaret Walsh, "The Democratization of Fashion: The Emergence of the Women's Dress Pattern Industry," *The Journal of American History* 66, No. 2 (September 1979): 299–313.

38Elizabeth Da[i]ngerfield, "Kentucky Mountain Patchwork Quilts," *Ladies' Home Journal* (July 1909), transfer pattern no. 14170; "The New Flower Patchwork Quilts; Designs by Marie D. Webster," *Ladies' Home Journal* (January 1912), transfer pattern no. 14474. Each pattern was fifteen cents, postage free.

39"Fancy Work for Christmas," *Farmer's Wife* (December 1912).

40Jinny Beyer, *The Quilter's Album of Blocks & Borders* (McLean, VA: EPM Publications, 1980), 3–9.

41Cuesta Benberry, "The 20th Century's First Quilt Revival," Parts 1–3, *Quilter's Newsletter Magazine* 114 (July-August 1979): 20–22; 115 (September 1979): 25–26, 29; 116 (October 1979): 10–11, 37.

42Charlotte F. Boldtmann, "Quaint Patterns for Quilts with Diagrams Showing Sizes and Shapes of Patches," *Farm and Fireside* (Nov. 11, 1911).

43"Quilt Patterns for Busy Fingers," *Farm and Fireside* (March 16, 1912).

44"Quaint Designs in Quilt-Blocks," *Farm and Fireside* (Jan. 4, 1913).

45Oma Haines, taped interview with author, Wichita, KS, Sept. 23, 1986. Oma Belle Pixley Myers Haines (1914–). Maternal grandmother: Sarah Belle Maltby McCain (1869–1938). Paternal great-grandmother: Melissa Amanda (?) McCain (ca. 1831–1932).

46Lillie Webb, taped interview with author, Wichita, KS, Sept. 20, 1986. Lillie Mae Hutcherson Webb (1909–). Mother: Elvalena Turner Hutcherson (1870–1943). Maternal grandmother: Sarah Owens Turner (1851–1923).

47Pansy Smith, taped interview with author, Wichita, KS, Oct. 7, 1986. Pansy Ellen Caldwell Smith (1907–1992). Mother: Margaret (Maggie) Ellen Thomas Caldwell (1874–1959). Paternal grandmother: Minerva L. Childress Caldwell (1856–1933).

48Hinson, 14.

Opposite: Quilt top of pieced pattern blocks, print and solid-color cottons, 75" x 66", made in Columbia County, Pennsylvania. Collection of Howard and Andrew Sechler. Courtesy of Oral Traditions Project.

Amish quilt block collection from Baltic, Coshocton County, Ohio, dates from circa 1962 and is made of the solid-color cottons of their dress fabrics. Private collection. Courtesy of the Ohio Historical Society.

A. ...

Co...

Am...

an...

Vis...

A. H. who enters our school.   I returned-that "my wife" about six o'clock & found Alfred just ready to go after me poor man! he had a dreadful time of it. from the account I find recorded in this journal.   Had a good visit at home. Helped Sarah quilt, on her pink & white quilt, like mine- Also assisted Charles & Augustus in their Algebra- My cold instead of growing better grows worse, and I am comforted this day with a bad cough & an extreme head ache. Took some medicine- It is customary when women leave their children at home to bring them something- I brought my boy a large water-melon & some apples

The Production of Cloth, Clothing, and Quilts

In Nineteenth-Century New England Homes

Lynn A. Bonfield

The daily routine of New England women changed dramatically during the first half of the nineteenth century. At the beginning of the century, the production of cloth and clothing was home-based but by mid-century was concentrated in factories. In 1800, women spent part of every day at home in the work of textile manufacturing; by 1850, few women produced cloth at home. During the same period, as fashions became more complicated, women increasingly spent time sewing. An increase in shopping also can be noted as women became consumers of cloth products. Quilting, which was rarely mentioned at the beginning of the century in comparison to the many references to spinning, twisting, and weaving, continued to be a seldom performed activity in contrast with sewing by the 1850s.

This chapter focuses on this change for New England women as documented through their own words in diaries, letters, account books, reminiscences, memoirs, and interviews. Personal documents are quoted in preference to published histories that often reveal the interpreter's bias rather than the woman's intended meaning. Created for their own eyes, as in diaries, or for other women's eyes, as in letters to mothers or sisters, these private writings reveal the activities and thoughts of ordinary women.[1]

Because of the reliance on primary sources, this chapter has a bias toward the better educated woman. Although eighteenth-century literacy estimates are unreliable, it is known that almost all New England women could read and write by 1840.[2]

Lynn Bonfield, *an archivist for more than thirty years, is director of the Labor Archives & Research Center at San Francisco State University. She and Mary Chase Morrison tell the story of quilters Chastina and Sarah Walbridge in their book,* Roxana's Children: A 19th-Century Vermont Family Biography, *forthcoming from the University of Massachusetts Press. Labor Archives & Research Center, San Francisco State, San Francisco, CA 94132.*

Less educated and presumably less affluent women probably were subjected to harder labor, were less able to afford "store-bought" goods and other amenities of the machine age, and therefore continued longer in the personal process of cloth production. In other words, those less educated women probably produced cloth at home longer than did the women whose writings are quoted here.

In addition, clothing production and particularly quilting were modes of expression for women, and it is possible that women who learned to express themselves by writing might have found less need and less time to express themselves in their former creative ways.[3]

Background

Many of the English who settled in America brought cloth-producing skills with them, so that from the beginning colonial women engaged in home textile production as a routine part of their daily life.[4] This industry included producing the raw material, either wool or flax, on the farm, through the various stages to clothing or bedding.

An elderly farmer reminiscing in the 1860s about Hollister, Vermont, before 1812 said that a farmer kept only as many sheep as "would produce enough wool to clothe his family with their winter garments, or as much as the women could work up."[5] Although farmers in other New England states had produced a surplus of wool earlier, Vermonters did not see a significant increase in the number of sheep until the state legislature passed an act in 1801 saying "every person shall be entitled to a deduction from his list of polls [tax] and rateable estate, of one dollar for each and every sheep not exceeding twenty." Thereafter sheep began to multiply, including the fine-wooled merino sheep that were imported from Spain. In Peacham, Vermont, for instance the Great Registers show a steady increase

in the numbers of sheep in the first decade of the century. Almost every farmer registered his sheep, indicating that each household had the raw product necessary for yarn making.

Other factors that influenced New England home production of textiles included the New England weather. With long winters, combined with inadequate heating of bedrooms, survival dictated ample cloth and clothing production for heavy clothing during the day and warm bedding at night.

Before 1800, cloth production at home was time-consuming and difficult, but by the turn of the century two inventions greatly reduced the labor required. In the South, the cotton gin, invented in 1793, allowed this field crop to be used by family industry. In New England, where wool and flax were the raw materials, the carding machine, after its introduction in North Bennington, Vermont, in 1801, reduced labor by up to one-third. A farmer from that area noted that before then "the wool was carded by hand by the farmers' wives and daughters and spun into yarn upon the 'great wheel,' and then woven into flannel by them or, being doubled and twisted properly dyed, was made into coverlets for beds."[6] The carding machine meant that women could dispense with the card, which resembled a large, oblong wire hairbrush with short bristles set in parallel rows. Once the carding machine was in use, women could send out the "wool to be carded" as Sarah Snell Bryant of western Massachusetts did on July 22, 1804, after "the girls [her daughters and Celia, the hired girl] picked the wool." On July 26, her diary recorded that "Celia went to Mr. Torreys after wool," presumably to pick up the carded wool.[7]

Flax too was a raw material used in home cloth production. One of the reminiscences recorded among Vermonters in the 1860s noted: "The flax, after being retted in the field was prepared . . . for further work of the

family. Here the hetchel separated the tow from finer flax . . . the flax being wound upon the distaff was spun upon the 'little wheel' which was turned by means of a footboard and made into linen yarn. This yarn, being woven into cloth, was used for sheets and pillow-cases, tablecloths, towels, and undergarments." Another man described his earliest recollections including "the buzz of the wheel and the thumping of the old loom; and whenever there came a sunny day in March, the flax-break might be heard at almost every farmer's barn, and very well do I recollect the big bunches of woolen and linen yarns which ornamented the kitchens of the old homestead, spun by my mother and sisters."[8]

Women's Work

The production of cloth depended entirely on women's muscles, stamina, good health, and ability to organize. Of course, this was not the only major chore in women's realm in the early nineteenth century. "In those days women manufactured the cloth with which they and their families were clothed, knit the stockings for themselves, their husbands and sons, as well as leggins for the latter, as boots were not known for boys; did their own housework and made up the clothing for their families."[9] A sixty-year-old housewife, Martha Moore Ballard, wrote in her 1795 diary after midnight on November 26, "A Woman's work is never done."[10] During that day she had been preparing wool for spinning, as well as caring for her house and family. Her diary entries tell of housekeeping and domestic manufacture for a farm in Hallowell, Maine, "where she baked and brewed, pickled and preserved, spun and sewed, made soap and dipped candles." In addition, "she was a trusted healer and midwife," having delivered over a thousand babies.[11]

Like Ballard's, Sarah Snell Bryant's diary revealed a woman whose work

*Weeping Willow counterpane of cotton
yarn on birds-eye weave ground, 99" x
103", made by Laura Collins of Gilford,
Connecticut, 1825. Collection of Shelburne
Museum (#10-390), gift of Mrs. George A.
Comstock. Courtesy of Shelburne
Museum.*

kept her busy from morning to night and beyond. For over fifty years Bryant wrote daily, usually noting the weather, the major household chores, and community events such as marriages, births, and deaths. Only on days when visitors came to her home in Cummington, Massachusetts, was no major chore listed. In 1804, the work recorded throughout the year included "spooled & warped a piece," "mended," "sewed," "hatcheled some flax," "sheep sheared," and "colored yellow." In this year when Bryant was thirty-eight years old, there were 189 entries listing the major work of the day as part of cloth or clothing production.

Bryant made clothes for twelve identified people, including herself, her husband, six children, a hired girl who lived in, and three nonfamily members. In 1804, she produced twelve shirts, seven short gowns, four "tyens" [aprons], nine trousers, five jackets, and three frocks. In addition, she made stockings, nightgowns, petticoats, overalls, pantaloons, breeches, handkerchiefs, and a cooler [short jacket]. For the hired girl she made two short gowns, a shirt, and a spencer. Presumably for exchange, she produced for nonfamily members six pairs of mittens, a coat, a bonnet, a pair of drawers, a blanket, a cravat, and a pair of calfskin shoes. She also "spun a mop," "wove tape," altered her husband's "great coat," and "made bags." Only one cloth purchase was described in this 1804 diary. On November 16, she "rode to Mr. Hubbards store in a sleigh bought me a gown and a set of chelsea ware." The next month she "began to make my gown," indicating that her purchase had been the cloth.[12]

Mrs. Louisa Storrow Higginson, the mother of ten children, resided in Cambridge, Massachusetts, where her husband worked for Harvard College. Most of her letters written during 1827 and 1828 to one of her children concerned the activities of family and friends, although some household chores were mentioned, such as "I was engaged in stewing apples." In almost every letter there is mention of "work," which indicated sewing.

Oct. 22, 1827   We came home and have been quietly seated at our work since.

Thursday, Oct. 25   Stayed at home all the morning quietly sewing.

Tuesday, Dec. 4   Engaged in making my little boy's clothes all day, while he by my side, reading or playing, has been my comfort and delight.

Monday, Dec. 24   I have had a rather tired, confused sort of day—not working to much profit, though working—tomorrow I hope I shall do better.

March 6th [1828]   I have still been engaged in the arduous duty of mantua making which is the most tiresome of all employments—but I have almost got through.[13] [A mantua is usually a loose-fitting gown.]

No matter what their age, women participated in the work of the household. Mrs. Jane Hazelton of Newfane, Vermont, the story goes, celebrated her 100th birthday in 1807 when "she spun a full day's work, and then called her son and told him to set her wheel away, as she had spun her last thread."[14]

Girls' Work

Girls were often "taught to sew sometimes when four years old," remembered a Vermonter.[15] Young Lucy Larcom (1824–93) learned to sew from two maiden aunts, "aunts by courtesy, or rather by the privilege of neighborhood . . . it was one of the earliest accomplishments of my infancy to thread my poor, half-blind Aunt Stanley's needles for her. . . . Many an hour I sat by her side drawing a needle and thread through a bit of calico, under the delusion that I was sewing . . . Another adopted aunt lived down-stairs in the same house. This one was a sober woman; life meant business to her, and she taught me to sew in earnest, with a knot in the end of my thread, although it was only upon clothing for

Counterpane of white twill woven wool blanket embroidered with indigo wool yarn, 87" x 82", marked "M S" in counted cross-stitch, made by Louisa Maria Smith (1851–79) of Vermont, circa 1835. Collection of the Shelburne Museum (#10-160), Shelburne, Vermont. Courtesy of the Shelburne Museum.

my rag-children." Later in her 1889 autobiography, Larcom told of her quilting experiences:

We learned to sew patchwork at school, while we were learning the alphabet; and almost every girl, large or small, had a bed-quilt of her own begun, with an eye to future house furnishing. I was not over fond of sewing, but I thought it best to begin mine early. So I collected a few squares of calico, and undertook to put them together in my usual independent way, without asking direction. I liked assorting those little figured bits of cotton cloth, for they were scraps of gowns I had seen worn, and they reminded me of the persons who wore them. One fragment, in particular, was like a picture to me. It was a delicate pink and brown sea-moss pattern, on a white ground, a piece of a dress belonging to my married sister, who was to me bride and angel in one.[16]

While little girls learned to sew, those past the age of ten were spinning. Hannah Hickok Smith of Connecticut wrote to her mother on June 5, 1800: "The girls [her five daughters] . . . have been very busy spinning this spring and have spun enough for about seventy yards besides almost enough for another carpet."[17] The Walbridge sisters of Wolcott, Vermont—Martha, Chastina, Sarah, and Clara—spent their adolescent years in the 1830s at the wheel. When reviewing Chastina's life in the first pages of a diary begun in 1849, her husband wrote teasingly of the differences between her and her older sister.

The course of our heroine's life till she reached her thirteenth year [1837] was the same as that of most girls in the country— the daughters of farmers—that is, labor six days in the week, attend church on Sunday. . . . We can now see in the eye of imagination and memory, the little fair faced Chastina at the wheel—while scarcely tall enough to reach the spindle— drawing out the thread from morning till night and humming to herself some favorite ditty. Sometimes the thread would break. On such an occasion it was possible to mark the differences of disposition in the two girls Martha & Chastina, the

former would bite her lip, seize hold of her wheel and give it a hearty shaking, while the latter would half say and half sing as she was mending the break, "Fish-fiddle-dum!"[18]

Even the sick were expected to do what they could. Sarah Mills, who lived near Hadlyme, Connecticut, kept a diary in 1809–10, when she was eighteen, in which she recorded her continual poor health as well as her work.

Jan. 5, 1809   have done very little of any thing except braiding a little trimming for Eliza.

Jan. 10   braided 3 yards of straw

Jan. 13   weaving

Jan. 18   Unable to do anything scarcely . . . knit a little.

Jan. 21   Enjoyed tolerable health. And some mending braided a little.

Jan. 23   I feel pretty feeble but have been able to sew a little, mended John's clothes a little.

Jan. 24   I have pulled out my needles and began another stocking today.

Jan. 25   Better today, have had a pretty comfortable day. Made me a work bag.

Jan. 26   Spent my time in sewing, and a little knitting.[19]

Advice Books

The most popular advice book for homemakers in the first half of the nineteenth century was Lydia Maria Child's *The American Frugal Housewife*. The introduction of the thirty-first edition, published in 1845, summarized the philosophy of thrift of that period:

The true economy of housekeeping is simply the art of gathering up all the fragments, so that nothing is lost. I mean fragments of *time*, as well as *materials*. Nothing should be thrown away so long as it is possible to make any use of it, however trifling that use may be; and whatever be the size of the family, every member should be employed either in earning or saving money. . . . In this point of view, patchwork is good economy. It is indeed a foolish waste of time to tear cloth into bits for the sake of arrang-

Bed rug made of dyed wools and embroidered on plain weave wool fabric, 100″ x 89½″, for "John and Dorothye Seabury of Stow[e], Vermont, March 1819." Collection of the Shelburne Museum (#10-615), Shelburne, Vermont. Courtesy of the Shelburne Museum.

ing it anew in fantastic figures; but a large family may be kept out of idleness, and a few shillings saved, by thus using scraps of gowns, curtains, &c.[20]

A successful author and editor, Child lived a life of economy herself. Her 1864 diary listed her domestic activities for the year, including 44 separate chores, such as "Cooked 360 dinners," "Filled lamps 362 times," and "Mended 70 pair of stockings." In comparison, only seven intellectual pursuits were outlined, including "Wrote 235 letters," "Read to myself 7 volumes," and "Corrected Proofs for Sunset book." Two quilt references showed up among her list of domestic work. In 1864, Child "Made a starred crib quilt, and quilted it; one fort-nights work," and sewed "1 quilted petticoat."[21]

By the 1860s, another advice book gained recognition, *The American Woman's Home*, by Catherine E. Beecher and Harriet Beecher Stowe. These famous sisters mentioned sewing for girls: "When a little girl begins to sew, her mother can promise her a small bed and pillow, as soon as she has sewed a patch quilt for them."[22]

Quilts

From the turn of the century to about 1850, quilting appeared to be of secondary concern to the production of cloth and clothing, which was a daily activity in most households. Letters and diaries written during the period referred to quilts and quilting very few times. On the other hand, memoirs, autobiographies, reminiscences, and interviews written *after* the time often mentioned quilting, indicating more quilt-related activity taking place than probably did. In addition, these writings from later years often romanticized quiltmaking. One of these later recorders wrote: "The odd bits and ends of calico dresses were cut and basted for bed-quilt blocks by the mother and given to Miss to sew. The cover to her quilt she was expected to finish by the time she became marriageable, and it was

to be part of her marriage outfit. When the girl had attained somewhere near her majority, eighteen or somewhere near, a quilting was given. All the young ladies of the neighborhood assembled at her house to complete the bed quilt."[23] No diary or letter written at the time noted anything similar to this type of quilting that was common in reminiscences.

Another term not found in private writings from the first half of the nineteenth century was "quilting bee," meaning a social gathering of women to quilt. The word "quiltings," as a neighborhood gathering, was used in diaries and letters written at the time. "Bees" was found in reference to "paring-bees" or "sewing bees," as in an 1849 letter by Fredrika Bremer, well-known Swedish novelist, who came to the United States for a visit.

I have been at a "bee!" And if you would know what this creature is in society here, then behold! If a family is reduced to poverty by fire or sickness, and the children are in want of clothes or anything else, a number of ladies of the neighborhood who are in good circumstances immediately get together at some place and sew for them. Such a sewing assembly is called a *bee*! And now there was a bee at the house of Mrs. Sparks, the wife of the president of the university [Harvard], to sew for a family who had lost all their clothing through fire, and I was invited to be present at it. The beehive was fine, busy, and gay, and had, if not honey, remarkably good milk and cake to offer the working bees, among whom I took my place, but not to do very much.[24]

Bees in relation to quilting turned up in reminiscences and private writings later in the century.

Bryant's 1804 diary gave strong evidence of almost daily cloth-production activity but mentioned quilting only four times. At this date, it is likely that the quilting was on a coat or petticoat rather than a bedcover.

May 30 [1804] went to quilting to Mr. Porter

June 20 girls went to quilting to

Mr. Nortons

September 14 went to Mr. Porters quilting

September 17 girls went to Mr. Porters quilting.

Because the only community social event Bryant described was a lecture at the meeting house, these "quiltings" must have been an important way for women to visit with other women.[25]

The diary of Elizabeth Porter Phelps covered more than fifty years, beginning in 1763 when as a teenager she lived with her widowed sick mother in Hadley, Massachusetts. In the early years, her weekly diary listed only the Sunday sermon subjects. Soon she expanded to community events such as births and deaths, and finally she began to describe the many comings and goings within her upper-class home. Living in a household with servants, both before and after her marriage to a prominent lawyer, she participated in few domestic chores. The only ones listed were "made candles," "made soap," "filled sausages," and "made mince meat pies." Throughout the diary, there is mention of seamstresses, usually young girls, coming "to make me a dark calico Gown," "to make a pair of stays for my Mother and alter a gown," "to taylour mens cloaths," and "to help make a cloak." These same girls and others were also often noted as coming to the house to spin or weave. Sometimes as many as three different names were mentioned in a week, such as in April 1768.

The one household activity that Phelps participated in with regularity was quilting, usually with family members. While an adolescent, she noted almost monthly that "this day have been a quilting." Her diary recorded quilting five times during the summer of 1767, six times in 1768, and eleven times in 1769. At this time, quilting commonly referred to petticoats and only to bed quilts where specifically noted. Entries that gave details of the quilts or the quilting experience include:

June 8. [1767] Tuesday Sally Goodrich came here to help me quilt—at night Miss Patty came to help me. Thursday about noon we finished the quilt (twas a black one for mother).

August 2. Wednesday went to Esq. Porters to quilt on Sally Goodridge's Blue Quilt.

August 9. Wednesday went to Esq. Porters to quilt upon a Blue Downy quilt for Mrs. Porter.

June 26. [1768] Tuesday Morning I went to quilt on a quilt for my aunt Porter—we finished the quilt before 11.

July 3 Wednesday morn, my Aunt Porter came here to stay to have me go to quilting for Miss Patty upon a Crimson Duerant returned on Fryday night.

March 26. [1769] Tuesday Mr. Porter came here—I went with him into town to Quilting at his house—finished the Bed-quilt.

June 25. Tuesday I went to quilt for Mrs. Dean.
Wednesday morning went into town to the Esq. to quilt upon a brown callimeno coat for Mrs. Porter.

July 30. Tuesday I went to My Aunt Marshes to quilt a coat for her and one for her Daughter Becky. Miss Polly Miss Pen and others helped.

August 13. Wednesday went to quilt upon a black Callimineo coat for Mrs. Hop.

August 27. Thursday morning went to quilt upon a bed-quilt for my aunt Porter.

Two weeks after her marriage in 1770, she "went into town to quilting on a coat for Polly." Then for the next seventeen years, during which she had four children and assumed the total responsibility for running her household, she rarely mentioned quilting. In 1788, however, when she was forty years old, there were five entries relating to quilting, not much different from her earlier notations.

August 17. [1788] Thursday to Mr. Hop. to help Quilt.

Sep. 28 Tuesday sister Warner here in the morn to help me Quilt a Bedquilt for sister Dickinson.

October 5 I at Brothers to help Sister Quilt.

Oct. 12 Wednesday sister Warner here to help me Quilt Thankfuls [her daughter] Quilt; did Bettys [possibly her other daughter, Elizabeth] yesterday.

Oct. 26 Thursday sister Warner and Mrs. Shipman here to help me Quilt a Bed quilt for Porter. Fryday here again.
Satt. Porter got home—the Bed-quilt got off just at night.
Soon her two daughters had taken up the skill of quilting and their visits to family and friends were noted.

August 1. [1790] the girls went to Mr. Gaylords. Fryday just at night got home—stayed to help quilt.

June 16 [1793] Wednesday the girls to quilt at Mr. Hop.

Dec. 7 [1794] Thursday the girls at Dr. Porter's quilting.

Throughout most of her life, Phelps quilted with other women often. Her last quilting entry in her weekly diary told of the quilt for her youngest daughter, now herself a mother.

May 12. [1805] Wednesday about noon the Miss Cutlers came here to help us quilt a green crape bed-quilt for daughter Huntington—we had jest got it on when they came. Polly Warner came here this morning. Mitte West came last night. Thursday forenoon the Miss Cutlers left us. Fryday about 3 we got it off.[26]

During the last decade (the 1830s) of extensive spinning, twisting, and weaving at home, Sally and Pamela Brown of Plymouth Notch, Vermont, kept diaries that detailed these daily duties. During the summer months, they taught school, as did a quarter of all New England-born women sometime in their lives between 1825 and 1860.[27] Even while teaching, their fingers were never idle, for the Browns had eleven children who needed warm clothing and bedding. Quilting was mentioned regularly. From November 1836 to March 1838, their mother, who was about fifty, attended at least two quiltings, while they went to five. Of the latter, one was at their married sister's and another—which continued

Counterpane of glazed indigo wool, 93¼" x 91⅛", made by Esther Wheat (1774–1847) of Conway, Massachusetts, circa 1790–99. The original wool back has been replaced with a quilted red wool/ cotton twill and a new machine-stitched applied binding. Quilting was in a two-ply dark blue wool, 8 stitches per inch. Collection of the Smithsonian Institution, gift of Mrs. Olive E. Hulbert, great-great-grand-daughter of maker.

This glazed indigo wool counterpane features the richness and grand expanse of its fabric surface as well as its quilted designs: a large feathered star and two pineapples surrounded by a scrolling vine with large flowers. The background quilting is diagonal lines set 3/8" apart.

for three days—at Capt. Wilder's. At the last one, Pamela wrote that she "Made up my blue coverlet that Mrs. Ordway made last spring." The sisters also helped quilt "a woolen petticoat," "pieced a bed quilt of old calico," and "quilted the lining for [their sister's] cloak."

Once, after a month of continual sewing, including a nightgown, muslin gown, cloak, and shirt, Pamela wrote, "I have a sore thumb." Again after a lengthy period of sewing, she complained of sore fingers, which kept her from sewing for two weeks, although she was able to continue her teaching. This temporary soreness seemed slight in comparison to the problems of a factory girl whom Pamela wrote about in March 1837: "Orpha Sawyer came out spent a week with us. She has had one of her fingers taken in the factory a few weeks since. We feel very sorry for her."[28]

Domestic Service or "Working Out"
The labor of young unmarried women was often needed to help sustain their families. Wages earned outside the home sometimes provided support for younger siblings, helped pay off the farm's debts, and allowed brothers to gain an education. Some girls worked as hired help on a daily basis, as those who helped in the Phelps household.[29] Others lived in, as did the series of young girls recorded in Bryant's diary, who "wove," "got out a piece," "drew in the aprons," and "spun."[30]

Chloe Samson, both a seamstress and a laundress, in Pembroke, Massachusetts, occasionally did domestic service outside her home, such as "when Sophia died" and she spent ten days at that household, charging two shillings per day. For one shilling on March 19, 1822, she listed in her account book "3 days making a bed quilt." She also made "Thomas's uniform," "wedding coat," and various "baby's clothing."[31]

Sometimes the need for additional

funds in a household coincided with the need for more help in another home. At age thirteen, the death of her father changed the life of Chastina Walbridge. While her three sisters remained at home, she was sent from their farm in Wolcott, Vermont, to the home of her uncle in Dunham, Canada. Recalling this event over ten years later, she wrote in the third person of the 1837 adventure: "This being the first time that she was ever far from home—a long journey it seemed to her—from W. [Wolcott] by way of Stanstead about seventy-five miles. She had scarcely ever seen her relatives there, so that it was among strangers that she was going to reside. Her aunt was very kind to her, taught her in many useful branches of home industry."[32] Even young girls fortunate enough to attend schools such as Miss Pierce's School in Litchfield, Connecticut, were expected to work as well as to study. Catherine van Schaack wrote in her journal for the summer of 1809: "Thursday attended school in the Morning—recited a lesson in Grammar and painted. In the evening went to Conference. Saturday Morning, wrote journal, in the afternoon quilted for Miss Anne Baldwin. After tea took a short walk, in the evening, sung psalms and heard prayers."[33]

The possible wage-earning occupations of teaching, needle trades, and domestic service were expanded to factory work by the 1840s. The first industrial spinning machinery came to New England at the turn of the century, but even then, the yarn that was produced was given out to women for weaving within their households. The power loom appeared around 1814, and eventually by the 1820s factory mass production of cloth was accomplished. By 1830, industrial manufacturing had surpassed home production in New England.[34] The result was a radical change in family routine as home production was reduced or ceased, but also the change forced the unmarried young women

Counterpane of wholecloth with appliqué print cottons, 91" x 80", made by Jeriesha Kelsey, Boston, Massachusetts, circa 1800–10. Back is plain cotton with cotton tape as edge treatment. Collection of the Shelburne Museum (#10-698), Shelburne, Vermont. Courtesy of the Shelburne Museum.

to leave home to earn wages, often to leave the state for lengthy periods of time.

In 1840, the women residing in Lowell, Massachusetts, numbered 6,320 with the majority coming from the farms of Maine, New Hampshire, and Vermont. For these girls the in-dustrial revolution meant the separation of workplace from home, the replacement of family production with wage earning, and the institution of time-discipline by machine regularity rather than the natural pattern of farm life. Historian Nancy F. Cott calls this the division of "work" from "life."[35]

Sewing

After the production of cloth was no longer a predominant home-based activity, sewing continued to occupy much of each woman's day. For instance, Anna and Georgia Whitwell of Fairhaven, Massachusetts, where their father ran a successful whaling ship business, were very clothes conscious. They exchanged long detailed letters after Anna married and then throughout their lives, describing the kinds of material purchased and the style of clothes they created. In September 1843, the fashion-setter Georgia wrote her sister:

I have been busy, so busy, I could not write you; but now I can. I have sewed so much that I have cut my fingers bad with the thread. I cannot sew so steady. I have a silver fender for my third finger, bought it in Boston. It is a blessing—looks quite like a thimble. About your dress and the bodice point—I have one dress made very long under the arms and then plain across the front. Not the least point. We have nothing prettier than tight sleeves—perhaps a cuff over the top, trimmed with fringe. Fringe is *awful* fashionable. Skirts gathered always. If you wear an apron, I would have it gathered and a plain place left in front. To line the dresses makes them hang prettier and as for skirts, the more the better.

Often Georgia's letters were a veritable compendium of sewing instructions with sketches she had drawn and long descriptions of how to make a coat out of a shawl, the style of collars, and directions for trimming a hat. But what is most noteworthy about all this is that these yards and yards of material were sewn by hand. Voluminous skirts and enormous detail in bodices were quite the style set by *Godey's Lady's Book*, first appearing in 1837. The benefit of the sewing machine did not come for twenty years, and was first mentioned by Anna's daughter in a letter of March 1867. "I wish I was one of those sassy sorts that never gets in a fret over anything. Didn't this sewing machine help me along fast. I never

mean to sew by hand any more if I can help it."[36] The same sentiment of saving time with a sewing machine was expressed often in women's letters of the 1860s.

Women as Consumers

Wealthy women, subjected to less strenuous work than their poorer sisters, often supervised servants in home production of cloth and clothing. From their diaries and letters, however, these women began noting shopping trips by the end of the eighteenth century. Phelps wrote often of going "into town to do some arrands" or "Went out a shopping." Usually the purchases were not listed, although in 1804, she did note that she "rode to Northhampton to get shades & lace."[37] Hannah Hickok Smith, in her 1821–24 account book, listed the purchase in Glastonbury, Connecticut, of at least eleven different kinds of fabric including dimity, brown holland, "factory cloth," four kinds of yarn and thread, leather, and buttons. She also bought silk, shawls, bonnets, dresses, stockings, and kid gloves.[38]

Although the Walbridge sisters were brought up making cloth at home in the 1830s, by 1850, like most women, they had begun to purchase material for their clothes. When Chastina noted in her diary that she "went to the Corner," she meant the general store, located where two roads crossed. This would be followed within a few days with a diary entry such as "C at home on her dress," or "C making a shirt." Christmas 1849, Chastina found a thimble in her "well filled stocking," which she put to good use the next month.

Thursday 10 [1850]   Alfred [her husband] went to the Hollow [to a store] with me to get me a new dress.

Saturday 12   making Tina's [Chastina's] new dress.

Monday 21   Chastina making her dress

Wednesday 23   I have at last finished my dress, which has been on hand for two weeks.

The importance of the local store was noted in Alfred's entry the next week:

Saturday 26   Chastina darned a darned pair of breeches and began to make another of the "same sort" but gave it up on a promise of one from the store.[39]

The Story of a Vermont Quilt

Chastina Walbridge Rix's life illustrates the changes in domestic routine for women described in this chapter. As a young girl and through adolescence, she helped in home cloth production; as a wife and mother, she purchased material from the store, which she then sewed into clothes for her family.

The traditional song "When I Saw Sweet Nellie Home," first published in 1858, may have been based on fact as well as sentiment. It may even have been describing the manner of the meeting of Chastina Walbridge and Alfred Rix, who began a diary together on their wedding day, July 29, 1849, in Peacham, Vermont. The first few pages were devoted to their biographies and the history of their courtship.

In the spring of the year 1841 the usual quiet of our maiden's life and heart was slightly disturbed by the arrival in her neighborhood of a young man by the name of Alf. Rix who was just commencing his studies preparatory to entering college. . . . On the very important and ominous occasion of a quilting at Mrs. Stevens where Alfred resided the two were introduced to each other. The mutual impression was favorable and from that hour until the present each has not ceased to be of more importance in the eyes of the other than any other individual.

A few paragraphs later, Alfred continued: "'Quiltings,' 'paring-bees' etc. brought them more or less together that autumn." After the wedding and a short trip, they moved into their "new apartments" near the Peacham Academy, where he served as principal. In August, on the day after their move to their new home, they wrote:

Thursday 23 [1849] Rainy. We wrote on Chastina's life as found in the first of this volume. C. trims her quilt and A. tinkers & laughs.

Three additional references to her quilt were added in November:

Monday 26 C. washed & got to the frames her quilt.
Tuesday 27 Chastina got out her quilt.
Wednesday 28 Sewing.

The quilt referred to was presumably a bed quilt for her new home. A similar bed quilt was made in September for her sister Sarah before her marriage.

Saturday 22 Helped Sarah quilt, on her pink & white quilt like mine.[40]

Thus two sisters made similar quilts around the date of their marriages.

It is possible that in this rural Vermont town there may have been a traditional quilt pattern. In the 1970s, old-timers remember the popularity of pink and white quilts in the early twentieth century. A visitor to Peacham in 1927, Mrs. A. E. Harrington of Petersfield, England, described the quilts she found there, perhaps similar to the ones the Walbridge sisters made: "I must not forget to mention the patchwork quilts . . . handed down from mother to daughter. The favourite design seems to have been rows of pink cotton baskets, with white spaces between filled in with maple leaves, cleverly outlined in darning stitch."[41] Two years after their marriage, Alfred caught gold fever and left for California. Chastina remained in Peacham with their son, Julian, and after several months, moved back to her mother's house. There her daily routine revolved around housekeeping and child care. Mondays without fail she washed, a difficult chore for a household of at least eight people. One Monday in July 1852, she noted, "We have washed, and besides the weeks washing I have washed three bed quilts."

Perhaps to give herself something to do or because wool was plentiful,

Chastina returned to an old skill that summer. "Have been spinning some. The first I have spun for about three years. I make rather bad work to what I used to & it makes me rather tired. Have spun little more than half a days work." Through the summer she spun often, dwelling in her mind on a plan Alfred had proposed from San Francisco, where he was now teaching. At last on September 21, she decided to join her husband and wrote in her diary that she "had made up my mind to go to California." On November 16, 1852, she "began packing my box again for California. I feel many doubts about my ever seeing it again, and it is with feelings of regret that I put in *my all* that has cost me so many hard days of labor, for first *earn* & then make. Many an hour & day & week I have labored for them & should they all be lost this testimony of my regrets will also be lost. I must bid adieu to this our journal."[42]

The diary from which these lines were quoted was nestled among the handmade clothes and linens, including possibly her pink and white quilt. Around the Cape the box traveled while Chastina and Julian journeyed via the Isthmus, arriving in San Francisco almost three months before their box. In Alfred's May 10, 1853, letter to Chastina's family in Peacham, he wrote: "By the way I ought to tell you that on opening the box everything was found as perfectly clean, dry & whole as when it was packed—not a shilling's damage in all."[43] In this manner, a Vermont quilt may have found its way to California.

Conclusion

By the middle of the nineteenth century, women's personal writings in New England indicated an elimination of home cloth production, an increase in cloth and clothing purchasing, and the continuation of home sewing, often highly complicated. During this same period, there appeared to be only scarce mention of quilting by women who kept diaries and wrote

letters. Where it was noted, it was in small proportion to cloth making at the beginning of the century and to sewing later on. Frequently quilting was described as a gathering of two or more women, thereby serving as a social event as in the lives of Bryant, Phelps, and the Brown sisters.

When writing of colonial times, quilt historian Sally Garoutte concluded "that quilts were not common or ordinary articles." She went on to point out that American colonial women who made quilts did not do so for "either economic or practical" reasons.[44] These same conclusions seemed to apply equally to the first half of the nineteenth century, according to women's writings from the period. There was mention of quilts presumably for babies in the diaries of Child and Phelps and for the weddings of Chastina and Sarah Walbridge. In addition, quilting or patchwork was noted as a means of teaching young girls to sew, as in Lucy Larcom's early years.

Historians are now in a new phase of women's scholarship that began in the late 1960s. Many of the misconceptions of male-dominated history have been corrected. Notable women and heroines have been identified. Credence has been given to women's role in family and community life. Now the facts about women's lives, the daily experiences of ordinary women, are being reconstructed. The history of quilts and quilting belongs in this study of women's friendship, collective housekeeping, sibling relationships, women's aesthetics, domestic routines, and the role of women at different ages and in different economic classes. Women's personal documents, the diaries, letters, scrapbooks, and accounts kept at the time must be the basis of this historical research.[45]

Notes and References

[1]Nancy F. Cott, *The Bonds of Womanhood, "Woman's Sphere" in New England, 1780–1835* (New Haven, CT: Yale Uni-

versity Press, 1977). Throughout this chapter the author is indebted to Professor Cott for providing background on nineteenth-century women's activities and their changes, and for referring her to the writings of Ballard, Bryant, Higginson, Mills, and Smith (see below). The use and meaning of women's private writings are discussed brilliantly in Cott's introduction, 1–18. For additional material on Bonfield's view of women's diaries and letters, see her articles in *California Historical Quarterly*, (Winter 1975), 359–72; (Spring 1977), 72–81.

[2]Cott, 30.

[3]The author thanks the participants at the American Quilt Study Group 1981 Seminar for suggesting this idea.

[4]Sally Garoutte, "Cloth in North America in the 17th and 18th Centuries: Sources and Distribution," *Book of Papers* (Research Triangle Park, NC: American Textile Chemists and Colorists, 1979), 132–36.

[5]Bertha S. Dodge, *Tales of Vermont, Ways and People* (Harrisburg, PA: Stackpole Books, 1977), 104.

[6]Dodge, 50.

[7]Sarah Snell Bryant Diary, July 22 and July 26, 1804. *Sarah Snell Bryant Diaries, 1795–1847*, Houghton Library, Harvard University, Cambridge, MA.

[8]Dodge, 50, 85. Abby Maria Hemenway (1828–90) collected Vermont reminiscences and published them in *The Vermont Historical Gazetteer*, 1867–91. Dodge has excerpted these.

[9]Dodge, 49.

[10]Cott, 19. According to Bartlett's *Familiar Quotations*, the first reference to "A woman's work is never done" was by Laurence Eusden at a Cambridge commencement in 1714.

[11]Martha Ballard, "Mrs. Ballard's Diary," in *The History of Augusta, Maine*, Charles E. Nash, ed. (Augusta, ME: Charles Nash and Sons, 1904), 229–464. Since I wrote this article, Laurel Thatcher Ulrich has published *A Midwife's Tale: The Life of Martha Ballard, Based on Her Diary, 1785–1812* (New York, NY: Knopf, 1990), which is more accurate and more complete than the version I used.

[12]Bryant Diary, 1804.

[13]Thomas Wentworth Higginson, ed., "Cambridge Eighty Years Since, [Letters in the form of a diary by Louisa Higginson, 1817–1829]," *Cambridge Historical Society Publications II* (Cambridge, MA: Cambridge Historical Society, 1907), 20–32.

[14]Dodge, 51.

[15]Dodge, 64.

[16]Lucy Larcom, *A New England Girlhood* (Gloucester, MA: Peter Smith, 1973), 27–29, 122.

[17]Cott, 26–27.

[18]Alfred & Chastina W. Rix Diary, biographical pages, Rix Family Papers, California Historical Society Library, San Francisco.

[19]Sarah Mills Diary, January 1809, Selden-Conant Papers, Vermont Historical Society, Montpelier.

[20]Lydia Maria Child, *The American Frugal Housewife* (New York: S&W Wood, 1845), 1.

[21]Lydia Maria Child [Diary, 1864] in Gerda Lerner, *The Female Experience: An American Documentary* (Indianapolis, IN: Bobbs-Merrill, 1977), 124–26.

[22]Catherine E. Beecher and Harriet Beecher Stowe, *The American Woman's Home* (New York: Ford, 1869), 298. The author is indebted to Jane Begos for this reference.

[23]Dodge, 64.

[24]Adolph B. Benson, ed., *America of the Fifties: Letters of Fredrika Bremer* (New York: The American-Scandinavian Foundation, 1924), 54.

[25]Bryant Diary, 1804. Nineteenth-century households were identified by the husband's name.

[26]Thomas Eliot Andrews, ed., "The Diary of Elizabeth (Porter) Phelps," *The New England Historical and Genealogical Register*, 1964–1968: 118–22.

[27]Cott, 34–35.

[28]Blanche Brown Bryant and Gertrude Elaine Baker, eds., *The Diaries of Sally and Pamela Brown, 1832–1838, Hyde Leslie 1887, Plymouth Notch, Vermont* (Springfield, VT: William L. Bryant Foundation, 1979), 7–94.

[29]Andrews, Phelps Diary.

[30]Bryant Diary, 1804.

[31]Chloe Samson, account book, 1819–64, Schlesinger Library, Radcliffe College, Cambridge, MA, esp. 1820, 1822, 1825.

[32]Rix Diary, biographical pages.

[33]Mirra Banks, *Anonymous Was A Woman* (New York: St. Martin's, 1979), 37.

[34]Cott, 36.

[35]Cott, 56, 60–63.

[36]Mary Rathbone Acker, *My Dearest Anna, Letters of The Richmond Family, 1836–1898* (Chicago, IL: Adams Press, 1981), 42–43, 200.

[37]Andrews, Phelps Diary, Aug. 12, 1804.

[38]Cott, 43–44.

[39]Rix Diary, Dec. 6, 25, 1849; Jan. 2, 10, 12, 21, 23, 26, 1850.

[40]Rix Diary, July 29, Aug. 23, Sept. 22, Nov. 26, 27, 28, 1849.

[41]Mrs. A. E. Harrington, "Some Impressions of America, 1927," 3, Peacham Historical Association, Peacham, VT.

[42]Rix Diary, July 20, 26; Sept. 21; Nov. 16, 1852.

[43]Alfred S. Rix in San Francisco, CA, to "Dear Friends" in Peacham, VT, May 10, 1855, Edward A. Rix Collection, Bancroft Library, University of California, Berkeley.

[44]Sally Garoutte, "Early Colonial Quilts in a Bedding Context," in *Uncoverings 1980*, ed. Sally Garoutte, (Mill Valley, CA: American Quilt Study Group, 1981), 25.

[45]For further documentation on nineteenth-century New England quilting, see the author's article, "Diaries of New England Quilters Before 1860," *Uncoverings 1988*, ed. Laurel Horton (San Francisco, CA: American Quilt Study Group, 1989), 171–97.

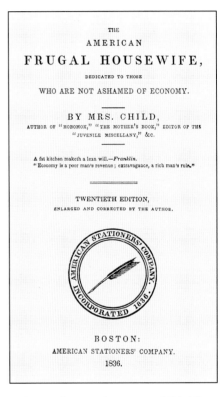

THE

AMERICAN

FRUGAL HOUSEWIFE,

DEDICATED TO THOSE

WHO ARE NOT ASHAMED OF ECONOMY.

BY MRS. CHILD,

AUTHOR OF "HOBOMOK," "THE MOTHER'S BOOK," EDITOR OF THE "JUVENILE MISCELLANY," &c.

A fat kitchen maketh a lean will.—*Franklin.*
"Economy is a poor man's revenue; extravagance, a rich man's ruin."

TWENTIETH EDITION,
ENLARGED AND CORRECTED BY THE AUTHOR.

BOSTON:
AMERICAN STATIONERS' COMPANY.
1836.

Title page from Lydia Maria Child's The American Frugal Housewife, *the twentieth edition, 1836. This book was first published in 1829 as* The Frugal Housewife. *The title was changed in 1833 to distinguish it from editions published abroad. The author explained her ideas on how people ought to manage on a small income and still maintain their self-respect. A popular subject—then and now.*

Detail of white-on-white cotton candlewick counterpane worked by Eliza Magdadien of Annapolis, Anne Arundel County, Maryland, in 1809. Private collection. Courtesy of the Museum of Early Southern Decorative Arts.

Double woven wool and cotton coverlet made in Frederick County, Maryland. Collection of the Maryland Historical Society, gift of Miss Mary Falconer (#53.90.1). Courtesy of the Maryland Historical Society.

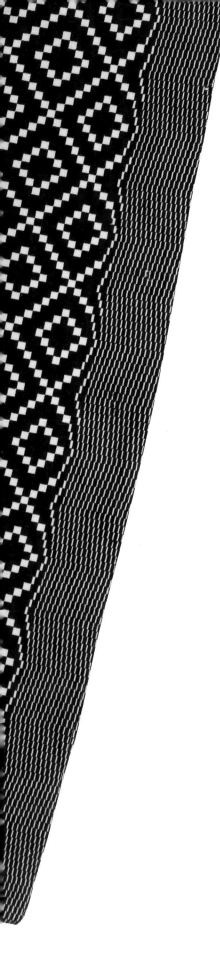

Bedcoverings in Kent County, Maryland 1710–1820

Gloria Seaman Allen

Textile furnishings made during the eighteenth century and used in Southern homes are today very rare. Only a few examples, which were very costly or had a ceremonial or personal significance, have been preserved. These were usually the possessions of the upper classes. Probate inventories extend our knowledge of eighteenth-century textiles beyond the holdings of the wealthy. They record the possessions of a large socioeconomic cross section of society from the very wealthy to the relatively poor. An analysis of 360 estate inventories, recorded between 1710 and 1820, reveals considerable information about the textile furnishings of residents of one small Southern community—Kent County, Maryland.

Setting

By the end of the first decade of the eighteenth century, Kent, the second oldest county in Maryland, had been reduced in size to its present boundaries.[1] Located on the Eastern Shore, the county totaled 223,163 acres of primarily tillable land with considerable water access along estuaries of the Chesapeake Bay. The population of 2,750 people was essentially native-born and stable. The vast majority of the people were descended from British immigrants and followed the Anglican religion. Plantations were strung out along the waterways rather than clustered around village settlements. The agrarian economy was originally based on tobacco, but by 1750 a diversified agricultural system placed Kent County at an advantage over other Maryland and Virginia counties still dependent on tobacco as their primary source of income.

Gloria Seaman Allen *is the former director and chief curator of the DAR Museum in Washington, DC. She is a doctoral candidate in American Studies/Material Culture/Folk Life at George Washington University and is writing a book based on the Maryland quilt documentation project. She is the author of* Old Line Traditions: Maryland Women and Their Quilts, First Flowerings: Early Virginia Quilts, *and numerous articles on textiles and ceramics. 9009 Clewerwall Drive, Bethesda, MD 20817.*

Active export trade with the West Indies centered on the Eastern Shore, particularly at the county seat of Chestertown, a port of entry with authority to collect customs. In return for exports of tobacco, corn, wheat, lumber, and naval stores, Chestertown received raw materials and manufactured goods from the West Indies, Azores, Europe, and England. Brisk trade stimulated agricultural production and fostered related industries in the form of flour milling and bread making. Ship building, ship refitting, ship stores, and the manufacturing of cordage and rope were also important to the economy of Kent County. A ferry system provided access to imported luxuries from Annapolis and later from Baltimore, and the post road, which passed through Chestertown, linked the county with the port of Philadelphia.

Prosperity continued up until the 1770s when increasing restrictions, resulting from hostilities with Britain, finally curtailed trade in the network of waterways forming the Chesapeake Bay system. After the Revolution, Chestertown never regained its former prominence as a port and customs clearinghouse. Commerce in the Chesapeake region centered in Baltimore with its accessible harbor and expanding inland trade.

Economic Background of the Chesapeake Region

The Chesapeake region is part of the Atlantic community, and in the colonial period it was closely linked with the economy of Britain. Starting in the late seventeenth century and continuing through the eighteenth century, a significant change took place in the ability of British people to acquire consumer goods. During the second half of the eighteenth century there was a dramatic increase in the purchasing power of the middle class.[2] The opportunity to accumulate additional money for purchasing goods beyond those required for sub-

sistence paralleled increased production of goods and diversification within a specific classification of manufacturers. The trend toward conspicuous consumption and the new ways of using available goods were contributing factors to the industrial revolution. In Maryland and in other English colonies, consumption patterns followed, at a slightly later date, those of England.[3] More people were able to acquire more goods regardless of their wealth or social standing. By

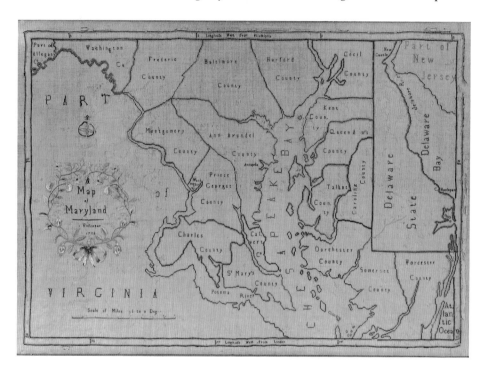

the close of the eighteenth century, the greater availability of manufactured goods contributed to a "common standard of refined living" where almost everyone could aspire to own what had once been confined to ownership by the elite.[4]

Textiles constituted a major category of British consumer products. With technological innovations, increased selection, graduated pricing, better marketing, and improved communications, more textiles became available to more people. The rapid increase in the use of textiles and textile furnishings can be confirmed by the findings from Kent County. Between 1740 and 1780 there was an increase in both the number and vari-

ety of textile goods as well as democratization of ownership. Liberal extension of credit contributed to expanded use. However, this steadily increasing demand varied with specific furnishings and with fashion, and it was temporarily curtailed during the Revolution.

Probate Records and Methodology

The analysis of probate records for evidence of consumption patterns of textile furnishings is an interdisciplinary study touching on areas of social and economic history as well as decorative arts and its subspecialty of textile history.

Probate records provide a wealth of information about the nature, use, and assemblage of material possessions owned by a broad spectrum of society. They contain evidence of the daily existence of ordinary people who made up the majority of the eighteenth-century population. Probate records also provide evidence of the consumer preferences and financial means of people who left no artifacts or written documents. These records are, therefore, valuable sources of information for many aspects of historical study from various geographical areas, but they are especially valuable for areas where documentation about all classes, including the upper class, is scant or where archaeological evidence is not widespread. Kent County, Maryland, is such an area.

Probate records consist of estate inventories, wills, and administration accounts.[5] Inventories are both fascinating and frustrating, but unquestionably they are invaluable historical documents in which ordinary people describe the ordinary objects of daily living. Inventories list and value goods and chattels, or all property that could be physically removed from the premises. Objects attached to the architectural framework were not included because, in theory, they were considered part of the real estate. In Maryland, inventories did not include land holdings or improvements, but they did include crops in the field or recently harvested, all livestock, and all bound labor. Maryland law did not require that an inventory be taken at the time of death, but it was customary to have one made to protect the interests of the legatees and to satisfy the creditors.

This study of bedcoverings and other textile furnishings spans the time period from 1710 to 1820. The beginning date of 1709–10 corresponds to the earliest available volume of Kent County inventories. These early inventories reflect consumption at the end of the seventeenth century and in the first years of the eighteenth century. The terminal date is arbitrary, but was selected to include inventories that would reflect postwar consumption. The Kent County probate inventories from 1710 to 1820 are compiled in sixteen volumes, each of which contains several hundred entries. It was therefore not possible to study all of the inventories recorded during the time period.[6] Instead, sixty inventories from six time periods were carefully analyzed: 1709–11, 1738–42, 1759–62, 1781–83, 1798–1800, and 1819–22, for a total

of 360 inventories.[7] In each volume the inventories were studied in order of appearance, eliminating only those that fell outside the time period. Otherwise, all inventories were included, whether they contained textile furnishings, or whether they had an estate value of £2 or £2,000. Each estate was assigned to one of six wealth groups: under £50, £51–125, £126–225, £226–500, £501–1,000, and over £1,000.

For each inventory, all bedcoverings, their descriptive adjectives, and values were recorded onto take-off sheets. The frequency of each item, as well as color, texture, condition, etc., was noted under the appropriate category on a spreadsheet for each time period. From these sheets, the totals of all bedcoverings were tabulated. The use of bedcoverings was then analyzed in relation to wealth and to time. The inventory evidence was further manipulated to study textiles in relation to bound labor, gender, and religion.

The results from this or any other inventory study must be viewed with caution. Although inventories are especially useful in areas like Kent County where little material culture remains and archaeological excavations are unsystematic, they do not provide evidence of the consumption patterns of the total community. In Maryland, unlike some of the other colonies, inventories do not include real estate holdings, but only goods and chattels or personal property. In an agrarian society, this omission can cause considerable distortion in total wealth or in a comparison among members of different wealth groups. Inventories are biased toward the wealthy while the poor are often overlooked. Because inventories were not required by Maryland law, the more affluent, with more property to protect and more money to spend on the probate process, and the better educated, who had some knowledge of estate laws, were more likely to be inventoried than men or women with

Opposite: Sampler in silk on wool of "A/ Map /of Maryland," 30" x 20¾", made by [?] Falconar of Kent County, Maryland, in 1798. Collection of the Maryland Historical Society, gift of Mrs. Francis H. Jencks and Miss Delia Pleasants (#59.34.1). Courtesy of the Maryland Historical Society.

Opening page from the 1762 estate inventory of Alexander Williamson of Kent County. Collection of the Maryland State Archives/Kent County Register of Wills/(Inventories) (5 [MSA C1059–11]).

negligible estates. Freemen, inmates, and small landowners fell into this category. Slaves and indentured servants never had estates to be inventoried. Therefore, the low end of the economic spectrum was underreported.

Inventories favor the older, free adult male population, which had had many years in which to acquire wealth and material possessions. Women's possessions were included in the husband's estate unless the decedent was a widow or spinster. Widows were also under-reported because many had minimal estates and were in reduced financial circumstances after their husbands' deaths.[8] Children's estates were almost never inventoried. A survey of the living population, which would include young people in the beginning stages of wealth and material acquisition, would produce different results.

Inventories reflect past acquisitions. In dealing with changes in consumption patterns, the data is distorted by an inability to determine when goods were acquired. The textile holdings of one decedent might have been purchased within a few years prior to death, while those of another might represent acquisitions over a long lifetime.

Inventories are further biased by the experience and interests of the appraisers. Although the appraisers generally came from the same socioeconomic background as the decedent and were knowledgeable in the terminology of farm, craft, and household equipment, some listed objects by generic names such as "bed furniture" or "bedcover" without attempting specific descriptions. Others lumped goods into "parcels" or "pieces." Still others may have overlooked some items completely. And because it was not customary to list nonportable items, one can only speculate about how many looms or quilting frames, which might have been attached to the wall, ceiling, or floor, were also omitted.

In spite of their shortcomings and biased reporting, probate inventories are important to the study of material culture. Although they do not encompass the total population of a community, they provide detailed information about the possessions of a far broader economic segment than that which is possible to obtain from viewing the preserved heirlooms of the affluent in museums or from reading the personal and business documents of the literate. For an area like Kent County, Maryland, inventories are a valuable resource that must be tapped in order to broaden our knowledge of a particular locality and to understand its place in the historical development of the pre-industrial Atlantic community.

Bedcovers

The original study encompassed all aspects of textile furnishings in Kent County, but this chapter focuses on the outer bedcovers, that is—rugs, quilts, coverlets, and counterpanes.[9] Outer bedcovers were owned by 85% of the total surveyed population. The percentage of ownership remained fairly constant from a low of 75% in 1710 to a high of 88% in 1760 and 1820. Bed rugs accounted for 46% of the bedcovers used in Kent County during the survey. When use of specific bedcovers is analyzed over time, it can be seen that the majority of covers used before 1780 were rugs, and that the lighter weight quilts, coverlets, and counterpanes accounted for the majority used thereafter. The actual number of rugs in use peaked in 1740, although rugs were more widely distributed in 1760. Quilts increased in number and distribution up to 1820, while coverlets were more widely held in 1780 but fewer in number than in 1820. Counterpanes, like bedcovers in general, peaked in use in 1760 and 1820.

Outer bedcovers were expensive and usually imported or made from imported textiles. A rug was valued at about twice the cost of a pair of wool blankets or a simple wooden bedstead, but was comparable to a pair of linen sheets. Quilts were even more valuable. Averaging between twenty and thirty shillings, depending on fabric and condition, they were nearly equal in worth to bed hangings and they were considerably more valuable than window curtains, bed sheets, or table linens.

Rugs

The rug was a wool pile outer bedcover that was widely used in England and the colonies in the seventeenth and eighteenth centuries. The 1730 edition of Bailey's *Dictionarium Britannicum* defined "rug" or "rugg" as a "shaggy coverlet for the bed." In Kent County the number of rugs increased up to 1740 and then sharply declined. Between the 1740s and 1760s there was an average of three rugs per household, but in 1820 there was a total of only three rugs in the entire county survey. Rugs were owned by 57% of the inventory population in the 1710 study, 87% of the 1760 population, and only 5% of the 1820 population.[10]

The use of rugs was not related to wealth alone even though rugs were imported and more expensive than a pair of blankets. Forty-seven percent of all the decedents with estates valued below £125 had rugs, and 45% of all decedents with estates valued over £500 also had rugs. In looking more closely at changes over time in use of rugs by the lowest and highest economic groups, it becomes apparent that when rugs were declining in use, they were used for a longer period in the households of the lower classes. In 1710, 100% of the decedents with estates over £500 had rugs, while 51% of those with estates under £125 had rugs. In 1780, 65% with estates over £500 had rugs, and 47% of those with estates under £125 had rugs. By 1820, no one in the higher wealth level owned rugs, while 14% of the lower group still owned them. Therefore rugs, which had been fashionable in middle- and upper-class homes, were

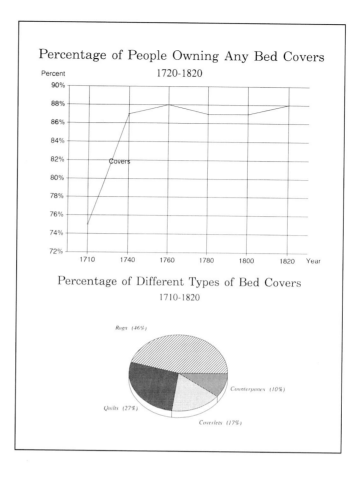

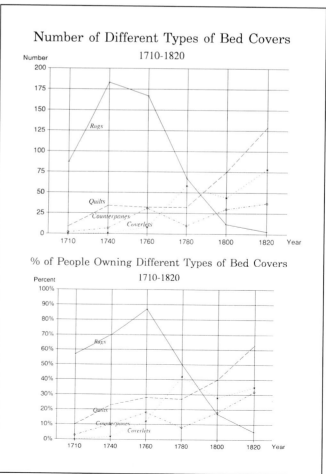

Graphs showing percentage of people owning bedcovers of any type in estate inventories in Kent County, Maryland, from 1710–1820, as well as the comparative number of different types of bedcovers and the percentage of those who owned any given type.

Quilted Indian palampore of mordant-painted and resist-dyed cotton, 111¼" x 87½", owned by the Augustine Boyer family of Kent County, Maryland, circa 1700–60. Collection of the Henry Francis du Pont Winterthur Museum, gift of Miss Gertrude Brinckle (#60.780). Courtesy of Winterthur Museum.

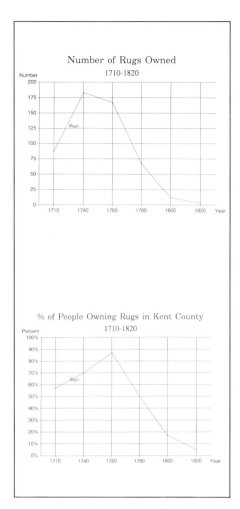

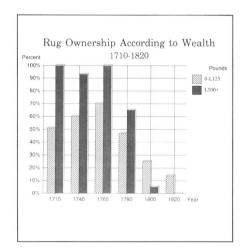

Graphs showing the number of bed rugs in estate inventories in Kent County, Maryland, from 1710–1820, as well as the percentage of rug ownership and the relationship to wealth.

Detail of woven, dyed wool English bed rug, 58″ x 48″, similar to those used in Kent County. Collection of the Henry Francis du Pont Winterthur Museum (#58.62.3). Courtesy of Winterthur Museum.

found only in homes of people in the lowest economic group in the nineteenth century.[11] It is surprising that such a popular bedcover could peak in use in 1760 and almost totally disappear from households sixty years later. It is not a question of rugs being put aside in storage in favor of lighter weight quilts and coverlets, but rather, it appears that rugs were totally removed from the premises.[12]

Kent County probate inventories provided evidence about the appearance of bed rugs. The eighteenth- and early nineteenth-century type of rug, found extant in New England, especially in eastern Connecticut, was made from wool sewn in a running stitch through a coarse woolen or linen backing. These rugs were worked by women and usually made in muted, multicolor floral patterns. It is apparent from the descriptive evidence that the majority of rugs listed in Kent County and other inventories did not resemble the sewn rugs. Rather, they were woven on a loom in England and exported to the colonies. They probably had a wool or linen twill web and a supplemental coarse wool weft drawn up in loops to create a shag.[13] The rugs that were used in Kent County during the eighteenth century were imported from several areas in England. They were variously described as·"4 West country ruggs," "2 Wiltshire rugs," or "1 worsted shag."[14] In the more than 500 references to rugs in Kent County inventories, there was only one that would indicate that rugs might have been made locally. In 1740, the Catholic farmer Daniel Flynn had "1 country rug."[15] With one exception, bed rugs were listed as "rugs" or "ruggs" in inventories, not "carpets."[16] The value of rugs changed little during the period of the study, and color or pattern had little effect on price except that dyed rugs were valued higher than undyed rugs. Bed rugs used in Kent County were available in several monochromatic colors,

the color of rugs than of other furnishings.[17] The preferred colors were green, blue, and red, in descending popularity. Although the green dying process was more labor intensive, green rugs dominated the inventories.[18] Most of the households with rugs had rugs in different colors, and some had one in each of three colors: green, blue, and red.[19] White or undyed rugs were uncommon, but the 1738 inventory of widow Mary Dunn listed "1 white shag rug."[20] The only suggestions of pattern were the frequent references in the 1760s to "spotted" or "mottled" rugs. George Copper's inventory listed "2 spotted" rugs in addition to "2 Wiltshire rugs, 1 worsted shag."[21] The blending of different shades of natural wools probably produced the variation in color or mottled effect. Differing

from the Connecticut rugs, the ones in Kent County were without personalization, names, initials, dates, or added decoration.[22] The only exception was found in the inventory of Michael Miller, which included a reference to "1 old gallen do [rug]."[23] This notation probably referred to a rug with a galloon or braid trimming.

Several inventories taken between 1740 and 1780 listed an unusual type of bed rug. Ten references to silk rugs appeared in connection with bedding.

A silk bed rug is difficult to imagine. Did it have a heavy texture like its wool namesake or was it a silk quilt?[24] The 1740 inventories of Dr. Alexander Adair and Dr. Thomas Williams referred simply to silk rugs, but the inventory of Captain Thomas Smyth listed "1 silk thrumd" rug at 1.5.[25]

Lightweight Bedcovers

There was considerable imprecision among the appraisers of Kent County estates in listing lighter weight bedcoverings. They used such catchall words as "bedcover" and "spread" as well as the more precise "quilt," "coverlid," and "counterpane."[26] Generic bedcoverings were variously described as woolen or yarn, cotton or calico, and might have been more precisely defined as coverlets, quilts, or counterpanes. Collectively, lighter weight bedcovers rose in popularity as bed rugs declined.

Appraisers used the terms "quilt," "coverlid," and "counterpane" somewhat interchangeably. All three terms were occasionally found in the same inventory indicating that a distinction was made between bedcovers of different construction, but more often, when descriptive adjectives were used, the terminology was contradictory. Appraisers listed such objects as "7 coverlids quilted," "1 counterpane quilt," "3 cotton coverlids patchwork," and "1 double woven counterpane."[27] Of these contradictory terms, only the coverlid with patchwork suggests a recognizable object. Patchwork probably signified chintz appliqué because the word "patch" was used in England and America during the eighteenth and nineteenth centuries as a synonym for chintz.[28] In the Baltimore area in the 1830s, chintz motifs were occasionally appliquéd to woven coverlets or Marseilles spreads and left unquilted.

Quilts

Quilts are mentioned in the earliest Kent inventories from 1709–11. Their number increased slowly during the eighteenth century, then increased dramatically between 1800 and 1820. Of the 311 quilts identified in the inventories, two-thirds were found in inventories dated 1800 or later. In 1710 quilts were used by less than 10% of the decedent population, in 1760 by 28%, and in 1820 by 63%. In addition to replacing rugs for warmth, quilts served a decorative or sociotechnic function as display pieces. Their dualism of purpose suggests that their use was subject to wealth. This theory is borne out by the evidence from 1760 that indicates that only 6% of the decedents with estates worth less than £125 had quilts compared with 50% with estates over £500. By 1800 these extremes had modified somewhat, when 19% in the lower group had quilts compared with 50% in the upper wealth group. By the second decade of the nineteenth century, quilts were in popular use by a wide economic segment of the population.

The wealthier estates were generally those with the largest slave holdings. When ownership of quilts is compared with ownership of slaves, 82% of all quilts were owned by men with slaves, and of that number 75% were owned by men with four or more slaves. All of the quilt frames found in the survey, with one exception, were owned by slave owners. This evidence suggests that slaves may have made quilts used in the big house, or that there was more time available for white women to pursue needlework when slaves assumed many of the household chores.[29] It is not possible to determine if any quilts listed in Kent County inventories were found in the slave quarters. Occasionally appraisers noted the presence of "Negro bedding," but this bedding was probably used by slaves who slept in the big house.

Ownership of quilts in Kent County can be further broken down by gender and religion. Women, who made up 9% of the decedent survey, owned 13% of all quilts in contrast to only 5% of all rugs and 3% of all coverlets and counterpanes. Clearly quilts, which symbolized women's artistic accomplishments, were valued possessions and frequently retained in female households.

Quakers in Kent County were conspicuous consumers especially in terms of their household textiles.[30] In almost every category of furnishing textiles as well as textile yardage and textile production tools, they owned more than their non-Quaker neighbors of approximately the same wealth. Although Quakers only made up 9% of the population, they owned 16% of all bed hangings found in the survey, 13% of all sheets, 12% of all blankets, and 10% of all bed rugs. Paradoxically, they owned only 8% of the quilts. Although Quakers in Kent County owned slaves, by 1820 many had divested themselves of slaves through manumission. The evidence suggests a correlation between a lower percentage of ownership of quilts by Quakers and their declining ownership of slaves.

The inventories provide some information about the appearance of eighteenth-century Kent County quilts. Unfortunately almost no Maryland quilts survive from that period to give dimension to the written descriptions.[31] The earliest quilts probably had a top layer made from large pieces of matching cloth as indicated by descriptive references to calico, India chintz, silk, calamanco, worsted, and linsey quilts.[32] Rarely mentioned quilt colors included blue, yellow, and green. The adjective "patched" was not used before 1760. When it was used it probably referred to quilts or coverlets with decoration formed by appliquéing large-figured printed textiles or chintzes. It may also have referred to wholecloth quilts made from boldly printed textiles. Appraisers did not describe quilts as "laid," "inlaid," or "appliquéd." The term "piecework" was also not used in Kent County inventories, yet quilts

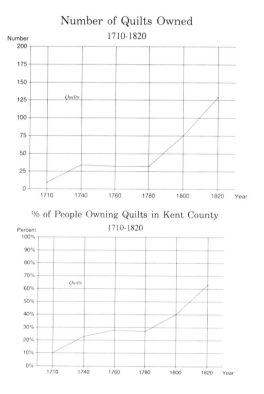

Number of Quilts Owned
1710-1820

% of People Owning Quilts in Kent County
1710-1820

Pieced and appliqué quilt of white and printed cottons, 87½" x 80½", attributed to Mary Eby (b. 1759) of Frederick County, Maryland, 1803. Private collection. Courtesy of the Maryland Association for Family and Community Education Quilt Documentation Project. Photo by Richard and Ann Rohlfing.

Graphs showing the number of quilts in estate inventories in Kent County, Maryland, from 1710–1820, as well as the percentage of quilt ownership and the relationship to wealth.

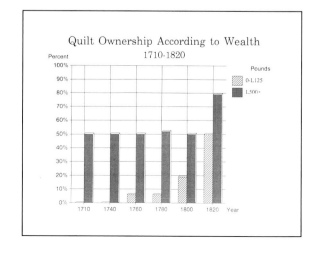

Quilt Ownership According to Wealth
1710-1820

made from small geometric pieces of textiles were used in Maryland toward the end of the eighteenth century. Other quilts may have been embroidered or worked with multicolor yarns or white thread. In 1773, Nicholas Riley's estate included "1 Pattern of a Work'd Bed Quilt."[33]

Inventories suggest that the fabrics used for Kent County quilts were imported, and extant early nineteenth-century quilts support that conclusion. However, a 1780 reference to a "new Linsey quilt country made" may indicate that quilts were also made from domestically woven cloth.[34]

It is generally assumed that the assembling and stitching of quilts were done in the home. However, the number of quilt frames found in Kent County inventories was in no way comparable with the number of quilts. Only two frames were listed before 1800, and only fifteen in all. Usually frames were found in pairs. To explain this discrepancy, one can speculate that quilting was done without a frame, that the frames were attached to the walls or ceilings and therefore omitted by the appraisers, or that quilting was done outside the home.[35] In 1749 Anne Griffith advertised in the *Maryland Gazette* that she did "Plain or Figured Corse or Fine quilting in the best and cheapest manner at her house" in Annapolis, and in 1751, Mary Anne March, an Annapolis teacher of needlework, also advertised that she took in quilting or needlework. Another quilter had a questionable past. Elizabeth Crowder, an English convict, ran away from her indenture with quilter Sarah Monroe in 1746. By 1747, she had established herself in Annapolis and advertised that she did "all sorts of Quilting in the best manner."[36] The practice of engaging outside assistance continued. In 1794 a Mrs. Polk offered her services in drawing patterns, perhaps for quilts or needlework, and in 1816 a Mrs. Hamilton of Baltimore advertised that she continued "to ornament

bed quilts, table covers & c."[37]

Ready-made quilts were available from England. The September 24, 1753, edition of the *South Carolina Gazette* advertised that "mattrasses and bed quilts" had just been imported from London. Similar merchandise may have been shipped to Annapolis or the Eastern Shore port of Chestertown. By 1820 the Baltimore merchant W. M. Stewart was able to advertise a recent shipment of "Counterpanes & Quilts."[38] Quilted fabric was also available to Kent County residents. Quilted cotton and Marseilles quilting were sold by local merchants from the 1760s on, and Baltimore merchants advertised "plain or bordered" Marseilles quilting and Manchester quilting during the 1780s and 1790s.[39] Surprisingly, Kent County appraisers did not record any "Marseilles quilts" in household inventories.

The cut-off date of 1820 for this research corresponds to the earliest period of extant Maryland quilts. Only a few quilts with Maryland histories can be dated prior to 1820 with any certainty. From the 1820s on quilts made in Kent County and elsewhere in Maryland can be found in increasing numbers. A study of estate inventories from 1820 to 1860 would indicate if descriptions in later inventories conform to the appearance of extant quilts.

Coverlets

The term "coverlid" (coverlet), signifying a pattern-woven bedcover, first appeared in Kent County inventories recorded in the early 1740s. Seventeenth-century English inventories frequently listed coverlets but rarely mentioned quilts and counterpanes. In England, coverlets were used in conjunction with rugs until around 1715. After that time they were used as an outer covering over blankets.[40] It is therefore surprising, with the strong English heritage of the residents in Kent County, that coverlets were not used in the county

until the middle of the eighteenth century. Additional research may determine if coverlets were woven in England primarily for local consumption rather than for export. Weavers resided in Kent County throughout the eighteenth century, but they may have lacked skills or equipment necessary for complex pattern weaving.

After coverlets first appeared in Kent County inventories, they increased in number up until 1780, declined after the Revolution, and then regained popularity in the nineteenth century. Only in 1780 did coverlets surpass quilts in total numbers, but their overall total of 191 was considerably lower than that of quilts or rugs. The popularity of coverlets at the time of the Revolution suggests that domestically woven coverlets replaced quilts and counterpanes made from imported fabrics. In 1740 coverlets were used by 2% of the decedent population, in 1780 by 42%, and in 1820 by 35%. A continuation of this survey through the 1840s would probably show increased usage.[41] Like quilts, the use of coverlets can be correlated with wealth and slave ownership. In 1760, 5% of the decedents with estates under £125 owned coverlets compared with 28% with estates over £500. By 1800, 19% of the lower group owned coverlets compared with 40% of the upper group. In the 1820s when coverlets increased in usage, they were used by only 7% of decedents with estates below £125 but by 50% with estates over £500. Therefore, coverlets in Kent County were found more frequently in houses of the wealthy in the eighteenth and early nineteenth centuries, in contrast to the later jacquard coverlets that were owned by people of modest wealth in the mid-nineteenth century.[42] When the ownership of coverlets is compared with slave holdings, it is found that 80% of all coverlets were owned by slave owners. The production and use of coverlets, as well as quilts, in Kent County may have depended on

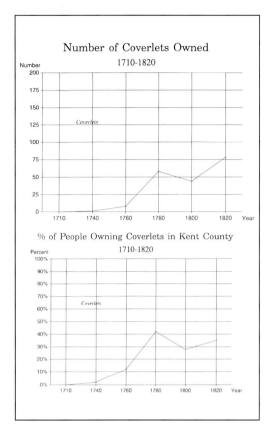

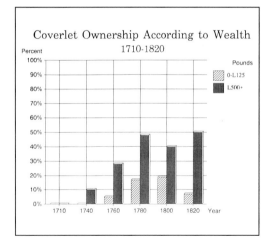

Graphs showing the number of coverlets in estate inventories in Kent County, Maryland, from 1710–1820, as well as the percentage of coverlet ownership and the relationship to wealth.

bound labor. Coverlets were most frequently described in inventories as "country," which indicates that they were woven by local weavers. A number of independent weavers in the county can be identified from their estate inventories, but many of the plantations may have had a slave or indentured servant who was trained as a weaver. Newspapers serving the Kent County area frequently advertised runaway servants and slaves. In 1755 Alexander Garvey lost an "Irish Servant Man and Weaver by Trade," and in 1791 John Beal Bordley advertised for the return of "Jim, a dark mulatto . . . a good weaver."[43]

A study of ownership of coverlets by special groups indicates that women did not usually acquire coverlets for bedcoverings. Women owned only 3% of the total number, far fewer than their 9% share of the surveyed population. Quakers owned 10%, which was consistent with their 9% share of the population.

After 1780 Kent County appraisers occasionally noted the fiber content of coverlets, thus providing clues about their composition. The majority of those described were cotton or a combination of wool weft with cotton or linen warp. These coverlets were variously listed as "cotton and yarn coverlid" or "cotton and wool coverlid."[44] Descriptions like "1 lincy coverlet," "1 yarn coverlid," and "4 yarn bed covers" may refer to coverlets made totally from one fiber, but it is more likely that coverlets were woven from a combination of fibers, using linen or cotton for strong warp threads and wool yarn for the warm weft filling.[45] Because many inventories listed several pounds of thread (linen) and yarn (wool), it is likely that clients provided the processed fibers for the weaver to weave into coverlets or other textiles. Because color and pattern were never mentioned in connection with Kent County coverlets, it is not possible to determine appearance. One 1780 reference to "1 double wove woolen

counterpine—£1.5.9" may indicate that some coverlets were of the double-cloth type with geometric patterns rather than "overshot" with a floating pattern weft.[46]

Counterpanes

The term "counterpin" or counterpane appeared in Kent County inventories throughout the period of study and seems to have been a catchall for a variety of different kinds of bedcovers.[47] Although never very numerous, counterpanes increased, declined, and increased again in number during the eighteenth and early nineteenth centuries. In 1710 only two households owned a grand total of two counterpanes, while in 1760 and in 1800, households with counterpanes averaged three apiece. In 1820 there were more counterpanes in use than ever before, but they were more widely distributed at the rate of two per household. In 1710 counterpanes were owned by 3% of the decedent population, in 1760 by 18%, and in 1820 by 32%. But in 1780, during the Revolution, counterpanes were only owned by 7% of the surveyed population. Ownership of counterpanes, like quilts, was a function of wealth. In 1740, no one with an estate valued under £125 owned a counterpane, but 40% with estates over £500 did own counterpanes. In 1820 counterpanes were only owned by 14% in the lower wealth group, but 54% of the upper wealth group. Eighty-five percent of all the counterpanes in the survey were owned by slave owners. Of this group, 75% were owned by families with four or more slaves.

Women preferred quilts to counterpanes. Paradoxically only two out of the 117 counterpanes in the survey, or less than 2%, were found in probate inventories belonging to women. Quakers, on the other hand, had a preference for counterpanes over quilts. They owned 18% of all the counterpanes in the survey, twice their 9% share of the population. Two thirds of the Quaker-owned counterpanes were listed in inventories recorded in 1800 and 1820. The evidence suggests that, because Quakers did not own as many slaves as non-Quakers and therefore did not have slaves available to do quilting, they used decorative but unquilted and, perhaps, store-bought bedcovers.

A few counterpanes were listed as being "country made," but others were available ready-made from local or nearby suppliers. "Cotton counterpanes" were advertised as early as 1748 by Philadelphia merchants, in 1784 by Baltimore merchants, and in the 1790s by various Easton, Maryland, merchants.[48] The earlier counterpanes used imported printed cottons or linens variously described as "flowered," "stampt cotton," "stampt linen," or "calico." These were probably lightweight, one- or two-layer bedcovers. After 1780 counterpanes are simply described as cotton, linen, calico, or white. A 1760 reference to "1 figured cotton napt counterpin" and an 1800 reference to "1 knotted do [counterpin]" may refer to candlewicking or needlework, but the references could also refer to woven bedcovers.[49] Counterpanes described as "yarn," "wool and linen," and "wool" were probably coverlets. White was the only counterpane color mentioned. Counterpanes described as diaper and calico may also have been white. In the 1820s there were four references to "white" compared with one earlier one. In a small way, these findings confirm a growing preference for white textile furnishings during the neoclassical period.

Conclusion

The findings for Kent County do not significantly contradict the perception held by social and economic historians of rapid change and an emerging consumer culture in eighteenth-century America. As textile furnishings were becoming more readily available and more economically accessible, the community of Kent County was moving toward greater prosperity. In Kent County, ownership of most textile possessions increased over time. With the exception of bed rugs, which went out of fashion, other bedcovers slowly increased in number up until the Revolution, leveled off, and then increased again at a more rapid rate of consumption. The wealthy had more bedcovers in all time periods, but certain coverings, which at one time had only been affordable by the wealthy, were eventually affordable by almost everyone. Some groups had more bedcovers than others due to greater financial means, wider opportunity, available labor, or personal preferences.

The inventory evidence from Kent County, Maryland, has provided specific information about the bedcoverings of a particular group of people. The findings suggest regional and temporal variations, but it is hoped that these variations will contribute to an understanding of the whole and add credence to a larger historical view of consumerism in the pre-industrial Atlantic community.

Notes and References

[1]In 1642 when Kent County was established, it encompassed all of the Maryland Eastern Shore. The modern boundaries date from 1706 and include the area of land south of the Sassafras River, north of the Chester River, and west of the state of Delaware.

[2]Lois Green Carr and Lorena S. Walsh, "Inventories and the Analysis of Wealth and Consumption Patterns in St. Mary's County, Maryland, 1658–1777," *Historical Methods* 13 (Spring 1980): 29.

[3]Barbara and Cary Carson, "Styles and Standards of Living in Southern Maryland, 1670–1752," paper delivered at the Southern Historical Association meeting, Atlanta, GA, 1976.

[4]Richard D. Brown, *Modernization: The Transformation of American Life* (New York: Hill and Wang, 1976), 89.

[5]The originals of the probate records cited in this report are located in the Maryland State Archives, Annapolis.

[6]All of the material is in original manuscript form.

[7]There are approximately twenty-year

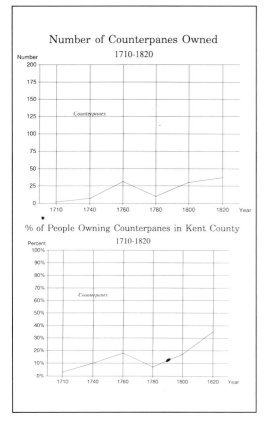

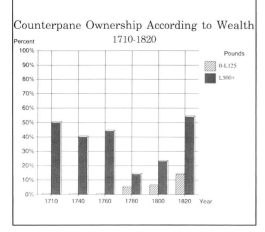

Graphs showing the number of counter-panes in estate inventories in Kent County, Maryland, from 1710–1820, as well as the percentage of counterpane ownership and the relationship to wealth.

gaps between each time period with the exception of the first where the gap is almost thirty years. It would have been preferable to read inventories from every decade or from 1710, 1730, 1750, 1770, 1790, 1810, but the sequence was established by an earlier study. Volumes consulted were: Vol. 1, 1709–20, 1730–32; Vol. 2, 1732–40; Vol. 3, 1720–30, 1740–41; Vol. 3[A], 1728–49; Vol. 5, 1759–67; Vol. 8, 1776–88; Vol. 11, 1799–1807; Vol. 16, 1820–22.

[8]Of the 33 women in the survey whose estates were inventoried, the majority died after 1800. There were probably just as many widows earlier in the century, but they were not inventoried. Estates of low value were not worth the cost of probate.

[9]The original study was "Textile Furnish-ing: A Case Study of Kent County, Maryland, 1710–1820," thesis, George Washington University, 1983.

[10]Schoelwer's study of Philadelphia fur-nishings shows that rugs declined substantially in the eighteenth century, from 43% of the households with bedding in 1700–04 to 20% in 1775. Susan Pre-dergast Schoelwer, "Form, Function, and Meaning in the Use of Fabric Furnishings: A Philadelphia Case Study, 1700–1775," *Winterthur Portfolio* 14 (Spring 1979): 80.

[11]Rugs lost their popularity in England at an earlier date. From inventories recorded by Steer, it is evident that after 1715 there was greater use of blankets with coverlets and quilts than with rugs. Francis W. Steer, *Farm and Cottage Inventories of Mid-Essex 1635–1749* (London: Phi-llmore, 1969). Samuel Johnson's dictionary of 1755 defined rugs as "coarse nappy coverlets used for mean beds" thus indicating that rugs were held in low es-teem in England by the middle of the eighteenth century.

[12]One can only speculate about the disap-pearance of bed rugs. When wool was scarce during the war years, rugs may have been used for other functions like outfitting the military and burying the dead. To aid the depressed woolen indus-try and discourage the importation of foreign linen, the Parliamentary Acts of 1666, 1678, and 1730 required that the dead in England and in the English colo-nies be buried in wool clothing and wrapped in wool shrouds. Failure to com-ply with the law was punishable by a substantial fine. The shroud may have dis-pensed with the need for a coffin. Perhaps, for lack of a bay or flannel winding cloth, an old woolen rug or blanket was used to conform to the law. A 1690 court account-ing for the estate of John Culle, formerly of Albermarle County, NC, included the following item: "To the Trubell of my House and the Lone of my bedding: and a Ruge he was bured in." (*North Carolina Higher-Court Records 1670–1696*, 15–16,

Museum of Early Southern Decorative Arts Research Files.) After the colonies established their independence from Eng-land, the tradition of burying in wool may have continued. While woolen imports were scarce until the early nineteenth cen-tury, unfashionable woolen rugs were readily available.

[13]A 1634 letter from John Winter on the coast of Maine to his factor in Plymouth provides evidence that rugs were woven on a loom: "2 dozen of Barnstaple ruggs wove without seam," quoted by Sally Garoutte in "Early Colonial Quilts in a Bedding Context," *Uncoverings 1980*, ed. Sally Garoutte (Mill Valley, CA: American Quilt Study Group, 1981), 21.

[14]West Country rugs probably came from around Barnstaple in Devon. The county of Wiltshire was known for its pure white sheep; and the "worsted" rugs may have come from Worsted, a town near Nor-wich. Florence Montgomery, *Textiles in America* (Winterthur, DE: Winterthur Museum, 1984).

[15]Inventories, Vol. 2, 316 (1740).

[16]Inventories, Vol. 2, 337 (1740). Two "caddow rugs" were listed, and Peter Thornton notes that in the seventeenth century the word "caddow" was a syn-onym for "rug." Peter Thornton, *Seventeenth-Century Interior Decoration in England, France, and Holland* (New Haven, CT: Yale University Press, 1978), 112.

[17]The local Kent merchant, William Bathurst, had red, green, and blue rugs in his shop inventory, and merchants in An-napolis advertised Torrington rugs, while one in Baltimore listed ¾ x ¾ yarn and worsted rugs. *Maryland Gazette*, March 22, 1764.

[18]The red dye probably came from mad-der or cochineal and the blue from indigo or woad. Green dying required that the yarn first be dyed in yellow and then overdyed in blue. Yellow rugs were not mentioned in Kent County inventories, but they were recorded elsewhere.

[19]Late-seventeenth-century and early eighteenth-century inventories from Essex in England also contained numerous refer-ences to "green," "blue," and "worsted" rugs.

[20]Inventories, Vol. 2, 290 (1740).

[21]Inventories, Vol. 5, 12 (1740).

[22]Refer to J. Herbert Callister's introduc-tion to *Bed Ruggs, 1722–1833* (Hartford, CT: Wadsworth Atheneum, 1972).

[23]Michael Miller was a gentleman and wealthy slave owner with many unusual possessions, such as a monogrammed bed-stead. Inventories, Vol. 3, 363 (1740). "Do" is an abbreviation for "ditto."

[24]References to silk rugs have been found by Barbara Carson in St. Mary's County

inventories from the 1740s. Florence Montgomery and Linda Baumgarten were also familiar with the term, but not the appearance. Peter Thornton found at Ham House "quilted silk blankets," which may have been similar to silk rugs. Thornton, 113.

[25] Inventories, Vol. 3, 350 (1740); Vol. 2, 323 (1740); Vol. 3a, 324 (1740). "Thrumd" refers to the warp ends left over from the weaving process.

[26] The words "bedcover" and "spread" were uncommon before 1800.

[27] Inventories, Vol. 8, 165 (1780); Vol. 16, 194 (1820); Vol. 11, 56 (1800); and Vol. 8, 209 (1780).

[28] Elisabeth Donaghy Garrett quoted two uses of patch in connection with chintz in "The American home (Part III): The bedchamber," *The Magazine Antiques* 123 (March 1983): 617. A bedchamber in Newburyport, MA, was described as "elegant with gay patch (chintz) hangings to the square post bedstead." *Reminiscences of a Nonagenarian* (Newburyport, MA, 1879), 32. Caroline King described her bedroom in Salem: "By the side of the bed was placed a high-back so-called easy chair . . . covered with gay colored chintz ('patch' it was called then) where very long tailed birds sat upon impossible trees surrounded by gorgeous flowers, never dreamed of in our philosophy or botany," *When I lived in Salem 1822–1866* (Brattleboro, VT, 1937), 1985.

[29] For a study of the correlation between slave holding and quilt ownership in Virginia see Gloria Seaman Allen, *First Flowerings: Early Virginia Quilts* (Washington, DC: DAR Museum, 1987).

[30] The probate inventories of Quakers can be distinguished from those of non-Quakers because Quakers did not swear oaths. A Quaker would "affirm" rather than swear to the accuracy of an inventory. For example, on April 4, 1760, Writson Browning "did solemnly affirm and declare that the within is a just and perfect Inventory of all and singular the Goods and Chattels, which were of the deceased [Christopher Vansant] at the time of his Death," Inventories, Vol. 5, 24. Quakers, who had an extensive kinship network, customarily inventoried the estates of other Quakers.

[31] The earliest quilt of the more than 2,500 recorded by the Maryland Association for Family and Community Education Quilt Documentation Project (formerly, the Maryland Extension Homemakers Council Quilt Documentation Project) is dated 1803. The project, which documented quilts made between 1634 and 1934, started in 1988 and will publish its findings in 1994 or 1995.

[32] The Maryland Quilt Project documented one quilt with large pieces of a plate-printed textile. The history of the quilt is sketchy, but from the photographs the quilt appears to have been made in the nineteenth century from late-eighteenth-century textile furnishings.

[33] Maryland Prerogative Court, Inventories, Vol. 3, 32 (1773). Museum of Early Southern Decorative Arts Research Files.

[34] Inventories, Vol. 8, 209 (1780).

[35] Because quilting frames were simply constructed out of a few boards, some appraisers may not have recognized a disassembled frame.

[36] *Maryland Gazette*, Dec. 27, 1749; March 27, 1751; Oct. 28, 1747.

[37] *Maryland Gazette*, July 28, 1774; *Federal Gazette*, Aug. 7, 1816.

[38] *Baltimore American*, Aug. 21, 1820.

[39] *Maryland Journal*, Dec. 12, 1784, and 1791, various.

[40] These conclusions are based on material presented by Steer and Machin in their respective inventory studies. Robert Machin, ed., *Probate Inventories and Manorial Excerpts of Chetnole, Leigh, and Yetminster* (Bristol: University of Bristol, 1976).

[41] The jacquard apparatus was used by weavers in Maryland by the 1830s but jacquard coverlets are only known from three western counties with large German immigrant populations.

[42] These findings are suggested by the research I have done concerning owners of New York and Pennsylvania coverlets owned by the DAR Museum. See, *The Magazine Antiques*, January 1985 and February 1986.

[43] *Maryland Gazette*, Dec. 4, 1755; *Maryland Herald*, May 10, 1791.

[44] Inventories, Vol. 8, 171; Vol. 8, 211 (1780).

[45] Inventories, Vol. 8, 186 (1780); Vol. 11, 81 (1800); Vol. 16, 20 (1820).

[46] Inventories, Vol. 8, 209 (1780).

[47] In inventories from affluent seventeenth-century English households, "counterpanes" referred to highly decorative covers, which were placed over quilts or coverlets. Thornton, 179.

[48] *Pennsylvania Journal*, Jan. 5, 1748; *Maryland Journal*, Dec. 9, 1784; and the *Eastern Shore Intelligencer*, various.

[49] Inventories, Vol. 5, 139 (1760); Vol. 11, 50 (1800).

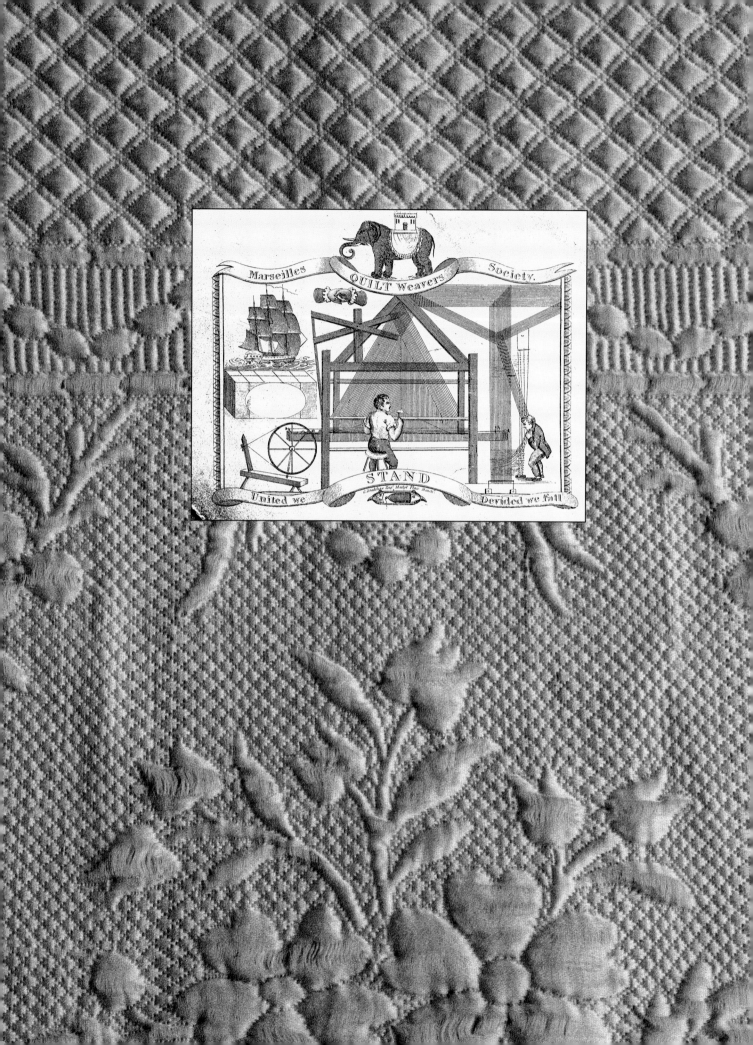

Marseilles Quilts and Their Woven Offspring

Sally Garoutte

Detail of a Marseilles loom-quilted silk and cotton petticoat, 38½" x 110" at lower edge, maker unknown, possibly of English manufacture circa 1780–90. Collection of Bonnie Martin. Courtesy of Tandy Hersh.

The pale robin's-egg blue silk double-cloth required the interaction of closely set threads in the upper cloth, a lower cloth with fewer warp and weft threads, and a thick loosely spun cotton fiber filling between the two silk cloths. This loom-quilted yardage was 32" wide.

The diamond pattern at the top and the ornamental border were designed to copy proportions of background to border found on mid-eighteenth century hand-quilted silk petticoats. A 6⅜" piece of unquilted silk fabric joins the quilted portion of the petticoat to the waist band.

Marseilles Quilt Weavers Society card circa 1875, which warns fellow manufacturers that "United we STAND Devided we Fall." Collection of Bolton Museum and Art Gallery, Bolton, England (#13.32). Courtesy of the Bolton Museum and Art Gallery.

The French input to early American quilts has been surprisingly ignored. The relations between the French and English American colonies were very close in the late-colonial period, and one would expect to find some influences. The influences, however, came through England and so their origins have generally been lost. In the politics of that time (not too different from our own), France supported the American colonies in their bid for independence, while carrying on an extensive British trade.

For the most part England monopolized the North American trade through control of colonial ports and import fees. Few French ships visited ports in America between the French islands in the Caribbean and eastern Canada. But English traders bought vast quantities of wine, and cotton and silk textiles from France, and shipped great amounts to the colonies, making their profit on the markup.

In the seventeenth and eighteenth centuries, France, England, Spain, Portugal, and Holland were all vying for the trade routes of the world. At that time, the products shipped from the New World eastward to the Old World were nearly all raw materials in the form of lumber for shipbuilding, chemicals, food items such as fish and grain, fur for making hats, and, of course, tobacco. The products shipped westward from Europe were all finished consumer goods—textiles, furniture, nails, iron pots, tools, utensils, paper, and books. By far the largest and most frequent shipments were of textiles of all kinds.

Sally Garoutte (1925–89) was a founder of the American Quilt Study Group in 1980, and served as its director, treasurer, and editor of its journal, Uncoverings. *Her own careful research and insistence on accuracy have set high standards for the field of quilt scholarship. Her collection of quilt-related books forms the core of the American Quilt Study Group's Research Library.*

Textile production in those times in Europe was the most extensive kind of manufacture. Even the word "manufactures" was almost synonymous with textiles. (Our modern word "fabrics" means manufactures and is again almost synonymous with textiles.) It is difficult to comprehend the enormous place textiles once had, before fuels made engines possible. But there simply were not a lot of other man-made things in the world of that time except what people made for their own use. Most people who made things to sell made textiles in one form or another.

Among things made to sell in the seventeenth century in the area of southern France known as Provence were quilts. Three seventeenth-century quilts from Arles are in the collections of the Museon Arlaten, a folk art museum displaying the ancient crafts of Provence. Descriptions and photographs of the quilts were published in France in 1926. Two of the quilts shown were all white, with elaborate stuffed and corded motifs. The third had a center of the type of printed cotton known as *indienne* quilted in double diamonds, surrounded by a border of plain dark cloth heavily quilted in what appears to be a floral design, and completed at the outer edges with several straight parallel rows quilted very close together—typical of all these quilts.[1]

The all-white stuffed and corded quilts may not have originated in Provence. Certainly there were similar examples in nearby Sicily in the fifteenth century.[2] Provence was the "province of Rome" from the second century B.C., and the connections between southern France and Italy are ancient.

The making of these quilts in Provence in the seventeenth century was not just an occasional event. It was a widely practiced folk art, developed to a high degree and well known as a regional tradition. Much quilted clothing·was made, in particular petticoats and outer skirts called *cotillions*.

These provincial skirts were usually made of indienne. On feast days, particularly the feast of Corpus Christi, the all-white bed quilts were hung outside the houses to honor the procession to the church.[3]

One of France's nineteenth-century poets was Frederic Mistral, a native of Provence, who received a Nobel Prize in 1904. His lengthy poems were about the old days and simple folk of Provence. In his poem "Calendral," published in 1867, Mistral referred to the traditional white quiltings, calling them "divine work that recalls a meadow when frost embroiders in white all the leaves and branches."[4] In an earlier poem, "Mireio" (1859), Mistral wrote:

A smart red petticoat she first prepares
Which she herself had quilted into
     squares,—
Of needlework a very masterpiece;
And round her slender waist she fastens
     this;
And over it another finer one
She draws[5]

The fabric of these quilts was usually white silk or linen, although other colors were used, and woolen fabric as well. Cotton imported from India was also used early in Provence. Prints from India and, later, French indiennes were used also.

The corded quilts were made by using a special instrument called a *boutis*. This was a thin, flexible rod around which a soft cord was wrapped. It was then inserted between the lines of quilting, held at the far end, and the boutis removed, leaving the cord in place. Large pieces such as bed quilts and petticoats were quilted on large wooden frames.[6]

For 2,500 years the major seaport of Provence has been Marseilles, a port of call for traders of many nations. The quilts of Provence inevitably found their way into the international trade, probably during the seventeenth century. When they arrived in England, they were referred to by their place of purchase as "Marseilles quilts." They appear to

have arrived in sufficient numbers for the name to be commonly understood in England to mean a wholecloth stuffed or corded quilt. "Quilt" in England might mean either a bed quilt or a petticoat. Beyond the bed quilts and petticoats, southern France also exported a great deal of quilted silk yardage to be fashioned into petticoats, linings, waistcoats, and as the basis for embroideries.

An early reference to a Marseilles quilt in England is contained in two letters from Henry Purefoy to Anthony Baxter in London. Purefoy, on July 15, 1739, sent an order for a "neat white quilted calico petticoat for my Mother which must be a yard and four inches long." On August 5 he wrote again to say "I received all the things in the box and have returned you the Marseilles Quilt petticoat. . . . It is so heavy my mother cannot wearing it."[7]

The early quilts that came to America came through English merchants and appear to have lost the French designation on the voyage. They are much more likely to be referred to by their fabric. In some orders sent from Virginia to the London merchant John Norton, the following are included: Sept. 16, 1760—"a Redd Sarcenett Quilted Petticoat" and "2 bedd quilts" ordered by John Baylor; August 18, 1768—"several bundles of best quilt" [yardage] ordered by George Wythe; Sept. 25, 1771—"One green peeling [peelong] Satin quilted Petticoat for a tall Woman" ordered by Peter Lyons; and Jan. 31, 1772—"4 White Quilted Peeling Child Bed Basket & Pin Cushions well & safe Packed up or the Satin will Mildue" ordered by Catherine Rathell, a shopkeeper in Williamsburg.[8]

England and France were still traditional rivals during this period. In America they competed for the fur and textile trade in Canada and along the whole length of the Mississippi. England was almost fully occupied with weaving. Her foreign trade depended heavily on the sales and shipment of cloth. The English weaving industry was characterized by doing the same thing over and over—very well and with a high degree of dependability. France also had important weaving centers. Her forte was in producing fancy fabrics: silks, brocades, ribbons, laces, and very fine woolens.

In the first half of the eighteenth century, however, a number of new inventions greatly altered the weaving trade, and now innovation became a way to meet the competition. In England and France, and later in the young United States, great efforts were made to develop new techniques and to steal industrial secrets from the other countries. What could be patented in one country was no protection from its free use in another country.

In 1762, a patent for a new type of weaving was recorded in England by George Glasgow. It was "a method of weaving cloth in imitation of women's stiched stays." The drawings submitted showed the specifications for "weaving together two, three and four pieces of single cloth, so that they will appear as if stitched together."[9] On March 9, 1763, Glasgow and Robert Elder jointly registered a patent for a "new method of weaving and quilting in the loom, in every method, fashion and figure, as well in imitation of the common manner of quilting, as of India, French and Marseilles quilting." The method specifies the need for a drawboy to pull up the many different shafts in the proper order to create the pattern.[10] The language used in this patent record tells us that Marseilles quilting was different from the "common manner" of quilting, and that it was fully recognizable in England by name.

A word about nomenclature is in order. In the England of the seventeenth and eighteenth centuries, there is no evidence of a widespread hand-quilting tradition such as in Provence. Existing records suggest that quilting

in England was specialized rather than commonplace. The English were weavers. When they first imitated Marseilles quilts, they simply called the procedure "quilting in the loom" and the products "quilts." They have retained this usage and, even today, a particular kind of wool honeycomb blanket woven in Wales is called a Welsh quilt. American usage has followed British usage, especially among merchants and manufacturers. The handmade quilts of Provence do not seem to have been called by their French title in America as they were in England. Therefore, in an American reference after 1800, a "Marseilles quilt" is confidently a loom-made bedspread. Now, in the United States, a distinction is made between an article made from two separate layers of cloth stitched together—with or without a batting—(a quilt) and a bedcover made on a loom (called either a coverlet, counterpane, or bedspread). For American scholars the modern term for the type of bedspread to be considered here is "Marseilles spread."

The news of the "new method of quilting in the loom" traveled fairly rapidly. In 1765, the *Georgia Gazette* of Savannah published this item:

London, February 7. The business of quilting bed-carpets and petticoats, which formerly the females engrossed, is now totally going into a different channel, the weavers in Spittalfields having struck upon a method of quilting in their looms, which is much cheaper and neater than any person with a needle can do.[11]

In 1776, in London, the Society for the Encouragement of Arts, Manufactures, and Commerce published a book describing items contained in its repository. Chapter XI is titled "Linen, Woolen, Silk, and Cotton, Quilted in the Loom, in Imitation of Marseilles and Italian Quilting," and in it the author remarked that "the advancement of the art of Quilting in the Loom is very extraordinary." The chapter ends: "Specimens of the different sorts of Quilting are preserved

Toilet and Marseilles as illustrated by swatches in W. Hough's Cotton Fabrics *(pp. 69–70). Collection of the Bolton Museum and Art Gallery, Bolton, England. Courtesy of the Bolton Museum and Art Gallery.*

in the Society's Repository of Manufactures."[12]

Ten different weavers were named in the chapter as having received a premium from the society for their work in the years 1762–65. The two men who submitted the patent application in 1763 were not among the winners. It would appear that the method was already known by other weavers before the patent application.

In 1783, the society published its *Transactions*, giving a summary of its rewards for the year. Included for the class of manufactures was a total of 597 pounds awarded for "Quilting in the Loom, and spinning several sorts of Yarn." Also in a paragraph titled "Quilting in the Loom," the compiler commented:

When the proposition was first made in the Society, of offering a premium to encourage the making in the Loom, and imitation of that species of Needle-work, long known by the name of Marseilles Quilting, it was almost rejected as visionary and impossible; but the laudable spirit of enterprize, which has always distinguished this Society, determined them to publish the premium, and the consequence has justified the measure. This success animated them to continue their premiums, in hopes of further improvement, in which they were not disappointed. The manufacture is now so thoroughly established, and so extensive, being wrought in all the different materials of Linen, Woolen, Cotton, and Silk, that there are few persons of any rank, condition, or sex, in the kingdom, (and we may add, within the extent of British commerce, so greatly is it exported) who do not use it in some part of their clothing; so that we may safely say, if the whole fund and revenue of the Society had been given to obtain this one article of Trade, the national gain in return should be considered as very cheaply purchased.[13]

Despite the hyperbole in this paragraph, it is still clear that loom-made Marseilles quilting was greatly singled out for praise. In the brief twenty-year period following the first premiums awarded, the new product had established an important place in the British family of fabrics. From the early frank imitations of the needle quilting of Provence, the English weavers were developing a whole new family of woolens. This new family was called by the name of "quiltings." The basic construction of quiltings consisted of a double-cloth made on a drawloom so the two layers could be "stitched" together, and containing an unwoven stuffing layer.

The drawloom had been in use for the weaving of intricate patterns for many centuries. Large looms required the help of one or more persons (known as drawboys) to pull predetermined warp yarns out of their ordinary position during the weaving. The sequence in which this was done determined the resulting pattern. By

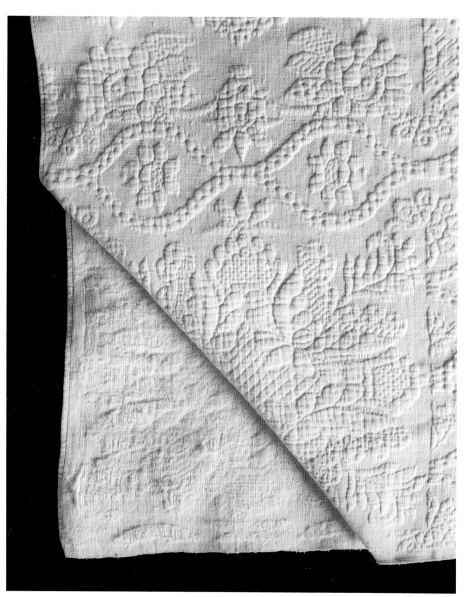

Detail of Marseilles spread circa 1860–85, showing both the woven spread's front and back. Courtesy of Ohio Historical Society.

the seventeenth century the drawloom was well known throughout Europe, being used mostly for patterned silks.

Double-cloth is also an ancient technique, known very early in China and in prehistoric Peru. Double-cloth can be woven on a very simple four-harness loom. If the two faces are of different yarns, they can be interchanged to form designs, as is done in Jacquard coverlets.

In quiltings, the two faces are not interchanged. The top face is constructed of finer yarns in a finer weave than the back face. The only interchange comes at the "stitches," where a single pick of yarn from the back comes to the front and holds the front face at that point. Such "stitch" picks can be arranged in *any* design. During the row-by-row weaving, the soft unspun filling layer is laid down and held in place by the "stitches."

What was new to the English weaving scene in the second half of the eighteenth century was the combination of double- (or triple-) cloth with the intricate patterning of the drawloom. This innovation, creating a three-dimensional cloth, was a great departure from a smooth, continuous, flat surface—previously a hallmark of Britain's fine woolens. Introduced at a time of other new developments in spinning, weaving, and the use of cotton in England, quilting in the loom combined with them in the production of cotton quiltings. Probably the English-French rivalry played its part. The English weavers could now make "Marseilles" quiltings faster than the women of Provence, and English merchants could market them readily through their superior trade routes.

These woven quiltings took many forms. Just as the needle-made quilts of France were made as often for clothing and furnishings as they were for bedding, so were the woven quiltings. Many new sorts of quiltings were developed using the ever finer and stronger cotton yarns. It is probably these new fabric variations rather than the bedcoverings alone that were

so popular a manufacture as to warrant the high praise given them in 1793 by the Society for the Encouragement of Arts. In 1800, in the *Commercial and Agricultural Magazine* of London, in a brief history of the society, the author wrote: "The art of QUILTING IN THE LOOM was one of the most generally useful of all those which, in the preparation of elegant cloth, this society's exertions gained to Britain."[14]

In a comprehensive study of British overseas trade, Elizabeth Boody Schumpeter calculated the amounts of cotton textiles exported from Britain during the years 1697 through 1807. Compared with the amount of exported woolens, cottons were a minuscule part of the export trade until 1782 when they took a significant rise. In every year after that, cotton exports increased, and in 1802 they outdistanced woolens in value to Britain.[15] The export of (undifferentiated) cotton counterpanes is separately listed from 1798 when almost 14,000 were shipped overseas. In the years following (to 1807—the final year of the study) the numbers were fewer—rising to more than 12,000 only in 1804, 1806, and 1807. Cotton "manufactures," which may be supposed to be quiltings and fancies, doubled in the value of exports between 1799 and 1807, and far outdistanced the value of counterpanes. In this same period the number and value of printed cottons and linen-and-cotton also rose dramatically and accounted for almost half of the total cotton exports.[16]

The quiltings were sold widely in America. Presumably they would have been in greatest abundance on the Eastern Seaboard, but they made their way early into the interior as well. Among early mentions is one in the sales records of a Bowling Green, Kentucky, general store in 1806, when "1 yd Marseillez" was sold.[17] Another "account of Goods Put in Red Store" (probably in Massachusetts) lists "2½ yds Marsails at 9/" on the first of May 1806.[18] In 1808, in St. Louis, J. Philipson's accounts show the sale of "¾ yds Marseills—$2.50"—a rather high price for a fabric less than a yard wide.[19] Although the spelling may have been as fancy as the fabrics, the handed-down name "Marseilles" perhaps gave them the image of being French and therefore, in American eyes, particularly desirable.

Cotton "fancies"—meaning fabrics of complex structure—of this early period were all made on the drawloom. As the major place of their manufacture was Bolton, in Lancashire, they were also referred to as "Bolton quiltings." Later weavers formed their own association called the Marseilles Quilt Weavers Society. Their card illuminates the connection between the drawloom (complete with drawboy) and overseas commerce represented by the sailing vessel, with an Indian elephant probably representing the early source of cotton.

It would be nice to know what the very earliest quiltings looked like, particularly those in the Repository of Manufactures of the Society of Arts. However, according to the curator-librarian of that institution, "the contents of the Society's Repository were dispersed in the 1850s" and "the specimens have not survived."[20] In the Colonial Williamsburg collections, there is a sample book from about 1783, containing quiltings of that date. The sample book was almost certainly made up as a catalog by a merchant in Manchester, England.[21] It contains more than 500 samples of different cotton fabrics—plain, printed, or fancy-woven. Two swatches of quiltings exhibit simple designs of diamonds. The size of each swatch is approximately 1 by 1½ inches; thus, the woven pattern is quite small.

Samples of twenty-five years later can be found in Ackermann's *Repository*. In each monthly issue of that periodical, Ackermann pasted in three or four swatches of fashionable fabrics. Four of these in 1809 were quiltings called "marcella"—a takeoff on Marseilles—and were recommended for gentlemen's waistcoats. The woven designs are fine and small and are further embellished with printed designs. Close examination of these small swatches reveals the unwoven stuffing layer in these quiltings.[22]

In the archive of the Borough of Bolton, Lancashire, is an 1841 pattern book of James Hardcastle & Company, Ltd., Bolton, that contains samples of similar quiltings for vesting, with overprinted fine designs. Another book in the Bolton Museum includes undated samples of a number of different kinds of quiltings traditionally made in Bolton.[23]

Some of these early "Marseilles" fabrics have been used as foundation fabrics for quilts and unquilted appliqué coverlets. Dunton, in *Old Quilts*, recorded eight appliqué coverlets from the period 1820–30 in which the foundation fabric was Marseilles quilting. The coverlets were attributed to the design of Achsah Goodwin Wilkins of Baltimore. Dunton carefully noted some of the details of fabrics. Designs were recorded as: "a repeat pattern of diamonds"; "a diapered pattern of flat lozenges 14 by 20 mm. with separating bands 4 mm. wide"; "a diamond design 30 by 40 mm. wide, or about twice the size of the diamonds of the marseilles" noted before; "marseilles of a different pattern"; "a rosebud design with a woven border"; and "a marseilles more elaborate in design . . . a braided or basket effect as though made with fancy ribbon." Dunton also noted that one of the eight coverlets was constructed on a Marseilles base of two strips of four-foot width, and three others on four strips ranging in width from 27½ to 30 inches.[24]

Existing early drawloom-made Marseilles spreads of full size are difficult to date with any confidence. They

Marseilles spread of machine-loomed cotton, 86¼" x 77½", made in Stronghurst, Illinois, circa 1860. Collection of the Fine Arts Museums of San Francisco, gift of Mrs. R. R. Newell (#67.19). Courtesy of the Fine Arts Museums of San Francisco.

are widely scattered and, being difficult to photograph, are hard to study on a comparative basis. They are easily recognizable—all being made of white cotton, having a fine-woven face cloth, a coarser back cloth, and a heavy unspun cotton roving as a stuffing layer. Many have worn areas where the roving is readily seen.

The old spreads are quite large and without a center seam. One such spread at Connor Prairie Pioneer Settlement measures 105 by 114 inches,[25] while another at the DAR Museum measures 105 by 104 inches.[26] Old Sturbridge Village collections include a Marseilles spread measuring 100 by 109 inches,[27] and a mid-nineteenth-century example of smaller size is in the collections of the M. H. de Young Memorial Museum.[28] Most Marseilles spreads have a round or oval central medallion with various surrounding designs and borders.

It is difficult also to determine which of the spreads may have been made in America. An effort was made in Fredericksburg, Virginia, in 1777, to establish a manufactory that was "capable of manufacturing . . . drawboys, quiltings, figured work of all sorts."[29] In Beverly, Massachusetts, in 1788, a Mr. Leonard and a Mr. Somers, who were setting up a carding and spinning mill, "understood the making and finishing of velverets, corduroys, jeans, fustians, denims, marseilles quiltings, dimity, and muslins."[30] A newspaper advertisement in Baltimore in 1792 offered the publication titled *The Weaver's Draught-Book and Clothier's Assistant*, which included drafts for "Diapers, Counterpanes, . . . Mock-Marseilles," and other fabrics.[31] There is no indication that any Marseilles spreads were actually produced by those early enterprises.

At some time, production did begin in the United States. The catalog of the Great National Fair of 1844, held in Washington, DC, includes as part of entry No. 301 from Yates & Canby, Baltimore: "From Joseph

Haslam, Patterson, N.J., 1 bale specimens counterpanes and quilts prices from $1.50 to $3.00 each," and as entry No. 440: "Lancaster Mills, Lancaster, Mass., 3 cases quilts, different sizes."[32] By this date, however, the Jacquard loom was certainly a part of the picture.

Between 1810 and 1820 the Jacquard mechanism had begun replacing the drawboys of England. The process was adopted slowly, partly because of the great height of the mechanism. Placed on top of the already large handlooms, they required a room with a twelve-foot ceiling—not readily available to many weavers. Gradually, improved and smaller versions were developed, and weavers began to use them for their convenience and versatility.

During the nineteenth century, the character of Marseilles spreads changed. They gradually became thinner, flatter, lighter in weight, and with smaller and more elaborate patterning. They no longer looked at all like the quilts of Provence. Some even lost their stuffing layer, reverting to a simple double weave though retaining the name Marseilles. As recently as 1902 in the Sears, Roebuck and Co. catalog, and 1916 in a wholesale catalog issued by J. H. Dunham & Co., New York, "Marseilles quilts" were included with other bedspreads. Oddly enough, some of the twentieth-century Marseilles spreads again tried to look like quilts, but now it was American quilts they imitated.

Other bedspreads and fabrics belong in this woven family of discontinuous surface textiles. Not all have a fully hidden third layer, and many were developed after the Jacquard loom fully replaced the drawloom. Although not inspired directly by true quilts, they owe their origins to the needleworked Provençal quilts and are still called by the general name of "quiltings." Some of the nineteenth- and twentieth-century variations are named: Mitcheline, patent satin, matelas, Alhambra quiltings, piqué, honeycombs, Bedford cord, and toileting or toilets. Loom-made double-cloth quiltings went out of fashion after 1925. References in most textbooks and glossaries after that time—if they include them at all—refer to them as "obsolete" curiosities.

Two more British patents are of interest in this development. Oddly enough, ninety-seven years after the first patents were recorded in England, and long after the weaving technique was fully understood and utilized, quilting in the loom appears again in the patent records. On January 6, 1859, James Kirkman and Isaac Grundy stated in their description: "This invention is applicable to the manufacture of fabrics known as Bolton or Marseilles quilts, or others of like texture and materials." On January 7, Edwin Heywood offered a patent statement that is worth quoting at some length.

The improvements relate to the production of a peculiar description of double fabrics united in the weaving at parts, and enclosing between them thread or yarn as stuffing; such fabric being adapted to be used for skirts, ladies petticoats, the lining of coats and other garments, and for other uses in imitation of where two fabrics are united by stitching in various forms, and enclosing wool or other matter as padding. . . . The imitation of or resemblance to stitching is obtained by the weft and warps in the lines or forms desired, being caused to unite the two fabrics, and at the same time hold in position the thick or soft threads between them. Such uniting threads may be of silk or other material, different from that used for the general surface of the fabric in order that as it appears on the surface of the fabric produced it may represent stitching or other sewing.[33]

Thus, in 1859, recognition was again paid to the quilters of France of three centuries ago.

UPDATE:
The term "Marseilles" has been used to refer to a variety of textiles: hand-quilted material, loom-woven material that imitated hand-quilted material, and loom-woven material that did not imitate hand-quilted material. Because its meaning continues to interest American quilt researchers, an update on the literature is appropriate.

Garoutte's chapter provides a historical overview that is most specific about loom-woven quilting made in England. This product was called "Marseilles" in eighteenth- and early nineteenth-century documents in both England and America. Photographs of swatches of fabric woven in England show quilted products woven after an English patent was granted in 1763. The patent concerned "a new method of weaving and quilting in the loom . . . as of India, French, and Marseilles quilting." These draw-loom products are followed by fabrics woven on the Jacquard loom in the nineteenth century.

In 1983, an English translation of a 1770 French source (Charles Germain de Saint-Aubin, *Art of the Embroiderer*, Los Angeles, Los Angeles County Museum of Art, 1983, 56–57, 123) provides instructions for two techniques of "Embroidery of Marseille" current in 1770. Saint-Aubin first describes stuffed-work quilting and how to cover the flat background surfaces with knot-stitch embroidery. His second technique is for quilting, using two fabric layers and a center layer of combed cotton wadding. A photograph of a cord-quilted, knot-stitch embroidered stomacher is presented in this edition.

The hand quiltings of Marseilles from the seventeenth to the nineteenth centuries are described in a 1989 article by Eymar-Beaumelle (Marie-José Eymar-Beaumelle, "Les Toiles Piquées de Marseille et leurs mules," *CIETA Bulletin* 67, 1989: 51–55). There are three different techniques, with photographs of the first and second. The first, "les toiles piquées," has two layers of fabric decorated with extensive, fine cord quilting. The second, "la broderie emboutie," has two layers of fabric decorated with cord quilting and stuffed work. The third, "le matelassage," has two layers of fabric and a center layer of wadding, quilted together as in most quilting. Each type differed in the quality of materials used as well as in quilting proficiency. The first type was made by professionals in the seventeenth and eighteenth centuries. The second was made in the eighteenth century by less skilled craftsmen, many working in their homes. The third type was made from the seventeenth century into the twentieth century.

Because these methods of quilting were used in other areas of Europe in the seventeenth and eighteenth centuries, it is not clear what peculiar characteristics of quilts exported from Marseilles or Provence distinguished them from others made outside of France.

Janniere, in a 1993 article (Janine Janniere, "The 'Hand Quilting' of Marseille," *The Quilt Journal*, Vol. 2, No. 1, 1993: 5–9), discusses the published literature on hand-quilted Marseilles, but concentrates on the history of the French government's prohibition on importing Indian cotton into France in order to protect the French silk, wool, and linen industries. However, Marseilles, a free port, was exempted from the prohibition to this extent: the forbidden fabric could enter the port, wait in transit, and be shipped; and white toiles from the Levant could be imported, quilted in Marseilles, and exported.

For the seventy-three years of the prohibition, white Marseilles quilting had special significance in commerce and must have been popular in England for the name Marseilles to have commercial value there and in its colonies. The term "Marseilles quilting" was exploited to refer to loom-woven quilting and bedspreads. The result is that when we use the terms "Marseilles quilting" and "Marseilles" to refer to fabric, it is necessary to describe the fabric in technical detail and locate its manufacture in time and place if we wish to be understood.

Tandy Hersh

Notes and References

[1] Henri Algoud, "Toiles ornées au boutis et Indiennes de Provence," *La Soierie de Lyon* (Lyon: 1926), 636–42. Courtesy Musée des Tissus, Lyon, France.

[2] Two corded and stuffed quilts from Sicily, ca. 1395, are in the collections of the Victoria and Albert Museum, London, and the Bargello, Florence. Photographs and discussion in Averil Colby, *Quilting* (London: Batsford, 1972), 13–16.

[3] Algoud, 637.

[4] Ibid.

[5] "Mireio" is the poem for which Frederic Mistral was given a Nobel Prize. It is published (in English) in *Nobel Prize Library*, Vol. 15, (New York: Helvetica Press, 1971), 188.

[6] Algoud, 636, 638.

[7] Janet Arnold, *Patterns of Fashion* (London: Wace, 1964), 4. Quoted in: Mildred B. Lanier, "Marseilles Quiltings of the 18th and 19th Centuries," *Bulletin de Liaison du CIETA* 47/48, (1978): 74. Courtesy Musée des Tissus.

[8] Frances Norton Mason, *John Norton and Sons: Merchants of London and Virginia* (Newton Abbot: David & Charles, 1937) 10, 58, 190, 218.

[9] B. Woodcroft, ed., *Patents for Inventions: Abridgments of Specifications Relating to Weaving* (London: The Great Seal Patent Office, 1861), 8–9.

[10]Woodcroft, 9.

[11]*Georgia Gazette*, Savannah, June 6, 1765. Courtesy Museum of Early Southern Decorative Arts, Winston-Salem, NC, hereafter cited as MESDA.

[12]Alexander Mabyn Bailey, *The Advancement of Arts, Manufactures, and Commerce* (London: Society for the Encouragement of Arts, Manufactures, and Commerce, 1776), 130. Courtesy Merrimack Valley Textile Museum (now Museum of American Textile History) Library, North Andover, MA, hereafter cited as MVTM Library. A curious comment in this chapter: "This new and useful manufacture was invented by a poor obscure journeyman weaver, whose views, at first, extended no farther than to make a small quantity of it for the use of his wife and children; but, before it was made into garments for them, it was shewn, as a matter of curiosity, to a gentlewoman, who . . . mentioned it to the author of this book; and he . . . with great difficulty, found out the ingenious invention." The author, however, does not name the ingenious inventor!

[13]*Transactions of the Society* (London: Society for the Encouragement of Arts, Manufactures, and Commerce, 1783), 25. Courtesy MVTM Library.

[14]"History of the Society of Arts, etc.," *Commercial & Agricultural Magazine* (February 1800): 109. Courtesy MVTM Library.

[15]Elizabeth Boody Schumpeter, *English Overseas Trade Statistics 1697–1808* (Oxford: Clarendon Press, 1960), 12.

[16]Schumpeter, "Table XI: Quantities and Values of the Principal British Exports of Textile Goods (excluding Woolens) for the Years 1772–1807," 31–34. Courtesy MVTM Library.

[17]Ms. SC. 294 BSB: day book, Gatewood and Chapline, merchants, Bowling Green, KY, 15. Account of Robert Magness. Manuscript Division, Kentucky Library, Western Kentucky University, Bowling Green.

[18]Ms. 1964.61: "An account of Goods put in red Store," Old Sturbridge Village Research Library, Sturbridge, MA.

[19]Day book, "Joseph Philipson Merchant St. Louis 1807," 42. Account of Alexr. McNair, March 29, 1808. St. Louis Mercantile Library, St. Louis, MO.

[20]Letter: D. G. C. Allan, Curator-Librarian, the Royal Society of Arts, London, letter to author, Feb. 26, 1982.

[21]#G 1974–570: Swatch book ca. 1783, "#50," Textiles Department, Colonial Williamsburg Foundation, Williamsburg, VA.

[22]R. Ackermann, *Repository of Arts, Literature, Commerce, Manufactures, Fashions, and Politics*, London, 1809, issues for May, June, August, and September. Courtesy Winterthur Research Library, Winterthur, DE. Printed descriptions read:

May: "No. 4 is called printed India rib. It is a species of marcella, and is, at this moment, a very fashionable article for gentlemen's waistcoats."

July: "No. 4. This chintz, or shawl pattern marcella, ⅔ wide, is a truly elegant and fashionable article for gentlemen's waistcoats."

August: "No. 4 is a printed diamond marcella quilting, for gentle men's waistcoats. On this article there is little need of comment, except to call the attention of our readers to the peculiar delicacy of the printed stripe, which has perhaps rendered it so universal a favorite with men of high fashion. It is ¾ wide, and from 9s to 10s per yard."

September: "No. 4 is a unique article in silk striped quilting, combining much delicacy and utility; and which the inventor, after much labour, and considerable expence, has brought to its present high state of perfection, at his manufactory in the north of England."

[23]W. Hough, *Cotton Fabrics* (Typed manuscript with swatches, 1922). Archives, Bolton Museum, Bolton, Lancashire.

[24]William Rush Dunton, Jr., *Old Quilts* (Baltimore: privately published, 1946), 184–98.

[25]CPM–1134. Marseilles spread ca. 1825, 105″ x 114″. Connor Prairie Pioneer Settlement, Connorsville, IN.

[26]5255. Marseilles spread, 105″ x 104″. Gift of Mrs. C. Edward Murray. Daughters of the American Revolution Museum, Washington, DC.

[27]26.10.127. Marseilles spread ca. 1810–40, 100″ x 109″. Old Sturbridge Village, Sturbridge, MA.

[28]67.19. Marseilles spread ca. 1860, 86¼″ x 77½″. M. H. de Young Memorial Museum, San Francisco, CA.

[29]Advertisement, *Virginia Gazette*, Fredericksburg, Jan. 1, 1777. Quoted in: Lanier, "Marseilles Quiltings," 76.

[30]Salem Mercury, (May?) 1788. Quoted in Perry Walton, *The Story of Textiles* (Tudor, NY, 1925), 154.

[31]*The Maryland Journal and Baltimore Advertiser*, March 16, 1792. Courtesy MESDA. The booklet advertised, "The Weavers Draught Book and Clothiers Assistant, by John Hargrove, is the earliest draft book known to be printed in America." It was republished in facsimile by the American Antiquarian Society in 1979. None of Hargrove's 52 drafts is called "mock-Marseilles" in his book, although he did include three different bird's eye designs and a "deception diaper."

[32]*The National Magazine & Industrial Record*, 1 (1845): 161.

[33]Woodcroft, *Patents for Inventions*, 955, 957.

Nine Patch quilt pieced of print cottons, 65" x 44", made by the Dublin Ladies' Soldiers' Aid Society, New Hampshire, inscribed in ink with names and dates from September and October 1863, and stamped with oval of Sanitary Commission. Collection of Jan Coor-Pender Dodge. Photo by Sharon Risedorph.

The ink stamp used to mark textiles sent from the Soldiers' Aid Society of Northern Ohio (Cleveland Branch of U.S. Sanitary Commission), illustrated in Our Acre and Its Harvest, *1869.*

U.S. SAN. COM.
S.A.S.
NORTHERN OHIO

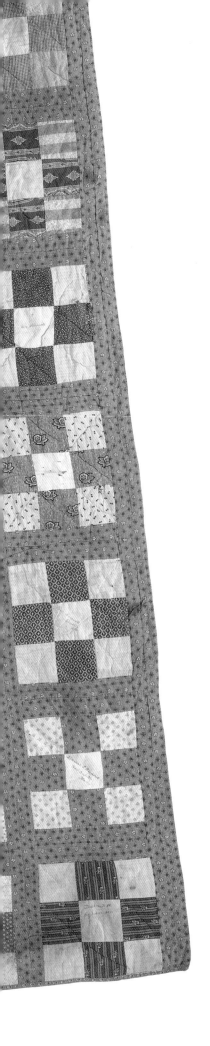

Quilts for Union Soldiers in the Civil War

Virginia Gunn

On April 20, 1861, five days after President Abraham Lincoln issued the call for 75,000 militia, a group of ladies in Cleveland, Ohio, assembled "to inquire how the charity of woman could best serve her country in its impending peril." Two companies of city militia had already left for Washington, DC, so the women took up a collection to aid the soldiers' families, some of whom had been left in desperate circumstances. Two days later they began to prepare bandages and lint, a dressing for wounds made from scraped or unraveled linen. A gentleman from the nearby military camp interrupted their efforts to inform them that one thousand volunteers from nearby districts were marching into camp. Expecting to be fully equipped in Cleveland, these men "had brought no blankets, and had now the prospect of passing a sharp April night uncovered on the ground." The ladies of Cleveland quickly procured carriages and set out on a door to door "blanket raid." They found that "a word of explanation sufficed to bring out delicate rose blankets, chintz quilts, thick counterpanes, and by nightfall seven hundred and twenty-nine blankets were carried into camp." They resumed efforts the next morning, and "before night every volunteer in Camp Taylor had been provided for."[1]

Now aware of the lack of necessities, the women set to work. Obtaining army flannel from the nearby post commandant, patterns and cutters' services from local tailors, sewing machines from city merchants, and workspace at the YMCA, the women turned out one thousand shirts in two days.

Virginia Gunn, *Ph.D., is a professor of Clothing, Textiles, and Interiors at the University of Akron in Ohio. She teaches and publishes in the areas of historic costume, history of furnishings, textile conservation, and women's history. 215 Schrank Hall South, University of Akron, Akron, OH 44325-6103.*

Next they participated in the ill-advised fad of making havelocks, linen cap covers such as British soldiers wore for protection from the sun, producing enough for each northern Ohio regiment. Looking around for further work, they began gathering hospital supplies for the sick troops at Camp Taylor. Soon they elected officers and established committees for hospital clothing and bedding, bandages and lint, fruit and groceries. By June 1861, they had formally organized as the Ladies' Aid Society of Cleveland.

Similar series of events took place in other cities across the country.[2] Northern women had long been used to group work for worthy causes. Therefore, with the framework for service already in place, "home mission societies, church sociables, sewing circles, and various benevolent organizations were converted into Soldiers' Aid Societies without change of organization." As one participant explained, "A vote of the members to work for sick and wounded soldiers while the war should last, was all the formality necessary. This enabled them to enter at once upon their new duties."[3] A lady from Wisconsin recalls "as a rule the women who had been prominent in the earlier organizations, became the leaders in the aid societies, so that the movement . . . went rapidly forward."[4]

Women, sending their loved ones off to war, eagerly sought ways to contribute to their well-being. The great desire to help spared the government any necessity of having to gain support. It is estimated that more than twenty thousand soldiers' aid societies were formed in the entire country, with approximately two-thirds of them in the North.[5] Aid society members cut, sewed, and knitted thousands of articles for Northern soldiers during the four years of the Civil War, including significant numbers of quilts and comforters.

In contrast to the women, the federal government found itself totally unprepared for even a peacetime provision of clothing, food, shelter, and medical supplies for the huge number of men called up so rapidly. Clothing and bedding became especially critical, for these items could not successfully be foraged for and took a good deal of time to prepare. The primitive industrial conditions of the wholesale trade, coupled with a shortage of prepared textiles, made efficient manufacture a slow development. The federal government urged the states to clothe and equip their own volunteers and to forward the bills. In spite of the best efforts of contractors and government agencies, the army could not fully equip soldiers for all occasions through official channels. Throughout the war, the government depended on philanthropic efforts to supplement its provisions of food, clothing, shelter, and medical supplies.[6]

Early efforts to help soldiers had a local emphasis. Towns shipped donations directly to local regiments or units. But as difficulties of transportation and mailing mounted, it became increasingly necessary to organize a more efficient system of getting donated supplies to their proper destinations. Local groups began to send their contributions through state commissions and national agencies such as the U.S. Sanitary Commission, the Western Sanitary Commission, or the Christian Commission.

According to Charles Stille, about seven thousand of the local soldiers' aid societies served as auxiliaries of the U.S. Sanitary Commission, the largest private national agency channeling donated supplies to soldiers.[7] This agency committed itself to a national effort to help any needy soldier regardless of his background—including enemy wounded. It believed that work done in an orderly, disciplined fashion assured the best interests of each soldier. By the end of the war, the value of women's contributions made through the U.S. Sanitary

Commission totaled $25,000,000. The effort took the cooperation of thousands of women of all ranks and stations who worked their volunteer efforts into the routines of their daily lives. Women committed to the philosophy of helping any Union soldier develop a national spirit and a will to win. By 1863, a Sanitary Commission officer believed that "while our Government has one great army in the field, of those who are pouring out their life-blood in its defense, the Sanitary Commission has in the home field another great army, composed of the mothers and sisters, wives and sweethearts of our brave soldiers, working scarcely less earnestly and efficiently for the same great end."[8]

The Women's Central Association of Relief, organized in New York City in April 1861, played an instrumental role in the formation of the U.S. Sanitary Commission. This association sent four male representatives to the nation's capital to find out what their organization could do for the war effort. The representatives included Henry W. Bellows, minister of a large Unitarian Church in New York City, and Elisha Harris, a doctor much interested in sanitary work. In Washington these men became convinced of the soundness of their idea to establish a sanitary commission, similar to a British example formed to improve conditions during the Crimean War. They made their way through the Washington bureaucracy, and President Lincoln officially approved their goals on June 13, 1861. The newly formed U.S. Sanitary Commission opened an office in the city and began work. It planned to investigate troop and hospital facilities and to advise the Medical Bureau and the War Department on ways to improve sanitary conditions in the army.[9]

The commission did not originally intend to distribute donated supplies; however, contributions from the women in New York and from other societies poured into its office follow-

Vintage photograph of the United States Soldiers' Aid Society storefront at 95 Bank Street, Cleveland, Ohio, circa 1864–65. Collection of the Western Reserve Historical Society.

ing the battle of Bull Run in July 1861. The commission officials, well aware of the government's deficiencies and inadequacies, deviated from their purposes of inquiry and advice and began distributing the badly needed supplies. One need only read about the terrible conditions following this battle to understand why the commission added relief work to its original purposes.[10]

After becoming committed to relief work, the Sanitary Commission hired relief agents who worked in the field with the sanitary inspectors. These agents reported to Executive Secretary Frederick Law Olmstead in the East, or to Secretary John S. Newberry in charge of the West. These two men, in turn, made needs known to branch organizations of women (and sometimes men) located in major cities. By 1863 the commission had regional branches in Boston, New York, Buffalo, Philadelphia, Pittsburgh, Cincinnati, Cleveland, Columbus, Chicago, Detroit, Louisville, and Bal-

timore. These branches were central receiving centers for the local aid societies of the surrounding districts. Some branches collected from as many as twelve hundred local auxiliaries.[11] The amount of food, clothing,

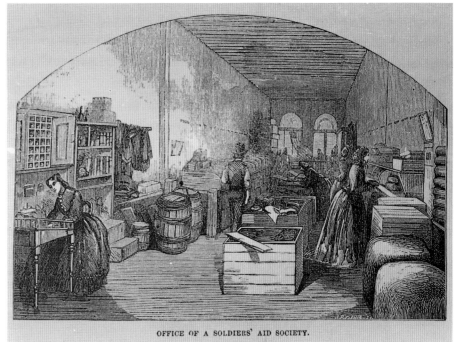

OFFICE OF A SOLDIERS' AID SOCIETY.

An engraving of people working in the interior of an unidentified office of a soldiers' aid society as it appeared in The Tribute Book *by Frank B. Goodrich, 1865.*

and bedding shipped, received, and distributed by the regional branches and local societies was staggering. It is even more impressive when one remembers that most articles had to be handmade by the donors.

Local newspapers helped the cause by focusing on the work of nearby societies. They regularly published lists of donors and the articles they contributed. Editors also printed appeals for more goods, reports of aid societies' meetings, and publicity for fundraising events such as festivals, suppers, and dime societies. Utilizing the paper, local aid society officers urged women to attend work sessions to help make and send needed materials on a systematic, rather than spasmodic, basis. They wanted women to consider themselves enlisted for the duration of the war. As the Akron, Ohio, officers stated, they expected members to be present at meetings "unless detained by more sacred motives than patriotism, or more urgent duties than helping to save our country."[12]

When crates and boxes of textiles and food sent by local societies arrived at a branch office, volunteers unpacked each one and checked the contents against the enclosed invoice before recording the contributions in the branch records. A typical box of textiles sent by a local auxiliary to a branch office might include "15 comforters, 9 blankets, 29 shirts, 9 pairs drawers, 14 pillows, 15 sheets, 30 pillow cases, 11 cushions, 21 cushion covers, 38 towels, 3 double gowns, 12 napkins, 12 handkerchiefs, 13 pairs socks, 2 Testaments, 1 Bible, books, magazines, papers, and rags."[13] Branch volunteers stamped all unmarked textile items with the identifying mark of the branch commission in indelible ink. The branch secretary sent an acknowledgment and thank-you back to the local society. This letter included advice as well as encouragement to keep up the good efforts. At the branch the donated supplies could be handed out to

needy or sick soldiers on furlough or in nearby soldiers' homes, but workers sorted and repacked most items. Associate members of the Sanitary Commission helped ship the repacked boxes of goods to temporary field depots or to one of the central supply depots established in Washington, Louisville, and (earlier) New York City. From these depots supplies could be shipped quickly to camps and battlefields and to field, post, regimental, and general hospitals.[14]

Relief supplies for sick and wounded soldiers always included large quantities of bedding—quilts, comforts, blankets, sheets, and pillowcases. Careful record keeping and reporting by the men and women at each end of the supply line built accurate records of the amounts of supplies shipped and received. Regional and branch records of donations and shipments reveal, for example, that during the year 1863, people contributed 5,459 quilts to the Hartford, Connecticut, association.[15] The Sanitary Commission gave out supplies on the field or in hospitals by requisition only, a practice often criticized by outsiders but in keeping with military protocol and the commission's belief in disciplined management as an essential ingredient of its work. Requisitions show, for example, that Grant's army at Vicksburg received 9,029 sheets and 2,429 comforts from May through August 1863.[16] They record that, during the month of May 1864, the commission issued 2,932 blankets and 1,203 quilts to the Armies of Virginia.[17]

Each Union soldier was to be furnished with two wool blankets every other year.[18] Blankets issued early in the war, however, often proved to be of inferior quality and fell apart when used or wet. Unscrupulous contractors made large fortunes on such "shoddy goods."[19] Quality controls improved, but the shortage of warm covers remained acute as each cold weather season approached. In October 1861, U.S. Quartermaster

---

Report of the "Girls' Soldiers' Aid Society."

This Society was organized August 9th, and the following are the cash receipts for two months, ending October 9th, 1862:

Memberships	$ 6 09
Dime Society	21 00
Contribution Box in the Post Office	70
A Friend	2 00
Stand on the Fair Ground	62 00
Mozart Society	8 21
Total	$100 00

We have sent off one box containing the following articles: 45 pillow cases, 2 rolls of cotton, 3 pairs of socks, 1 package of magazines, 4 quilts, 20 pairs of slippers, 16 handkerchiefs, 6 towels, 7 needle-books, 6 boxes of lint, 100 compressess, 133 bandages, 90 pin-balls, 2 bags of dried cherries, 1 bag of dried corn, 1 bag of dried currants, 4 ounces of cloves.

We have also sent 2 jugs of wine, and 2 cans of fruit, in a box which contained other articles belonging to the Ladies' Aid Society.

The following are the articles donated to the Society: Anna Manly, 3 lbs of bandages, 1 lb of linen, 1 bottle of wine; Mattie Sabin, 2 quilts, 2 lbs of bandages, 1 can of raspberries, 1 jug of wine, 1 bag of dried cherries; Flora Hanchett, 1 quilt, 1 lb of bandages; the little girls 14 blocks for patchwork; Laura Balch, 10 handkerchiefs; E.P. Green, 1 piece of cotton cloth; Minnie Wheeler, 1 bag of dried corn, 1 bag of dried cherries; Olive Wheeler, 1 package of magazines; Lizzie Ladd, 10 bandages, 6 compresses, ½ lb of lint; Emma Ladd and Lottie Baldwin, 4 blocks for patchwork, 4 bandages, 1 linen table-cloth; Mr. Fay, 5½ lbs of tow; Libbie and Manda Wills, 1 quilt, 6 bandages, 17 compresses, ½ lb of lint; Olive Henry, 1 roll of linen, 1 roll of cotton; Mrs. White, 1 roll of linen, 1 roll of cotton; A Friend, 1 package of lint; Fannie Belden, 1 roll of cotton; Mrs. Scott, 1 roll of linen; Mrs. Sabin, 3 pairs of socks; Mrs. Burton, 1 roll of linen; Nellie Abbey, 1 can of cherries; Fannie Viele, 1 bag of dried currants, Grace Ferkina, 1 box of lint.

L. O. BALCH, Secretary.

Summit Beacon, October 16, 1862.

General Montgomery Meigs issued a call for contributions of blankets:

The troops in the field need blankets. The supply in the country is exhausted. Men spring to arms faster than the mills can manufacture, and large quantities ordered from abroad have not yet arrived. To relieve pressing necessities, contributions are invited from the surplus stores of families. The regulation army blanket weighs five pounds; but good sound woolen blankets weighing not less than four pounds, will be gladly received at the offices of the United States Quartermasters in the principal towns of the loyal States, and applied to the use of the troops. To such as have blankets which they can spare but cannot afford to give, the full market value of suitable blankets, delivered as above, will be paid.[20]

With inspectors in the field, the Sanitary Commission had anticipated such a shortage and on October 1, 1861, had issued its own letter of appeal to the loyal women of America urging all neighborhoods without an aid society to organize one and to send committees from "house to house and store to store to obtain contributions in materials suitable to be made up, or money for the purchase of such materials." The commission's list of most needed articles included "blankets for single beds; quilts, of cheap material, about seven feet long by fifty inches wide."[21] The Soldiers' Aid Society of Northern Ohio (formerly the Cleveland Soldiers' Aid Society) suggested making "comfortables, 8 feet long, 4 feet wide, of cheap dark print, wadded with cotton."[22] In December 1861, the Sanitary Commission stated that "never, probably, was so large an army as well supplied at a similar period of a great war," but noted that in the regiments it had inspected, 75% of the soldiers had one good blanket, 20% had two blankets, but of inferior quality, and 5% had never received a blanket.[23]

Women, hearing of the lack of bedding, often sent their sons and husbands off to war with a quilt from the family supply. During this first winter, "long hoarded treasures of fine linen spun by grandmothers, and relics of revolutionary times, which had been reserved in all previous emergencies, now came to light and were freely offered."[24] People generally acknowledged that many heirloom-quality quilts had been donated to the cause. Other quilts offered for Northern soldiers, however, could not be classified as either of heirloom quality or newly made to suggested measurements. In November 1861, Mrs. A. M. Coburn of the Akron Soldiers' Aid Society noted in her letter to Mrs. Rouse of the Cleveland Branch that "you will find some of the old quilts much worn and soiled. You will of course use your discretion whether to send them to a hospital or to Camp Wade."[25]

Some donated quilts resulted from group projects where each contributor made a patchwork square. Children in schools or "alert clubs" sometimes worked on such projects in addition to collecting and raising funds for the local societies.[26] In 1864, a group of school children made patchwork blocks "with a white center, on which the name and age of the one who gave it was to be written" with indelible pencil. In this class the girls sewed most of the blocks, but one boy "sewed his own block with the nicest little stitches you ever saw." The other boys earned the $3.00 for cotton and batting. With group effort, the children finished "thirty-five blocks in the quilt; thirty-four of them had names and ages on them—none over twelve years—and on the centre one was written 'Bradford County. For any soldier who loves little children.'" The class sent the quilt to the Sanitary Commission with a note urging the recipient to correspond. In November 1864, a Minnesota soldier in Tennessee reported that, being unable to get a blanket from Uncle Sam, he had gone to the Sanitary Commission and had been given "that splendid quilt that your pennies and busy little fingers made." He noted

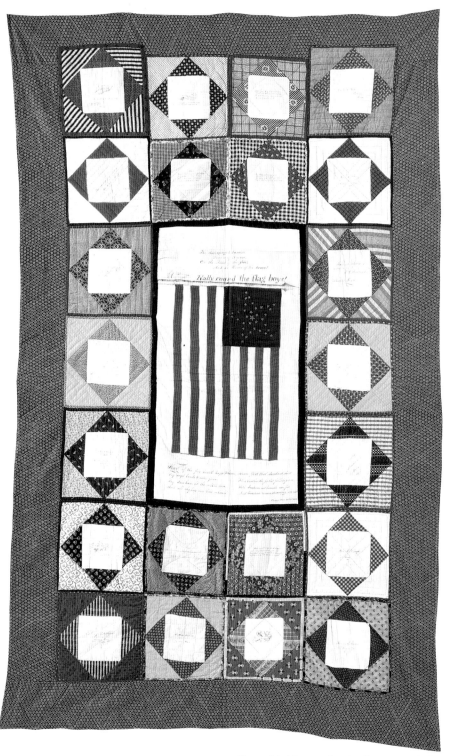

Civil War soldier's quilt of pieced cottons, 85" x 53", with inked inscriptions, 1865, Florence, Massachusetts. This cot-size patriotic quilt with the striking flag and message "Rally round the flag boys!" appears to be unused. It may have been made just as the war came to an end. Courtesy of America Hurrah Antiques, New York City.

Opposite: Summit Beacon, *March 17, 1864.*

"how highly I value it, how carefully I shall preserve it, and how I shall take it home with me (if I don't wear it out, and live to go home)."[27]

Such letters provided important encouragement for men, women, and children laboring on the home front. Local newspapers regularly published letters from soldiers. Ladies could read that their men "are glad to feel and know, that they are not forgotten by their friends at home, but feel extremely thankful, for the valuable supplies they have received from time to time."[28] *The Sanitary Commission Bulletin* and *The Sanitary Reporter*, official organs of the commission, published letters from field agents that informed the women back home that soldiers appreciated their efforts. One sanitary agent reported that he had just seen the wounded "lifted from rough blankets and undressed from the soiled clothes of march and battle, and laid, in your clean sheets and shirts, upon your comfortable quilts and pillows."[29] Another reported giving out more than eighteen hundred blankets and nine hundred quilts to alleviate suffering and cold and assured women that "could they have observed the change produced when the soiled and bloody garments were replaced by clean and warm clothing that they had sent, they would be eager to replenish our storehouses and keep our hands filled with the means to accomplish these purposes."[30]

The branch societies sometimes sent their own female representatives to check on hospitals or to help on hospital transport ships. These women returned to give eyewitness accounts of conditions at the front. One woman wrote her fellow workers at home that "blessings on the Aid Societies were invoked when the stores of sheets and comfortable quilts were brought from their hiding place, and the cots made, one after another, by their cleanliness and comfort, as inviting as those of a fine hotel."[31]

Difficulties in transporting supplies to distant battlefields and the rigors of campaigns in which supplies became lost or discarded in the heat of battle meant that men sometimes lacked essential supplies, including bedding. The Sanitary Commission tried to anticipate and have supplies on hand near the site of an impending battle. But still notices would be sent back that sick and wounded Union soldiers could be found "lying on bare floors mostly without blankets, pillows, mattresses, or even straw. Their clothing fetid with filth and blood, without proper or sufficient food," and to make matters worse, "Government supplies were wholly inadequate to the wants of these men even if they had not been wounded."[32] Such reports kept the problems of the soldiers uppermost in women's minds.

Never could women rest assured that their men were well taken care of. Thus their efforts continued unabated throughout the war. One woman pinned a note to her quilt stating, "My son is in the army. Whoever is made warm by this quilt, which I have worked on for six days and most of six nights, let him remember his mother's love."[33] As women labored to make and send supplies, as well as carry out their other duties, many probably felt like the volunteer who wrote "I am so weary tonight that I have begged the assistance of my daughter in making out the invoice which I enclose."[34]

Huge battles in the summer of 1862 drained supplies. By the fall of 1862, nearly one million soldiers served in the Union army. The army had a constant sickness rate of one-seventh of its total. This meant that more than 100,000 sick and wounded soldiers filled the hospitals, almost totally dependent on gifts for their supply of special foods, bedding, and hospital clothes.[35] Women set aside frivolous needlework and responded to increased needs. At a county fair held in Ohio in the fall of 1862, a reporter noted that scarcely any of the usual fancy work articles could be seen on exhibit. Instead, fairgoers

might see in every corner, on every shelf and platform and in every part of the Hall the sad effects of war. And well it is, for although fancy stitching and sewing are lain aside, and the brush and pallet have been forgotten, yet thousands of march-worn, sick and wounded soldiers will testify that the good ladies of our land have not been idle, and that although the handy work is not seen as much in Floral Halls as in years past, still they have been busy

in preparing articles of diet and clothing for those truly in want.[36]

An overwhelmed Medical Bureau gratefully received the systematic aid of the Sanitary Commission on the battlefield and in camps and hospitals. Weary surgeons sometimes took time to write branches of the Sanitary Commission acknowledging their indebtedness. One stated that he "particularly noticed a large invoice of quilts from your society, received here just when fly-blown blankets could not be endured another day, and one of the most timely of all of your favors."[37]

Throughout the fall and winter of 1862–63, the demand for bedding continued. In January 1863, the Soldiers' Aid Society of Northern Ohio (Cleveland) informed its five hundred auxiliaries:

Sheets and Quilts are now very much wanted. The latter should be seven feet long, four and a half feet wide, and may be made of old calico or delaine, with cotton quilted firmly between, so that it will not lose its place on being washed. Carpeting cut into pieces seven feet long, four feet wide, thoroughly washed and bound around, makes a good bedcovering. It must be remembered that hospital cots are very narrow, and second hand bedding, before being sent to us, should be cut down to a proper size. Two half quilts of ordinary size can be altered into three hospital quilts. The same advice will apply to half-worn sheets. . . . The yet unsupplied wants of hundreds of our suffering friends and brothers, whose cries ascending from hard-fought fields or ill-conditioned hospitals, should incite our utmost exertions.[38]

The final winter of the war, like the preceding ones, "brought on a heavy and sudden pressure for blankets, quilts, underclothing and shoes." Hospitals found supplies of quilts most welcome and "by far preferable to the rough woolen blankets."[39] In January 1865, the Sanitary Commission reported the need for "flannel clothing, bed quilts, socks and mittens."[40] As the war dragged on,

A Voice from the Hospital.
—

BATH, March 5, 1864.

MR. LANE—The enclosed letter was received by a member of our society, and she is quite willing (if you think proper) to have it published, hoping it may meet the eye of some who are depriving themselves of the enobling pleasure and great privilege of assisting in the work of alleviating, in some degree, the sufferings of our brave soldiers, through doubts as to the proper appropriation of their gifts, or the less pardonable excuse of penuriousness or indifference. Permit me to add that we have heard directly from four of the bed quilts sent by our society within the past year.

A MEMBER OF THE SOCIETY.
—

GENERAL HOSPITAL, KANSAS CITY, MO.,
January 23d, 1864.

FIDELIA NASH—You will excuse the boldness of one that is a stranger to you in thus addressing you. I am a sick soldier in hospital at this place, and one day while reading the names of ladies, written on a quilt, I saw your name subscribed Fidelia Nash, Bath, Summit County, Ohio. I presume you are a member of a sick soldiers' aid society, and are doing all that you can to support the general Government, and to cheer and gladden the hearts of soldiers. I have visited a great many hospitals in Arkansas and Missouri, all of which were supplied with clothing by Aid Societies, principally from Northern Ohio. I am a native of Ohio, and it does my heart good to know that the ladies of my native State feel such an interest in the success of this war, as to make such ample provision for the comfort of us soldiers that are obliged to face the enemy. If fighting was the only danger and hardship that we have to endure, we would call it fun; but hard marching, wading rivers and laying on cold, wet ground, eating poorly cooked food and drinking bad water is more to be dreaded than the roaring cannon, or the flashing sword. Our hospitals are filled with sick, and if it were not for your Aid Societies there would be an untold amount of suffering. Having received the benefit of a quilt made by your society, you will permit me to thank you, and through you the kind and benevolent ladies of your Aid Society. May God bless you all is the sincere wish of a sick soldier.

My dear Madam, I do not know whether you are an old or a young lady. I wish to know if your maiden name is Nash—the reason of my inquisitiveness is, that my mother's name was Nash—and this fact is the excuse that I offer you for this intrusion; we may be cousins. My mother was Elizabeth Nash, the daughter of Samuel Nash. He had sons named Uriah, Henry, Chester and David. You may be daughter or granddaughter, or if a married lady, your husband may be a son or grandson of one of my uncles. Kin or no kin, you will do me a favor by writing me a letter. Please direct to General Hospital, Kansas City, Missouri.

I am, very respectfully, yours &c.

R. FULLER.

growing numbers of destitute families of absent soldiers, increasing numbers of widows and orphans, disabled veterans, loyal refugees from the South, and freedmen also needed material aid.[41]

Northern families found it increasingly difficult to supply all the needed items. In 1862 about 90% of the supplies had been donated, often from goods people had on hand. By 1863, however, supplies in homes had become exhausted. Often aid societies needed to purchase raw materials that could be given out and made up by their members.[42] They found cotton and wool in scarce supply and increasingly expensive. Calico cost forty to fifty cents a yard.[43] The Cleveland Branch gave donated quilts a value of four dollars each, approximately the cost of the materials used to make them.[44] In addition to local needs for money, the Sanitary Commission needed cash to continue paying its agents, to transport supplies, and to purchase in bulk the huge quantities of food it provided for hospitals. A timely and significant monetary gift from supporters in California helped to keep the commission's work going.[45]

To help raise needed funds, Northern women decided to try their traditional fundraising techniques on a grand scale. Beginning in the fall of 1863 and continuing through 1864 and 1865, they organized great Sanitary Fairs in cities across the country. Mary Livermore and Jane Hoge of the Chicago Branch planned the first fair, which opened in Chicago on October 27, 1863. It raised $78,000 and set off a chain reaction. Boston held a fair in December, which netted $145,000. Cincinnati's fair started on December 21 and made $235,000. On Washington's birthday in 1864, fairs opened in Albany, Brooklyn, Buffalo, and Cleveland. The New York Metropolitan Fair, the largest of all, took place in April 1864 and netted $1,200,000. Philadelphia, St. Louis, and Pittsburgh, as well as many

smaller cities, also sponsored successful fairs. This series of Sanitary Fairs raised an amazing $4,500,000 for the cause.[46]

The planning, preparation, and execution of these huge projects involved hundreds of men and women from all walks of life. Humble farmers from outlying districts linked hands with the crème de la crème of metropolitan society in a concerted effort to make each city's fair a grand success. The fairs became regional social events and provided a means of cultivating patriotism as the war became prolonged and depressing. Some fair committees erected special buildings, which they decorated with greens, flags, patriotic motifs, and pictures of military and civilian leaders. Fairs opened with parades and ceremonies. In a spirit of friendly competition each city tried to outdo the others, but they also cooperated by sharing ideas. Branches sent delegates to visit fairs in other cities. People often contributed to several fairs. *The New York Times* devoted a special daily column to fair announcements.

Although patriotic women had temporarily laid aside leisure pastimes of fancy needlework when they turned to making garments and doing plain sewing for hospitals, the great fairs gave an excuse to do fancy work once again. A ladies' bazaar featuring a great variety of fancy articles "formed the staple of each Sanitary Fair."[47] People made and bought frivolous items without feeling guilty because the money raised went to a worthy cause.

Quilts ranked among the more expensive items made and donated to the fairs. At Cleveland, quilts and other fancy items could be seen on display in county booths in the great bazaar section of the fair. One reporter noted that "silk patchwork quilting of elaborate fashion, woolwork, pin cushions and cobweb knitting tempt the purses of buyers."[48] As in all commission work, volunteers kept records of do-

nations to the fairs. Records of the Cleveland fair show that the branch received six crib quilts, twenty-one bed quilts, and three silk bed quilts, as well as smaller quilted items. Donors placed a value on articles they gave. They valued the quilts from $1.75 to $18.00, for an average of $7.00 each. Silk quilts received values of $30.00 to $50.00 each. An American Flag quilt donated by the Christian Commission of Michigan had a value of $15.00. The most highly prized fancy item, a magnificent afghan, listed originally for $125.00, an amount later raised to $200.00.[49] Although considered by some to be a form of gambling, a number of fairs used raffling as a means of selling expensive items that were beyond the purchasing power of most fairgoers, because the annual income for a family was about $500.00 a year.

Of special interest is a money-raising event used at the Cleveland Fair. Organizers fashioned a " 'crazy bed quilt,' a grotesque piece of newspaper patchwork," which they hung in a busy corner of the building. It was "sold by lot every day, with the express condition that the unlucky possessor is not obliged to keep it, but will be allowed to present it to the fair." The newspaper reported that "a considerable sum of money and a great deal of fun are realized by this transaction, which takes place every noon just as the clock strikes twelve."[50]

The reports of the Great Western Sanitary Fair in Cincinnati give a few descriptive details about quilts, which highlight silk Log Cabin quilts. At the booth of the Willow Glen Aid Society, a reporter "observed a silk patchwork quilt, lined with silk valued at $50. This quilt was made by the ladies of the society in one week, expressly for the Fair. It is a beautiful quilt, of the 'log-cabin' pattern."[51] Another reporter mentions that this quilt was to be raffled off at $100.[52] The Morris Chapel Soldiers' Aid So-

The Hartford Booth at the New York Metropolitan Fair, April 1864, included patchwork pillows and a patchwork quilt. Photograph by M. Stadfeld appeared in A Record of the Metropolitan Fair, *1867.*

ciety displayed "a silk log-cabin quilt, by Mrs. Glenn, an elderly lady."[53] And in the booth of the Trinity Methodist Episcopal Church, fairgoers could see a "half-grown" marble-topped bureau and matching bedstead "furnished with a silk log-cabin quilt, and all the other indispensibles of a real bed."[54]

At the Brooklyn and Long Island Fair, visitors could look up and see "a spectacle of wonderful brilliancy . . . afghans, quilts, and spreads, of the most vivid colors" draped along the circular balcony of the academy where the event was held.[55] The fair committee sent several of the most noteworthy articles to President Lincoln as gifts. An anonymous donor gave $179.00 toward the "quilt for the President."[56] This "superb silk bed-spread . . . formed of the National Colors, and emblazoned with the Stars and Stripes and the National Eagle" had been made by an eighty-one-year-old woman. On April 1, 1864, Lincoln wrote expressing his "most cordial thanks for the beautiful present transmitted by you, and for the kind and graceful manner in which it was conveyed."[57]

The New England Kitchen became one of the most popular spaces at the Brooklyn and Long Island Fair. The committee decorated this section with genuine antiques in order "to present a faithful picture of New England farmhouse life of the last century." Tableaux events featured in this setting included a quilting party with "'old folks' industriously stitching on the quilt during the afternoon, while the 'young folks' were summoned in to close the evening."[58] Playing on this sentimental look at the past, the Brooklyn Fair closed with a "calico ball" to raise money for soldiers' families. More than half the ladies attending wore plain calico dresses, most of which they later gave to the wives and daughters of soldiers.[59] By the 1860s, urban dwellers considered quiltmaking a country craft of nostalgic interest.[60] A few weeks later,

An engraving of the women who dressed in old-fashioned clothing and quilted for the colonial tableaux featured at the Brooklyn and Long Island Fair and the New York Metropolitan Fair. From The Tribute Book *by Frank B. Goodrich, 1865.*

New York City's Metropolitan Fair featured a Knickerbocker Kitchen, which duplicated the quilting tableaux.

The splendor of the ladies' bazaar at the Metropolitan Fair proved to be, so reports claimed, beyond the descriptive powers of the male reporters sent to cover it. The fair's historian describes the great hall as "a realm of bewildering profusion, where one was smothered with afghans and sofa pillows, buried amid pincushions, tidies, and glove-boxes, and triumphed over by wax-dolls and fate-ladies." He goes on to say that "it was a true region of the indescribable, and those who went in to spy out the land, if they came back at all, came with no report."[61] Engravings and photographs show patchwork for sale and one record mentions "a silk quilt, representing a flag, made by a lady seventy years old."[62]

The correspondence of the Woolsey family of New York City provides further insights on quilts at the fair. Members of this prominent family made and donated large quantities of supplies to the commission. As the time approached for the city's Metropolitan Fair, Mrs. Woolsey wrote a letter to her two daughters serving as nurses. She described family preparations for the fair and reported that they were making "three silk comfortables, all spandy new, none of your old gowns, lined with silk and beautifully quilted in scrolls and medallions by a Fishkill woman, and trimmed with ribbon quillings. . . . I dare say we shall all do our full part, both in making and purchasing."[63]

As another special attraction, most fair committees arranged a museum or room of curiosities where a profusion of antiques, exotic treasures, and battlefield souvenirs lent for the occasion were on exhibit. Here valued quilts might be displayed next to Japanese and Chinese artifacts. In New York City, the Curiosity Shop included "a quilt that had once covered the beautiful Mary of Scotland . . .

and one made by one of the earlier among the American sovereign people—a patchwork quilt of calico—bought during the Revolutionary War, when calico was a dollar and a quarter a yard."[64] The Great Central Fair in Philadelphia displayed relics believed to have belonged to George Washington. These included "a bed-quilt, of elaborate patchwork, sewed by Mrs. Washington herself, after the fashion of that time."[65]

Although women made special quilts to raise money for the great fairs, they also fashioned unique quilts to send to unknown soldiers. One of the rare extant quilts bearing the identifying stamped mark of the Sanitary Commission is a Nine Patch album-style quilt sent "To the Soldiers with the best wishes of The Dublin Ladies Soldiers Aid Society" of New Hampshire. Names, dates from September and October 1863, poems, and the words "60 volunteers" are ink-inscribed on the center white squares of the forty blocks that form the quilt. The blocks are set straight and separated with lattice strips in a brown printed calico. The 44″ by 65″ dimensions indicate that the makers had a soldier's cot in mind. The recipient of this quilt must have treasured it enough to bring it home with him. His family must have continued to value it as a war memento for it was saved by several unknown generations before the current owner purchased it at a California flea market.[66]

During the Civil War, the Cleveland Branch reported that "'album quilts' were a favorite conceit of sewing circles, where each lady would contribute a patchwork square made from scraps of her own dresses, writing upon it her name and a patriotic sentiment or cheering couplet."[67] The Hartsville, Pennsylvania, Society made up twenty quilts, some of them "album quilts." They sent these to their contact, Mary Pollack, who distributed them in Washington, DC, hospitals. A regular visitor to one of these hospitals found a ward "quite in a commotion over some Album Quilts Miss Pollack had been distributing." One of the recipients, who had lost his leg in the Battle of the Wilderness, wished to take his quilt home with him. The visitor wrote the Hartsville Society stating that "if the ladies and gentlemen who have ornamented his quilt with their names think he is deserving of it for a keepsake, he would appreciate the gift highly."[68]

Northern patriots prominently displayed the American flag and patriotism prompted the making of flag quilts. Early in the war ladies made company flags and presented them to local units leaving home. They also made American flags. One family used "stripes of muslin and turkey-red calico, and a piece of the daughter's blue apron (for cotton cloth was dear) formed the background for the stars, which were six-pointed and patterned after a drawing by the younger son."[69] In April 1865, the New Haven, Connecticut, Society "received from a country town a quilt made in the form of a flag—red and white stripes and a blue field with the white stars sewed on, all nicely quilted." Members donated "this Union quilt," accompanied with a request for acknowledgment. In May, a Pennsylvania soldier at Fairfax Station, Virginia, replied that "the first night the flag quilt was spread over me, I did dream of the loved ones far away."[70] The New Haven Society received another flag quilt fashioned from a flag made by a mother and son shortly after the war began. The son later lost his life at Chancellorsville. When Lincoln died, the soldier's family mournfully draped the flag he had helped make and then a sister "converted it into a quilt, and wishes it sent to some one of our released prisoners still in hospital."[71]

A report of a quilt made in 1864 in Green Bay, Wisconsin, which turned up again in 1884 "in the cabin of a negro family living near Bentonville," gives insights on other special quilts

made for soldiers. It notes that "the piece that remained contained eight blocks, each of which had in the centre a white cross running diagonally, while the outside pieces were of colored calico, bordered with white. On each square was written the name of its maker in indelible ink; a few of the blocks bore also timeworn inscriptions." The reporter believed that the verses on the quilt illustrated "the sturdy and uncompromising spirit" of the quiltmakers:

For the gay and happy soldier
We're contented as a dove,
But the man who will not enlist
Never can gain our love.

If rebels attack you, do run with the quilt
And safe to some fortress convey it;
For o'er the gaunt body of some old
   secesh
We did not intend to display it.

'Twas made for brave boys, who went
   from the West;
And swiftly the fair fingers flew,
While each stitch, as it went to its place in
   the quilt,
Was a smothered "God bless you, boys,"
   too.[72]

Quilts purchased at sanitary fairs probably received careful treatment, but most of the quilts and comforts made for soldiers did not survive the war or hard use in the years that followed. Refugees and destitute families quickly picked up quilts laid aside by marching soldiers trying to lighten their loads. Other quilts became lost or destroyed in the heat of battle. The Sanitary Commission worked to install washing procedures for hospital textiles and saved some quilts for a second use by boiling them in kettles of water.[73] Still, when field hospitals moved, they often left behind piles of quilts and comforts caked with blood and dirt. All this helps explain why so few Civil War era quilts still exist, in comparison with the numbers thought to have been made before and during the war.

It is impossible to know exactly how many quilts and comforts women made and donated in this

Detail of Nine Patch quilt pieced of print cottons, 65" x 44", made by the Dublin Ladies' Soldiers' Aid Society, New Hampshire, inscribed in ink with names and dates from September and October 1863, and stamped with oval of Sanitary Commission. Collection of Jan Coor-Pender Dodge. Photo by Sharon Risedorph.

four-year period. Women gave quilts to Northern soldiers from the beginning of the Civil War until the very end. They made special quilts as well as utility quilts of cheap, practical materials, which were meant to be used up keeping soldiers warm; and, in desperate times, families also relinquished treasured textiles for the good of the cause.

While no one attempted to make a grand total of recorded donations, it is possible to make some estimates of the numbers of quilts donated based on data available. As aid societies gradually ended their work after the war, they often tallied up the records of their achievements and sent in reports. Some branches circulated

summary reports and others published reports in books. While some records became misplaced or lost, archival holdings of U.S. Sanitary Commission records are sizeable, though fairly widely scattered. Remaining records show that Chicago received a final total of 15,131 donated comforts.[74] Cincinnati reported a total of 13,892 comforts.[75] Cleveland's final totals included 13,473 comforts and quilts.[76] The New York Central Association ended with a record of 26,408 quilts.[77] The final report of the Philadelphia Branch recorded 4,986 comfortables and quilts.[78] These figures are from only five of the twelve branches, but the total is 73,890. Even if these five branches had provided over half of all bedding taken in by the Sanitary Commission, the total would have amounted to over 125,000 quilts and comforts.

Another way of estimating gives similar results. By October 1864 the Western Department of the Sanitary Commission had disbursed 50,177 comforts and quilts.[79] At a meeting in November 1864, delegates from the Eastern division, representing New York, Connecticut, Rhode Island, and parts of Vermont, New Jersey, Rhode Island, Massachusetts, and Canada estimated that they had issued 60,000 quilts.[80] This would be a conservative estimate for the East, as not all branches sent representatives to this meeting. Together these figures give a total of about 110,000 comforts and quilts issued in the Western and Eastern divisions by late 1864, for an average of about 30,000 per year. Because quilts continued to be issued throughout the following winter or for another six months, an estimated 15,000 more can be added to the total, again suggesting that the U.S. Sanitary Commission distributed at least 125,000 quilts and comforts.

The commission records probably account for only half the number of quilts and comforts donated during the war because aid societies also sent supplies through personal representatives and through other state and national agencies. Contemporaries felt that "not more than half of the supplies and stores collected throughout the country have ever been recorded; that is, that fully half have been employed in such a way as to preclude their entering into any general account."[81] Research in northern Ohio records upholds this assessment as fair. Members of the Canton, Ohio, Society, for example, noted that while they forwarded 255 packages to the Cleveland Branch, "many boxes were sent direct to regiments in the field, to hospitals at the front, and to State Relief agencies, with some supplies of money and stores to the Freedmen."[82] In addition, Canton fitted regiments for service, and aided soldiers in transit. Some societies sent all their contributions outside the U.S. Sanitary Commission channels.[83] Thus it would seem that 250,000 quilts and comforts is a conservative estimate of the number of quilts women made for Union soldiers in the Civil War. This number is even more impressive when one remembers that in addition to quilts and comforts, women of the North made thousands of other items of bedding, clothing, and food for the soldiers. The material aid provided by the soldiers' aid societies helped to significantly reduce the death toll of this war. Clothing and bedding played an important role in the success or failure of military units.[84] Before the Civil War, experts estimated that for every soldier killed in battle, four would die of disease. The efforts of agencies like the Sanitary Commission lowered these statistics to two Union soldiers dying of disease for every one who fell in battle. Some 186,000 Union soldiers died of disease. The total might have been as great as 372,000 without the concerted efforts of the commissions and aid societies.[85]

A comprehensive history of the aid societies has still not appeared among the thousands of books and pamphlets printed on the Civil War. While home front activity received much recognition in its day, later literature emphasized the work of soldiers and politicians, and "workers in benevolent societies were relegated to bit parts."[86] The men and women of the U.S. Sanitary Commission and its branches and auxiliaries, however, acknowledged the mutually beneficial aspects of their joint efforts. Henry W. Bellows, president of the commission, wrote that "it was another feature of the case that there was no jealousy between women and men in the work, and no disposition to discourage, underate or disassociate from each other."[87]

The New England Women's Auxiliary Association's final report comments on this universal cooperation, and states that "rich and poor, wise and simple, cultivated and ignorant, all—people of all descriptions, all orders of taste, every variety of habit, condition, and circumstances; joined hands heartily in the beginning, and have worked together as equals in every respect."[88] When Henry W. Bellows sent his greetings to the women of the Northwest assembled at the Chicago fair, he compared the women's work to a "great national quilting party." He considered:

the States so many patches, each of its own color or stuff, the boundaries of the nation the frame of the work; and at it they have gone, with needles and busy fingers, and their very heart-strings for thread, and sewed and sewed away, adding square to square, and row to row; allowing no piece or part to escape their plan of Union; until the territorial area of the loyal States is all of a piece, first tacked and basted, then sewed and stitched by women's hands, wet often with women's tears, and woven in with women's prayers; and now at length you might truly say the National Quilt—all striped and starred—will tear anywhere sooner than in the seams, which they have joined in a blessed and inseparable unity![89]

Using their traditional skills, women moved onto a new plane of responsibility. They became interested in causes outside their immediate circles and experienced the feelings of self-confidence that come from successfully completing a hard task. Women also began to see the power of networking with one another across class, social, and regional lines. Mary Livermore, co-director of the Northwestern Branch of the Sanitary Commission at Chicago, gave valuable insights from a woman's perspective:

Peace came at last, but during those days of hardship and struggle, the ordinary tenor of woman's life changed. She had developed potencies and possibilities of whose existence she had not been aware, and which surprised her, as it did those who witnessed her marvelous achievements.[90]

Numerous leaders of this volunteer home army would, like Mary Livermore, provide leadership for other social reform causes, including women's rights and suffrage, during the last quarter of the nineteenth century. Very early in the war the editor of the Akron, Ohio, newspaper perceived the way the war would change the lives of women as well as men. He predicted that "it is possible, that one of the great benefits which is to grow out of this wicked rebellion, will be the discovery of the important fact that the young ladies of our country can be useful as well as ornamental members of society."[91] From 1861 to 1865, women used their traditional skills to make thousands of quilts and textile items to help the soldiers and the country they loved. In the process they began to transform their own lives and to change the paths that they would follow.

Notes and References

[1]Cleveland Branch of the United States Sanitary Commission (written by Mary Clark Brayton and Ellen F. Terry), *Our Acre and Its Harvest: Historical Sketch of the Soldiers' Aid Society of Northern Ohio* (Cleveland: Fairbanks, Benedict, 1869), 17, 19–20.

[2]Ibid., 20–25.

[3]Ibid., 27.

[4]Ethel Alice Hurn, *Wisconsin Women in the War Between the States* (Madison, WI: Wisconsin History Commission, 1911), 22.

[5]Mary Elizabeth Massey, *Bonnet Brigades* (New York: Knopf, 1966), 32; Robert Bremmer, *American Philanthropy* (Chicago: University of Chicago Press, 1960), 77.

[6]One of the best sources for information on the problems of clothing the army is Fred A. Shannon, *The Organization and Administration of the Union Armies, 1861–1865*, Vol. I (Cleveland: Arthur H. Clark, 1928). See also: William Quentin Maxwell, *Lincoln's Fifth Wheel: The Political History of the United States Sanitary Commission* (New York: Longmans, Green & Co., 1956), 41–49.

[7]Charles Stille, *History of the United States Sanitary Commission* (Philadelphia: Lippincott, 1866), 172.

[8]Dr. J. S. Newberry, "Sanitary Commission Document No. 75: Report on the Operations of the U.S. Sanitary Commission in the Valley of the Mississippi Made September 1, 1863," in *Documents of the U.S. Sanitary Commission*, Vol. II (New York: 1866–71), 20.

[9]Stille, *History of the Sanitary Commission*, 40–62.

[10]For descriptions of conditions, see Horace H. Cunningham, *Field Medical Services at the Battles of Manassas (Bull Run)* (Athens, GA: University of Georgia Press, 1968) and George Worthington Adams, *Doctors in Blue: The Medical History of the Union Army in the Civil War* (New York: Henry Schuman, 1952).

[11]Linus Pierpont Brockett, *The Philanthropic Results of the War in America* (New York: Sheldon, 1864), 54–55; William Y. Thompson, "The U.S. Sanitary Commission," *Civil War History* 2 (June 1956): 46–52.

[12]"Report of the Akron Soldiers' Aid Society," *Summit County Beacon* (Akron, OH, newspaper), Feb. 13, 1862, microfilm frame 189.

[13]Hurn, *Wisconsin Women in the War*, 58.

[14]Sarah Edwards Henshaw, *Our Branch and Its Tributaries: Being a History of the Work of the Northwestern Sanitary Commission* (Chicago: Alfred L. Sewell, 1868), 153–60; *Our Acre and Its Harvest*, 60–74.

[15]United States Sanitary Commission, *The Sanitary Commission of the United States Army: A Succinct Narrative of Its Works and Purposes* (New York: U.S. Sanitary Commission, 1864; reprint, New York: Arno Press, 1972), 268–69. This work is hereafter cited as *Succinct Narrative*.

[16]Ibid., 141.

[17]"Issues of Stores to the Army in Virginia," in *U.S. Sanitary Commission Bulletin* 2, No. 16 (1866): 493.

[18]"How Soldiers Are Clothed," *Summit County Beacon*, Jan. 16, 1862, microfilm frame 172.

[19]See Robert Tomes, "The Fortunes of War: How They Are Made and Spent," *Harper's New Monthly Magazine* 29 (July 1864): 227–31.

[20]"Stockings and Blankets for the Soldiers," *The Scientific American* 5 (Oct. 12, 1861): 227.

[21]"To the Loyal Women of America!" *Summit County Beacon*, Oct. 17, 1861, microfilm frame 117. This letter, dated Oct. 1, 1861, appeared in other papers across the country.

[22]Mrs. B. Rouse, "Bulletin #6—Soldiers' Aid Society for the Relief of the Sick and Wounded of the Federal Army (in Co-operation with U.S. Sanitary Commission)," an undated pamphlet contained in bound Vol. 28 (a scrapbook for years 1861–63), in Manuscript #1012, titled *U.S. Sanitary Commission. Cleveland Branch: Soldiers' Aid Society of Northern Ohio. Records, 1860–1878*, Collection of Western Reserve Historical Society, Cleveland, OH. Hereafter, this collection is cited as WRHS Manuscript 1012.

[23]Frederick Law Olmsted, "Sanitary Commission Document No. 40—A Report to the Secretary of War of the Operations of the Sanitary Commission, and Upon the Sanitary Condition of the Volunteer Army . . . December 1861," 17, in *Documents of the U.S. Sanitary Commission*, Vol. I.

[24]*Our Acre and Its Harvest*, 48. See also "Meeting at New Haven, Connecticut," *The Sanitary Commission Bulletin* 3, No. 27: 856–57.

[25]A. M. Coburn, Akron, OH, letter to Mrs. Rouse, Cleveland, Nov. 4, 1861, in WRHS Manuscript 1012, Container 11, Vol. 1.

[26]"Alert Club" (June 8, 1863, newspaper article from Cleveland Branch), *The Sanitary Commission Bulletin* 1, No. 12: 371.

[27]"For the Children" (newspaper article from *New York Independent*), *The Sanitary Commission Bulletin* 3, No. 33: 1049–50.

[28]J. F. S., "From the 29th" (letter dated Dec. 10, 1862), *Summit County Beacon*, Dec. 18, 1862, microfilm frame 367. See also "A Word to the Aid Societies Contributing to Philadelphia Agency," *The Sanitary Commission Bulletin* 3, No. 35: 1091.

[29]Field Agent Edward P. Smith, of U.S. Christian Commission, letter to Dr. J. S. Newberry of U.S. Sanitary Commission, July 23, 1863, in *Succinct Narrative*, 248–49.

[30]"Sanitary Work in the Army of the Potomac during the Year 1863" (letter from commission agent on sanitary supply steamer in Fredericksburg campaign), *Succinct Narrative*, 146–47.

[31]*Our Acre and Its Harvest*, 52.

[32]"At Fredericksburg," *The Sanitary Commission Bulletin* 2, No. 20: 625.

[33]"Marked Articles," *The Sanitary Commission Bulletin* 1, No. 14: 443.

[34]Mrs. A. M. Coburn, Akron, OH, letter to Miss Brayton of Cleveland Branch, April 25, 1862, in WRHS Manuscript 1012, Container 11, Vol. 1.

[35]*Succinct Narrative*, 43.

[36]"Geauga County Fair," *Summit County Beacon*, Oct. 2, 1862, microfilm frame 322.

[37]"Testimony of Surgeon Hart" (A. G. Hart, letter to Cleveland Branch), *The Sanitary Commission Bulletin* 3, No. 18: 556. See also: "Letter from Dr. Woodward" in Appendix to "Sanitary Commission Document No. 64—What the U.S. Sanitary Commission is Doing in Valley of the Mississippi," 16, published in *Documents of the U.S. Sanitary Commission* 2.

[38]"Circular No. 10—Soldier's Aid Society of Northern Ohio, Branch of United States Sanitary Commission, January 15, 1863," in WRHS Manuscript 1012, Container 10, Folder 6.

[39]"The Commission In the Valley," *The Sanitary Commission Bulletin* 3, No. 25: 775.

[40]"Women's Central Association of Relief," Ibid., No. 31: 961.

[41]See Joseph E. Holliday, "Relief for Soldiers' Families in Ohio During the Civil War," *Ohio History* 71 (1962): 97–112.

[42]Frank B. Goodrich, *The Tribute Book: A Record of the Munificence, Self-Sacrifice, and Patriotism of the American People during the War for the Union* (New York: Derby & Miller, 1865), 88–93.

[43]Hurn, *Wisconsin Women in the War*, 47, 73.

[44]*Our Acre and Its Harvest*, 421. The 13,473 comforts and quilts were valued at $53,892, or four dollars each.

[45]Stille, *History of the Sanitary Commission*, 479.

[46]William Y. Thompson, "Sanitary Fairs of the Civil War," *Civil War History* 4, No. 1 (1958): 51–67.

[47]Henshaw, *Our Branch and Its Tributaries*, 222.

[48]*Our Acre and Its Harvest*, 163. General William Tecumseh Sherman donated a patriotic silk quilt he had been given to the St. Louis sanitary fair. The center field of the quilt features red and white bricks arranged in a Streak of Lightning diagonal variation. This is set off by a wide blue border appliquéd with white stars. The

quilt is now in the collection of Jefferson Memorial Missouri Historical Society in St. Louis. For further information, see Cuesta Benberry, "Epilogue: Quilt Patterns of the Late Victorian Era," *Nimble Needle Treasures Magazine* (Fall 1973): 2–3. There is a pattern for it in Mabel Obenchain, ed., "General Sherman's Quilt," *Bicentennial Quilts* (New York: Famous Features, 1976), 24–25.

[49]Information taken from invoices and receipts related to the Cleveland Fair contained in WRHS Manuscript 1012, Container #40, Vols. I and II.

[50]*Our Acre and Its Harvest*, 179.

[51]*History of the Great Western Fair*, (Cincinnati: C. F. Vent, 1864), 315–16.

[52]Ibid., 299.

[53]Ibid., 277.

[54]Ibid., 268.

[55]Executive Committee, *History of the Brooklyn and Long Island Fair, February 22, 1864* (Brooklyn: "The Union" Steam Presses, 1864), 47.

[56]Ibid., 183.

[57] "Presents to the President of the United States," Ibid., on unnumbered 190.

[58]Ibid., 73, 76.

[59]*History of the Brooklyn and Long Island Fair*, 93–94.

[60]See discussion of this in "What We Have and What We Need," *The Sanitary Commission Bulletin* 1, No. 1: 41.

[61]*A Record of the Metropolitan Fair in Aid of the United States Sanitary Commission Held at New York, in April 1864* (New York: Hurd and Houghton, 1867), 145.

[62]Ibid., 157.

[63]Georgianna Woolsey Bacon and Eliza Woolsey Howland, *Letters of a Family during the War for the Union 1861–1865*, Vol. II (Printed for private distribution, 1899), 569.

[64]*A Record of the Metropolitan Fair*, 76–77.

[65]Charles J. Stille, *Memorial of the Great Central Fair for the U.S. Sanitary Commission held at Philadelphia, June 1864* (Philadelphia: U.S. Sanitary Commission, 1864), 82.

[66]The description is based on the author's personal observation and on the documentation work done by owner Jan Coor-Pender Dodge and by Dorothy Cozart and Merikay Waldvogel.

[67]*Our Acre and Its Harvest*, 62. A cot quilt made in Florence, MA, in 1865 contained pieced blocks inscribed with patriotic messages that were arranged around a central section featuring the flag and an inked heading, "Rally round the flag boys!" It appeared in Robert Bishop and Carter Houck, *All Flags Flying: American Patriotic Quilts as Expressions of Liberty* (New York: Dutton, 1986). Courtesy of America Hurrah Antiques of New York City.

[68]Soldiers' Aid Society of Hartsville, PA, *History of the Hartsville Ladies' Aid Society* (n.p.: W. W. H. Davis, Printer, 1867), 13–14.

[69]Hurn, *Wisconsin Women in the War*, 9.

[70]"Flag Quilts," *The Sanitary Commission Bulletin* 3, No. 39: 1224–25.

[71]Ibid., 1225.

[72]Hurn, *Wisconsin Women in the War*, 26–27.

[73]Henry W. Bellows, "The Sanitary Commission," *North American Review* 97 (April 1864): 390; Henshaw, *Our Branch and Its Tributaries*, 90–91.

[74]Ibid., 379.

[75]William J. Jacobs, *Quiet Crusaders: A History of the Cincinnati Branch of the United States Sanitary Commission* (Master's thesis, University of Cincinnati, 1956), 60.

[76]*Our Acre and Its Harvest*, 421.

[77]Ellen Collins, *Women's Central Association of Relief Table of Supplies Received and Distributed from May 1, 1861, to July 7, 1865*, in WRHS Manuscript 1012, Container 10, Folder 6.

[78]Robert M. Lewis, *Report of the General Superintendent of the Philadelphia Branch of the U.S. Sanitary Commission to the Executive Committee, January 1, 1866* (Philadelphia: King and Baird Printers, 1866), 41, 50, 61, 64.

[79]Dr. J. S. Newberry, "Sanitary Commission Document No. 84—Report on The Operations of the U.S. Sanitary Commission in the Valley of the Mississippi for the Quarter Ending October 1, 1864," 21, published in *Documents of the U.S. Sanitary Commission* 2.

[80]"The New York Meeting—Meeting of Delegates From the Soldiers' Aid Societies," *The Sanitary Commission Bulletin* 3, No. 27: 874, 879.

[81]Goodrich, *The Tribute Book*, 156.

[82]*Our Acre and Its Harvest*, 469.

[83]Brockett, *Philanthropic Results of the War in America*, 85–87.

[84]See John D. Chapla, "Quartermaster Operations in The Forty-Second Virginia Infantry Regiment," *Civil War History* 30 (March 1984): 5–30.

[85]Frank Moore, *Women of the War: Their Heroism and Self-Sacrifice* (Hartford: S. S. Scranton, 1866), 592.

[86]William Y. Thompson, "The U.S. Sanitary Commission," *Civil War History* 2 (June 1956): 63. Also see Alan Nevins, Bell Wiley, and James I. Robertson, Jr., eds., *Civil War Books: A Critical Bibliography* (2 vols.) (Baton Rouge, LA: Louisiana State University Press, 1967–69).

[87]Linus Pierpont Brockett and Mary C. Vaughn, *Woman's Work in the Civil War: A Record of Heroism, Patriotism, and Patience* (Philadelphia: Ziegler, McCurdy, 1867), 42.

[88]Ibid., 555.

[89]Henry W. Bellows, "U.S. Sanitary Commission Document No. 63—A Letter to the Women of the Northwest, Assembled At The Fair at Chicago, for the Benefit of the U.S. Sanitary Commission," 3–4, in *Documents of the U.S. Sanitary Commission* 2.

[90]Mary A. Livermore, *The Story of My Life: Or, The Sunshine and Shadows of Seventy Years* (Hartford: A. D. Worthington, 1897), 484–85.

[91]"To Patriotic Young Ladies," *Summit County Beacon*, Aug. 7, 1862, microfilm frame 290.

Alabama Gunboat Quilts

E. Bryding Adams

In mid-February of 1862 an article titled "A Southern Woman" appeared in the *Mobile Register and Advertiser*. The female author appealed to the patriotism of Southern women and particularly those of Alabama, to make contributions for an Alabama gunboat to defend the city of Mobile. Even though the author had a "house full of children," she proposed to contribute her five dollars "earned by her needle." Further, she stated that "were she a man, she would be in the harness of the soldier and grasping the firelock in some expectant camp; being a woman, she has but her prayers . . . and her noble thoughts to lay upon the altar of love of her dear country."[1] Thus began the inspiration for a statewide campaign in Alabama for the women's gunboat fund.

Alabama, however, was not the only state where women were raising money for gunboats. The first of these societies appeared in New Orleans late in 1861, and from there the idea spread to the February appeal in Alabama.[2] The *Charleston Daily Courier* of March 1, 1862, printed a letter from a lady of Summerville, South Carolina, suggesting contributions,[3] and on March 14, 1862, the *Georgia Daily Enquirer* proposed that the South Carolina lady's suggestion be followed in Georgia.[4] Within a week, twelve Georgia cities had organizations and were forwarding the funds to Savannah.[5]

On March 17, 1862, the *Richmond (VA) Daily Dispatch* appealed for funds for a gunboat, citing inspiration from the women of South Carolina and Georgia.[6] The women of Williamsburg responded by forming a society as reported on March 28, 1862,[7] and by April 4 the Ladies' Defense Association of Richmond was formed.[8]

Gunboat quilt A, 66" x 66", made by Martha Jane Singleton Hatter (1815–96) of Greensboro, Alabama, before 1862. Pieced and appliqué wool challis on silk taffeta with cotton backing and applied binding. Museum purchase with partial funds from the Quilt Conservancy. Collection of the Birmingham Museum of Art (1985.209). Courtesy of Birmingham Museum of Art, Alabama.

CSS Georgia. *Engraving from* Harper's Weekly, *February 14, 1863.*

E. Bryding Adams *is the curator of decorative arts at the Birmingham Museum of Art. She is the project director for the Alabama Decorative Arts Survey and co-director of Alabama Quilt Sharing. She is conducting research and writing about quilts, as well as other Alabama decorative arts. Birmingham Museum of Art, 2000 8th Avenue North, Birmingham, AL 35203-2278.*

The exact sum of funds raised by these organizations is not known, but at least $30,000 was raised in Charleston and Richmond. The *Charleston, Fredericksburg,* and *Georgia* came to be known as "ladies gunboats," or, derisively, "petticoat gunboats." Other ironclads, most notably South Carolina's *Palmetto State,* were also financed in part by contributions from women. The *Georgia* is currently being examined and researched by the Coastal Heritage Society of Savannah and the United Daughters of the Confederacy.[9] Newspapers throughout the Confederacy reported with great fervor the contributions toward the gunboats from early March through midsummer of 1862.[10] Communities developed rivalries, and even states competed for the greatest contributions. An Alabama newspaper urged, "we would state that the women of Georgia and South Carolina are also engaged in the same noble work . . . and unless the women of Alabama bestir themselves their sisters will snatch from them the honor of having the first of the women's gunboats built and ready for service."[11]

Research in extant Alabama newspapers reveals the overwhelming effort of the ladies of this state to secure the funds for a gunboat. Notices of contributions appear from February 18 through May 23, 1862, in the *Mobile Register and Advertiser,* the *Weekly Montgomery Advertiser,* the *Alabama Beacon* of Greensboro, and the *Selma Morning Reporter.* Individuals held concerts and dinners and contributed everything from actual funds to objects to be raffled at bazaars and fairs.

The *Mobile Register and Advertiser* should be given the credit for instigating the Alabama effort as reported on February 18, 1862:

Who speaks next. Let us hear from town and country, from village and hamlet, mountain and plain of our great state. . . . We call upon the women of the interior to take the matter in hand. . . . If

the response is general and the one feeling is enkindled from the Promethena spark struck from the mind of "A Southern Woman" it will be easy to organize. . . . The cause is a noble one, the effort is sublime, and the moral effect will reach far beyond the deadly projectiles which the contemplated gunboat can send. If the women take it up with a will, there is no such word as fail.

The *Weekly Montgomery Advertiser* of February 26, 1862, reported a similar appeal. "We commend it to our noble women, who have already done so much to clothe our brave troops with wool and to soothe and tend them when sick. The women of the South wield an influence in the struggle for her independence, which is impossible to estimate. They should exert it." Indeed, contributions did come from throughout the state, including thirty-six cities.[12]

Money was contributed in small donations ranging from one dollar to $303.95 by women, children, and slaves.[13] Others who could not give money gave objects, quite often precious to them due not only to their sentimental value, but also to their monetary worth. Objects given to the cause included a bell, a kettle, brass and irons, a fender, a lamp, oak timbers, a breast pin, gold pencils, a lead pipe, gold thimbles, peafowl flybrushes, a map, jewelry, a decorative pincushion, a silver cup, a silver fish knife, wine, butter, paintings, a silver goblet and waiter, cotton, quilts, and even a sewing machine. Concerning the sewing machine the lady wrote: "I have no money nor valuables, my only treasures being my children and I cannot offer them to my country for they are daughters. I have a sewing machine, though, which I offer to be disposed of for the benefit of the fund."[14] The paper replied: "This patriotic offer affords another proof of the deep hold our case has taken upon the affections of our noble women. We advise our correspondent to hold on to her sewing machine for the present."[15]

By April 4 the *Mobile Register and Advertiser* reported a total of $2,246.25 with another $1,500 to $2,000 expected. Still the total cost of the gunboat was estimated to be $80,000. Naval disasters suffered by the Confederate forces in the spring of 1862 fueled public dissatisfaction. With the increasing ineffectiveness and loss of the blockade gunboats, contributions declined. This outpouring of patriotism for a gunboat came to an end in late May when the *Alabama Beacon* and *Selma Reporter* reported: "In view of the probability that Mobile will fall into the hands of the enemy, the project for building the women's gunboat for the defense of the State will be either abandoned or indefinitely postponed . . . it has been proposed . . . that the gunboat fund be applied in providing Hospitals and in procuring hospital stores for the use of the sick and wounded in our armies."[16] Thus the project came to an end with the funds applied toward hospital supplies.

Of particular interest to this study were the donation and raffling of six quilts for the benefit of the Women's Gunboat Fund. From Whistler, Alabama, on March 30, 1862, a lady, M. D. Resor, wrote to the *Mobile Register and Advertiser*: "Messrs. Editors: This unholy war has bereaved me of my husband, leaving myself and little son depended upon my father, who is in very limited circumstances. I have no money, and I wish to contribute something to the ladies' gunboat; so if you will dispose of this quilt, as you see proper, for the gunboat, you will oblige me."[17] In Eutaw, Alabama, on April 19, 1862, $108.00 was raised from the "Raffle of a fine silk quilt. It was made by a patriotic young lady of Demopolis, Miss C ."[18] Oddly enough, the "Miss C____" did not want her name used.

In Greensboro, Alabama, recorded in the *Alabama Beacon,* "Two very handsome quilts have been left with Col. Chadwick . . . to be raffled off—the proceeds to be applied to the

Gunboat quilt B, 71" x 68", made by Martha Jane Singleton Hatter (1815–96) of Greensboro, Alabama, before 1862. Appliquéd wool challis on cotton with cotton backing and applied binding. Collection of the First White House of the Confederacy, Montgomery, Alabama, gift of Mrs. Mary Hutchinson Jones. Courtesy of Birmingham Museum of Art, Alabama.

Women's Gunboat Fund. One is the handiwork of ladies residing in the Havanna neighborhood—the other was made by Miss Josephine Bayall."[19]

Unfortunately, the whereabouts of the four above-mentioned quilts are unknown; however, two quilts recorded in the *Alabama Beacon* are now in the collections of the First White House of the Confederacy in Montgomery, Alabama, and the Birmingham Museum of Art. The *Alabama Beacon* on April 4, 1862, tells their story:

A widow* of our town of Greensboro, who had two sons in the army, had made two quilts of most rare and beautiful workmanship; the proceeds from the sale of which she proposes to devote to the building of the gunboat. One of the quilts was placed in my charge on my visit to Marion, Perry County, on Thursday last. At a public meeting there, I offered the same for sale to the highest bidder. It was bid off for the sum of one hundred dollars! Their money was immediately contributed by the persons present, and the quilt replaced in my hands to be resold

for the same patriotic object.
Yours respectfully,

J. J. Hutchinson

*The lady referred to is Mrs. Hatter. That quilt or the other contributed by her has been sold in Tuscaloosa for $400.00-ED.

One week later the *Alabama Beacon* reported again on the status of these quilts.

You noticed the sale of a quilt at Marion, made and presented by a lady of Greensboro as a contribution to the ladies' gunboat fund. The quilt . . . returned to me with a request to sell it again . . . was bought by a gentleman of Tuscaloosa for $100—thus making $200 realized. . . . I have the pleasure to state, the same lady has placed in my hands another quilt of still richer workmanship, devoted to the same object. . . . Offered for sale in Tuscaloosa . . . it was first bought by the contributions of several citizens for $115, who directed me to sell it to a larger company I expected to address, in the same place, that day, and devoted the proceeds of the sale to providing for the families of absent soldiers. At this second sale in this city, the sum of $500 was realized, and the quilt again presented to the gunboat enterprise. Last night, at Summerfield, in your county, I offered the quilt for sale again . . . the sum of $250 was bid for the same. . . . The sale of that object is expected to come off, in Selma, tomorrow, 3rd of April.

Yours,

J. J. Hutchinson[20]

In essence, Mrs. Hatter of Greensboro offered two quilts for sale with the proceeds going to the gunboat fund. Quilt A, most probably the one at the Birmingham Museum of Art, was sold at Marion and Tuscaloosa for $100 each sale. Quilt B, more elaborate and probably the one now owned by the First White House of the Confederacy, was sold four times, twice in Tuscaloosa for $115 and $500; in Summerfield for $250, and in Selma, the price unknown.

Quilt A descended in the Hatter family with the oral history that it was made by Mrs. Hatter and that this quilt and another quilt were auctioned off to support the Con-

Child's quilt D, 60" x 33", made by Martha Jane Singleton Hatter Bullock (1815–96) of Greensboro, Alabama, after 1863. Appliqué cotton on cotton with cotton backing and crocheted cotton edging with fringe. Collection of Dr. and Mrs. Robert Cargo. Courtesy of Birmingham Museum of Art, Alabama.

federacy. "A wealthy Texan bought the quilt and then gave it back to Martha Hatter. Martha then decided she would honor her own mother, Elinor Singleton, by leaving the quilt to be passed down to future Elinors in the family." This story was told to the author by Elinor Wesley Weinberg Strickland, having been passed down from her mother, Elinor Singleton Hatter (who died in 1960), after hearing it from Martha Jane Hatter Bullock, who died in 1896.[21] In 1985 Quilt A was purchased by the Birmingham Museum of Art from Mrs. Strickland with financial assistance from the Qult Conservancy.

Quilt B, owned by the First White House of the Confederacy, was a gift of Mrs. Mary Hutchinson Jones in 1928. She was the daughter of Alfred H. Hutchinson and granddaughter of the J. J. Hutchinson who auctioned the quilts and reported the event to the newspaper. He must have kept the quilt for his family or have been given the quilt by Mrs. Hatter.[22]

Three other quilts are now thought to have been made by Martha Jane Hatter. These attributions are made on the extraordinary fine needlework, overall framed-center design, similar appliqué fabrics, and provenance.

A crib-size quilt, Quilt C, now also in the collection of the First White House of the Confederacy, was a gift in 1979 of Panthea Mary Reid Fischer and her mother, Nell Marshall Reid (Mrs. John Reid). It was made for Panthea Coleman Baltzell by the great-grandmother and grandmother of the donors listed above. They are direct descendants of Colonel William Henley Bullock and his first wife, Panthea Coleman Birchett Bullock. Martha Jane Hatter was the second wife of Colonel Bullock.[23]

Some controversy has arisen between the descendants of the Hatter family and the Bullock family as to which Mrs. Bullock, the first or the second, actually produced this crib quilt. It is the contention of this author that they were made by the second Mrs. Bullock, Martha Jane Singleton Hatter Bullock. Martha Jane Hatter's first husband was Richard B. Hatter, who died on February 14, 1849. She married Col. William Henley Bullock (1797–1870) on July 30, 1863.[24] The first Mrs. Bullock died on October 19, 1860, and the crib quilt was made for her future step-granddaughter, Panthea Coleman, born in 1861. Thus it is concluded that Martha Jane Hatter Bullock also made the crib quilt after her marriage to Colonel Bullock in 1863.

A child's quilt, Quilt D, like crib-size Quilt C descended in the Bullock family to Nell Marshall Reid. The quilt was purchased by Dr. Robert Cargo in 1989 from Mrs. Reid's estate.

A carriage quilt, Quilt E, has descended in the Greensboro family of John Erwin, where it is still located today. The family was unaware of the Hatter origin, but due to the many similarities in the design, appliqué, and quilting as compared with the other Hatter quilts, in addition to the Greensboro location, the quilt has been attributed to Martha Jane Singleton Hatter Bullock. The date of production is unknown.

Finally, a brief analysis of the technique of the five quilts is pertinent to this study.

Quilt A is sixty-six inches square, obviously conceived by Mrs. Hatter not as a bed quilt but as a showcase for her considerable needlework skills. The main feature of the quilt is an embroidered basket with wool challis appliquéd flowers surrounded by an embroidered wreath. The appliquéd flowers are individually cut from printed cretonnes, then heavily stuffed and embroidered. Most of the flowers are attached with a buttonhole stitch, sometimes in dark thread, which outlines the design visually. Two tiny strawberries, completely three-dimensional, stuffed and embroidered, are attached to the flower basket on the quilt surface. The basket itself is outlined in a split-stitch and decorated with button-like embroidered circles. Such highly detailed beauty is un-

Crib quilt C, 37" x 31½", made by Martha Jane Singleton Hatter Bullock (1815–96) of Greensboro, Alabama, after 1863. Appliqué cotton on cotton with cotton backing and cotton torchon lace fringe. Collection of the First White House of the Confederacy, Montgomery, Alabama, gift of Panthea Mary Reid Fischer and Nell Marshall Reid. Courtesy of Birmingham Museum of Art, Alabama.

usual even for very fine chintz appliqué quilts of the mid-nineteenth century. Yet another feature sets this quilt apart from others of its era. The framed-center motif is applied not to a piece of fine domestic but to a background of chocolate-brown silk taffeta.[25]

Silk became a popular quilt fabric in the mid-nineteenth century. American ladies' magazines in the 1850s and 1860s began to publish articles on making template-pieced quilts from silks.[26] Some known quilts from the Charleston, South Carolina, area from the 1870s are pieced from squares of silk remnants. However, the use of silk as a background fabric is, if not unprecedented, quite rare for the mid-century.

Small, dark blue taffeta squares lined up corner to corner form a frame around the central design. Instead of being pieced into the brown taffeta as one might suppose from viewing the quilt at a distance, the squares are applied over the seamed brown surface with a visible whip-stitch. In the corners of the quilt are four additional floral bouquets, also stuffed and embellished with embroidery.

The quilting is very fine. The center area is covered by a fine crosshatch of diagonal lines. The outer areas are quilted in double clamshells. The quilt is backed with a medium-brown polished cotton and bound with blue taffeta.

Martha Hatter's handiwork has held up remarkably well. The silks, while fragile, are only slightly fraying, except for the binding, which shows some breakage of the fibers. There is apparently some dye change in the printed cottons, as the present blues and tan were probably greens and reds originally.

This quilt combines the framed-center floral-appliqué format of early nineteenth-century quilts with the use of silk, characteristic of quilts of the late nineteenth century. While it links two temporally separate nonutilitarian styles of quiltmaking, it ignores all that came between, that is, repeated block styles of appliqué and piecework with the predominant use of red, green, and yellow, and the influence of English-style template piecing. If Martha Jane Hatter was following a trend rather than creating her own style, other examples have not come to light.[27]

Quilt B is in every way as important historically as Quilt A, yet its technical virtuosity and attention to detail are even more outstanding. The appliqué floral bouquets in the corner of Quilt A are taken from the same wool challis fabric as that surrounding the outer edges of Quilt B. There are twenty-one bouquets, stuffed and embroidered, framing the edge. Quilt B also has a large embroidered basket in the center, with heavily stuffed appliqué flowers and four three-dimensional stuffed strawberries. These flowers and a flower wreath surrounding the center basket were cut from the same fabric used in the border. Nine birds and four butterflies are appliquéd on or around the central basket.

The quilt is quilted in a small diamond pattern above the outer floral appliqué. There are four corner blocks of quilting, each with four inner blocks of alternating hanging diamond and clamshell quilting. Filling in among these large blocks are a double diagonal crosshatch forming framed diamonds. A small block quilted with hanging diamonds extends to the center wreath from each corner block. The area within the floral wreath itself is quilted in a small-scale diagonal crosshatch. The background fabric of the quilt is cotton throughout.

Crib Quilt C depicts in its center a basket of flowers, cut from printed floral chintz fabric and carefully appliquéd, with a surrounding appliqué floral wreath. Although not as heavily stuffed as the two larger quilts, the flowers throughout are outlined by white embroidery. The basket is depicted by quilting beneath the center floral spray. Inside the floral wreath is small-scale diagonal crosshatch quilting, and outside the wreath is large diagonal crosshatch quilting. The staining around the appliqué on Quilt C and Quilt E may be the result of a paste used to stiffen the applied work. The paste consisted of either carpenter's glue and flour or shoemaker's paste of rye flour. Each corner is

quilted in a fishscale pattern within a block. The background of the quilt is a plain ecru muslin.

Typical of Mrs. Hatter's work, the child's Quilt D has the framed-center medallion of multicolor floral appliqué, with eight smaller flowers surrounding it. At the bottom of the rectangular quilt is another bouquet, this time medium-size as compared with the framed-center medallion. The appliqué is of cotton, applied with a white cotton binding stitch, and stuffed to a height of about ¼ to ½ inches. The ground is a plain white cotton, which is quilted overall in a one-inch diamond pattern with six ½-inch squares in each corner quilted in half-inch diamonds. The knotted, white cotton fringe is handmade and attached by two rows of crochet.

Quilt E is called a "carriage coverlet" by the family. This white cotton quilt has a "U"-shaped edge with fringe around two sides and the bottom. Like the two large quilts, this piece depicts a framed-center embroidered and quilted basket/vase holding a multicolor bouquet of appliqué and stuffed flowers, one butterfly, and a bird on the top. The basket and flowers are surrounded by two outer borders, one a vine of stuffed work and the second a wreath of stuffed and appliqué flowers. The quilting throughout is a fine crosshatch of diagonal lines, except for the four corners, which are quilted in a diamond pattern accented by two scroll-ended vines with leaves that separate the diamonds from the crosshatched quilting. The appliqué flowers may be of the same multicolor fabric as on quilts C and D. The five-inch knotted fringe is attached to the quilt by a two-inch machine-made insertion trim.

In summary, the two gunboat quilts plus the three additional examples provide a most interesting window into the skill of the needleworker, Martha Jane Singleton Hatter Bullock, and the efforts of Southern women to save their homeland during the Civil War. It is indeed amazing and wonderful that these quilts have survived, especially in very good condition. They are exceptional examples of needlework with or without their history. Further, we are most fortunate that three are in public museums where they can be enjoyed by many people. It is hoped that through future quilt research as part of the Alabama Quilt Survey, other quilts that were mentioned in the old newspapers and examined during the course of this research may be located and connected with their history. These quilts prove that with continued cooperative efforts among the quilt projects throughout the United States, more quality quilts and their histories will be known and made available for study and public viewing.

Notes and References

[1] *Mobile Advertiser and Register*, Feb. 17, 1862, 29:271.

[2] William N. Still, Jr., *Iron Afloat: The Story of the Confederate Ironclads* (Nashville, TN: Vanderbilt Univ. Press, 1971), 85.

[3] Ibid., 85.

[4] Ibid., 86.

[5] Ibid., 86.

[6] Ibid., 86.

[7] Ibid., 86.

[8] Ibid., 86.

[9] Tim Callahan, personal correspondence with author, May 5, 1987, and telephone conversation with author May 15, 1987. Mr. Callahan, who is with the Coastal Heritage Society, Old Fort Jackson, Savannah, Georgia, is currently researching information on the *CSS Georgia*, which is submerged in the Savannah River at Old Fort Jackson.

[10] *Mobile Advertiser and Register*: March 7, 1862, 29:287; March 13, 1862, 29:292; March 18, 1862, 29:296; March 19, 1862, 29:297; March 21, 1862, 29:299; March 22, 1862, 29:300; March 25, 1862, 29:302; March 26, 1862, 29:303; April 3, 1862, 30:3; April 4, 1862, 30:4; April 5, 1862, 30:5; April 6, 1862, 30:6; April 8, 1862, 30:7; April 24, 1862, 30:21; April 29, 1862, 30:25.

Weekly Montgomery Advertiser: Feb. 26, 1862, 28:23; March 22, 1862, 28:26; April 15, 1862, 28:29.

Alabama Beacon (Greensboro): March 7, 1862, 6:8; March 14, 1862, 6:9; March 21, 1862, 6:10; April 4, 1862, 6:12; April 11, 1862, 6:13; April 25, 1862, 6:15; May 23, 1862, 6:19.

Selma Morning Reporter: March 10, 1862, 4:7; March 19, 1862, 4:16; April 10, 1862, 4:135; April 21, 1862, 4:144; March 13, 1862, 4:163; May 14, 1862, 4:164; May 15, 1862, 4:165; May 16, 1862, 4:166.

[11] *Alabama Beacon*, March 21, 1862.

[12] The cities from which contributions were received included: Benton, Black Bend, Blakeley, Brewerville, Buena Vista, Cahaba, Camden, Citronelle, Clinton, Columbiana, Dayton, Demopolis, Eutaw, Evergreen, Fayetteville, Ft. Gaines, Forts, Gainesville, Greensboro, Jackson, King's Landing, Kymulga, Linden, Livingston, Locust Laws, Marion, Montgomery, Pikeville, Prairie Bluff, Selma, Sidney, Summerfield, Sumterville, Tomkinsville, Tuskegee, Yellow Bluff.

[13] *Montgomery Daily Advertiser*, April 15, 1862.

[14] *Mobile Advertiser and Register*, March 13, 1862.

[15] *Mobile Advertiser and Register*, March 21, 1862.

[16] *Selma Reporter*, May 16, 1862, and *Alabama Beacon*, May 23, 1862.

[17] *Mobile Register and Advertiser*, April 6, 1862.

[18] *Mobile Register and Advertiser*, April 24, 1862.

[19] *Alabama Beacon*, April 25, 1862.

[20] *Alabama Beacon*, April 11, 1862.

[21] Birmingham Museum of Art Accession File #1985.209. Information and correspondence from Elinor Strickland.

[22] Joseph Johnston Hutchinson (1810–69) was a Methodist minister for Summerfield, AL. The Alabama Census of 1850, Dallas County, lists a "Rev. Joseph Johnston Hutchinson, born in Georgia, age 40 years, and a Methodist minister with seven children." Marion Elias Lazenby, *History of Methodism in Alabama and West Florida* (North Alabama Conference and Alabama-West Florida Conference of the Methodist Church, 1960), 295.

[23] Birmingham Museum of Art Accession File #1985.209. Information and correspondence to and from Mrs. John Reid and Mrs. John H. Napier III. Telephone conversation with Mrs. John Reid and the author on Sept. 7, 1987.

[24] Marriage Records. Greene County Courthouse, Eutaw, AL.

[25] This description was taken from an unpublished report by Laurel Horton sent to the author in a letter of April 21, 1986. This report and letter are in the Birmingham Museum of Art Accession File #1985.209. The author is most appreciative of Ms. Horton for the use of this description as well as her assistance in the final disposition of this quilt to the Birmingham Museum of Art.

[26] Virginia Gunn, "Victorian Silk Template Patchwork in American Periodicals, 1850–1875," *Uncoverings 1983*, ed. Sally Garoutte (Mill Valley, CA: American Quilt Study Group, 1984), 9.

[27] Horton letter and report.

The quilt box. Photo by David R. Bennion.

Typical wool quilt circa 1920, made by Mary Mortensen Bjork (1869–1951) for her daughter Nettie at the time of her marriage to Angus P. Bennion. Photo by Richard N. Peaden.

Mary Mortensen (Bjork) with baby sister, Amalia, and grand-mother, Else Marie Jacobsen in early spring, 1876. Photo by H. A. Hald, Aalborg, Denmark.

Donated Quilts Warmed War-torn Europe

Joyce B. Peaden

An hour spent in the World War II section of the history stacks in any library is a grim reminder of the depths of human need. Need translates in the mind of a quiltmaker to warmth and the vestige of security a quilt can provide.

It would seem you could give quilts away, along with food and clothing. Not in 1945. In Norway, for instance, only relatives could send packages in, and then only by license.[1]

Finland, Norway, Denmark, the Netherlands, Belgium, France, and Czechoslovakia had been liberated from Germany but travel was restricted in these countries, even one unofficial or foreign person being a burden from the standpoint of food and transportation. Postal service had to be reestablished, and, initially, the weight of individual packages was limited to eleven pounds.

Allied military occupation forces in West Germany and Austria denied entry to civilians. Red Cross workers, in military uniform, assisted the army with domestic relief.[2] The Russians did not allow people or relief to come into East Germany and Poland. Thousands of Finns were living in the underground bunkers left from the Finn-Russian War of 1939–40.[3] Greece was being consumed by guerrilla warfare because of Russia's effort to find a way to the sea.[4] The shipping organization and capacity of our own country was diminished.

The relief operation that is the subject of this chapter is one of many. In the beginning, help was given family to family, church to church, and ethnic group to mother country. Private agencies contributed as well as the Red Cross and the United Nations Relief and Rehabilitation Administration.

Joyce B. Peaden *is a quilt historian, and a teacher and author of quiltmaking techniques. She is the author of* Irish Chain Quilts, A Workbook of Irish Chains and Related Patterns, *published by the American Quilter's Society, and historical and technical magazine articles. She has an avid interest in primitive cultures and crafts. 910 Roza Vista Drive, Prosser, WA 99350.*

Many churches were involved. In Salt Lake City, September 4, 1945, two days after the peace treaty was signed with Japan on board the battleship *USS Missouri* in Tokyo Bay, 6,000 people of all faiths (Catholic, Episcopal, Jewish, Protestant) and Sons of the Revolution met at the invitation of George Albert Smith, president of the Church of Jesus Christ of Latter-day Saints (LDS) in the LDS Tabernacle on Temple Square to offer gratitude for peace. J. Reuben Clark (counselor to President Smith) spoke of the responsibility of the victor for the vanquished, and of the "hundred odd millions of people whose very existence lies in our hands."[5]

I will only attempt to tell about one phase, the provision of quilts, of the relief work of my own group, the Relief Society of the Church of Jesus Christ of Latter-day Saints and its members. The relief society is the women's organization of the LDS Church. Its functions cover every phase of a woman's life, one of which is a provision for physical welfare. Each relief society is a part of a "ward" and its membership includes the people within a specified geographic area. Approximately five to nine wards comprise a "stake." A variable number of stakes comprise a "region."

Each ward relief society produced and donated quilts to the Church Welfare Program, a central administrative organization directly under the president of the church that provides for members of the church who for one reason or another cannot provide for themselves. It also meets some national and international disasters. The program is supplied by its own agricultural/limited manufacturing system as well as by donations.

Relief supplies are kept in regional and local warehouses. This storage system was the first means by which relief supplies were sent into war-torn countries as quickly as shipping arrangements could be made in the fall

of 1945. That relief included a stockpile of quilts.

The first relief was sent into liberated countries of Europe in eleven-pound Parcel Post packages. While they were being shipped, LDS Church President George Albert Smith visited U.S. President Harry Truman and secured his cooperation to ship bulk relief supplies to Europe. At the same time, November 1945, other leaders of the church arranged with shipping companies and relief agencies for bulk, or carload, shipments to Europe.[6]

President Smith chose a member of the Council of the Twelve, Ezra Taft Benson, who was then president of the church, to go to Europe and open the missions in all the countries. It was necessary to get inside the German and East European countries to contact and arrange with civil and local church leaders to receive supplies, and to negotiate for warehouses and transportation to provide both security and orderly distribution. Fred Babbel accompanied Elder Benson as secretary and later wrote an account of their experiences.

Carload shipments including food, clothing, and bedding began February 15, 1946, to the liberated countries and to West Germany, Austria, Poland, and Syria. By December 1946, 92 carloads (2,000 tons) of relief supplies had arrived in Europe. By March 1947, the way was prepared for shipments to LDS Church members in East Germany. Relief was given to the general population as well as to church members, particularly in areas of the worst devastation.[7]

The European Recovery Program, commonly known as the Marshall Plan, was enacted into law in April 1948. The first Marshall Plan ship, the *Noordam*, arrived in the Netherlands on April 26.[8] Thereafter the LDS Church Relief Program tapered off, having sent 133 carloads of relief goods to Europe.[9]

With this background information in mind, I turn now to a discussion of

VOL 34 NO. 2   Lessons for May   FEBRUARY 1947

A Marshall Plan wheat delivery at Rotterdam, the Netherlands. A variation of the shield from the United States Seal, with seven red and six white stripes, and four white stars on the blue field, or chief, was used to mark the shipping cartons of all Marshall Plan products, and the vehicles in which the products were delivered. They were generally labelled "For European Recovery. Supplied by the United States of America." Courtesy of the George C. Marshall Foundation.

the quilts in this operation. Each relief society in the war risk zones of the United States (California, Washington, Oregon, and the North Atlantic coastal states) had been instructed, in December 1942, to keep first-aid supplies in a locked cupboard in the relief society room. These supplies were to include twelve quilts or blankets with wool content, at least two of these being blankets.[10] Inland relief societies followed this instruction as well.

Quiltmaking had been a part of the Church Relief Society program from its inception in 1842. Each ward relief society made and gave one or more quilts to the Church Welfare Program each year after 1936. Most had already been given to the needy, but there were 3,326 left in the church welfare storehouses in the fall of 1945. Individual ward relief societies then allocated 6,636 more quilts and 1,941 blankets specifically for Europe from their so-called war emergency kits.[11]

A mass drive for bedding, clothing, and soap was conducted by the Church Relief Society on December 10–11, 1945. The count for the December drive, a total of 5,044 quilts and 1,403 blankets, includes quilts from these ward kits sent to the regional warehouses at this time.[12] It is reasonable to believe that stake and mission relief societies on the East Coast held their quilts for packages sent directly from their own areas. These figures indicate that there were sufficient quilts for the Parcel Post packages, local need, and the beginning of the collection that would go later in the boxcar loads.

The aim of the Church Relief Society and the Church Welfare Program was to send one eleven-pound pack-

Opposite: The Church Relief Society Seal. The motto "Charity Never Faileth" is taken from I Corinthians 13:8. Courtesy of the Relief Society of the Church of Jesus Christ of Latter-day Saints.

Opposite: The February 1947 Relief Society Magazine *carried Elder Marion G. Romney's report of welfare sent by the Church of Jesus Christ of Latter-day Saints (LDS) to church members and others in Europe between October 29, 1945, and December 1946. The* Relief Society Magazine *was the official publication of the Church Relief Society from 1914 through 1970. It was preceded by the* Woman's Exponent, *1872–1914, which was owned and printed by LDS women and served the Church Relief Society. Photo by Peter Jenkins.*

age of bedding and one eleven-pound package of clothing to each member. Packages also included soap, sewing supplies, vitamins, and treats such as cake mix or dried fruit. There were believed to be 7,245 members of the church in the liberated countries. Consequently, 15,112 packages (one-half were bedding and one-half clothing) were mailed to Norway, Finland, Denmark, the Netherlands, Belgium, France, Czechoslovakia, and also to Japan, the majority between October 29, 1945, and March 31, 1946, and the remainder by December 31, 1946. Two hundred of the 354 packages to Japan were prepared by the relief societies in the Central Pacific Mission (Hawaii). No count was found for packages sent by Canada to England. Beautiful letters of appreciation were received by the leaders of the church, some of which were published in the *Relief Society Magazine* in February 1947 in the report by Marion G. Romney.[13]

Quilts were needed to continue the program for the boxcar shipments. The annual statistical report of the general board of the Church Relief Society of the entire church gives the total number of quilts made in all the workday meetings of the individual wards during one year, but does not indicate clearly what percentage were given to the Church Welfare Program. The percentage figure includes all sewn items, "quilts, other bedding, and clothing," therefore any estimate must be approximate. Quilts were made for the welfare program more commonly than clothing, which was mainly nightwear, men's work clothing, or practical children's clothing. In 1945, 20% of all sewn items made in the relief societies of the entire church were given to the Church Welfare Program. The remainder were for local need. The individual relief societies responded to the crisis in the war-torn countries by giving 50% of sewn items in 1946 and 62% of sewn items in 1947 to the welfare program. There was an in-

crease in the number of quilts made as well as a higher proportion sent to the welfare program. There were 27,310 quilts made in the relief societies of the entire church in the two years 1946–47.[14] During this time, the number of women participating in the sewing program increased from less than 30% to almost 40%.[15]

There were approximately 1,200 relief societies in Utah-Idaho-California alone, the three states with 80% of the church population and large ward memberships. The statistics, consistent with the understanding of the author from former relief society presidents of the post-war era, show that each relief society gave one or two quilts to the Church Welfare Program in an ordinary year but made five or more quilts for the welfare program each year right after World War II. Quilts made in the home, donated to the relief societies, and earmarked for war relief, are not included in the statistical report.

Relief societies throughout the United States and the world participated in the relief program according to their numbers and their means. Denmark and Sweden in particular sent packages into Norway and Finland immediately after the war. England, Sweden, Switzerland, and the liberated countries as well contributed to Germany as their own most immediate needs were met.

In the summer of 1947 the Netherlands Mission, men and women alike, raised potatoes in road medians, vacant lots, and backyards and gave the harvest of seventy tons of potatoes to the East and West German missions. There was a corresponding sewing project for those who did not have a place to plant potatoes. The potato project was expanded in 1948 to include the purchase of herring to be sent to Germany. This story is told in an article by William G. Hartley, research historian in the church historical department.[16]

The Church Welfare Program continued providing supplies to the

needy in the United States, but the great focus was on Europe, specifically Germany and Austria, and the eastern European countries. Recollection of comments by those involved in my own area indicated there was a desire and an effort to insure that quilts for Germany and Japan were as good in quality as the quilts that went to the liberated countries.

A second major drive was conducted by the Church Relief Society May 26–27, 1947, as a result of messages delivered in the April 1947 churchwide conference.[17] According to the conference report, a plea was made by President J. Reuben Clark on behalf of the people of Germany. He read a letter from Walter Stover of the East German mission, which related an account of his visit to one sister whose husband was killed in action in Russia. She lived with her three children in an attic that had no heat, no glass in the windows, no water, frozen toilet facilities, and little bedding. The family was given welfare supplies, clothing, food, and bedding, and their windows were boarded up for them, but no one could supply heat.[18] The scenario was undoubtedly a common occurrence.

The feeling for the plight of the people of Germany, now almost two years after the close of the war, was such that our whole neighborhood sought out my mother as a relief society worker and volunteered their clothing and bedding. May 26, the first day of the great collection, was also my youngest brother Frank's birthday. In the morning a woman came to our door with a considerable amount of clothing and bedding. I helped her lay it out on the living room couch. She was about to leave, but turned back with a stricken look on her face to pick up a particular blanket. "I can't give this!" she said, and took the blanket and left. A couple of hours later she came back. She neither knocked nor spoke, but walked right in, put the blanket down, and left. It made such an impression on me that the scene and the time on the clock made a photographic image in my mind. It was five minutes to eleven.

This lady was not a member of our church. The counterpart to this story was told to me by a friend in Prosser, Washington, when I read to her from this section of my chapter. She told me about a woman who comes from Germany occasionally to visit her sister in our town. When she first came to visit years ago she met my friend and discovered she was a Mormon. She exclaimed with joy, because she had always wanted to meet the people who sent those good packages to Germany. She and her husband were friends and neighbors of a Mormon family in Germany, and whenever they got supplies from the church after World War II they shared with her. A special friendship has developed over the years between this woman and my friend.

The church news section of the *Deseret News* reported on May 31, 1947, that the Church Relief Society was swamped with clothing, shoes, blankets, and quilts. The response astonished the leaders of the church. It was noted that warm Arizona sent more than a hundred quilts and blankets.[19] Total numbers were not readily available.

The quilts kept coming. The spirit of the time is shown in an article in the 1973 *Ensign*, on the life of Mary Smith Ellsworth, the wife of the president of the Northern California mission, based in San Francisco. She listened to an account of the suffering of the members in Germany given by the wife of the West German mission president, who had just come from Germany for the April 1947 conference. Mary Ellsworth Smith raised her hand and said, "Northern California mission will send 100 quilts!" That mission had 145 beautiful quilts and blankets for Europe by the end of June.[20]

Quilts made in relief societies were quilted, both to teach the members and to inspire the recipients. The women were taught that it was well to perpetuate the art of quilting. There were 64 to 74 hours spent per quilt on the quilting, each woman who worked on the quilt giving 3.5 to 6.25 hours.[21] Pieced tops were generally contributed by members. Wool quilts were not common in relief societies but were made in the home and were generally tied. They were emphasized greatly in the 1947 drive.

The quilt chairman put a quilt on the frame early in the morning of relief society workday to have it ready by 9:30 or 10:00 A.M. Sixteen women could quilt until it was necessary to roll the sides. The business meeting was conducted and lesson given during lunch to save time. Quilting continued until 4:00 or 5:00 P.M., and then the quilt frame was tipped up against the wall until the next meeting.

An accepted policy was to finish a quilt in two meetings, even one, lest the quilters get tired of working on the same quilt. It might be finished by the quilt chairman with volunteers in her home, or by the president and her counselors. Enthusiasm was maintained by the expediency of the work.

Quilts for war-stricken people have particular meaning for me because of my mother, Nettie Emily B. Bennion, and her work with relief society quilts, and because of my grandmother and aunt. I remember specifically the cold Saturday morning in November 1945 when I was home from school for my birthday. The house was charged with feeling for the project to be done, that of tying a quilt for Europe. This quilt was one of many family quilts to be tied, bound, and donated or mailed as part of the Church Relief Society project.

The quilt tops had been made over the years by my grandmother, Mary Mortensen Bjork. I first saw them when I was about sixteen. They were stored in a large wooden box and a steamer trunk along the north wall in the granary on the Bjork farm in Hol-

laday, a farm community ten miles from downtown Salt Lake City, and in three steamer trunks in my grandmother's house. They were heavily mothballed.

The material in the quilts came from clothing given to my grandmother by affluent people in the city to whom she peddled fruit, flowers, and eggs over a period of many years. Some of the material had been diverted by my mother to make silk, velvet, and lace dresses for my sister and me, and even for our dolls.

My mother told me about riding to town with her mother when she was a

The Bennion home with Mt. Olympus in the background, as it appeared in 1941. Although two bedrooms were added in 1943–45, it was in the original structure that many of the donated quilts were tied. Courtesy of Joyce B. Peaden.

child. Grandmother would leave the farm in Holladay at daylight or after the first "picking" and sell from her wagon all day. In the late afternoon she would start home, and being very tired, she would sleep, just tying the reins to the wagon and letting the horses find their way home.

From the fancy clothing of the early 1900s, my grandmother had made beautiful velvet, silk, and wool embroidered Victorian quilts for her five children, as well as practical wool quilts for everyday use. After her own children married, she went on to make quilts for her grandchildren. The store of quilts, mostly Crazy Patch, grew each winter in a never-ending sewing project.

I was often the grandchild on call to help lay out the blocks on the floor, moving them about one by one to balance the colors and achieve the greatest visual effect. There would be enough blocks for three or four quilts, and by the end of an afternoon, they would be matched and pinned, ready to sew.

On the day of the radio broadcast of the meeting of all faiths in Salt Lake City, September 4, 1945, my mother and grandmother, and my aunt, Nellie B. Peterson, talked about giving some quilts. I went away to school, but they began their project, tying and finishing the quilts in our home in the spare hours after each worked a full-time job as well as keeping house. My mother tended between two and three thousand chickens while my father worked, still trying to recover from the Depression. My aunt worked at a bakery. My grandmother was raising and selling flowers in the summertime.

Only wool quilts were sent to Europe from our family. My mother was adamant about this. They were warm and tough. She said the family could do with cotton and silk. The batts were wool, carded by my grandmother, or worn wool or wool and cotton blankets. The wool batts were best. The backings were from my mother's collection of dark plaid flannel or soft paisley cotton kept for this purpose. The collection was supplemented by any suitable material my mother and aunt could find for ten cents per yard.

A typical quilt was made of 14-inch blocks, five across and six down (70″ x 84″). Pieces were sewn with inside construction to a 14.5-inch square of cotton. Each quilt required two lengths of 36-inch material for backing. Edges were turned in to each other, so that no flannel would show on top, and stitched by hand. The quilt would weigh about seven pounds. A similar wool quilt made by Mary Björk, and retained by the family, has been in use for over sixty years.

I helped some by cutting apart beautiful clothing to be made into quilts. At one time we cut for three days, the clothing and cut material covering the entire kitchen floor. On the third day I realized I had lost the feeling in the nerve of my thumb, and I did not regain it for six months.

The quilts were given to the relief society and earmarked for Europe. Later a contribution of $5.00 per quilt was sent to pay shipping costs. The quilts were given freely but it was sometimes a problem to find the $5.00.

The stories told in the April 1947 general conference about the sufferings of the German people were so heartbreaking that our family sent several quilts as tops, just adding a smooth cotton edge to put by the face, in addition to finished quilts.

After the carload shipments from the Church Welfare Service tapered off, our family sent boxes, primarily quilts, to Austria and Czechoslovakia. Greece was on my mother's list, but I found no record in the church historian's office of relief to Greece. Some relief societies also served as Red Cross units, and our box for Greece may have gone through the Red Cross. For forty years, as I watched movies about Greece or the Mediterranean, I watched for American quilts, even knowing the movies were mere stories made on sets!

After the European project my grandmother continued to make quilts, but her health was failing. These quilts had some poor materials in them, and they were smaller. She called them "buggy" quilts, from horse and buggy days.

However, in August 1951, there were sufficient quilts from the original collection to send boxes to Korea. Boxes also included homemade wool clothing, bandages, quality white flannel for diapers, and sewing supplies. As one box was prepared my mother scooped three or four double-handfuls of buttons from her button box (these were buttons from the elegant clothing), packed them, and

dropped them in the box. The box was no more than shipped when she realized she had been hasty. Thereafter we never had a matched set of buttons. I'm sure they didn't in Korea, either.

At this time, the quilt box was in the basement of our own home. The box was almost empty with only five quilts left, and the errant thought flashed through my mind that there would not be a quilt for me. I as quickly said to myself, "For shame, a selfish thought!" and helped pull out another quilt to put on the frame. I was now married, and had stayed with my parents for the birth of our first baby, my husband having been drafted into the army.

Mary Bjork died in late October 1951. The quilt project was over. How many quilts of her making were sent overseas? No one had counted.

My brother David, of Menlo Park, California, moved the quilt box to his ridge property in the Santa Cruz Mountains in 1971. He photographed the box for me in 1986 and measured its capacity. The so-called "quilt box," which reminded us of the endurance and creativity of our grandmother, was apparently adapted by her for quilts, which overflowed the storage facilities in the farmhouse. It was a

Many buttons in this collection came from the clothing given to Mary Bjork. Photo by Richard N. Peaden.

practical all-purpose box, called a tack box, often used to hold harness, collars, horse blankets, combs, and curry brushes. It was commonly taken to county fairs to carry this gear. Boxes like this were also used for grain, the slant lid preventing a horse from "nosing" into it.

My brother folded quilt tops into the box, and estimated that it would hold fifty to sixty wool quilt tops. The four steamer trunks, now owned by granddaughters, may well have held another fifty wool quilt tops in addition to silk and cotton tops and household quilts. Tops were also made continuously during the relief project, as with the material I helped cut. A personal survey in 1986–87 of quilts inherited by the grandchildren of Mary Bjork included sixteen silk tops and approximately twenty-two cotton tops, but there were only six wool tops of the original collection in all the family. There surely were 125 wool quilts, and probably 150, sent by our family for war relief.

The Quilts for Europe research project was a surprise to most of the sixteen grandchildren of Mary Bjork, who had no comprehension of the number of quilts made, nor that they were sent for war relief. The exceptions were my sister, Dorothy B. Potter, and cousin, Shirley P. Petersen, eldest daughter of Nellie Peterson and wife of Gerald Petersen, whose memories have bolstered mine.

Shirley said, "I always wondered how they (our family) had a living room because the couch was always pushed up against the window, and the quilt frames were up." Shirley's family lived next door. Her memory is significant in the fact that only two quilts were finished for our own family after the war, these being for my sister when she married.

Shirley remembered the frames and quilts but had forgotten what they were for. With her memory prodded, she recalled and described the large wooden crates (slats nailed onto a frame over a cardboard box) being packed on our kitchen table, and

bringing her clothing to go into them. She added her special memories of Mary Bjork making quilts on the sewing machine on her sleeping porch.

My sister Dorothy said, "I used to stand in Grandmother's kitchen, and roll yarn into round balls as she pulled it from worn hand-knit sweaters and socks. This was the yarn that tied the quilts."

There was a quilt top saved for me. My grandmother had made three tops for granddaughters who married tall men. I have the only one that remains. My mother gave it to me when my husband and I returned from our travels with the army in 1953.

I like numbers, and would like to have known how many quilts the Church Relief Society made and collected for war-stricken countries after World War II. Some information is obscured by the grouping of items in statistics. Some work was never counted and some records were lost. I estimate, based on information gathered for this chapter, that thirty-eight to forty thousand quilts were made and donated by the Church Relief Society and its members to the war-stricken countries after World War II. Numbers are relative, but the selflessness of the women who gave the gift is an indelible memory, needing no count. The work was considered to be a personal responsibility.

My father, Angus P. Bennion, survived my mother by twelve years. In November 1970, in one of his last conversations with me, he asked me what our family should do about the quilts. Should he give his own family quilts to welfare? I told him that they would be treasured by his children. I also assured him that his family would always strive to meet the welfare calls of the church and community. And I promised him I would do the best thing I knew to do, and that was to teach others, quilting being one of the things I teach.

Notes and References

[1] "Mission Reports," *The Improvement Era* (October 1945): 582.

[2] Elizabeth W. King, "Heroes of Wartime Service and Mercy," *National Geographic Magazine* (December 1943): 719, 734.

[3] LaVerne Bradley, "Scenes of Post War Finland," *National Geographic Magazine* (August 1947): 240, 249, 259.

[4] Maynard Owen Williams, "War-torn Greece Looks Ahead," *National Geographic Magazine* (December 1949): 713–15.

[5] "V-J Mass Meeting," *The Improvement Era* (October 1945): 583; "President Clark Represents Church at Salt Lake Mass Peace Meet," *Deseret News* (Sept. 8, 1945).

[6] Marion G. Romney, "European Relief," *Relief Society Magazine*, (February 1947): 75–85; Frederick W. Babbel, *On Wings of Faith* (Utah: Bookcraft 1972), 168–69.

[7] Ibid.

[8] Sidney Clark, "Mid-Century Holland Builds her Future," *National Geographic Magazine* (December 1950): 754.

[9] M. Lynn Bennion and J. A. Washburn, *History of the Restored Church* (Salt Lake City: Deseret Sunday School Union Board, 1960), 133.

[10] *Relief Society Bulletin*, Salt Lake City: Historical Department, Church of Jesus Christ of Latter-day Saints (December 1942).

[11] Romney, 75–85.

[12] Annual Report 1945, *Relief Society Magazine* (September 1946): 620.

[13] Romney, 75–85.

[14] Annual Report 1949, *Relief Society Magazine* (September 1950): 610–11.

[15] Annual Report 1946, *Relief Society Magazine* (September 1947): 619.

[16] William G. Hartley, "War and Peace and Dutch Potatoes," *Ensign* (July 1978): 18–23.

[17] "Clothing to be Gathered for European Saints," Special Notice from Relief Society General Board, regarding May 26–27, 1947, Salt Lake City: Historical Department, Church of Jesus Christ of Latter-day Saints (n.d.); "Relief Society Sends Details On Church Clothing Drive," *Deseret News* (May 10, 1947).

[18] J. Reuben Clark, Jr., in *Conference Report*, 117th Annual Conference, April 4, 1947 (Salt Lake City: Church of Jesus Christ of Latter-day Saints, 1947), 18–19.

[19] "Clothes for Europe Swamp Relief Society," *Deseret News* (May 31, 1947): 4.

[20] Jaynann Morgan Payne, "Mary Smith Ellsworth: Example of Obedience," *Ensign* (April 1973): 39.

[21] Annual Report 1949.

The Sewing Machine and Visible Machine Stitching on Nineteenth-Century Quilts

Suellen Meyer

W hen Isaac Merritt Singer turned his considerable talents toward perfecting the sewing machine, he was looking only for a way to get rich quick. He succeeded— and in the process, he transformed sewing from a tedious, time-consuming task into a mechanized one. Seamstresses saved considerable time: by hand, a man's shirt required fourteen and a half hours of sewing time, but by machine, only a little more than one hour. Making coats, dresses, nightclothes, underclothes, and children's clothes became merely a nuisance, not the overwhelming burden it had been. Quiltmakers devoted their newfound time to making more quilts, some of which they embellished with visible machine stitching, an indication of the pride they felt in their sewing machines.

Many inventors had tried to perfect a sewing machine, some working to reproduce the movement of the human hand, others to duplicate the stitch. In 1755, a London mechanic, Charles Weisenthal, patented a machine with a revolutionary eye-pointed needle, later to be the central feature of all sewing machines.[1] In 1834, Walter Hunt, a New York inventor, duplicated the stitch, not the movement of handsewing. His machine included a spool above the fabric and one below with a shuttle between; as the shuttle moved the threads, it locked them together, making a lockstitch— a grand improvement over the chainstitch, which unraveled at any break.[2]

Suellen Meyer *is a professor of English at St. Louis Community College-Meramec. Her research interests include the role of quilts in social history, Mid-American quiltmaking, and early textiles. 11210 Still Lane, St. Louis, MO 63141.*

The Ohio Farmer, *January 7, 1860.*

Cherry Basket quilt made by Mary Parks (Lawrence) (1854–?) of Logan County, Kentucky, in 1870. Collection of Wichita-Sedgwick County Historical Museum. Courtesy of Kansas Quilt Project. Photo by Jim Meyer.

   Like many quiltmakers who were proud of their machines and their expertise with them, Mary Parks combined both hand and machine work on an elaborate quilt. She hand-appliquéd the flowers and baskets and machine-appliquéd the basket handles and stems. She hand-quilted the background and machine-quilted the borders.

Some elements of Hunt's machine resurfaced in the machine later developed by Elias Howe, a New England mechanic. Because Howe became too ill to work, his wife took in sewing to support the family. Howe saw firsthand the toll sewing took on her and became obsessed with inventing a sewing machine, finally patenting a practical one in 1846. Although an expert mechanic, Howe lacked merchandising savvy and proved unable to sell his machine. Meanwhile, other American inventors, among them Isaac Merritt Singer, were trying to invent a practical machine.

Singer had no interest in easing women's burdens. In fact, when a friend first suggested that he invent a sewing machine, Singer shouted, "You want to do away with the only thing that keeps women quiet—their sewing!" But once convinced that he could make a lot of money quickly, Singer improved on Howe's needle and shuttle, and, in a flash of mechanical genius, combined the ten components that became standard on all sewing machines. Even today, machines include the lockstitch, an eye-pointed needle, a shuttle for the second thread, continuous thread from spools, a horizontal table, an overhanging arm, continuous feed, tension controls that change the tautness of thread, a presser foot, and the ability to sew in a curving or straight line.[3]

In 1848, Howe returned from an unrewarding sales trip to England. In America, he learned that his wife was dying from consumption and that other men were selling sewing machines—machines suspiciously like his own invention.[4]

Howe and the sewing machine companies fought bitterly over patent rights in the design of different machines. Finally realizing that only the lawyers were getting rich, three companies—Singer, Wheeler and Wilson, and Grover and Baker—created the first patent pool, the Sewing Machine Combination. Each company contributed $15.00 for every machine sold; after expenses, they shared this money equally. To persuade Howe to join, the companies paid him $5.00 for each machine sold in addition to his share of the profits. Between 1856, the date the combination was formed, and 1867, when his patent expired, Howe earned at least $2 million—without ever manufacturing a machine.[5]

Before the outbreak of the Civil War, sewing machine companies concentrated on selling factory models to manufacturers who could afford the high prices. In 1862, clothing manufacturers owned three-quarters of all machines.[6] The larger market, that of women at home, was waiting to be tapped. The Singer Company led the way with its lightweight Turtleback machine and its inventive marketing strategies. The company combatted two entrenched myths held by Victorian men: first, that women couldn't control machinery, and, second, that, freed from some of their arduous labors, women would go wild.

Although campaigns to disprove both these myths took place simultaneously, the Singer Company found it simpler to prove that women could in fact handle machines. Up to the mid-1800s, people believed that men had the intelligence and temperament for machines; women, those delicate creatures, could use tools (needles, brooms, washboards) but not machines. In order to counteract the public's notions about machinery, I. M. Singer and Company insisted that all demonstrations be conducted by young women. (They paid sales agents $6.00 a month extra if their wives could demonstrate the machines.)[7]

Other sewing machine companies imitated Singer's approach. Grover and Baker's St. Louis agent advertised that "A Lady will always be in attendance to exhibit the Machine and give instructions free."[8] Other brochures bragged that "It is so simple in its construction, so accurate and reliable in its execution, that even a child can manage it with success," a not-too-subtle suggestion that if children could control a machine, their mothers might also manage.[9] *Godey's Lady's Book* assured its readers that women could learn to operate sewing machines. The editor added that the machines would not only teach some science to the wives, but that "the boys under their charge, the men in miniature, would have their curiosity aroused in contact with the finest and most effective . . . machinery of modern times."[10]

Sewing machine companies soon won the war of ability. Convincing men that women would use their additional time wisely took longer. Most companies interpreted "wisely" as meaning women would devote more time to the needs of their families, particularly of their husbands. Singer's ads insisted that women would be more rested, more able to supervise the children, and more capable of providing their husbands with comforts previously available only to the wealthy.[11]

Godey's also encouraged this view. In 1863, it devoted its frontispiece to two views of the sewing machine: "The Old Sewing Machine" pictured a bare room, with a plainly dressed woman hunched over her work, sewing by candlelight, a mound of other sewing before her. The next month featured "The New Sewing Machine"—a lovely bright parlor, a woman instructing her elder daughter on the machine, a younger child sitting at her feet playing with her doll, an open magazine beside her.[12]

Women had to find the money to purchase machines—and they were not cheap. When introduced, sewing machines sold for $125, a steep price when the average annual family income was only $500.[13] In contemporary terms, the machine equalled a car—paid for in cash, with no chance of credit. A farmwoman, Elizabeth Welty, figured the family would have to thresh more than 1,600 bushels of wheat for her to get a machine.[14] Even after the price fell, many families couldn't afford machines. *Godey's* encouraged groups of families to unite, each contributing a portion of the cost and each getting use of the machine for two and a half days per month.[15]

Many women who owned machines did share them. Alceste Huntington wrote her mother that she "was so excited with the thought of the amount of sewing I had to do that I was awake at daylight. . . . Julia Gritten [a neighbor] is helping with her machine."[16] Talula Bottoms used her mother-in-law's hand-turned machine until 1895, when she bought her first pedal machine.[17] When Maria Wicker visited St. Louis, she learned to sew on a machine and proudly wrote her son, "Lou is making some clothes for Millie. . . . I have learned to run a Wheeler and Wilson machine that Mrs. Ronlet left in the house and am able to help considerably."[18]

In order to discourage sharing, Edward Clark, Singer's partner, offered a solution few families could resist. In 1856, he suggested that a family lease the machine ($5.00 down, with the rest paid in monthly installments of $3.00 to $5.00). Immediately, sales skyrocketed from 883 in 1855 to 2,564 in 1856. Singlehandedly, Clark created the installment plan, still used in many consumer sales.[19]

Amanda Slaughter, in a time-honored rural tradition, combined the installment plan with bartering. The peddler brought a machine to her Missouri farm home and offered to leave it for a few days. Amanda got it on Tuesday; on Wednesday, they came to terms—a total of $75.00 with a down payment of Rose, a cow valued at $35.00, and monthly payments of $5.00 until the remaining $40.00 was paid.[20]

In 1857, Edward Clark introduced the trade-in allowance. He offered $50 for every old sewing machine of any make, promising to destroy them, because they couldn't possibly match Singer's quality. Clark's move was

brilliant marketing; he enticed owners of machines made by other companies to trade for Singer's machines, ensuring that these machines could not be sold on the secondhand market. At the same time, by giving customers a trade-in allowance even for old Singer machines, he encouraged brand loyalty. Singer's sales rose half again from 2,564 to 3,630 for that year.[21]

Machines sold first to women living near the manufacturers—the Singer Company and Willcox and Gibbs in New York City; Clark and Baker in Orange, Massachusetts; Bodgett and Lerow in Boston; and Wheeler and Wilson in Watertown, Connecticut. Because most factories were in the Northeast, women there were most likely to have machines. In 1860, the Civil War brought a disruption of transportation and trade between the regions and delayed the widespread sale of sewing machines in the South.

Real-photo post card of a Singer Sewing Machine store, circa 1910. Courtesy of Barbara Brackman.

Detail of machine-quilted white cotton percale quilt, 82" x 83". Applied cotton binding, filled with thin layer of cotton, machine stitched, 22 stitches per inch. Machine-quilted in script caps 2½" high: "SINGER MACHINE WORKS," and in Roman face in upper and lower case 1" high: "By M. J. Foster Ottawa Illinois." Collection of the Shelburne Museum (#10-405). Courtesy of the Shelburne Museum, Shelburne, Vermont. Photo by Ken Burris.

Trade cards issued by the Singer Sewing Machine Company. Collection of George and Annette Amann. Photo by Terry Wild Studio.

Singer and other sewing machine companies regularly used children and domestic images in their advertising cards to suggest that owning a machine would give women more time for their families and that the machines were so simple even children could work them.

Women, both North and South, sewed for their men in uniform, providing clothing, sheets, blankets, and quilts. In the industrial North, women organized themselves into sewing groups and, using machines lent by merchants, sewed for the army, turning out 1,000 shirts in two days. By 1865, women had made 250,000 quilts and comforts for the Union soldiers, many of them probably pieced by machine.[22]

Southern seamstresses lucky enough to·own machines used them heavily. Judith Brockenbrough McGuire of Alexandria, Virginia, confided to her diary, "Our soldiers must be equipped. Our parlor was the rendezvous for our neighborhood, and our sewing-machine was in requisition for weeks. Scissors and needles were plied by all."[23] Judith and her friends switched to handsewing when the blockade prevented the importation of factory-made thread. Homemade thread proved too uneven for machine use.[24] Because machine sewing required from two to five times as much thread as hand sewing, Southern women with limited access to thread were more likely to sew by hand. Northern soldiers searching Confederate homes seized guns and

damaged sewing machines. After one party searched her home, Judith McGuire reported:

I believe they took nothing but the rifle, and injured nothing but the sewing-machine. Perhaps they knew of the patriotic work of that same machine—how it had stitched up many a shirt and many a jacket for our brave boys, and therefore did it wrong.

But this silent agent for our country's weal shall not lie in ruins. When I get it again, it shall be repaired and shall "Stitch, stitch, stitch, Band, and gusset, and seam" for the comfort of our men, and it shall work all the more vigorously for the wrongs it has suffered.[25]

Deprived of the necessary thread and replacement parts, Southern women depended on the needle for their tasks.

Thus, Northern women developed their technical expertise and expanded their uses of the machine earlier than did Southern or Western women who did not have access to sewing machines. Once the war was over in 1865, the distribution of the sewing machine widened dramatically, as did women's experimentation with it.

Women began by learning to control the machine, a task more difficult than it appeared. Instruction in the salesroom or the card of directions enclosed with mail-order made the machine appear simple to operate. However, machine sewing required practice, as a California woman discovered in 1860:

The next day my precious machine was unpacked, and following the printed directions, I succeeded in fixing the cotton and threading the needle, which was already properly set. It seemed so perfectly easy to work, as I had seen the man at the store operating upon it, that I spurned the idea of trying on a rag, and confidently put under the cloth-presser a leg of a pair of drawers for one of the children, that I had just cut out and basted. . . . [I] put my foot upon the treadle and started off. The wheel made a revolution forward, and then came back with great facility; my work moved the wrong way; the cotton became mixed up in a lamentable manner, and when I endeavored to pull the work into place, crack! went the needle. . . . Early on Monday morning I was again at work, and had the happiness of actually making stitches. To be sure they were in all directions, of various lengths, as I had pulled or held back the work, and their loose appearance was not very satisfactory to a neat seamstress as I profess to be. Still, there was no getting over the fact that they were actual stitches.[26]

Such time-consuming practice proved worthwhile. The machine not only stitched ordinary items quickly, but it also served as an important status symbol. So important was the machine that Worth of Paris, a major couturier, used the machine for the top-stitching on his fabulously expensive gowns, which were otherwise entirely handsewn.

Seamstresses developed their expertise by sewing clothing on the machine. Next they eyed the inevitable bedding. The large families of the nineteenth century—and the servants who worked for them—needed many bedcovers. According to an 1883 issue of *Arthur's Home Magazine* three-quarters of these covers were quilts.[27] If so, a sizeable number must have been utility quilts, quickly made with inexpensive domestic cloth and the sewing machine.

Women probably made many machine-quilted, utility coverings. In doing so, they adapted the machine beyond the companies' imagination. Early ads promoting quilting attachments and touting machine quilting were aimed at tailors who bought hand-quilted fabric for linings of vests and coats. When cost-conscious factory owners replaced hand-quilted linings with machine-quilted fabric, women applied the idea to bed quilts, which they quilted in squares, from one to four inches wide—much like the grid of the commercially quilted lining materials.[28]

No doubt seamstresses found it difficult to control the three layers of top, batt, and lining while treadling

the machine, for the working space was shallow, and the thread often broke. Once adept, however, some turned their attention to their fine quilts, where the visible machine stitch testified to their skill.

It is difficult to determine how many nineteenth-century quilts have visible machine stitching in the appliqué or quilting. Such quilts are much rarer than quilts that include machine piecing. Jonathan Holstein asserts that while machines were seldom used for appliqué or quilting, they were commonly employed for piecing. He reports that about half of the quilts he has seen that date after the 1860s are machine pieced and that the edges of both appliqué and pieced quilts are commonly finished by machine.[29] While machine-stitched bindings have been accepted, collectors and dealers have devalued other visible machine stitching, so these examples tend not to be displayed for sale or in shows. Still, such quilts exist in private, family collections and in some museum collections. Perhaps as many as 10% of all quilts during the period from 1865 to 1900 in some areas bear some machine appliqué or quilting.

Sometimes machine quilting appears as a grid over the surface of a full-size quilt, or individual blocks may be quilted and then joined in the quilt-as-you-go manner. Robert Cargo owns a curious small piece, just twenty inches square, with a bright red-and-green Feathered Star in the center.[30] Using the machine, the quilter has quilted around each piece making up the star, has quilted the ground in close parallel rows, and has quilted the center in small squares. This unusual piece from the fourth quarter of the nineteenth century may have been designed as an entry for a fair or to demonstrate the maker's proficiency with her sewing machine.

Women across the country tried their hands at machine quilting. Some sewing machine companies provided quilted pieces for inspiration. In 1859, Grover and Baker entered quilting in

Feathered Star, 20" x 20", maker unknown, fourth quarter nineteenth century. Collection of Robert Cargo. Courtesy of Suellen Meyer.

Probably a specimen piece designed as an entry for a fair or to show what the maker could do with her sewing machine, this Feathered Star is entirely machine-quilted.

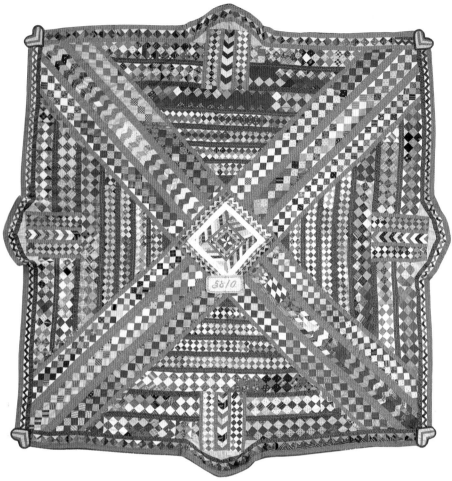

Pieced quilt, 94" x 94", made by Sallie Jane Edmisston Woodward (1843–1925) of Iredell County, North Carolina, circa 1870. Collection of Ethel Mason Campbell. Courtesy of North Carolina Quilt Project.

This incredible quilt of 5,810 pieces is machine-quilted without batting. It must have been difficult enough to control the machine's stitches over the myriad seams. In the center of the quilt, Sallie appliquéd a patch with the number "5810" embroidered in double rows of chain stitch.

Opposite: Stuffed whitework quilt, 76" x 62⅝", maker unknown, circa 1865. Collection of Smithsonian Institution (#1977.0101). Courtesy of Smithsonian Institution.

Stuffed and corded quilts, made from about 1800 through the Civil War, required quiltmakers to sew the design and then either stuff it with batting or pull a cord through it. Using a two-thread chain stitch, this quiltmaker machine-quilted and stuffed each block, then joined them by hand. Her motifs include floral sprays, baskets of flowers, hearts, birds, stylized star patterns, and a log cabin.

the sewing-machine work category at the Sacramento, California, fair. For a time in the late 1800s, Iowa fairs gave a premium for machine quilting. These may have been specimens (perhaps like Robert Cargo's piece), not quilts, but in 1882, Mrs. M. E. Shaffer of Ashew, Iowa, won $2.00 for her machine-quilted white quilt.[31] Many quiltmakers mixed hand quilting and machine quilting on the same quilt. In 1889, Mathursa Jane Craft received a sewing machine for Christmas. As she finished a Pine Tree quilt for her daughter Lucrita, she switched from her quilting needle to her sewing machine, quilting the border by machine and finishing with a flourish in one corner, "New Year's Eve 1889/ Crita."[32]

Very few quiltmakers used the machine for extravagant quilting. One who did created an amazing full-size white-on-white quilt, the entire surface closely quilted by machine. The center of the quilt features two doves

perched in a branch. They sit in a circle in which the free spaces have been filled in with six five-pointed stars. A circle of scrolls surrounds this center design. Outside the scrolls the maker has quilted a variety of designs including a cherub playing a triangle, a dove with a ribbon in its mouth, and a large public building with a flat roof and many arched windows. Below the building the quiltmaker has stitched "Singer Machine Work By M J Foster Ottawa Illinois." Other designs on the quilt include a large three-masted sailing ship with square sails and an American flag at the stern, two spread eagles holding in their beaks American flags with thirteen stars, another public building smaller than the first, and another ship with a triangle sail at its back. As if this tour de force were not enough, all free spaces on the surface have been stitched in crossed diagonals, with foliage patterns, or with scrolls so that the entire quilt is covered with stitchery.[33] Although the details of M. J. Foster's life are unknown, the quiltmaker was clearly a virtuoso with Mr. Singer's machine.

By the end of the century, machine quilting had become déclassé in fashionable circles. Rural readers still asked the editors of publications such as *Comfort* for instructions for machine quilting. In 1906, the editors obliged with these directions: "To quilt on the machine do one block at a time, making it so much easier to handle. You can have a gauge so that all will be uniform, the lining is put on afterwards, only needing some thin material for the lining of each block to quilt through."[34] More fashion-conscious magazines exhorted women to return to hand quilting even if they had to seek out older quilters. In 1894, after describing the way to piece a quilt, Sybil Lanigan suggested a quilting bee as "the merriest and quickest way of finishing the quilt," assuring the reader that "the worst way of all is to use a sewing machine for the purpose, and the best

is to find some skillful, old-fashioned sewing woman."[35]

Although most late-nineteenth-century quiltmakers preferred to finish their quilts with hand quilting, many used their sewing machines to construct the tops. Some used their sewing machines to appliqué, because this allowed them to show off both their machines and their skill. Most sewers found it more difficult to handle curves and points with the machine than by hand. Some women, like an anonymous slave in New Madrid, Missouri, used the machine for the entire top: Instructed to make a quilt for her mistress's birthday, she surprised her master by machine-appliquéing large, showy flowers.[36]

In the nineteenth century, certain appliqué designs such as Tulip, Princess Feather, and Cockscomb and Currant became recognized as show quilts, that is, quilts made for the pleasure of their artistry rather than for use. Some women used their sewing machines to create similar appliqué and quilted showpieces. About 1870, Jane Richey Morelock of Bradley County, Tennessee, designed an extravagant Cockscomb and Currant quilt constructed of four large blocks. The design included flowers, leaves, buds, vines, and grapes. Jane used both the sewing machine and the hand-held needle to appliqué the intricate design.[37] We don't know whether she began with the machine and finished with the needle or vice versa. However, her willingness to use the sewing machine to appliqué part of her Cockscomb and Currant design suggests her pride both in her dexterity with the machine and also in the machine itself.

Like Jane Richey Morelock, Harriet Powers used both the needle and the machine to appliqué her Bible quilts now housed in the Smithsonian Institution and the Museum of Fine Arts in Boston. She used the machine for all the figures—Adam and Eve, the serpent, animals of all kinds, and the angels—while she appliquéd the

folded stars by hand. This mixture of hand and machine sewing appears repeatedly in quilts in the fourth quarter of the nineteenth century. Toward the end of the century many quiltmakers pieced baskets by hand and appliquéd the handles by machine, combining their tools to complete one quilt. Quiltmakers could appliqué the handles more quickly by machine than by hand, but perhaps more importantly, this visible machine stitch reflected their pride in their machines.

Like many late-nineteenth-century quiltmakers, Mary Parks Lawrence of Logan County, Kentucky, experimented with the power of the machine. At the age of sixteen she was an accomplished seamstress, responsible for the family sewing. Her father gave her a machine when she promised to sew all the family's coats, and Mary used it as well in her 1870 Cherry Basket quilt. Using a needle, she hand-appliquéd the orange and red flowers and baskets; using the machine, she applied the green basket handles and leaves and stems. She hand-quilted exquisite feather wreaths and running feathers, filling in the background with one-quarter-inch diagonal lines. Still eager to try out her machine, she reserved the narrow white borders for machine quilting.[38] This masterpiece reflected both her traditional training (most girls learned to sew before they started school) and her acquisition of new techniques.

Yet another quiltmaker, Narcissa Black, a skilled professional seamstress in McNairy County, Tennessee, used both the hand-held needle and the sewing machine. In the 1860s, she made a red-and-white reverse appliqué quilt with hearts and stars, using both hand and machine appliqué. It suggests that Narcissa, who lived in southwestern Tennessee, got a sewing machine shortly after the end of the war. (During the same period, she stitched a Log Cabin quilt entirely by hand.) During the next decade, however, she made an intricate Pineapple quilt, entirely appliquéd by machine.

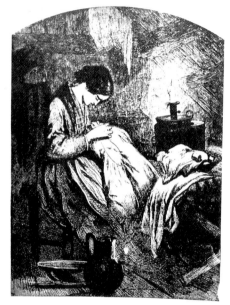

Contrasting frontispieces in Godey's Lady's Book *(1863) titled, "The Old Sewing Machine" and "The New Sewing Machine." As soon as sewing machines were available to the public, Godey's actively encouraged women to buy and use them. Because machines were so expensive, the editor suggested that women pool their finances and buy a machine to share.*

Perhaps she experimented with the reverse appliqué in the 1860s, learned to manipulate her machine, and chose to use it for her next appliquéd quilt.[39]

By the turn of the century, the sewing machine had ceased to be a status symbol. Most families had them, and women had learned to use them efficiently. With the passing of time, the machine turned into simply that—a machine. When the time came that women took the machine for granted, they—and the magazines they read—once again valued handwork for its own sake. By the end of the nineteenth century, handwork, not machine work, was the status symbol, for the handmade stitch spoke of leisure time and experience with the needle. Given this new attitude, women returned to appliquéing and quilting by hand—quiet, relaxing activities, which demonstrated that they had sufficient leisure to sew a fine seam.

Nevertheless, the sewing machine had revolutionized women's attitudes toward their work. Where before they had often complained about the never-ending sewing, they now adopted the machine wholeheartedly. One woman bragged, "I have . . . used it constantly for family sewing; have quilted whole quilts of the largest size and it is still in perfect order, runs like a top, and bids fair to be willed to those who come after me with better powers of production than an unbroken prairie farm."[40]

Few twentieth-century women can imagine the joy with which their great-grandmothers embraced the sewing machine, the first home appliance for women. When contemporary viewers disdain quilts showing machine stitching, they reveal our own age's preference for handwork. A nineteenth-century woman looking at the same quilt would have seen beauty, skill, and comfort, all embodied in the tiny stitches made by the metal workhorse that revolutionized women's sewing.

Notes and References

[1] Grace Rogers Cooper, *The Sewing Machine: Its Invention and Development* (Washington, DC: Smithsonian Institution Press, 1976), 4.

[2] John Kobler, "Mr. Singer's Money Machine," *Saturday Evening Post* (July 14, 1951): 39.

[3] Ruth Brandon, *A Capitalist Romance: Singer and the Sewing Machine* (Philadelphia: Lippincott, 1977), 73.

[4] Cooper, 219–21.

[5] Ibid., 41.

[6] Susan Strasser, *Never Done: A History of American Housework* (New York: Pantheon, 1983), 138.

[7] Penrose Scull, *From Peddlars to Merchant Princes: A History of Selling in America* (Chicago: Follett, 1967), 187.

[8] Broadside, Missouri Historical Society, St. Louis.

[9] I. Hale and Co., Broadside, Classified file 463, Smithsonian Institution, Washington, DC.

[10] *Godey's Lady's Book* 61 (September 1860): 271.

[11] Brandon, 126.

[12] *Godey's Lady's Book*, 1863.

[13] Brandon, 116.

[14] Elaine Hedges, *Hearts and Hands: The Influence of Women and Quilts on American Society* (San Francisco: Quilt Digest Press, 1987), 38.

[15] *Godey's Lady's Book* 61 (September 1860): 271.

[16] Letter, March 12, 1868, quoted in Harvey Green, *The Light of the Home* (New York: Pantheon, 1983), 80.

[17] Nancilu Burdick, letter to author, April 13, 1987.

[18] Maria Wicker, St. Louis, to Cyrus Wicker, June 25, 1871, Wicker Collection, Missouri Historical Society, St. Louis.

[19] Brandon, 117.

[20] Stephen S. Slaughter, *History of a Missouri Farm Family: The O. V. Slaughters, 1700–1944* (Harrison, NY: Harbor Hill, 1978), 55.

[21] Brandon, 119.

[22] Virginia Gunn, "Quilts for Union Soldiers in the Civil War," *Uncoverings 1985*, ed. Sally Garoutte (Mill Valley, CA: American Quilt Study Group, 1986), 95.

[23] Katherine M. Jones, ed., *Heroines of Dixie* (Westport, CT: Greenwood Press, 1955), 32.

[24] Laurel Horton, "South Carolina Quilts and the Civil War," *Uncoverings 1985*, ed. Sally Garoutte (Mill Valley, CA: American Quilt Study Group, 1986), 60.

[25] Jones, 39.

[26] Brandon, 122–23.

[27] Elaine Hedges, "The 19th-Century Diarist and Her Quilts," *American Quilts: A Handmade Legacy*, ed. L. Thomas Frye (Oakland, CA: Oakland Museum, 1981), 60.

[28] Virginia Gunn, conversation with author, March 28, 1987.

[29] Jonathan Holstein, *The Pieced Quilt: An American Design Tradition* (New York: Galahad Books, 1973), 84.

[30] Pieced quilt, Feathered Star, unknown maker, fourth quarter nineteenth century, collection of Robert Cargo, Tuscaloosa, AL.

[31] Carol Crabbe, letter to author, June 21, 1987.

[32] Peggy Potts, letter to author, Aug. 13, 1989.

[33] White stitched quilt, made by M. J. Foster, undated, collection of Shelburne Museum, Shelburne, VT.

[34] In December 1905, Rose Oliphant from Lexington, MS, asked *Comfort* for instructions for machine quilting. Instructions appeared in *Comfort* 18, No. 4 (February 1806). Letter from Katy Christopherson to author, June 1988.

[35] Sybil Lanigan, "Revival of the Patchwork Quilt," *Ladies' Home Journal* (October 1894): 19, cited in Jeannette Lasansky, *In the Heart of Pennsylvania: 19th and 20th Century Quiltmaking Traditions* (Lewisburg, PA: Oral Traditions Project, 1986), 55.

[36] Cuesta Benberry, letter to author, June 8, 1987.

[37] Appliqué quilt, Cockscomb and Currant, made by Jane Richey Morelock, collection of Mary K. Morelock Ledford, granddaughter of maker, pictured in Bets Ramsey and Marikay Waldvogel, *Quilts of Tennessee* (Nashville, TN: Rutledge Hill Press, 1986), 46–47.

[38] Katy Christopherson and Nancy Hornback, "Logan County Treasure—Found in Kansas," *Back Home in Kentucky* 10, No. 4 (July/August 1987): 48–49.

[39] Reverse appliqué quilt, Pineapple; and pieced quilt, Log Cabin, both in collection of Mississippi State Historical Museum, pictured in Mary Edna Lohrenz and Anita Miller Stamper, *Mississippi Homespun: Nineteenth-Century Textiles and the Women Who Made Them* (Jackson, MS: Mississippi Department of Archives and History, 1989), 5–7.

[40] Mills, Betty J., *Calico Chronicle: Texas Women and Their Fashions* (Lubbock, TX: Texas Tech Press, 1985), 84.

first Day of November 1870   Rile worked
on Middle River meeting house covering the shed room
Darling went to Mill Mr. D. Brown come & staid
all Night Peninnah put in the third quilt   Tues
I began to wash Eliza & Dora went to School   Tues
2nd, Wed, I finished washing, 4, Dozen, Nina quilted
ued .....   rank
Flor
4th,
5th,   the
6th,   eeting
Rile   me
7th   ashia
in the
8th   ed
9th
th   98
Nine
12th
13th
Midd
June
14th
until   dus
quil   snow
16th.
17th   Snow, Rile started to work and washing
Nina put in a Linsey quilt too, they had a spell
match tonight Allen went with the girls Nina Selby

Southern Linsey Quilts

of the Nineteenth Century

Merikay Waldvogel

November 1–17, 1870, entries from the Nancy Nash Holeman diary (1869–77) of Callaway County, Missouri, mention the weather and routine chores of the diarist, her family and friends. Their activities included digging potatoes, butchering, washing, visiting, going to meeting, holding a spelling bee, spinning flax, and quilting. In the eighteen days covered on this page, entries noted "Mr. D. Brown came & staid all night Peninnah put in third quilt"; "Nina quilted reddy to role"; "Jack Bartley helped us quilt"; and on the 17th "Rile started to move his father Nina put in a lincy quilt." Collection of the Western Historical Manuscript Collection, Columbia, Missouri. Courtesy of the Western Historical Manuscript Collection.

Fifty-four Forty or Fight pieced linsey, 78½" x 67", maker unknown. Back to front edge treatment, natural quilting thread, 3 stitches per inch. Collection of Merikay Waldvogel. Photo by Terry Wild Studio.

Every quilt, no matter how ragged it may be, carries important threads of history. The Southern pieced linsey quilt is just such a quilt. Coarse, heavy, and often tattered and dirty, these quilts today lie forgotten in garages, barns, and outbuildings of Southern farms. Yet these quilts contain fabrics whose manufacture was seen at times as a patriotic measure to circumvent British trade restrictions during colonial times, and to provide bedding and clothing to soldiers and families in the blockaded South during the Civil War. The fact that Southern women after the Civil War followed their instincts of thrift and resourcefulness by using the linsey blankets and garments in quilts became a final act of preservation of an important fabric. Little did they know that economic conditions would never again dictate the need for the fabric called linsey.[1]

The Southern linsey quilt is related in name only to linséy-woolsey quilts made during the colonial period. The wholecloth linsey-woolsey quilts are formal in their design and construction. The shiny surface cloth (correctly known as calimanco) of indigo, red, and green sets off the intricate feather and floral quilting patterns. The linings are generally of a coarser fabric. Montgomery believes some might have been imported already quilted.[2]

The name "linsey-woolsey" has confused people for many years. It suggests a fabric composed of linen and wool. When fibers from the linsey-woolseys at the Shelburne Museum were studied under a microscope, they were determined to be one-hundred-percent worsted wool in a twill or satin weave.

Merikay Waldvogel *is an author, curator, and quilt researcher. Her writings include* Quilts of Tennessee: Images of Domestic Life Prior to 1930, Soft Covers for Hard Times: Quiltmaking and the Great Depression, *and* Patchwork Souvenirs of the 1933 World's Fair. *1501 Whitower Road, Knoxville, TN 37919.*

The linings are also one-hundred-percent wool, but not worsted, and the weave was plain. The worsted yarn and/or the glazing may give the appearance of linen fabric in the quilt top, but otherwise researchers have not solved the mystery of the name "linsey-woolsey."[3]

Southern pieced linsey quilts contain quilt blocks and quilting designs that are among the simplest known. Many are simple Bar and String pieced quilts. As such, Southern pieced linsey quilts have not received much study by quilt historians. For textile and costume curators, the quilts may prove to be an important resource of data on home manufacture of textiles.

When a Knox County, Tennessee, woman told me the name of the fabric in her wool quilt was linsey, I doubted it because the fabric did not appear to contain linen. Later, when the fabric was determined to be a cotton-wool mix, the mystery was not solved but further complicated. Why was this fabric not called "cottonsy-woolsey"?

It is possible the name "linsey" persisted long after the fabric composition changed because it came to be associated with an inexpensive plain weave fabric produced in the parish of Linsey in Suffolk, England.[4] Linsey's cloth was originally made of linen and wool—two products readily available on English farms. In the American colonies, the cloth was also made of linen and wool, but when stronger mill-spun cotton thread became available, colonists changed from a linen warp to a cotton warp.

Leaving the unsolved mystery of the name to others, I have chosen to concentrate instead on the history of the fabric, especially on its economic and political significance to the people of this country. The changes in the production of linsey closely parallel the forces, both positive and negative, which impacted American families.

The first pieced linsey quilt I saw was at the home of a seventy-year-old

woman who grew up in Sevierville, Tennessee. She told me her great-great-grandmother (Margaret Burdine Connatser of Sevier County, Tennessee) had made it in the late 1800s. She said the quilt was made of fabrics from women's dresses and men's garments. Most of the fabric was called "linsey." She remembered sleeping under the quilt as a child. Some winter nights the snow fell through the cracks in the roof over her head; the layer closest to her body was a feather comforter, but on top of that was the heavy linsey quilt. The quilt

Star pieced linsey, 84" x 67", maker unknown from the Barren County area of Kentucky. Back to front edge treatment, natural quilting thread, 4 stitches per inch. Collection of Carole C. Wahler. Photo by Terry Wild Studio.

served three purposes: it kept her warm, it kept her dry, and it weighted down the feather comforter, which was prone to falling off in the middle of the night. She did not care for the quilt; it was coarse, it had raveled edges, and the dark colors were not to her liking.[5]

In 1982 a linsey quilt called Kentucky Sun was featured on the cover of *Kentucky Quilts, 1800-1900* produced by the Kentucky Quilt Project.[6] While the author, Jonathan Holstein, was intrigued by the "extraordinary" pieced design of this Kentucky linsey quilt, I was intrigued by the fabric. The quilt contained coarse naturally dyed striped and checked fabrics similar to those in the linsey quilt I had seen. Holstein pointed out:

The material is a type not often used, made of wool weft on a cotton warp, but is not one of the linsey-woolsey cotton and wool cloths seen in late eighteenth- and early nineteenth-century American quilts. These design and construction characteristics may indicate that the quilt represents a regional type rather than a single, creative insight.[7]

A Nine Diamond linsey quilt found during the Quilts of Tennessee survey had been on the floor of a deserted log cabin in Knox County, Tennessee.[8] Others have covered tobacco in wagons and machinery in barns. These cast-off quilts were not the ones proudly brought to quilt documentation days in Tennessee.

Therefore, we began to specifically ask for linsey quilts in publicity about quilt documentation days. Eventually, we documented three other pieced linsey quilts and three wholecloth linsey quilts. On a visit to the Blair Farm of Roane County, I examined several linsey quilts, linsey garments, and remnants of linsey cloth.[9] I have since studied other pieced linsey quilts from Tennessee, Georgia, Kentucky, North Carolina, and Missouri.

The following published sources include discussions and photographs of pieced linsey quilts: *Keep Me Warm One Night*, a book on early hand-weaving in Eastern Canada, by Harold and Dorothy Burnham,[10] *Traditional Quilts and Bedcoverings* by Ruth McKendry,[11] *The Pieced Quilt: An American Design Tradition* by Jonathan Holstein,[12] *America's*

Quilts and Coverlets by Carleton Safford and Robert Bishop,[13] *Quilts in America* by Patsy and Myron Orlofsky,[14] and *A People and Their Quilts* by John Rice Irwin.[15] Besides these few references, very little information exists about pieced linsey quilts, especially those made in the South during the mid- to late nineteenth century.

An important reference to a linsey quilt appears in *Marthy Lou's Kiverlid: A Sketch of Mountain Life* written in 1937 in East Tennessee. The young girl in the story, Marthy Lou, reports on a weekend visit with her grandmother. "I made two linsy quilts out o' squares o' linsy dresses an' some o' Granny's balmoral petticoats an' padded 'em with wool bats."[16] This fictional reference is further evidence of a regional type of quilt called a "linsey quilt" distinct from the colonial linsey-woolseys.

Construction of Linsey Quilts

Of the Southern linsey quilts studied, all contain a plain weave fabric of a wool weft and a cotton warp.[17] Dyed wool thread was carried back and forth on a shuttle through a web of long white cotton threads tied to a simple two-harness loom. The plain two-harness weaving limited the design of linsey to stripes, checks, and solids. In the striped and solid pieces, the white cotton warp threads appear as small white specks. The design limitation and the unusual combination of cotton and wool gave linsey its distinctive look and feel.

Linsey had much to commend it. It could be made with resources available on the farm, it could be made quickly, it was strong, and it was cheap. However, it was coarse and stiff, and it raveled easily. The raveling problem limited the size and type of quilt blocks one could make from linsey. The quilt pieces are rarely curved and never appliquéd. The coarseness and thickness of the cloth limited the quilting stitch length and the quilting designs. The following

pieced patterns are typically found in linsey quilts: Bar, One Patch, Nine Patch, Sixteen Patch, Streak of Lightning, and String. The quilting designs are limited to fans, diamonds, or straight diagonal lines, with four to six stitches per inch.

Ruth McKendry includes in her book a group of Canadian quilts she calls "hand-woven quilts," which appear to be similar to linsey quilts. The striped and checked fabrics are like those in Southern linsey quilts, and the blocks and quilting patterns are also as simple. She dates the Canadian hand-woven quilts from the third and fourth quarters of the nineteenth century. She points out that these quilts are most common in the areas settled by Scots, but they also appear in German areas.[18]

A similar type of thick woolen quilt, called a "hap," was made in Central Pennsylvania during the nineteenth century.[19] Haps, like the Southern pieced linsey quilts, do not often find themselves at the center of attention. Both are heavy, simply constructed, and made of recycled textiles. Jeannette Lasansky suggests that "they are rarely illustrated . . . because they do not fit into the present concept of what is salable, collectable, and therefore showable."[20] These rough quilts are valuable for many reasons, the most important being the record they hold of the many textiles whose history ended when the influences of the industrial revolution finally reached the interior of the United States.

Dating Southern Linsey Quilts

No linsey quilt found includes an inscribed date, and rarely are linsey quilts mentioned in women's letters and diaries. On the other hand, evidence of linsey fabric appears often in early travel accounts, in store records and advertisements, in estate inventories, and even in slave narratives.

According to Sadye Tune Wilson, a Tennessee weaving historian who wrote *Of Coverlets: The Legacies,*

Flying Geese pieced linsey, 76½" x 63½", maker unknown. Back to front edge treatment, natural and colored quilting thread, 4 stitches per inch. Collection of Diane Cormell. Photo by Terry Wild Studio.

Turkey Tracks pieced linsey, 79½" x 67", maker unknown. Applied linsey binding, blue quilting thread, 4 stitches per inch. Collection of Merikay Waldvogel. Photo by Terry Wild Studio.

The Weavers, linsey was woven with a cotton warp and wool weft "after machine-spun cotton became available [in Tennessee] around the 1820s. There were many small cotton gin operations for those who grew their own cotton in a community." According to Wilson, the same is true for coverlets. "Finding linen in a coverlet is very rare because most coverlets [in this area] were done after the 1820s." When asked to date linsey quilts she estimated linsey quilts were made from dress and suit scraps woven after 1850.[21]

Comparing pieced linsey quilts to other quilts made during the period of 1820–80, one sees the most similarities with quilts made during the 1870s. In the mid-1800s, appliqué motifs of pink, red, and green on a white background, or pieced baskets or stars on a white background were common. Delicately quilted vines, vases, and flowers filled the white areas. Women had the fabric and the time to make nonutilitarian quilts. Quilts made in the 1860s and 1870s, during and after the Civil War, reflect the need to make warm bedding quickly. Quilt blocks are larger, quilting stitches are longer, and quilting patterns typically include fans, diamonds, and parallel lines. Pieced linsey quilts fit perfectly this description of utilitarian quilts. They are warm, easy to produce, and the materials are inexpensive.

Another method of dating linsey quilts is to review the lives of the makers. Of the linsey quilts studied, five were attributed to women who were adults in the last half of the nineteenth century. Mary Blair and her three daughters lived in Roane County, Tennessee, during that time. The Blair family collection of nineteenth-century artifacts is particularly important to dating linsey quilts because so many different types of objects remain intact. Dozens of skeins of machine-spun cotton thread, coverlets of cotton warp and wool weft, weaving drafts, and spinning and carding tools are evidence of home manufacture of cloth, but that cotton warp thread was probably spun at a local gin.

The collection includes many linsey garments: dresses, petticoats,[22] and a man's jacket. None of these linsey items contains a fabric with a linen-wool mix. All of the garment fabric is a cotton-wool mix. Of the sewing scraps, bedding, lengths of cloth, and linsey quilts studied, only one length of cloth has a linen warp, but the weft was cotton.

Printed materials in the Blair collection include an 1873 store receipt for various fabrics, an 1882 letter from a relative in Arkansas mentioning the use of linsey to line a jeans jacket, and a steamboat bill of lading for a sewing machine dated 1878. Since none of the Blair quilts contains evidence of machine sewing, the linsey garment fabric in the quilts probably pre-dates 1878, but, of course, the quilts could have been constructed without machine stitching after 1878. I believe that most linsey quilts were constructed in the quarter century following the end of the Civil War. As women had a choice of fabrics to buy and as linsey garments were discarded, some women recycled the linsey fabric in their quilts. This fact is borne out in analyzing the Blair collection.[23]

Estate sale records reveal the value of linsey quilts. A preliminary review of estate sale records (1792–1874) in Knox County, Tennessee, revealed only one linsey quilt. The estate sale inventory of John Kirk (dated July 1864) includes "one quilt linsey," which sold for $1.00. For purposes of comparison, three counterpanes sold for $4.25, $5.00, and $5.75.[24]

The Greene County, Tennessee, will of Rebecca Hicks, dated 1890, states "To my son, James—one feather bed, three best calico quilts, one blanket, one linsey quilt, two sheets new domestic ones, two pillows and $5 cash."[25]

Linsey quilts were not often mentioned in women's diaries, but women's studies scholar, Elaine Hedges, located a series of diary entries that do mention weaving, sewing, and linsey quilts.[26] Nancy Holeman of Callaway County, Missouri, born 1806, kept a diary from 1869 to 1877, recording weather, daily chores, visitors, and happenings. On April 19, 1869, she wrote "I am about to begin to piece a Lincy quilt . . . it is raining." On October 18, "A cold cloudy day . . . I finished a new sheat and pieced a middle for a lincy quilt." During early 1870 Holeman records the progress of quilting her quilt on a frame: January 11, "Rain about all Day. I put my Lincy quilt." January 12, "we got out the quilt." January 25, 1870, "I finished my Lincy quilt." March 26, "Cloudy. I put a border on my lincy quilt." Later in 1870, Nancy Holeman described a female relative who came often to quilt: November 17, "Nina put in a Lincy quilt"; November 18, "[Peninnah] got out the Lincy quilt"; and November 26, "Peninnah finished the Comfort. Kitty and I hemed it."[27]

The entries are particularly valuable because they describe the process of making a linsey quilt and the length of time needed to quilt one. More importantly, they date the type of quilt as one being made in 1870. The November 26 entry, in which the word "Comfort" is used instead of "Lincy quilt," suggests that the terms may have been interchangeable.

The History of the Linsey Fabric

Southern pieced linsey quilts represent the end of the long, important, but confusing history of a fabric called linsey-woolsey. Weaving traditions brought from England were important in the production of sufficient clothing and bedding in America, but, more importantly, weaving also enabled the colonists to maintain a certain degree of economic independence from England.

A Mr. Denton living in New York in 1670, reported on the home manufacture of linsey-woolsey:

They sowe store of Flax, which they make every one Cloth of for their own wearing, as also woolen cloth, and Linsey-woolsey, and had they more Tradesmen among them, they would in a little time live without the help of any other Countrey for their clothing.[28]

England saw the colonies as a vast marketplace for its own expanding textile industry and, therefore, took drastic steps to limit the establishment of textile manufacturing in the colonies— even the home manufacture of textiles. The case of the spinning machine invented by Hargreaves in 1764 serves as an example. The spinning machine was a major labor-saving invention, and the English wished to maintain a monopoly on the manufacture and use of this device. American colonists constructed a wooden model in England, then cut it into pieces and shipped it to America, where it was reassembled in Philadelphia.[29]

During the eighteenth century colonial women felt encouraged to make their own cloth rather than import cloth from England. A New England preacher was quoted as saying "Wear none but your own country linen. Of economy boast. Let your pride be the most to show cloaths of your own make and spinning."[30] Weaving one's own cloth was patriotic. A visitor to New York commented upon the clothing he saw in that city:

Their petticoats of linsey-woolsey, were striped with gorgeous dyes . . . they were all of their own manufacture, of which circumstance, as may well be supposed, they were not a little vain. The gentle-men of those days, were well content to figure in their linsey-woolsey coats—domestic made, and bedecked with an abundance of large brass buttons.[31]

When the Revolutionary War began, direct textile trade with England ceased. Households were asked to furnish cloth for soldiers' uniforms, but there were two and one-half million citizens to be clothed as well.

According to Rolla Milton Tryon:

The fact that the people had within their own homes the means of supplying their needs for wearing apparel was one of the big factors that enabled them to continue their struggle to a successful termination.[32]

After the Revolutionary War, textile trade with England resumed so that by the mid-1800s, quiltmakers in the South were able to use fabrics imported from the British Empire. When William Grasty took over a general store in Mount Airy, Virginia, in 1838, the following items were among the dry goods listed in the inventory, including both domestic and imported fabrics: bobbinet, lawn, muslin, jaconet, gingham, cambric, pongee, oriental gauze, blue satin, linen, calico, flannel, oznaburg, bombazett, silk, velvet, sarcenet, vesting, linsey, and cassimere.[33]

The American textile industry grew rapidly after independence. With the invention of the cotton gin by Eli Whitney, cotton mills became commonplace in towns first in the North and later in the South.

On December 17, 1791, John Hague advertised in the *Knoxville Gazette* for weavers to work in his establishment in the town of Manchester in the Mero District (Middle Tennessee):

The subscriber has his machines in order for carding spinning and weaving, and is in want of a good number of GOOD WEAVERS. The greatest encouragement will be given to such as are acquainted with the weaving of velvets, corduroys, and calicoes.[34]

Textiles often appeared in lists of goods needed for sale and exchange. On December 17, 1791, in the *Knoxville Gazette*, Summerville and Ore announced the opening of their store on German Creek,

where they have a large and general assortment of well-chosen goods from the markets of Philadelphia and Baltimore, which they are determined to sell on the most reasonable terms that goods have

been sold for in the western country, for cash. The highest price will be allowed for good linsey, seven hundred linen, beeswax, bearskins, deerskins, fur skins, of all kinds, rye, corn and oats.[35]

On February 28, 1793, John Sommerville & Co. advertised in the *Knoxville Gazette*.

Wanted to purchase, a quantity of linsey, seven hundred linen, and public securities of every denomination, that are or may be issued for the protection of the Territory.[36]

On December 26, 1796, the *Knoxville Gazette* itself advertised for linsey as a means to settle debts.

Those persons who are indebted to the printer, for the *Knoxville Gazette*, or its former establishment, are informed, that the following articles will be received in discharge of their respective arrearages, if delivered on or before the first day of January next, viz—beef, pork, corn, flour, linsey, country linen and fire wood.[37]

The value of linsey is further evident in the fact that lengths of linsey cloth often appear in estate sale inventories along with bedsteads and bedding. In the June 1859 Knox County settlement of the estate of Catherine McHaffie, thirteen yards of linsey sold for $6.11.[38]

The April 1864 settlement in Knox County of the estate of Sarah Lovelace listed 1¼ yards of linsey at 35 cents per yard, three meal sacks for $2.00, 2½ yards of janes at $1.60 per yard, and three yards of check linsey at $1.60 per yard.[39]

The April 1865 Knox County settlement of the estate of William Davis listed 13½ yards of linsey for $7.89 and 15½ yards of gingham for $3.80.[40]

Slaves were clothed in linsey and other home-manufactured textiles. Linsey was one of the cheapest textiles available, and the raw materials were present on most Southern farms. Slaves worked in loom houses and sewing houses making clothing for themselves and other slaves. Inter-

views of surviving ex-slaves recorded by workers of the Federal Writers' Project of the Works Progress Administration in the 1930s provide a rich resource of information on the domestic lives of Southerners in the nineteenth century. The former slaves recalled their memories of home activities, food, and clothing. Several subjects mentioned home manufacture of cloth and homespun fabrics such as linsey. Robert Shepherd, age 91, of Athens, Georgia, reported the following:

De cloth for most all of de clothes was made at home. Marse Joe raised lots of sheep and de wool was used to make cloth for de winter clothes. Us had a great long loom house where some of de slaves didn't do nothin' but weave cloth. Some carded bats, some done de spinnin', and dere was more of 'em to do de sewin'.[41]

James Lucas, of Natchez, Mississippi, was 104 years old when he was interviewed in 1937 about his life as a slave.

When I got big enough to wait round at de Big House and got to town, I wore clean rough clothes. De pants was white linsey-woolsey and de shirts was rough white cotton what was wove at de plantation. In de winter de sewin' womens made us heavy clothes and knit wool socks for us. De womens wore linsey-woolsey dresses and long leggin's like de soldiers wear.[42]

Susan Snow, age 87, of Meridian, Mississippi, reported similar memories.

Dey made all de niggers' clothes on de place. Homespun, dey called it. Dey had spinnin' wheels and cards and looms at de Big House. All de women spinned in de winter time.[43]

Morris Sheppard, age 85, of Fort Gibson, Oklahoma, referred to a "stripedy" cloth, which might have been linsey.

Everything was stripedy 'cause Mammy like to make it fancy. She dye with copperas and walnut and wild indigo and things like dat, and made pretty cloth. I wore a stripedy shirt till I was about eleven years old.[44]

Blair linsey petticoats, maker unknown. Collection of Mary J. Browning. Photo by Terry Wild Studio.

Susan Caroline Blair (1846–1924), at the well beside her home in Roane County, Tennessee, was photographed circa 1915 wearing a linsey skirt similar to the two left in the family estate. Courtesy of Mary J. Browning.

And the "checkedy" cloth, which Martha Colquitt, age 85, of Athens, Georgia, remembered might also have been linsey.

[Grandma] worked in de loom house and wove cloth all de time. She wove de checkedy cloth for de slaves clothes. . . . She made heaps of cloth. . . . She brought her featherbed with her from Virginny, and she used to piece up a heap of quilts out of our old clothes and any kinds of scraps she could get a hold of.[45]

Charles Davenport, age 100, of Natchez, Mississippi, remembered fondly quilts in his childhood.

I growed up in de quarters. . . . Us had blankets and quilts filled with home raised wool and I just loved layin' in de big fat featherbed a-hearin' de rain patter on de roof.[46]

Domestic life in the South changed drastically when the Civil War broke out; sea ports were blockaded, and trade along the roadways leading north and south was stopped. While men went to war by the thousands, women proudly returned to their looms. Textiles were as important as guns and bullets to the Confederate cause. An appeal for clothing for sol-

diers appeared in the *Knoxville Daily Register* on April 22, 1862, requesting the following items:

Gray cassimere pants, shirts, homemade shoes, long boots for cavalry, heavy grained boots for infantry, brown flannel overshirts, linsey overshirts.[47]

Wives, sisters, and mothers shouldered the burden of making uniforms, bedding, and tents for the war effort while facing major changes in their domestic lives. In the years preceding the war, women had discussed which sewing machines to buy, and which mantua-maker to hire to cut a fancy

129

dress. They could choose from a wide variety of fabrics imported through the great seaports of the South, such as Charleston and New Orleans. With the blockade in place, women found themselves facing a serious textile and clothing shortage.

In some parts of the South, textile mills and carding factories were targets of military offensives. The factories that remained open apparently charged high prices for goods and services. One Georgia woman discussed the situation in a letter to her mother.

I wish we could spin by magic. It would assist us very much if we were near a carding factory. I am told there are plenty around this place, but I do not know what they charge per pound. What do you think of yarn selling for thirty to thirty-five a bunch in Marietta?[48]

The situation was especially serious for those women who had many slaves. Mary S. Mallard, whose family's letters make up the massive volume *The Children of Pride,* wrote the following in 1864:

Mr. Mallard wrote Mr. Quarterman last night to give out the osnaburgs to the people [the slaves]. I think there will be enough for all of the people at Arcadia. I am very glad we happened to have it on hand, for it would be difficult to get it at this time. Roswell factory is threatened, but I hope it will not be destroyed, for it would be a great loss.[49]

Out came the looms, spinning wheels, and cards. However, in 1863 in Arcadia, Georgia, Mary Jones wrote to her son that cotton cards were not to be found.

Mr. Russell, to whom we sent nine sheep skins to be exchanged for cotton cards some four months since, writes that they are not to be had. Can they now be had in Savannah? And at what price?[50]

By 1864, Loudon County, Tennessee, was under military occupation by Union troops. A Loudon County resident, Mary Jane Reynolds, was angered because she had to take an oath to the Union every time she made a purchase at her local general store. In letters to her husband, she reported on the shopping practices of the day.

March 13, 1864: I went down the other day and bought some dark calico for Mother, Lizzie and I. I would have gotten a balmoral but they were very common and they asked four dollars for them. Do you think that goods will continue to get higher. They did not require me to take the oath.

March 1864: We are pretty quiet now. Mrs. Franklin is here, came last night. Had been to Loudon to pick out some calico for Mr. Kline to buy [for her]. That is the way the ladies get out of taking the oath, but Andersons sell to almost any one.

April 1, 1864: They say they are not near so particular about selling goods as they were at first there. They asked a person if they were loyal now they ask them if they will trade.[51]

Some women seemed to make the most of the situation and even staged parties. Lucy Virginia French wrote in 1861 that she was "sewing, made the skirt of a new plaid linsey dress for myself for our Homespun party."[52]

A Georgia woman described a friend's "confederate" dress to her mother in a letter. "She has a black linsey dress that she dyed herself, and it is a beautiful black. She seems to have succeeded remarkably well with her experiments."[53]

One of the more poignant statements about the Civil War was stitched on a pillow by a Tennessee woman, Mary High Prince, in 1910:

Hoorah! for the home spun
dresses we southern ladies
wore in time of the war.
Ev'ry piece here.
Sad memories it brings
back to me.
For our hearts was weary
and restless.
And our life was full of care.
The burden laid up on us
seemed greater than we could bear.[54]

Although the pillow cover is made of scraps of checked, hand-woven, all-cotton fabric reminiscent of linsey, and not linsey itself, the statement expresses the sentiments of women who made many sacrifices during the Civil War.

Soon after the end of the Civil War, Northerners turned their attention to modernizing their major cities. Products from newly built factories streamed into all areas of the country as transportation systems expanded. Cloth production in homes and small mills declined in importance. Sewing machines and plows replaced bedsteads and bedding as the items on the top of estate inventory lists. Officials at a Knoxville fair continued for several years to offer a prize of $2.00 for the best eight yards of home linsey,[55] but for the most part the weaving of linsey had died out by 1900.

For some women linsey fabric elicited bitter memories— memories of a time of sacrifice for battles that were lost—and for that reason they may have quickly given up the home weaving of linsey as soon as they were able. However, the general demise of linsey was more likely due to the expansion of transportation systems, especially the railroad, and the return to active commerce after the Civil War. With the return of peace time, women once again faced a myriad of choices when shopping for fabrics, and the sewing machine was touted as the ultimate timesaver, bringing the age of weaving homespun and linsey to an end.

Linsey quilts are a record of the fabrics and garments made necessary by the politics and economics of slavery, the Civil War, and Reconstruction in the inland South. Since the 1870s, women in this country have faced similar times of economic and political distress with a spirit of resourcefulness. However, the need has never been so great that it required home manufacture of fabrics such as linsey. Linsey quilts represent a unique response to particular circumstances in nineteenth-century America. This fact alone makes the study of linsey quilts and quilts like them important.

Notes and References

[1]The term also appears as "lincy" and "linsy."

[2]Florence M. Montgomery, *Textiles in America 1650–1870* (New York: Norton, 1984), 279.

[3]Noordaa, Titia Vander, "The Linsey Woolseys at the Shelburne Museum," *Shuttle, Spindle, and Dyepot,* 62 (Spring 1985): 59–61.

[4]Montgomery, 279.

[5]Merikay Waldvogel, "Of Cotton Seeds, Calico and Boss Thread: Quilting in East Tennessee," *Quilts Close Up: Five Southern Views,* ed. Bets Ramsey (Chattanooga, TN: Hunter Museum of Art, 1983), 13.

[6]Jonathan Holstein, *Kentucky Quilts 1800–1900* (Louisville, KY: Kentucky Quilt Project, 1982), Cover.

[7]Ibid., 2.

[8]Bets Ramsey and Merikay Waldvogel, *The Quilts of Tennessee: Images of Domestic Life Prior to 1930* (Nashville, TN: Rutledge Hill Press, 1986), 98.

[9]Ramsey and Waldvogel, 81–92.

[10]Harold Burnham and Dorothy Burnham, *Keep Me Warm One Night* (Toronto: University of Toronto Press, 1975), 71.

[11]Ruth McKendry, *Traditional Quilts and Bedcoverings* (New York: Van Nostrand Reinhold, 1979), 124–26.

[12]Jonathan Holstein, *The Pieced Quilt: An American Design Tradition* (New York: Galahad Books, 1973), 30–32, 42–44.

[13]Carleton L. Safford and Robert Bishop, *America's Quilts and Coverlets* (New York: Dutton, 1980), 29–30.

[14]Patsy and Myron Orlofsky, *Quilts in America* (New York: McGraw-Hill, 1974), 85.

[15]John Rice Irwin, *A People and Their Quilts* (Exton, PA: Schiffer, 1983), 18–19; 161.

[16]Rebecca Dougherty Hyatt, *Marthy Lou's Kiverlid: A Sketch of Mountain Life* (Morristown, TN: Morristown Printing, 1937), 109. A balmoral petticoat is a striped or figured woolen petticoat worn beneath a skirt looped up in front.

[17]Thread samples from twenty-eight pieces of fabric from quilt tops, linings, garments, and sewing scraps were analyzed under a microscope by Jim Liles of Knoxville, TN. I thank him for his assistance and interest.

[18]McKendry, 123–27.

[19]Jeannette Lasansky, "The Role of the Haps in Central Pennsylvania's 19th and 20th Century Quiltmaking Traditions," *Uncoverings 1985,* ed. Sally Garoutte (Mill Valley, CA: American Quilt Study Group, 1986), 85–93.

[20]Ibid., 91.

[21]Sadye Tune Wilson, letter to author, Aug. 20, 1987.

[22]Mary Browning referred to the garments as "petticoats." They are similar to modern-day gathered skirts.

[23]Ramsey and Waldvogel, 81–92.

[24]Knox County Estate Settlements, 14 (July 1864): 155.

[25]Goldene Fillers Burgner, *Abstracts of Greene County, Tennessee Wills, 1783–1890* (Easley, SC: Southern Historical Press, 1983), 153.

[26]Letter from Elaine Hedges, Aug. 2, 1987.

[27]Diary of Nancy Nash Holeman, typescript, in Joint Collection, University of Missouri Western Historical Manuscript Collection—Columbia and State Historical Society of Missouri Manuscripts.

[28]Rolla Milton Tryon, *Household Manufactures in the United States, 1640–1860* (1917; reprint, New York: Augustus M. Kelley, 1966), 68.

[29]Ethel Lewis, *The Romance of Textiles* (New York: Macmillan, 1937), 314–15.

[30]Tryon, 108.

[31]John Fanning Watson, *Annals and Occurrences of New York City and State in the Olden Time* (Philadelphia: Henry F. Anners, 1846), 170, cited in Montgomery, 279.

[32]Tryon, 117.

[33]Lewis E. Atherton, *The Southern Country Store, 1800–1860* (1949; reprint, New York: Greenwood, 1968), 73.

[34]*Knoxville Gazette,* Dec. 17, 1791.

[35]Ibid., Dec. 17, 1791.

[36]Ibid., Feb. 28, 1793.

[37]Ibid., Dec. 26, 1796.

[38]Knox County Estate Settlements, June 1859, 13: 162.

[39]Ibid., April 1864, 14: 93.

[40]Ibid., April 1865, 14: 302.

[41]Norman R. Yetman, *Life Under the "Peculiar Institution": Selections from the Slave Narrative Collection* (New York: Holt, Rinehart, and Winston, 1970), 267.

[42]Ibid., 217.

[43]Ibid., 291.

[44]Ibid., 271.

[45]Ibid., 60.

[46]Ibid., 72.

[47]*Knoxville Daily Register,* April 22, 1862.

[48]Robert Manson Myers, ed., *The Children of Pride: A True Story of Georgia and the Civil War* (New Haven, CT: Yale University Press, 1972), 1126.

[49]Ibid., 1182.

[50]Ibid., 1064.

[51]Letters of Mary Jane Johnston Reynolds to her husband, Simeon D. Reynolds, Jan. 6, 1864—June 20, 1864, typescript, in Special Collections, University of Tennessee Library.

[52]Lucy Virginia Smith French, *War Journal, 1860–1865,* typescript, in State Library and Archives, Nashville, TN.

[53]Myers, 1140.

[54]Ramsey and Waldvogel, 22. The pillow is pictured in color in Pat Ferrero, Elaine Hedges, and Julie Silber, *Hearts and Hands: The Influence of Women and Quilts on American Society* (San Francisco: Quilt Digest Press, 1987), 79.

[55]*Premium List and Rules and Regulations of the Eastern Division Fair for East Tennessee—October 10–14, 1871,* 11–17. McClung Collection, Knox County Public Library, Knoxville, TN.

The Textile Industry and South Carolina Quilts

Laurel Horton

The development and expansion of the American textile industry during the nineteenth century had a marked effect on American quiltmaking. Imported chintzes and calicos had made quiltmaking the province of the well-to-do in the early part of the century, and quilts reflected an expenditure of both money and time. The increased availability and lower cost of domestic printed and plain fabrics during the second half of the century encouraged quiltmaking among the greater American population.

The influences of the American textile industry, however, went beyond providing locally manufactured cloth. In many Southern states the new industry transformed the daily lives of hundreds of thousands of people and created waves of change that are still felt a century later. Both textile production itself and the social changes wrought by the mills and mill villages influenced the way women in those villages made quilts.

Laurel Horton *is a folklorist, quiltmaker, and quilt researcher. She is the author of* Social Fabric: South Carolina's Traditional Quilts, *and numerous scholarly and popular articles. She served as editor for* Uncoverings *from 1988 to 1993. 302 East South Third Street, Seneca, SC 29678.*

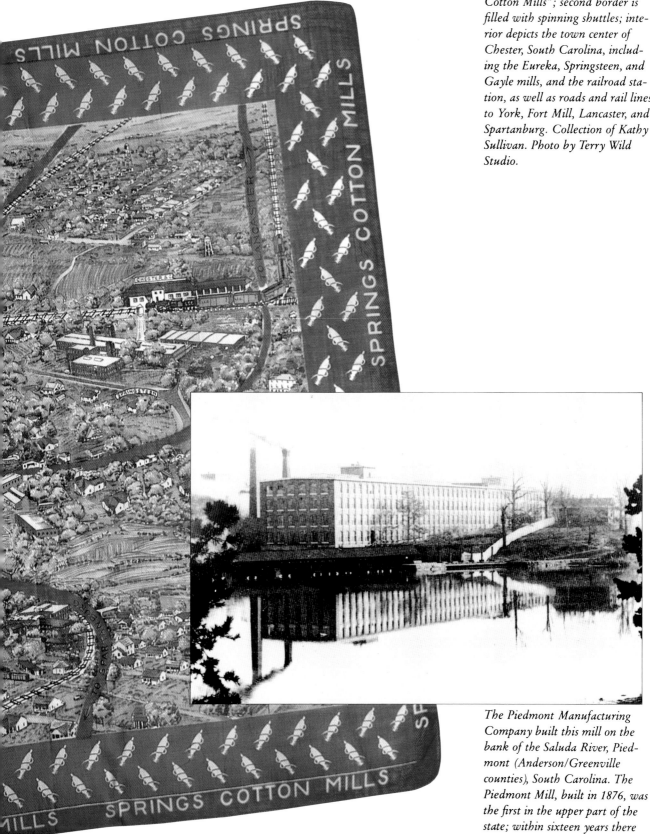

Printed cotton bandanna, 21" x 21". Outer border reads "Springs Cotton Mills"; second border is filled with spinning shuttles; interior depicts the town center of Chester, South Carolina, including the Eureka, Springsteen, and Gayle mills, and the railroad station, as well as roads and rail lines to York, Fort Mill, Lancaster, and Spartanburg. Collection of Kathy Sullivan. Photo by Terry Wild Studio.

The Piedmont Manufacturing Company built this mill on the bank of the Saluda River, Piedmont (Anderson/Greenville counties), South Carolina. The Piedmont Mill, built in 1876, was the first in the upper part of the state; within sixteen years there were fifty-one mills operating in the area. Courtesy of the Pendleton District Historical and Recreational Commission.

The establishment of textile mills transformed the Southern economy during the late nineteenth and early twentieth centuries. Before the widespread construction of textile mills, agriculture, specifically cotton, formed the economic base. Although cotton had been an important crop since the 1790s in the low country, farmers in the Piedmont, the higher red clay country between the Appalachian Mountains and the fall line, tended to be self-sufficient, growing their own food and raising livestock.

Before the construction of railroads in the Piedmont in the 1850s, it was difficult and expensive to market agricultural products. Some farmers periodically drove cattle and other livestock to markets near the Atlantic coast or hauled barrels of grain, preserved meat, and other products in wagons over poor roads to the nearest navigable waterway. There were a few large plantations but most farms were small, single-family operations.

Woven bedcovers, both plain-woven blankets and fancy overshot coverlets, were the norm in the early nineteenth-century Piedmont. Households raised sheep for wool and flax for linen. As cotton became more important, women grew, spun, and wove it into clothing and household textiles. During the first half of the nineteenth century, women used local cotton to make white wholecloth quilts and bedspreads. From the care and attention lavished on surviving examples we know they were highly prized by makers and their families.[1]

After the disruption of the Civil War the Piedmont economy changed radically. Surviving soldiers returned home to find buildings, fences, and fields in disrepair. Cotton prices (the amounts paid to the farmers) were high so that everyone who had land planted cotton to try to regain economic stability. Farmers needing loans to rebuild their holdings found that lenders were willing only if they planted a cash crop of cotton. As a result, land that might have been used to raise food for families was planted in cotton.

Following the official abolition of slavery, the system of sharecropping and tenant farming evolved. Affluent landowners divided their land into plots that could be worked by single families and leased them to freed slaves and other landless families in exchange for rent payments or a share of the crop at harvest.[2]

Even small landowners who previously had been nearly self-sufficient were drawn into the cash crop system in order to pay the higher taxes levied by reform-minded governments that needed revenue to fund road improvement and railway expansion. New fence laws, requiring containment of farm animals, also altered the landscape and reduced the ability of small farmers to raise livestock. Until the 1870s only crops had been fenced. Hogs and cattle foraged freely on public or private land. Fence laws limited livestock raising to farmers with larger plots.[3]

The prices farmers could get for their cotton remained high during the late 1860s, then fell heavily during the 1870s. High prices one year often led to overproduction the next, resulting in lower prices and less production the following year. This repeated cycle created a rollercoaster effect that persisted through the end of the nineteenth century.

Fluctuating cotton prices caused uncertainty among the vulnerable small farmers, tenants, and sharecroppers. Larger landholders and cotton buyers had enough reserves to enable them to withhold their crop from the market until prices were more favorable. Tenants, however, had to sell their cotton at harvest in order to pay rent and repay loans that covered fertilizer and operating expenses for that crop year. Few poor farmers were able to break the cycle of debt from one year to the next.[4]

In any community there was a range of economic situations with the large landholders and merchants at the top, farmers with sufficient land and labor to maintain independence in the middle, and tenants and sharecroppers at the low end of the scale. Large landholders generally did well under the sharecropping system but the real beneficiaries were the merchants. All farmers needed tools, seed, fertilizer, and household supplies while waiting for their cotton to mature. After selling their crop, farmers paid off their store credit account first, with interest. In a bad year there might be little or nothing left for the family.

Because there was a variety of economic situations among Piedmont farmers we would expect also a range of quilts. The wives and daughters of large landowners and merchants had their pick of fabric. During the late nineteenth century Piedmont quilts reflected the availability of an array of relatively inexpensive domestic printed cottons from Northern mills.[5]

Less affluent families purchased fabric for clothing and quilts after the crop was sold in good years and probably did without new cloth at other times. Fabric was customarily purchased by the bolt of ten or twenty yards, and in a good year there would be enough money to buy fabric to make new dresses for all the girls and shirts for the boys. Dress scraps might be saved until there was enough variety to make a special quilt, while everyday quilts could be made from heavier remnants left from making overalls and pants.

While scrap quilts remain from the late nineteenth century, in most cases we don't know much about the specific family situations in which they were made and used. A single quilt tells us less than would the entire range of household bedding, and few such laboratories exist for examining the textiles of a typical farm family.[6]

Ironically, the volatile economic conditions that crippled farmers improved the lot of merchants.[7] By the 1880s merchants had money to invest and began backing the construction of textile mills. Mill construction was seen as a progressive move, a way out of the post-war economic slump. Throughout the Piedmont small

towns were transformed into cities, as mill villages sprung up on the outskirts. Greenville, South Carolina, a small courthouse town of 1,500 before the Civil War, became an important cotton market with more than 10,000 people by 1900.[8]

Victoria Cunningham Bailey, of Bailey's Crossroads in Greenville County, made a Carolina Lily quilt about 1870. She was the wife of William Bailey, a cotton buyer who invested in textile mill construction. Victoria Bailey later owned controlling shares in the Victor Mill, which was named after her.[9]

Dependent on water power, early mill builders selected sites along the falls of rivers. Because there were few potential workers in these sparsely populated locations, mill owners built complete villages, including houses, churches, and stores, to attract workers. After construction was underway they sent recruiters through the countryside to entice families to trade the uncertainty of cotton farming for paid wages.

Among the first farm families to take up mill work were those headed by women or having more daughters than sons.[10] Widows, plentiful after the war, often had difficulty getting credit, and families without men or older boys to plow and do heavy work were usually at a disadvantage on a farm. Mill recruiters looked for families who could provide three or more workers. Large families continued to be an advantage in the mill just as they had been on the farm. The more workers a family could provide, the more money the family earned. A typical early twentieth-century flyer advertised for workers in this way:

Carolina Lily pieced and appliqué print and solid-color cottons, 84" x 73½", made by Victoria Cunningham Bailey (1842–96), Bailey's Crossroads (Greenville County), South Carolina, circa 1870. Front to back edge treatment, natural and brown quilting thread, 8–9 stitches per inch. Collection of Victoria Bailey. Photo by Terry Wild Studio.

Bailey's husband was a cotton buyer, and later the family owned textile mills. The Victor Mill was named after Victoria Bailey; she owned controlling shares in the mill.

The Pacolet Manufacturing Company, of Pacolet, SC, can furnish steady employment for over 300 days in the year for boys and girls over 12 years old, men and women at average wages, as follows: Experienced 12 to 16-year old boys and girls from $.50 to $1.25. Experienced boys and girls over 16, and men and women, $.75 to $1.50. Old men, 60 to 70 years old, $.75 to $1. We want whole families with at least three workers for the mill in each family.[11]

The wages quoted represented the daily, not hourly rate. One woman later recalled her family's move from the farm to the mill:

Mother decided she would sell the farm for she was in debt and the farm was poor and small. She did not get much for it but did pay all she owed and had enough to go to the city . . . I worked in a cotton mill and made between $4.50 and $7.00 a week. Mother washed, ironed and cleaned house for other people to keep the rest of the children in school.[12]

Lacking child-care facilities, some women brought their young children with them to the mill. Children growing up around the machinery learned

Workers in the spinning room of the Piedmont Mill, circa 1920. Operating spinning machines, which involved moving quickly up and down a row of spinning frames repairing breaks and snags, was generally considered women's work. Doffers, who replaced full bobbins with empty ones, were usually boys. Courtesy of the Pendleton District Historical and Recreational Commission.

to help their mothers and older siblings until they too were old enough to draw wages. Children as young as seven or eight were trained as doffers and sweepers. This use of child labor represented a continuation of rural practice. Farm children had regular chores that were vital to the family's well-being. Children in mill families were likewise expected to contribute to the family economy.

Textile factory production involved a number of tasks. Bales of cotton arrived in the opening room where machinery tore apart the packed cotton. A vacuum tube carried the fluffed cotton to the picker room where pickers removed debris and spread it into even, continuous sheets. Card hands operated carding machines that turned the sheets into loose ropes called "slivers." Other workers fed four or more slivers through a drawing frame that combined them into a single strand. Then the threads were roved and spun to permanently join and twist the fibers. The spun thread was collected on large bobbins. Workers called doffers replaced filled bobbins with empty ones. Each spinner maintained several spinning machines, repairing breaks and snags. Spoolers operated spooling frames that combined the thread from many bobbins.

In the weave room, warp threads (the long, lengthwise threads in a piece of cloth) were rolled onto the loom beam. A draw-in hand threaded the harness, then the beam and harness were placed on the loom. Weavers operated automatic Northrup looms, keeping the rotating battery of bobbins filled.[13]

Within the mill most jobs were segregated by sex. Spinners were always women, while only men worked in the card room. Weavers, however, included both men and women. Women's wages were generally about 60% of men's. The highest paid women's work was "drawing-in," the tedious process of threading individual warp threads through the harness, which was required every time the

loom pattern was changed.

Although black slaves had worked as weavers and spinners in home textile production and in antebellum factories, blacks were excluded from most mill work. Black men could sometimes unload cotton bales, load finished goods, and perform other heavy and less desirable jobs. For the most part racial segregation was merely accepted practice, but in South Carolina, the Segregation Act of 1915 made it illegal for mills to allow people of different races to work together in the same room.[14]

Opportunities for black women were even more limited, as only a few mills hired them for janitorial work. Many black women found employment doing laundry and domestic work for white families employed in the mills. Katie Geneva Cannon, of Kannapolis, North Carolina, recalled the experience of her family:

My mother worked as a domestic. At one point she made five dollars a week, and then she found by working for different people she could make five dollars a day. . . . It was always assumed that we would work. Work was a given in life, almost like breathing and sleeping. . . . The first work I did was as a domestic, cleaning people's houses. . . . All the black women I knew worked as domestics and all the black men I knew worked in Cannon Mills in the low-paying menial jobs. My father drove a truck and did whatever dirty work there was to be done.[15]

At first most mills hired workers for twelve-hour shifts, six days a week, but in 1907, South Carolina passed a law reducing the work week to sixty hours.[16] Surprisingly, many workers found the schedule and the work itself less demanding than farming. Others, however, accustomed to outdoor work and being their own bosses chose to return to farming rather than work in the confinement of the noisy mill. One woman later wrote, "At first I thought work in the mill a great experience, but I soon grew tired of working in such a place and would often long to be out in the open again."[17]

Some families maintained a compromise. Farm families living near mills sometimes kept their farms while some members commuted to mill jobs. Others farmed until harvest, then worked in the mill until spring planting time. During the mill expansion before World War I, labor shortages gave workers a high degree of flexibility in choosing when and where they would work.

Country people moving into the mill villages left behind the communities that had given them support and identity, but they adapted the established customs and habits of their rural heritage to their new living situation. Millhands tended livestock in barns provided by the company and planted gardens in community plots. The physical closeness of mill housing created a close-knit community among its inhabitants. Some millhands recalled communal work occasions held over from farming days: "They'd have women get together in the church basement. They'd have a quilting bee and they'd go down and they'd all quilt. One of them would have a good crop of cabbage, they'd get together and all make kraut. And up there at the barn they'd have a cornshucking."[18]

Companies established institutions such as churches and schools, aiming for control over villagers that was never fully achieved. Even the notorious company store, from which millhands were expected to purchase their necessities, operated in only one-third of Southern mills at the turn of the century and in only a handful by 1920.[19]

Many families tried to avoid running up accounts at the company store by gardening, preserving food, raising chickens, and fishing in the mill river during nonworking hours. Some women sewed for other people and made quilts to sell.[20]

Mill companies provided recreational activities for their villagers. Some sponsored brass bands that performed at public functions and competed with bands from other towns. Games between company-sponsored baseball teams were probably the most popular pastime in the villages. Mill management also set up sewing clubs, mothers' clubs, exercise classes, and other social clubs.

The first generation of mill families off the land may have continued to make clothing and quilts, from habit and from a continuing sense of thrift. Early Piedmont mills produced mainly coarser grades of cloth such as plain sheeting, suitable for quilt backs but less desirable for tops. By the 1930s local mill products also included printed cloth, and thrifty quiltmakers made use of mill ends and misprints discarded by the company. Mill workers used swatches of discarded mill ends as grease rags or sweat rags, and some women salvaged these and washed them for their quilts.[21] Some women had access to new fabrics as well. Lois Kay Spearman made an Indian Hatchet quilt about 1917. She got her fabric from the store of the Gossett Mill, in Williamston, where her father-in-law and husband worked.[22] She may have gotten her pattern from a magazine or other publication. Lois Kay Spearman made other quilts, including a 1918 Old Maid's Puzzle. The fabrics in her quilts may include some actually produced by the Gossett Mill.

The decades leading up to World War I represented a period of prosperity for textile workers. The expansion of Northern war-related factories drew off the surplus labor force, creating a seller's market for labor of all kinds. War preparations increased the demand for cotton goods, resulting in high cotton prices. Mill supervisors raised wages and shortened the work week in order to keep workers from returning to farming or seeking mill jobs elsewhere. Companies faced with large wartime orders paid large bonuses to keep their employees.[23]

The end of the war brought a sudden slump to the entire cotton industry. Suddenly faced with cancelled orders and stockpiled goods, mills cut back on wages and reduced production. In 1919 Southern textile workers, members of the United Textile Workers, staged a series of walkouts, beginning in Columbus, Georgia, and the Horse Creek Valley area of South Carolina. Unlike later strikes, the dispute of 1919 was settled equitably. In North Carolina, Governor Thomas W. Bickett defended the workers' right to collective bargaining, and workers and mill owners came to an agreement. In the wake of this success union membership increased and local chapters formed in many mills.

When the full force of the post-war textile depression hit the South in 1920, mills again reduced wages and cut back production. This time workers had fewer options. With little support from the business community during the economic downturn, strikers often were forced to go back to work to feed their families. Some mill owners welcomed strikes as a way of cutting back production and could easily "wait out" the strike. Since low cotton prices once again hit farmers hard, droves of potential new workers arrived to fill vacancies left by strikers.[24]

During the 1920s, mill owners faced severe price fluctuations. Firms facing bankruptcy were often taken over by competitors. Surviving companies sought to increase production by installing new, more efficient machinery and by using principles of "scientific management." Many workers lost their jobs. Remaining workers had to handle more machines for less pay, a situation they referred to as the "stretch-out."[25] A South Carolina woman described the new working conditions: "In the weaving department of a cotton mill we had been running around the average of twenty-four looms. After the stretch-out system was introduced, we were put on from eighty to one hundred looms and were given boys and girls to fill our batteries."[26]

In the earlier days millhands could

Sampler quilt pieced and appliqué print and solid-color cottons, 74" x 60", made by Winnie Marie Breazeale Roper (1910–80) with help from her sister Clara Breazeale Webb, Piedmont (Anderson County), South Carolina. Collection of Donna Roper. Photo by Terry Wild Studio.

Winnie Roper worked for Piedmont Manufacturing for 37 years, filling batteries in the weave room. Clara Webb had a deformed hand and could not work in the mill, but she worked at home and took in sewing. Pieced back, back to front edge treatment machine sewn, white quilting thread, 2–3 stitches per inch. An older quilt in the Chimney Sweep pattern forms the filling.

take short breaks or chat with co-workers while their machinery ran. The stretch-out created a less friendly work environment and diminished the importance of individual skill. Work, which had provided millhands with a degree of satisfaction, became more repetitive and routinized with fewer opportunities for individual control.

Some mill companies diversified operations to deal with the post-war slump. In Alamance County, North Carolina, J. Spencer Love experimented with rayon, the new "artificial silk," and his Pioneer Plant began to produce bedspreads. Although stiff, shiny, and woven on a narrow loom so that the finished spreads had a seam down the center, the bedspreads

became very popular. After upgrading equipment and technique, Love's Burlington Mills offered improved rayon bedspreads in more than ten patterns, including the Tree of Life, the Rose of Sharon, and the "basket number,"[27] creating interpretations of traditional quilt patterns using the new fabric.

The success of these spreads in the early 1930s shows that interest in Colonial Revival styles could be fulfilled in a variety of ways. At a time when a large number of middle-class women were making Double Wedding Ring quilts for their colonial style bedrooms, many working women preferred the modern luxury of rayon, though in patterns that reflected an older heritage.

By 1929 the crisis in textile employment erupted in a series of strikes across the Southeast. Beginning in the rayon mills in Elizabethton, Tennessee, walkouts quickly spread to other states. In South Carolina, thousands of workers in thirteen different mills struck to protest the stretch-out. This time government officials sided with manufacturers and called out the National Guard to put down strikes. In Marion, North Carolina, armed law officers attacked picketing mill-hands, killing six and wounding twenty-five.[28]

The most famous strike occurred at the Loray Mill in Gastonia, North Carolina. Bertha Hendrix, a Loray worker, described the conflict:

We worked thirteen hours a day, and we were so stretched out that lots of times we didn't stop for anything. . . . If we didn't keep our work up like they wanted us to, they would curse us and threaten to fire us. . . . One day some textile organizers came to Gastonia. . . . That night we had a meeting, and almost all the workers came. People got up and said that unless they got shorter hours and more money they would never go back to work. . . . The next morning, we were all at the mill at five o'clock to picket, but we couldn't get anywhere near the plant because the police and the National Guard were all around the mill and kept us a block away. We formed our picket line anyway, and walked up and down a street near the mill. . . . In the second week of the strike, the bosses went to other towns and out in the country and brought in scabs. The police and the National Guard made us keep away from the mill, so all we could do was watch the scabs go in and take our jobs.

We kept on with our picket line, though we didn't have much of a chance to persuade the scabs not to go in, because of the police and the guards. We were treated like dogs by the law. Strikers were knocked down when they called to the scabs, or got too near the mill. Every day more and more strikers were arrested. They kept the jail-house full of workers. Strikers were put out of their houses. All over our village you could see whole families with their household belongings in the street.[29]

The chief of police was killed, and Bertha's husband was one of seven strikers convicted of the murder. With the death of union leader Ella May Wiggins three months later, the Gastonia strike collapsed.[30] The stock market crash of 1929 and subsequent national depression effectively ended mill workers' hopes for improvement.

Although women were usually underrepresented in organized labor nationally, they took a major role in Southern labor disputes. Union organizers from the North, primarily men, often lacked the resources or motivation to help women improve the lives of their families.[31] Southern mill women walked picket lines alongside men, operated soup kitchens, and organized relief efforts for families made destitute by extended disputes. The important role of women in these efforts is underscored by historian Mary Frederickson: "The fact that so many Southern women became involved in protests, walk-outs, or clearly defined strikes during this period convinced [them] that as a group they had an important role to play in ongoing effects to organize workers across the South."[32] A South Carolina mill worker described such work by women in 1929:

I will tell you a little of our hardships during our strike for we did not have a union at that time although we have one now that is growing in number and enthusiasm. We organized a relief committee which traveled over different parts of South Carolina and collected money and food for the most destitute of us that we might hold onto our cause. Wherever our committee went they always met people who knew about us and what a fight we were making and everyone was glad to help.[33]

By 1932, nearly a quarter of the American labor force was unemployed. During his first year in office President Franklin D. Roosevelt created the National Recovery Administration (NRA) to deal with problems in American industry. Employers were encouraged to increase profits by controlling production, hours, and wages. NRA files in the National Archives preserve a remarkable series of letters written to the

president and the NRA Board by ordinary citizens. Letters from unemployed mill workers reveal great hardship mixed with hope that the president and the NRA might right the wrongs in their lives. Henry Coyle of Gaffney, South Carolina, wrote "I believe it will be a National Faith Recovery administration. I am a long ways from you in distance yet my faith is in you my heart with you and I am for you sink or swim."[34]

The hopes of 1933 gave way to despair by 1934 as workers saw

Indian Hatchet pieced print and solid-color cottons, 84½" x 66", made by Lois Kay Spearman (1897–1921), Williamston (Anderson County), South Carolina, circa 1916. Back to front edge treatment, pink quilting thread, 4–5 stitches per inch. Collection of Frank and Mary Spearman. Photo by Terry Wild Studio.

The fabrics for this quilt came from the Gossett Mill store where Lois Spearman's husband worked.

conditions worsen. "One of the boss men told my sister if they did go on eight hours and pay $12.00 a week they would sure put out some hard work for it," wrote a spinner at a North Carolina mill. "When I came out of the mill down here last Friday evening I had worked so hard till I felt like I was nearer dead than I was liveing. . . . I had worked so hard till I just staggered like a drunk man and I wasn't the only girl that come out of the mill in that condition."[35]

Ultimately the NRA was ineffective in controlling textile production or bettering the lot of mill workers. Manufacturers used the NRA to justify turning the twelve-dollar minimum wage into a maximum wage by requiring a certain level of production for full pay and firing workers who could not meet production.[36]

In 1934, in response to a call for further cutbacks in production, Southern workers conducted a series of wildcat strikes that started in northern Alabama and soon engulfed other states. Workers demanded a twelve-dollar minimum wage for a thirty-hour week, abolition of the stretch-out, reinstatement of workers fired for union activity, and recognition of the union. Within two months, more than 400,000 Southern textile workers had walked out, marking the largest single labor conflict in American history.[37] State government officials, including South Carolina Governor Ibra Blackwood, called out the National Guard to arrest picketing millhands and place them in barbed wire enclosures.[38]

Mills hired hungry farmers and nonunion millhands to replace strikers, and many conflicts between unionists and strikebreakers ended in violence. At Chiquola Mill in Honea Path, South Carolina, Mack Duncan recalled the bloodiest battle:

The people that had the guns were nonunion people. Nobody ever saw a striker with a gun. It was a regular riot, was what it was. . . . And when it was over there was a lot of people hurt lying on the ground. They'd been shot and beat. And seven people were killed. And some of the others were crippled for life.[39]

President Roosevelt set arbitration machinery in motion and asked the United Textile Workers (UTW) to break off the strike and employers to take back striking workers. The strike ended but reprisals against union members continued. Within a year the Supreme Court declared the National Industrial Recovery Act unconstitutional, thus effectively ending union hopes for federal support.[40] Blacklisted from textile jobs, unionists left the Southeast, found other work, or went on relief. These events left a legacy of profound distrust of mill owners, trade unions, and government that remains among Southern workers more than fifty years later.

World War II revived the textile industry to some degree. As male textile workers left to become soldiers, the percentage of female workers increased. Some young women made quilts during this time. Ruth Ellis, of Anderson County, made an appliqué Lotus Blossom around 1940 when she was twenty years old and working in a mill. In 1945 Inez Hudson appliquéd a Dutch Doll quilt top (also called Colonial Lady) for her hope chest. She worked second shift in a Pickens County mill and worked on the quilt top in the mornings. Her mother, Mattie Hudson, quilted it. Neither Ruth Ellis nor Inez Hudson married, perhaps because so many men of their generation died in the war. Both women selected popular mail-order patterns for their quilts.[41]

The Southern textile industry of the late twentieth century has changed dramatically from the two-room spinning factories of a century ago. Large, successful companies have diversified and taken over smaller concerns. Improved machinery has virtually eliminated manual work, so that only a small labor force can operate a large plant. Both women and men form the shrinking textile work force. Mill closings are traumatic and fearful, but regular occurrences, as older, less efficient operations are eliminated by multinational, conglomerate corporations. Manufacturers use textile imports as a smokescreen to cover automation's reduction of the labor force.

Remaining Piedmont mills produce not only plain woven cloth but also a wide range of synthetics, knits, and finished clothing. Mill outlet stores that sell off-prints and leftovers are frequented by thrifty quilters, but they are not the only ones who have made quilts using mill fabrics. In 1969 Mary Abrams made a quilt from shirting scraps from the Raycord Shirt Company in Greenville. Her husband was the president of the company.[42]

In many ways quiltmakers in mill villages were not so different from their cousins who stayed on their farms. Women in the cotton-growing and manufacturing area shared a number of options when it came to providing bedding for their families. The choice to buy blankets or make quilts depended largely upon the family's economic situation, which in turn was determined by changes in the national economy. The motivation to make quilts continued to depend upon personal and individual factors. Some women continued to make everyday quilts from a sense of thrift in order to save money for other expenditures, while their neighbors in similar circumstances decided to purchase blankets.

Likewise certain quiltmakers, both on the farm and in the mill village, made sacrifices in order to purchase new fabric for special quilts. A group of approximately two dozen South Carolina quilts known to have been made by women in textile mill villages includes both utilitarian and fancy quilts made from both local and nonlocal fabrics.

An awareness of Southern textile history does not always provide answers to specific textile puzzles. Sometimes it can lead to the formation of many new questions. A quilt made in the mill village of Newry, in Oconee County, South Carolina, demonstrates how much more there is to know about mill village women and their quilts.[43] At first examination the quilt appears to be a typical fundraising quilt, made from large, unpatterned square blocks embroidered with many names. While churches were the usual sponsors of such quilts,[44] this one was made by the Newry "Get Together Club."

The quilt is dated 1934, the nadir of the Great Depression and the year of the General Strike. People paid a nickel to have their names added and to have a chance on the quilt. That was a lot of money at a time when many Americans were out of work and mill workers were fighting or striking for the opportunity of earning twelve dollars a week.

We know that the quilt was not made to raise money for the union because right in the center, in the place of honor, is a block that represents the mill, "The Courtenay Manufacturing Company." What was the "Get Together Club"? Was it one of the social clubs formed by the company? What was the particular situation in Newry in 1934? Did the village somehow escape the conflict that raged around them? What occasion prompted the creation of this quilt? Who are the people whose names are listed? Were these loyal, nonunion workers celebrating having jobs? Were unionists excluded? Was the quilt made before or after the general strike? How was the money used?

When the quilt was displayed at the July 4, 1986, Newry Homecoming, and again in 1993 during Newry's Centennial Reunion, villagers and former villagers eagerly searched it for familiar names. Today's retired mill workers were children when the quilt was made. They have few memories or handed-down stories of the events of 1934. For them the quilt is a document of the participation of their families within the Newry community, which sets them apart from more

recent arrivals.

What appears at first glance to be a straightforward cloth document, providing its own interpretation through the words recorded on its surface, instead becomes an enigma in its own right. While research often turns up answers to historical inquiry, in this case it has presented additional questions to be pondered about the lives of Southern mill villagers and their quiltmaking activities.

Notes and References

[1]Laurel Horton, "Quiltmaking Traditions in South Carolina," in *Social Fabric: South Carolina's Traditional Quilts*, eds., Laurel Horton and Lynn Robertson Myers (Columbia, SC: McKissick Museum, 1985), 15–17.

[2]Harold D. Woodson, "Sequel to Slavery: The New History Views the Postbellum South," *Journal of Southern History* 43 (November 1977), 523–54.

[3]Steven Hahn, *The Roots of Southern Populism: Yeoman Farmers and the Transformation of the Georgia Upcountry, 1850–1890* (Chapel Hill, NC: University of North Carolina Press, 1982), 239–68.

[4]Gavin Wright, *Old South, New South: Revolution in the Southern Economy Since the Civil War* (New York: Basic Books, 1986) 55–57.

[5]Diane L. Fagan Affleck, *Just New From the Mills: Printed Cottons in America, Late Nineteenth and Early Twentieth Centuries* (N. Andover, MA: Museum of American Textile History, 1987), 11.

[6]An example of such a family textile collection is described in "News Far and Near: The Blair Quilts," *The Quilts of Tennessee: Images of Domestic Life Prior to 1930*, Bets Ramsey and Merikay Waldvogel, (Nashville, TN: Rutledge Hill Press, 1986), 81–92.

[7]Jacquelyn Dowd Hall, et al., *Like a Family: The Making of a Southern Textile Mill World* (Chapel Hill, NC: University of North Carolina Press, 1987) 31.

[8]Ibid., 25.

[9]Pieced and appliqué Carolina Lily quilt (GRE-104), made by Victoria Cunningham Bailey, Bailey's Crossroads, SC, ca. 1970, in private collection. Interview, South Carolina Quilt History Project, March 1984.

[10] Hall, 33.

[11]August Kohn, *The Cotton Mills of South Carolina* (Columbia, SC: South Carolina Department of Agriculture, Commerce, and Immigration, 1907), 23.

[12]Mary Frederickson, "Recognizing Regional Differences: The Southern Summer School for Women Workers," *Sisterhood and Solidarity: Workers' Education for Women, 1914–1984*, eds., Joyce L. Kornbluh and Mary Frederickson (Philadelphia: Temple University Press, 1984), 161.

[13]Hall, 49–50.

[14]Ibid., 66.

[15]Victoria Byerly, *Hard Times Cotton Mill Girls: Personal Histories of Womanhood and Poverty in the South* (Ithaca, NY: Cornell University Press, 1986), 35–36.

[16]Hall, 77.

[17]Frederickson, 163.

[18]Hall, 151.

[19]Ibid., 130.

[20]Interview (CHR-12, CHR-13), South Carolina Quilt History Project, 1985.

[21]Interview, South Carolina Quilt History Project, March 1984.

[22]Pieced quilt Indian Hatchet (AND-38), made by Lois Kay Spearman, Williamston, SC, 1920, in private collection.

[23]Hall, 183–84.

[24]Ibid., 185–90, 198.

[25]Ibid., 196, 211.

[26]Frederickson, 172.

[27]Hall, 247–48.

[28]Ibid., 212–14.

[29]Bertha Hendrix, "I Was in the Gastonia Strike," in Frederickson, 175–76.

[30]Hall, 215.

[31]Frederickson, 149.

[32]Ibid., 165.

[33]Frederickson, 177.

[34]Hall, 291.

[35]Ibid., 296.

[36]Ibid., 289–93.

[37]Ibid., 328–29.

[38]Ibid., 332.

[39]Ibid., 340.

[40]Ibid., 350.

[41]Appliqué quilt Lotus Blossom (AND-40), made by Ruth Ellis, Anderson County, SC, ca. 1940, in private collection; appliqué quilt Dutch Doll (PIC-79), made by Inez Hudson, Pickens County, SC, ca. 1945, in private collection.

[42]Unnamed pieced quilt (GRE-139), made by Mary Abrams, Greenville, SC, 1969, in private collection.

[43]Embroidered quilt (OCO-32), made by the Get Together Club, Newry, SC, 1934, in private collection.

[44]Dorothy Cozart, "A Century of Fundraising Quilts, 1860–1960," in *Uncoverings 1984*, ed. Sally Garoutte (Mill Valley, CA: American Quilt Study Group, 1985), 42.

Quilt
Cottage
Industries

A Chronicle

Cuesta Ray Benberry

I n addition to the provision of a practical solution for the making of necessary bedcoverings, and the provision of aesthetic satisfaction to the quiltmaker, a third factor as to why some quilts were made can be explored: the economic factor. Quilt lore is replete with stories of quilters who made and sold quilts individually, or who made quilts "on shares" with another person, or who made quilts to be sold in a variety of formal and informal arrangements.

Primarily in twentieth-century America, there came into being an organized group method of making and selling quilts: the quilt cottage industry. Cottage industries were so named because much of the work was done in the small homes or cottages of the workers. The antecedents of the quilt cottage industry can be traced to a centuries-old tradition: the Old World needlework cottage industries. To push the ancestry of this phenomenon back further in time, the needlework cottage industries can be shown to have more than a tenuous relationship to the medieval craft guilds of Europe. Over the years changes and adaptations occurred so that by the eighteenth century needlework cottage industries had their own configuration. The medieval craft guilds' rigid hierarchic classifications of apprentices, journeymen, and masters were not adhered to in the later, more informal needlework cottage industries.

Cuesta Ray Benberry, *quilt historian and archivist, has conducted quilt research since the late 1950s. She is the author of* Always There: The African-American Presence in American Quilts, *co-editor of* A Patchwork of Pieces: An Anthology of Early Quilt Stories, 1845–1940, *and has written numerous research-based quilt articles, 5150 Terry Avenue, St. Louis, MO 63115.*

Members of the Martin Luther King, Jr., Freedom Quilting Bee of Gees Bend, Alabama, pictured in the August 1968 issue of Fortune magazine, displaying one of their early quilts. This African-American quilting group, organized in 1966, was one of the first quilt cooperatives formed in poverty-stricken areas of the rural South. Collection of Cuesta Ray Benberry.

Sampling of promotional materials by various quilt cottage industries from the 1920s into the 1980s. From top to bottom, clockwise: the Gazebo, New York; Eleanor Beard Inc., Hardinsburg, Kentucky; Appalachian Craftsmen, Huntington, West Virginia; Wool and Woo, St. Louis, Missouri; Mary McElwain Quilt Shop, Walworth, Wisconsin; Allanstand Industries, Asheville, North Carolina; Grassroots Craftsmen, Jackson, Kentucky; Freedom Quilting Bee, Gees Bend, Alabama; Kay McFarland, Topeka, Kansas; Nancy Lincoln Guild, New York; Cabin Creek Quilters, Malden, West Virginia; Laura Copenhaver, "Rosemont," Marion, Virginia.

In 1782 in Edinburgh, Luigi Ruffini, an Italian, set up a professional shop for making tambour embroidery with twenty girls and three boys as apprentices. His male apprentices were trained to draw out the designs. Ruffini opened another tambour shop in Dalkeith in 1790.[1] In 1814, Mrs. Jamieson, wife of an Ayr cotton agent, organized a needlework cottage industry of Ayrshire embroidery. She taught the outworkers (a British term for cottage industry workers). No poor work was tolerated and it had to be finished on time. Designs were drawn by professional draftsmen.[2] In 1878, the New York Exchange for Women's Work was founded by Candace Wheeler. A variety of needlework items, including quilts, were among the handicrafts marketed by the organization. The New York Exchange was not merely a marketing vehicle. Standards were set as to the quality of the items to be sold and supervision was supplied.

In the United States, a tracing of the specific historical chronology of quilt cottage industries reveals that the concept was mainly a twentieth-century one, with perhaps a few examples dating from the late nineteenth century. The most historically significant early needlework cottage industry did not focus the bulk of its work on the making of quilts. Yet it was so outstanding that it is being used as the prototype with which ensuing needlework and quilt cottage industries, reported in this chapter, can be compared. That paragon of a needlework cottage industry was a Massachusetts organization, the Society of Blue and White Needlework of Deerfield. Two artists, Margaret Whiting and Ellen Miller, became very interested in the old Connecticut Valley blue and white crewel embroideries for their beauty and historical value. The majority of these lovely needlecraft pieces belonged to old families in the area. Some of the items were in fragile condition; the wool embroideries were often moth-eaten and in advanced stages of deteriora-

tion. Whiting and Miller wanted to preserve this unique body of designs and to foster a revival of interest in what they considered to be an indigenous American art form. So, in August 1898, they established the Society of Blue and White Needlework of Deerfield. An additional objective was to help relieve poverty in the area by hiring a number of local women to do the actual embroidering. To that end they decided to get a return that should make the effort profitable, to produce the best possible work, and to maintain that standard. They worked out their costs so that the full price of each piece was divided into ten parts: five parts to go to the embroiderer (who would be paid twenty cents an hour), two parts for the designer, two parts to the "fund" (which was used to pay the running expenses of the society), and the one remaining part to cover the cost of the materials used.[3] Miller and Whiting decided to work with flax rather than wool thread to prevent moth damage. Deerfield blue and white needlework was used to form small mats and larger items including embroidered

coverlets, curtains, dresses, and table linens identified by their coloring, generally blue on white, and also signed with a capital D surrounded by a spinning wheel.[4]

The Society of Blue and White Needlework was a successful endeavor. Its designs were a mixture of traditional patterns and original, tradition-influenced, yet simplified, designs. The society assiduously maintained strict quality control over workmanship and the materials used. Soon women from all over the United States were coming to buy the embroideries of the Society of Blue and White Needlework of Deerfield. Except for an interruption of services during the First World War, the organization continued to flourish until

The Deerfield Society of Blue and White Needlework exhibition catalog from 1911 and a pattern drawing seen here, along with four completed pieces, which used the indigo-dyed linen thread. Collection of Pocumtuck Valley Memorial Association, Memorial Hall, Deerfield, Massachusetts. Photograph by Joe Coca, copyright by Interweave Press. First appeared in PieceWork *magazine, March/April 1993.*

1925 when it was disbanded.[5] By 1925, Miss Whiting's eyesight had begun to fail, and she and Miss Miller both believed they had accomplished their original objectives. For its time, the Society of Blue and White Needlework was highly sophisticated.

Although not structured exactly as its predecessor, the Society of Blue and White Needlework of Deerfield, a true quilt cottage industry, the Quilting Bee of Rye, New York, evolved in a small Westchester County town in 1913. A 1916 newspaper interview with the group's organizer read:

"We started the Quilting Bee three years ago," says Mrs. J. B. Putnam, president, "to give congenial employment to women and girls here in Rye, who needed it and to revive the art of quilting, in which we were much interested. Three other Rye women and I originated the idea. Those three are Mrs. Daniel O'Day, Mrs. Edwin Binney and Mrs. Arthur Chester. Last year the Quilting Bee was incorporated. . . . We are self-supporting now and we hope to make this a paying business . . . to get an income out of it, so that we can make it a cooperative. There are twenty people on our payroll, and we have a waiting list of applicants."[6]

In the beginning, an exhibition of beautiful antique quilts, borrowed from Westchester County residents, was held. It generated much enthusiasm among the Rye village women, who then joined the Bee. The women were instructed in quiltmaking by Mrs. O'Day. Already famed in art circles, the talented Mrs. O'Day also did most of the designing of the appliqué quilts.[7] The first order for a quilt came to the Quilting Bee of Rye, New York, when a visitor, who had attended the exhibition, wanted a faithful reproduction of one of the displayed antique quilts. More orders came. By 1917, a leading woman's magazine reported: "And so the work of the Bee developed gradually and naturally and at the present time orders are being taken, received from cities all over the country and from points in China, Manila, and South Africa."[8] Prices for finished quilts

varied from $75.00 to $150.00. Basted quilts' prices ranged from $16.00 for Tulip; $18.00 for Poke Berry; $20.00 for Moss Rose; and $22.00 for Trumpet Creeper.[9] The Quilting Bee, Rye, New York, gave gainful employment to women and girls in the town. Historically, it is recognized as one of the early twentieth-century quilt cottage industries.

Concurrent with the existence of the Society of Blue and White Needlework of Deerfield and the Quilting Bee of Rye, New York, in the northeastern section of the country, a strong handicraft revival movement was developing in the Southern Highlands region. Schools and cottage industries were established that fostered handicrafts such as spinning, weaving, furniture making, wood-carving, and patchwork quiltmaking. Within this handicraft movement the weaving of coverlets held a more prominent place than the making of patchwork quilts. One can locate records of a number of cottage industries in the handicraft movement in the Southern Highlands devoted solely to weaving. There were few cottage industries in this movement solely devoted to quiltmaking. A cottage industry that included quilts in a diversified setting of offerings was Rosemont Industries, organized by Laura Copenhaver.

In 1920, the Farm Bureau at Marion, Smyth County, Virginia, at the suggestion of Mrs. Laura Copenhaver, who at the time was a member of the Bureau, organized an industry to utilize the surplus wool resulting from a depressed market following the World War. The wool was bought for cash from the farmers, and . . . was woven into coverlets

from old patterns that had been preserved as precious possessions. These coverlets were sold through women's clubs and parent-teacher associations.

The Farm Bureau was later moved from Marion but the coverlet weaving was left there in charge of Mrs. Copenhaver. . . . By this time many women were urging Mrs. Copenhaver to give them work, offering to weave, to hand-tie, to hook, to quilt. She responded by assuming personal responsibility for the undertaking and became deeply interested in reviving the old handcrafts for women of the mountains.[10]

The cottage industry was described thus in a periodical: "The Rosemont Workers, a group of women organized by Laura S. Copenhaver and whose work has its center at Rosemont, Mrs. Copenhaver's home, are busy all year 'round hooking rugs, knitting, crocheting, and weaving coverlets; hand-tying fringes and canopies for four poster beds; quilting, and weaving luncheon sets."[11] In an interview, Mrs. Copenhaver stated, "At Rosemont we are trying to develop the crafts which are native, and yet in the mood of today, crafts that are concerned with useful household furnishings and that have the simplicity and beauty of our mountains."[12] From a beginning in weaving coverlets to consume unsold wool, the endeavor became a double service enterprise in discovering and nurturing almost forgotten household handicrafts and turning them into lucrative and pleasurable employment for a group of mountain women.

An early, undated Rosemont catalog (circa 1930s) lists double-bed quilt prices as only a quarter of their cost forty years later (see below).

A 1974 letter from Laura Copen-

	1930	1971	1973
Wild Rose quilt	$40.00	$150.00	$200.00
Forget-Me-Not quilt	$40.00	$150.00	$200.00
Grandmother's Flower Garden	$25.00		
Feathers quilt (not listed in '30s)		$150.00	$200.00
All-white or Solid Color Whole-Cloth quilt (not listed in '30s)		$120.00	$155.00

haver, Inc., to a California customer stated, "Workers now charge the same for twin bed-size as double bed-size." Prior to this, twin-bed quilts were usually $30.00 less than double-bed quilts.[13]

An example of a Southern Highlands handicraft movement cottage industry devoted solely to quilts was the Mountain Cabin Quilters. "The Mountain Cabin Quilters, organized at Wooten, Leslie County, Kentucky, in 1931, comprises a group of women who are banded together under the leadership of Mrs. J. K. Stoddard, wife of the community doctor, for the purposes of reproducing old mountain and colonial quilt patterns. The work is done entirely in the homes, some of the quilters often having to walk or ride 10 miles to get the order and instructions for a quilt." The group included both women who could sew quilts, as well as women who could "card the wool or cotton and make the batts that go into the quilt for padding. . . . During the summer of 1935 the business office for Mountain Cabin Quilters was moved to Cashiers, Jackson County, North Carolina."[14]

At the time the handicraft movement in the Southern Highlands was launched and was growing, in other parts of the country a quilt revival was occurring. A change in architectural and home furnishings styles from the gingerbread houses and fussy, crowded, over-decorated furnishings of the late Victorian period to a preference for the Cape Cod and Colonial-style homes in the early twentieth century can be considered a factor in the renewed interest in quilts. Just as in the 1980s the popularity of the Country style of home furnishings increased the demand for patchwork quilts, so in the early twentieth century did the Colonial style stimulate a desire for patchwork quilts. The Southern Highlands region's contribution to the quilt revival was not inconsiderable. Quilt scholars and researchers went into the South-

ern Highlands and found old and often unique quilt patterns and a veritable treasure-trove of colorful, orally transmitted quilt lore.[15] Their reports also indicated that a characteristic much admired by Americans, conscientious craftsmanship, was endemic to the Southern Highlands. This information was often published in periodicals of national circulation, and helped to create an aura for quilts. Frequently when a person bought a handmade quilt, she believed she was purchasing more than an attractive bedcover. She was acquiring history, folklore, and legend. So cottage industries solely devoted to quilts began to flourish.

An early twentieth-century quilt cottage industry was the organization that came to be known as the Wilkinson Sisters of Ligonier, Indiana. Two sisters, Rosalie and Ona Wilkinson, headed a cottage industry that eventually was nationally famous for its expensive silk, satin, or sateen quilts, which the Wilkinsons called "Art Quilts." Most of the full-size quilts in their catalog were wholecloth quilts with perhaps a large personalized monogram in the center. A few appliqué patchwork quilts, such as the Rose of Sharon, were sold by the Wilkinson sisters.

Rosalie Wilkinson started the company after she became dissatisfied with the Ladies' Aid Society, for whom she worked. The Ladies' Aid Society made quilts for sale—"Pretty quilts, well-made and substantial." Rosalie wondered why they did not make something different and something really artistic. When an order came to the society for a bridal quilt, she was asked to design this "different" quilt. She worked out a pattern that was a creation of soft rose pink satin quilted with hearts. From that day on, the design was known as the "Honeymoon Quilt."[16] As more and more orders came in, Rosalie Wilkinson traveled twice a year to places such as Atlantic City, Palm Beach, or California's fashionable Coronado

Beach to show her "Wonder Quilts." The Wilkinson baby quilts were sateen, filled with lamb's wool from Australia, and designed specifically to appeal to the owner's desire for cultural refinement.[17] Here's a present-day author's assessment of the Wilkinson baby quilts: "The ultimate effect was more precious than charm-

A baby quilt from the catalog of the Wilkinson Sisters, "Art Quilts," of Ligonier, Indiana, 1921. The Wilkinson Sisters, Rosalie and Ona, catered to the luxury market and used only fine silks, satins, and woolens in their quilts. Collection of Merikay Waldvogel.

ing, lacking the true artistry of the crib quilts produced by America's nonprofessionals."[18] What does seem apparent is that the Wilkinson sisters aimed their quilts at the luxury market.

Indiana was also the location for other successful quilt businesses, the Practical Patchwork Company of Marion and the Esther O'Neill Company of Indianapolis. Practical Patchwork was a mail-order quilt cottage industry established by Marie D. Webster, circa 1920. Marie Webster, whose influence as a quilt designer, author, and entrepreneur is today a matter of historical record, wrote the first full-length quilt text, *Quilts, Their Story and How to Make Them,* in 1915. When she formed the Practical Patchwork Company, Webster had already attained national prominence by having a number of her beautiful, tradition-changing quilts published in the most prominent women's magazine of that time, *Ladies' Home Journal.* Always the innovator, Webster produced paper quilt patterns for Practical Patchwork that were unlike patterns available from other sources. Her patterns, original designs only, were printed on draftsman-type blueprint paper and on colored tissue paper in the colors of the original quilt. Practical Patchwork regularly published editions of an illustrated catalog titled *Quilts and Spreads* that divided the company's inventory into listings of full-size and baby quilts. Paper quilt patterns, basted quilts, and fully completed quilts were sold directly from Marion, and from outlets such as Marshall Field, in Chicago, and Eleanor Beard, Inc., in Kentucky. Marie Webster's legacy not only included her landmark book and her successful pioneer quilt cottage industry, but she also helped to change and modernize the American appliqué quilt. A letter of admiration for Mrs. Webster's work was sent by Mrs. J. B. Putnam, organizer of another quilt cottage industry that specialized in appliqué designs, the Quilting Bee of Rye, New York.[19] One can gauge Marie Webster's effectiveness by the number of imitators who commercially reproduced her designs or copied her style.[20] Esther O'Neill Company, Indianapolis, sold stamped quilt kits, mostly appliqué, to be completed by the buyer.[21] The Esther O'Neill operation predated Practical Patchwork Company.

It was in this early twentieth-century period that the contemporary Kentucky quiltmaker's sewing prowess became legendary. Cottage industries located inside and outside of Kentucky proudly advertised that their quilts were handmade by the women of Kentucky. This is not meant to imply that Kentucky quiltmakers' reputations were not

well-deserved. It is simply that their skill became a strong selling point for cottage industries. The sewing prowess of the Kentucky quiltmakers was highly advertised and commercialized almost to the point of constituting a Kentucky quiltmaker's mystique, as indicated in a 1934 article:

Here in America the lifting of this rather pastoral art up to the place of really amazing expression of fine craftsmanship has been accomplished by the American Needlecraft Guild, which has its home in the mountains of Kentucky. . . . In fact, with original designs, executed with such perfection of detail, there seems no limit to

Poinsettia *quilt, pieced and appliqué of solid-color cottons, 94" x 62", designed by Marie D. Webster (1859–1956) of Marion, Indiana, in 1915. Courtesy of the Indianapolis Museum of Art, #IMA79.99, © Indianapolis Museum of Art. Gift of Mrs. Garrish Thurber.*

Her cottage industry, called Practical Patchwork, was organized in 1921 in response to the great demand for patterns of her quilts that had been widely publicized in issues of Ladies' Home Journal *and in her book,* Quilts, Their Story and How to Make Them. *The* Poinsettia *and nine other Marie Webster quilts are in the collection of the Indianapolis Museum of Art.*

the accomplishment of these craft workers of the Kentucky mountains.[22]

The Nancy Lincoln Guild, 514 Madison Avenue, New York, advertised itself as "A Product of Kentucky." On the cover of its catalog a specially designed logo read "Exquisite Hand Sewn Things from Kentucky." (It does seem the organization's very name—Nancy Lincoln Guild—had Kentucky connotations: that the company was named for Nancy Hanks Lincoln, Abraham Lincoln's mother). The company's brochure proclaimed "Quilts may come and quilts may go, but these will always be the most desirable for colonial rooms and for houses in summer." It described "Sweet Home," a floral appliqué quilt, as "one much favored in Kentucky and in the early colonies." A double-bed quilt sold for $39.50.[23]

In the January 1932 issue of *Good Housekeeping* there was an article, "New Quilts With Rugs to Match," by Anne Orr. A section of the page told of the possibilities of having one's quilt made by others. It stated, "There is a woman in Kentucky with sixty mountain women working under her direction, who will do your quilting. This work is exquisite. Write to Anne Orr for prices." An Anne Orr letter to a customer, who evidently had not followed the *Good Housekeeping's* directions and had by-passed Anne Orr by writing directly to the magazine, was a somewhat miffed reply explaining the correct procedure for getting quilts made by the Kentucky women.[24]

One of the most successful of the Kentucky quilt cottage industries was the Eleanor Beard Hedgelands Studio of Hardinsburg. By 1929, Eleanor Beard had offices and outlets in New York City (across the street from the Nancy Lincoln Guild), Pasadena, Santa Barbara, and Chicago.[25] An account that relates a personal experience with Eleanor Beard's Studio states, "Eleanor Beard's Studio

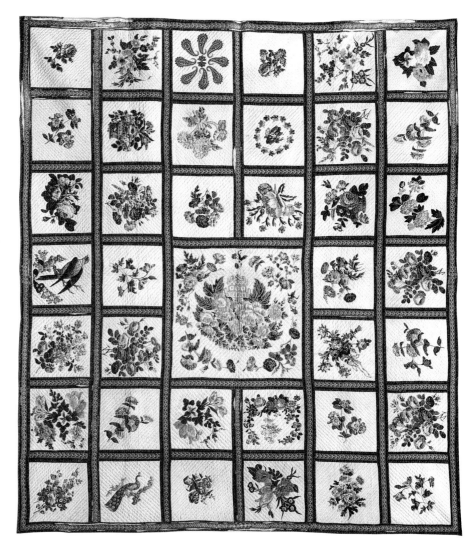

Broderie Perse quilt designed by Eleanor Beard Studio, "Hedgelands," Hardinsburg, Kentucky, circa 1921. Collection of the Metropolitan Museum of Art (#1971. 180.126). Courtesy of The Metropolitan.

meant the survival of the small town of Hardinsburg, Kentucky." Eleanor Beard's husband, Marvin, was the owner of a general store. He had accepted much raw wool from farmers in payment for merchandise instead of money because it was a time of great depression, and the farmers were strapped financially. The raw wool was stored in an attic where Eleanor Beard found it. She had the wool cleaned and processed in Louisville. Then she began a project of making silk quilted comforters, or whole-cloth quilts. She employed the women of Hardinsburg, including one who had professional designing experience. Eleanor Beard's organization grew and she engaged more and more of the town's women. Some quilters worked in her studio; others, especially those with small children, worked at home.[26]

As her business expanded, Eleanor Beard advertised in such publications of national circulation as *House Beautiful* and *Good Housekeeping*. Her advertisements were labeled as "Hand Quilted Things" and the list of items offered included bedspreads, comforters, chaise covers, pillows, travel sets, robes, and blanket covers. Examples of quilts in her 1920s advertisements were Windblown Tulip (72" x 90"), $22.50; Daisy (42" x 54"), $19.50; and Wild Rose (66" x 84"), $17.50. All these quilts made in cotton. The silk and taffeta items were more expensive. An unusual offering was a quilted chaise lounge throw called "French Pouf," taffeta on the topside, satin on the underside. The pouf was rectangular in shape, 35″ x 54″, with a matching oval pillow. There was a pocket on the underside for one's feet—"perfect for those half hour before dinner naps"—the ad promised. The cost of the throw was $40.00 and the matching oval pillow was $20.00.[27]

Additional Kentucky-based quilt cottage industries were conducted by Withers at Kirk, the Caden Sisters at Lexington, and Mrs. Dale Combs at Pebworth. Withers was best known in the 1920s for its quilted clothing, cushions, and baby things. A knee-length quilted robe in satin was $50.00, and in taffeta, $55.00. One of the Caden sisters, Margaret Rogers Caden, acquired fame by winning the Grand Prize of $1,000 in the 1933 Sears, Roebuck Century of Progress Quilt Contest at the Chicago World's Fair, for her Unknown Star quilt. As an honor, the winning Unknown Star quilt was presented to President Franklin D. Roosevelt's wife, Eleanor.[28] (The Unknown Star pattern later was popularly called Star of the Bluegrass.) The three Caden sisters ran their business from a shop in Lexington. Mrs. Dale Combs received so many orders for quilts after her lovely handwork got exposure at various fairs that she engaged her quilting neighbors to help her fill the orders. A favored quilt with Mrs. Combs' customers was the Beautiful Star of France, a Home Arts Studio, Des Moines, Iowa, 1930s pattern—a large, showy, pieced medallion.[29]

During the early twentieth century there were a number of quilt cottage industries located at various sites around the country. No quilt cottage industry elsewhere, however, seems to have acquired the panache of the ones that could state their quilts were made by the women of Kentucky.

In an interview with Mrs. Ralph E. Foster, Dorothy Cozart learned of an Oklahoma quilt cottage industry leader, Edna Foster of Perry. Mrs.

Foster made her first quilt in 1929, an embroidered quilt that ended up being too small. Her second quilt was Turkey Tracks, which she quilted herself. After some experience with quiltmaking, Mrs. Foster got an idea for a business venture. She cut and basted appliqué quilt blocks and sold them, ready to finish. When the buyer finished sewing the blocks, they were returned to Mrs. Foster, who set them together and did the quilting. Early in the venture Mrs. Foster realized she could not do all of the quilting by herself, and so she employed a group of Catholic women of St. Genevieve, Missouri. There were eleven of these women who quilted for Mrs. Foster until they were too old to quilt any longer. Several Amish women in Indiana, Iowa, and Missouri now do quilting for her during the winter, as summer is reserved for other Amish chores.[30]

Operating a quilt cottage industry as a component of a full-scale quilt service organization was the idea of Mary McElwain of Walworth, Wisconsin. Available from her Mary McElwain Quilt Shop were completed quilts and comforters, a large inventory of paper patterns, cotton and wool battings, waxed thread, needles, various quilter's notions, percale sheets, pillowcases, and a variety of fabrics. Mary McElwain hired a number of women to complete the appliqué and pieced quilts, to prepare some appliqué quilts by basting only, to stamp the cloth, to cut the patches, and to send the quilts out in kit form. Examples of Mary McElwain's 1936 prices: the elaborate appliqué Indiana Wreath quilt, finished $85.00, basted $45.00; a finished crib quilt (ABC quilt), $12.00, and a finished pieced quilt (Shoo Fly quilt), $40.00.[31]

Mary McElwain's mail-order service, which went all over the country, made her a well-known figure in the 1930s. She was one of the judges in the famous 1933 Sears, Roebuck Century of Progress Quilt Contest at the Chicago World's Fair. If her 1938 let-

ter to Betty Harriman, Bunceton, Missouri, is any indication, it appears that Mary McElwain's business practices were very personalized. In this letter she wrote that she did not have a fabric that Betty Harriman had requested, but she listed sources where she believed the fabric was available.[32] Mary McElwain's offerings increased over the years. It is believed she may have bought some of Marie Webster's inventory after Marie Webster retired. The Marie Webster catalog *Quilts and Spreads* was reprinted bearing the names Mary Ann McElwain and D'Ette McElwain, "The Mary A. McElwain Quilt Shop, Walworth, Wisconsin, near Lake Geneva." No paper patterns were offered in that catalog. She presented the Webster quilts only as boxed kits, basted quilts, or finished quilts. For example, the prices for the Marie Webster quilt Wreath of Roses were: stamped kit $12.50, basted top $22.50, and finished quilt $65.00.[33]

A rare occurrence happened within Mary McElwain's quilt cottage industry. One of its members became a prominent, one-woman quilt industry, sending out basted tops nationwide, as she did only the appliqué work on quilts that she sold. Lillian Walker of Fairfield, Iowa, was a master quiltmaker and designer. She contributed several original quilt patterns to the Mary McElwain inventory. Two of the original Lillian Walker patterns in the McElwain collection were Grandmother's Fancy and Garden Symphony with 10 Song Birds. Lillian Walker's trademark was featuring birds on her quilts. A May 1955 cover of *Sports Illustrated* inspired Lillian Walker to make a spectacular quilt, Bird Watcher's Guide, with various species of birds reproduced in minute detail. Lillian Walker's quilts were highly valued even then. Today they are collectors' items.[34]

In the 1930s, Marion Cheever Whiteside (Mrs. Roger Hale Newton) organized a quilt cottage industry named Story Book Quilts. Although the themes of her quilts were juvenile, the quilts were sold as both full-size and crib-size. Marion Cheever Whiteside was an artist; her base of operations was New York City, where she designed the quilts at her 1212 Fifth Avenue home. Two artists cut out the patches. Then the work was sent to home sewers all over the country for completion of the quilts. All of the quilts were pictorial appliqué. Whiteside received national publicity for her Story Book Quilts cottage industry when pictures of her quilts appeared in such magazines as *Ladies' Home Journal*, *Woman's Home Companion*, *McCall's*, and *Today's Woman*. *Ladies' Home Journal* ran an entire series of Marion Cheever Whiteside's Story Book Quilts, including Little Women, Peter Pan, Bridal quilt, Pinocchio, the Fireman quilt, and the Circus quilt. The quilts were featured in 1940s and 1950s issues of *Ladies' Home Journal*.[35] An interesting personal assessment of the Story Book Quilts was written in a letter by noted quilt authority Florence Peto to Emma Andres of Prescott, Arizona. Florence Peto disliked the sparse amount of quilting on the Whiteside quilts and the format of alternating large blank squares with the appliqué blocks. Nevertheless, some of the Whiteside quilts were accorded recognition by becoming a part of the permanent collection of prestigious museums, such as the Alice in Wonderland quilt owned by the Metropolitan Museum of Art in New York.[36]

In the late 1950s, Kay McFarland of Topeka, Kansas, operated a quilt cottage industry selling quilts by mail-order. She included both commercial quilt kits and "made from scratch" quilts in her catalogs. Pattern names of the commercial quilt kits were given but not the name of the company that designed them. Typical prices in Kay McFarland's listings were: Shirred Camellia (Paragon kit), double-bed size, $135.00; May Basket (scratch quilt), $90.00; Grandmother's

Pieced Tulip (scratch quilt) $90.00; and Double Wedding Ring (scratch quilt), $110.00. Most quilts were promised completed to the buyer within six to eight weeks. The majority of the quilters who participated in McFarland's cottage industry lived in Kansas. While conducting her cottage industry, McFarland attended law school. When she became a practicing attorney in 1965, she gave up her quilt business. Now Kay McFarland is a State Supreme Court judge in Kansas.[37]

A development occurred in the 1960s that could be termed a variation

Alice in Wonderland *quilt pieced and appliqué print and solid-color cottons, 65-5/8" x 45". Designed by Marion Cheever Whiteside Newton*, Story Book Quilts of New York City, *in 1945. Collection of the Metropolitan Museum of Art, Purchase, Edward C. Moore, Jr. Gift, 1945. (#45.38). Courtesy of The Metropolitan.*

of the traditional quilt cottage industry. This was the rise of quilt cooperatives. Many of the quilt cooperatives stemmed from the national anti-poverty programs engendered by President Lyndon B. Johnson's

"Great Society" initiatives. A number of the quilt cooperatives were projects of VISTA and the Office of Economic Opportunity and its various agencies. Some of the better-known quilt cooperatives were:

1. The Freedom Quilting Bee, Alberta, Alabama, a group of black quiltmakers, formed in 1966, later renamed the Martin Luther King, Jr., Freedom Quilting Bee. It became one of the first quilt cooperatives to gain national recognition.

2. Mountain Artisans, Sod, West Virginia, chartered in 1968. The group became famous partially from the very powerful support of Sharon Percy Rockefeller, wife of the Governor of West Virginia, and the innovative designs contributed by the New York-based professional artist, Dorothy Weatherford.

3. Cabin Creek Quilters, Eskdale, West Virginia, begun in 1970.

4. Dakotah Handicrafts, Webster, South Dakota, begun in 1970. Dakotah is the name given to the products of the cooperative titled TRACT. TRACT, composed of Sioux Indian women and rural white women, drew participants from the Sisseton Sioux Indian Reservation and three counties in South Dakota.

5. Grass Roots Craftsmen, Jackson, Kentucky, is a diverse group, with a quiltmaking component. It was incorporated in 1968, and includes persons who also practice crafts other than quilting.

Additional quilt cooperatives were Storm (White Hall, IL), Tennessee Craftsman (Columbia, TN), Ridge House Side Crafts Association (Sugargrove, NC), and the Sunflower County Quilters (Sunflower County, MS). The Sunflower County Quilters was a black quilting group.[38]

Dolores Hinson, a noted quilt author, worked with quilt cooperatives overseen by the Tennessee State Arts Commission and the Office of Economic Opportunity in the early 1970s. Her assignment was to help the groups make their quilts salable. The workmanship was fine but the quilters had been compelled to sell their quilts quite cheaply. Fabrics such as used materials, "seconds," and

throwaway materials had cheapened their products. With a combination of instruction and practical advice, Dolores Hinson was able to upgrade the work of the Tennessee groups. Her next step was to take these rural women to Nashville, Tennessee, and to other urban centers to see what the women called "durn fool" city folk were willing to pay for quilts. The quilters had practically been giving their quilts away for extremely small sums—ten to fifteen dollars each. Now they were motivated to do better work and to use finer fabrics. Working closely with the cooperatives, giving advice on marketing strategies, and observing a continual improvement of the product, Dolores Hinson was gratified when the women were finally engaged in a profitable business.[39]

In the 1980s, it appeared that the chapter on quilt cooperatives might be coming to an end. Those cooperatives that were able to establish a firm commercial base may survive. Other cooperatives still linked to federal and state funding agencies have faced an uncertain future. In some cooperatives, workers are paid by the piece. A U.S. Labor Department study has determined that wages in cooperatives often averaged out at below the minimum hourly wage of $3.35. In labor-intensive crafts such as quilting, if the workers are paid the minimum hourly wage, the cost of the quilts may be boosted so high that an increase in the sales of cheaper quilts from Haiti and China would result. The firm espousal of the International Ladies Garment Workers Union of laws against home work is creating additional problems for quilt cooperatives.[40]

Like electronics, steel, shoes, leather goods, textiles, and manufactured apparel, the quilt cottage industries now have foreign competition. Some of the American businesses that use foreign women to make quilts do not publicize that fact. One very chic New York boutique, however, states quite openly that its quilts are made by the women of Haiti. So Haiti's needlework connection is not confined to the sewing of baseballs for major league teams.

In the early 1970s, two New York women formed a cottage industry using home sewers in Connecticut. Their company was called Hands All Around. They took antique quilts and had them cut up to make pillows that were then sold in many big-city department stores. Some of the cut-up quilts were advertised as dating from 1850 and earlier. At that time, Hands All Around believed the antique quilt pillows gave Americans "a share of their history."[41]

In the 1980s, there were still traditional quilt cottage industries. Tricia Woo of St. Louis, Missouri, established the first Wool and Woo shop in 1971. Today nearly one hundred women in Missouri and Illinois piece traditional quilt patterns and newer designs for Tricia Woo's three St. Louis stores. Some of the best-selling designs are Missouri Waltz, Lone Star, Variable Star, Log Cabin, Double Wedding Ring, and a Tricia Woo original, City Blocks.[42]

Bryce and Donna Hamilton of Minneapolis, Minnesota, have a flourishing quilt cottage industry. Their quilts are sold on a consignment basis to twenty-five or thirty shops around the country. The favorite designs requested by their customers are Lone Star, Double Wedding Ring, Irish Chain, Louisiana Star, and Trip Around the World. In addition, the Bryce and Donna Hamilton Company takes orders for custom work. Although some of their quilters live in close proximity to the company, others are located in four or five Midwestern states.[43]

Preserving the craft of quilting and creating a steady market for their quilts seem to be the major objectives of most quilt cottage industries. Numerous cottage industries in New England, Pennsylvania, throughout the South, and on the West Coast appear to be thriving and prosperous.

Research on the topic of quilt cottage industries provides a sense of the history of these organizations, their origins, their structures, and their offerings to the public. Their quilts were made to meet a perceived demand. As people most often demand what they already know, the quilt cottage industries almost invariably produced familiar, traditional patterned quilts. New and original designs from these sources appeared on their quilts to a lesser degree. The Domino quilt from the Freedom Quilting Bee (during its early stages), the ethnic flavored designs from Dakotah Handicrafts, Lillian Walker's Grandmother's Fancy and Little Brown Church in the Vale, and Marion Cheever Whiteside's Story Book Quilts represent examples of original works from quilt cottage industries. As quilt cottage industries are expected to provide economic betterment for the quilters, I hoped to form some generalizations about the degree that financial arrangements made an impact on quilters' lives, but generalizations were not possible. Each cottage industry studied varied widely from unit to unit. Yet as we look at the larger picture of masses of unknown, unheralded quilt cottage industry quiltmakers whose handwork has beautified countless homes for many years, we know we are looking at one reality of American quilt history.

Members of Bear Soldier Quilters, a Lakota Sioux quilting group from the Standing Rock Reservation, contributed to the design of the All-American Quilt. *The quilt represents the combined efforts of three quilt cooperatives: Cabin Creek Quilters, West Virginia, Freedom Quilting Bee, Alabama, and the Bear Soldier Quilters. Courtesy of James Thibeault, Coordinator of Cabin Creek Quilters.*

The All-American Quilt *was an American response to the Smithsonian Institution's controversial licensing agreement that allowed its quilts to be replicated in a foreign country.*

Epilogue

When the report on quilt cottage industries was written in 1986, it did appear the end was near for the quilt cooperative movement that had begun in the 1960s. The loss of federal funding meant the loss of administrative workers paid by federal agencies. Those workers were to develop marketing strategies and to institute, within the organizations, training programs in sound business procedures. They were to enable the quilt cooperatives to become ongoing, stable, and successful commercial ventures capable of providing steady incomes for the members. Conflicts with the U.S. Labor Department's guidelines for minimum hourly wages, and the International Ladies Garment Workers' Union's opposition to textile work conducted at home were additional obstacles faced by the quilt cooperatives.

When the quilt cooperatives were able to secure a contract with a major merchandiser, the problem was to reconcile the rather slow process of sewing handmade quilts to the demands of the marketplace. To produce in large quantities, to obtain a semblance of uniformity in the quality of the product, and to meet the retailers' shipping deadlines frequently required the cooperatives to purchase expensive commercial sewing equipment, buy fabrics in huge quantities, and to organize the work force in an assembly line kind of production. When the Freedom Quilting Bee, in Gees Bend, Alabama, signed a contract with the Sears chain of stores, it was not for the unique handcrafted quilts that first gained recognition for the group. Instead, the Freedom Quilting Bee was to supply Sears with a large and continuous stream of corduroy pillow shams.[44] For the Freedom Quilting Bee, the Sears contract was a good source for a steady income. At times the contracts signed by the quilt cooperatives were not renewed at their expiration date because the retailers could get the work done more

cheaply by workers in such places as Taiwan, Haiti, the Philippines, Korea, and China.

In the interim between the early 1980s and the early 1990s, some of the quilt cooperatives ceased operations, while others suffered greatly reduced incomes. The surviving quilt cooperatives experienced troublesome times. The Freedom Quilting Bee went from an annual sale of 400 quilts and the income from their Sears contract, to a low of 8 quilts in a year, and the expiration and nonrenewal of the Sears contract. The Bee, in 1989, even after joining the Artisans Cooperative, a large organization in Chadds Ford, Pennsylvania, was compelled to send out a pleading letter soliciting charitable funds.[45] Yet today, the quilt cooperative movement is not dead. Supported by limited funding from local and state agencies and the private sector of local businesses, religious organizations, and concerned citizens, new quilt groups are pursuing the dream of making handmade quilts as a profitable business.

Two African-American sisters, Graffie Jackson and Jean Johnson of Lexa, Arkansas, started the quilt organization, Arkansas Country Quilts, and with the assistance of the Arkansas Industrial Development Commission were able to expand their building and the number of quiltmakers needed to make the quilts.[46] An example of the melding of religious entities and private businesses to support income-generating quiltmaking can be seen in the Mississippi Delta town of Tutwiler. Since the late 1980s, Catholic nuns, who staff the Tutwiler Clinic, have fostered a group of twenty-five impoverished local African-American residents' quiltmaking project. A 1989 article stated: "Bearing the label, 'Handmade by the Women of Tutwiler, Miss.,' 85 colorful quilts already have been sold through the Tutwiler Clinic Outreach Program, which is blossoming into a thriving cottage industry."[47]

An appeal published in the Tutwiler

Clinic newsletter, mailed to thousands of parishes and persons around the country, generated gifts of materials, patchwork scraps, much publicity, and welcomed orders for quilts. Angelica Uniform Company, of nearby Tallahatchie County, generously donated thread and materials. Led by the project director, Sister Maureen Delaney, the Delta Patchwork Quilts organization has accomplished much, raising both the quiltmakers' income levels and their self-esteem.

Another model for the initiation of a quilt project that later developed into a quilt cottage industry is represented by the nonprofit educational and cultural organization, Mississippi Cultural Crossroads, in Claiborne County. In the early 1980s, Mississippi Cultural Crossroads sought four African-American women to teach traditional quiltmaking to area middle school children. From securing a grant from the Mississippi Arts Commission for an especially gifted quiltmaker, Hystercine Rankin, to teach apprentices to make quilts, to sponsoring quilt exhibitions of local women's works, to holding quilt workshops, Mississippi Cultural Crossroads became more and more involved with Claiborne County quiltmakers. Under the leadership of Patricia Crosby, Mississippi Cultural Crossroads has combined forces with area women to market their quilts by providing space for a shop. In addition, they have sought marketing information from the Governor's Office of Economic Development.[48]

A dramatic development in the quilt cooperative movement resulted from one of the most rancorous situations ever to occur in the quilt community. As a fundraising effort, the Smithsonian Institution, Washington, DC, licensed American Pacific Enterprises to manufacture quilts copied from outstanding antique quilts in the collection of the National Museum of American History. The reproduced quilts were manufactured in the People's Republic of China, returned to the United States, and offered for sale in mail-order catalogs from such companies as Speigel's, Lands' End, Robert Redford's Sundance, and in numerous stores nationwide. The first four quilts replicated—the Bible quilt of Harriet Powers, a freed slave; the Great Seal of the United States quilt; an 1851 Maryland Bride's album quilt; and an 1850 Sunburst quilt—are so revered as to be considered cultural and artistic icons by Americans. Indignation and outrage from most of the quilt community greeted this transaction.[49] On National Quilting Day, March 20, 1992, incensed quilters from Everybody's Quilt Guild formed a picket line in front of the Smithsonian.[50] Hundreds of protest letters and signed petitions poured into the Smithsonian director's office and were sent to U.S. Congressional members who comprised the oversight subcommittee that funded the tax-supported national museum. A committee of prominent and influential persons in the quilt world met with Smithsonian and American Pacific Enterprises officials to dissent and to discuss possible means of rectifying the matter.[51] Aware of how the political process works effectively in Washington, DC, an American Quilt Defense Fund committee was organized to pursue an alternate strategy: lobbying.

Although the majority of quilt lovers expressed anger, severe disappointment, and even amazement at what they believed was the Smithsonian's extreme insensitivity to Americans' appreciation of these highly regarded artifacts of American folk culture, a smaller number of persons agreed with the Smithsonian's and American Pacific Enterprises' decision. These persons' statements, more or less, centered on the practical aspects of the endeavor, such as the relatively inexpensive retail costs of the Chinese imitations of American quilts, the copied quilts' wide availability, that licensing of museum

artifacts for reproduction was common, and the Smithsonian's very real financial straits. A vigorous debate on proper import labeling, ethical concerns of a tax-supported institution undercutting American quiltmakers for foreign labor, the choice of Smithsonian quilts to be replicated, the future of the imported quilts when acquired by unscrupulous dealers, and the overall impact of the massive importing of quilts on quiltmaking in the United States rages even today.

One worthwhile outcome of the debacle was the joining forces of three struggling quilt cooperatives to make truly American quilts. One counter claim of the manufacturer was there were not enough available American quilters to produce the quilts in the large quantities needed. Under the leadership of James Thibeault, Cabin Creek Quilters, Malden, West Virginia, a group of Appalachian quiltmakers; the Freedom Quilting Bee, Gees Bend, Alabama, an African-American quilt organization; and the Bear Soldier Quilters, a Lakota Sioux association from the Standing Rock Reservation in the Dakotas, joined forces to produce the "All-America" quilt, that Lands' End, a large mail-order company, has featured in its catalog.[52] High hopes for the cooperatives have been raised as Lands' End has promised to promote their future quiltworks.

Like Phoenix arising from the ashes, so has the quilt cooperative movement renewed itself. Who can predict what lies ahead for these grass-roots organizations?

Notes and References

[1]Margaret Swain, *Ayrshire and Other White Work: Shire Album 88* (Bucks, UK: Shire Publications, 1982), 11.

[2]Ibid., 15

[3]Margery Burnham Howe, *Deerfield Embroidery: Traditional Patterns from Colonial Massachusetts* (Deerfield, MA: Pocumtuck Valley Memorial Association, 1976), 23.

[4]Mary Taylor Landon and Susan Burrows Swan, *American Crewelwork* (New York: Macmillan, 1970), 87.

[5]Martha Genung Stearns, *Homespun and Blue: A Study of American Crewel Embroidery* (New York: Scribner's, 1940), 73.

[6]"Rye Revives the Quilting Bee as a Village Industry," *The Evening Sun* (Sept. 1, 1916). Collection of the New York Quilt Project. Phyllis Tepper provided valuable information about the Quilting Bee of Rye, New York.

[7]Irene Vandyck, "The Old Time Quilting Bee Is the New Fangled Thing," *The New York Press* (July 12, 1914). Collection of Joyce Gross.

[8]Lydia Littlefield, "The Quilting Bee Lives Again, First As A Socializing Influence and Then As A Paying Industry," *Modern Priscilla* (November 1917): 9.

[9]*The Quilting Bee, Rye, NY, Price List* (1923–24). A sales catalog. Collection of the New York Quilt Project. "The New Kind of Patchwork: Designs for Porch Furnishings," *Ladies' Home Journal* (June 1915): 22. "Full information as to the size, quality and price of each design will be given upon receipt of an addressed, stamped envelope," wrote the needlework editors of *Ladies' Home Journal.*

[10]Allen H. Eaton, *Handicrafts of the Southern Highlands* (New York: Russell Sage, 1937): reprint edition (New York: Dover, 1973): 76–77.

[11]Anne Ruffin Sims, "Rosemont Workers," *The Commonwealth* (February 1937): 12.

[12]Ibid., 13.

[13]Laura Copenhaver, Marion, VA, letter to Mrs. R. E. King, Napa, CA, June 17, 1974. Author's collection.

[14]Eaton, 87–88.

[15]Elizabeth Daingerfield, "Patch Quilts and Philosophy," *The Craftsman* (August 1908): 532–37.

[16]Maude Bass Brown, "Dollar Signs in Quilting," *Modern Priscilla* (October 1920): 3.

[17]*The Wilkinson Art Quilt* (Ligonier, IN: The Wilkinson Sisters, n.d.), 16. A sales catalog.

[18]Thomas K. Woodard and Blanche Greenstein, *Crib Quilts and Other Small Wonders* (New York: Dutton, 1981), 15–16.

[19]Letter to Marie Webster from Mrs. J. B. Putnam, director of the Quilting Bee, Rye, New York. "My dear Miss Webster, I wish to write and tell you that I appreciate [ ] about Quilts to the fullest extent— somewhat, perhaps [ ] especially interested in the subject. Your writing is exceedingly interesting, as well as most instructive. All that information about the Egyptian, Persian, Old English, and Armenian patchwork is not to be found every day, and you deserve much credit for laying it before us in so delightful fashion. The modern quilts are charming,

not the least so being your own designs of Grapes and Vines, and the very attractive 'Keepsake Quilt.' The Poppy design is beautiful, and the Morning Glory too, but so are all of them. It is difficult to choose. Altogether it is an exceedingly artistic book. I enclose a leaflet which shows our three cottages which are very old, having had only this third purchase since the Colonial days. Then there is a shop adjoining, where we display and sell our goods. So we are doing very well indeed, and we are looking forward to further progress. I hope very much that when you come to New York you will be able to take the trip to Rye, and look us over. It takes only an hour by train or automobile, and I think you would find it worth while. We have some good patrons, and we shall take great pleasure in calling their attention to your book, which is so deserving of credit, particularly by any one attracted to old-fashioned 'Quilts.' Trusting to have the pleasure of meeting you sometime, I am Yours very truly, Frances F. Putnam (Mrs. J. B. Putnam)." Collection of Rosalind Webster Perry.

[20]Cuesta Benberry, "Marie D. Webster: A Major Influence on Quilt Design in the 20th Century," *Quilter's Newsletter Magazine* (July/August 1990): 32–35.

[21]*Esther O'Neill Designs* (Indianapolis, IN: Esther O'Neill Needlework and Stamping, n.d.). A sales catalog.

[22]"Hand Quilting: A Craft De Luxe in the Hands of the Kentucky Mountaineer Women," *Arts and Decoration* (May 1934): 54–55.

[23]*Nancy Lincoln: A Product of Kentucky,* (New York: Nancy Lincoln Guild, n.d.), 4. A sales catalog.

[24]Anne Orr, "New Quilts With Rugs to Match," *Good Housekeeping* (January 1932).

[25]"Eleanor Beard, Inc., Hand Quilted Things," *House Beautiful* (July 1929): 8.

[26]Gladys Dill, "Dill-Lightful Doings: Eleanor Beard's Studio," *National Quilting Association's Patchwork Patter* (February 1977): 3–4.

[27]"Window Shopping," *House Beautiful* (October 1927): 338.

[28]Alice Beyer, *Quilting* (Chicago: South Park Commissioners, 1934; reprint, Albany, CA: East Bay Heritage Quilters, 1978), 3; Merikay Waldvogel and Barbara Brackman, *Patchwork Souvenirs of the 1933 World's Fair* (Nashville, TN: Rutledge Hill Press, 1993), 42–61.

[29]Clara Belle Thompson and Margaret Lukes Wise, "Quilts That Went to the County Fair," *Country Gentleman* (November 1942).

[30]Mrs. Ralph Foster, interview by Dorothy Cozart, June 19, 1978.

[31]Mary McElwain, *Romance of the Village Quilt* (Walworth, WI: Mary A. McElwain Quilt Shop, 1936), 22, a sales catalog. Nickols, Pat L., "Mary A. McElwain: Quilter and Quilt Businesswoman," *Uncoverings 1991*, ed. Laurel Horton (San Francisco: American Quilt Study Group, 1992), 98–117.

[32]Mary A. McElwain, letter to Betty Harriman, Natural Bridge, VA, Feb. 19, 1938.

[33]*Quilts and Spreads: Original Designs by Marie Webster,* (Walworth, WI: Mary A. McElwain Quilt Shop, n.d.); Marie Webster, letter to Bertha Stenge, Chicago, Sept. 24, 1946.

[34]Maxine Teele, "Something Worthwhile," *Nimble Needle Treasures Magazine* (Summer/Fall 1974): 8–9; Joyce Gross, "Lillian Walker," *Quilters' Journal* (Spring 1981): 1–3.

[35]Marion Cheever Whiteside, "Story Book Quilts" appeared in the following magazines. *Ladies' Home Journal*: Bridal quilt, February 1949; Little Women quilt, Circus quilt, October 1950; Lucky Day quilt, March 1954; Peter Pan quilt, December 1956; Pinocchio quilt, January 1958; Fireman's quilt, November 1961. *McCall's Needlework and Crafts*: The Three Little Kittens Who Lost Their Mittens quilt, Summer 1947. *Today's Woman*: Hansel and Gretel quilt, n.d. *Woman's Home Companion*: The House That Jack Built quilt, August 1944.

[36]Amelia Peck, *American Quilts and Coverlets in the Metropolitan Museum of Art* (New York: Metropolitan Museum of Art and Dutton Studio Books, 1990), 102–03.

[37]*Quilts from Kay McFarland*, Topeka, KS, (Christmas 1964; other issues, n.d.). A series of sales catalogs.

[38]"Freedom Quilting Bee," *St. Louis Post-Dispatch* (Oct. 13, 1968); "Craze for Quilts," *Life Magazine* (May 5, 1972): 74–80; Two Routes to a Better Life—Co-ops and Job Training," *Fortune* (August 1968); "Quilting Co-op Starts with Sewing Scraps," *Capper's Weekly* (Feb. 11, 1972); Barbara Cloud, "Mountain Artisans Create in Patchwork," *Pittsburgh Press* (Jan. 24, 1971); *Cabin Creek Quilt Collections* (Eskdale, WVA: n.d.). A sales catalog; Patricia Degner, "Quilts Spread Out from South Dakota," *St. Louis Post-Dispatch* (Feb. 25, 1976): *Grass Roots Craftsmen of the Appalachian Mountains* (Jackson, KY, n.d.). A sales catalog. Thomas Newsom, "A Passion for Patchwork," *St. Louis Post-Dispatch* (May 9, 1971); "Handmade Quilts: Sunflower County, MS," *American Teacher* (September 1968).

[39]Dolores Hinson, letter to the author, July 29, 1986.

[40]Peter Breslow, "The End of Rural Arts and Crafts," *Country Journal* (June 1968): 16–18.

[41]Marilyn Hoffman, "Antique Quilts Made into Pillows," *Flint (MI) Journal* (April 17, 1972).

[42]*Missouri Quilts by Tricia Woo* (St. Louis, n.d.). A sales catalog.

[43]Bryce and Donna Hamilton, Minneapolis, MN, letter to the author, June 5, 1985.

[44]Jennifer Lin, "Reaping More for Their Sewing," *Philadelphia Inquirer* (March 13, 1984); Nancy Callahan, *The Freedom Quilting Bee* (Tuscaloosa, AL: University of Alabama Press, 1987), 114.

[45]"Ladies of the Quilt," *Crafts News* (March 1988).

[46]Jan Tyler, "Folks Warm Up to Arkansas Country Quilts," *Rural Arkansas* (November 1988): 4.

[47]Penny Mayfield, "Colorful Patchwork Quilts Propel Tutwiler's Cottage Industry," *The Clarksdale Press Register* (May 30, 1989).

[48]Carter Houck, "Cultural Crossroads," and Patricia Crosby, "Traditional Quilting Alive and Well in Mississippi," *Lady's Circle Patchwork Quilts* (July 1989): 50–57.

[49]Position Paper, National Quilting Association, Marie Salazar, President, *Quilting Quarterly* (Summer 1992): 4.

[50]Jura Koncius, "The Quilts That Struck A Nerve," and Patricia Dane Rogers, "A Bible of Black History," *Washington Post* (March 19, 1993).

[51]Bonnie Leman, "The Needle's Eye," *Quilter's Newsletter Magazine* (May 1992): 4f.

[52]Katherine Webster, "The Quilt Is Making a Comeback across the Rural South," *Capper's Weekly* (Jan. 19, 1993); Jura Koncius, "The Power, The Glory, The Quilts: A Tale of Survival in a Small Town in America," *Washington Post* (March 11, 1993): 14–22.

A Century of Fundraising Quilts, 1860–1960

Dorothy Cozart

Waterlily fundraising quilt of pieced solid-color cottons, 75" x 65½", made by women of Mt. Pleasant Baptist Church near Westminster, South Carolina. Back to front edge treatment machine and blue quilting thread 7 stitches per inch, as well as colored threads in French knot, outline, and buttonhole stitches. Collection of Frances Harbin. Photo by Terry Wild Studio.

When this chapter was published in its original form in *Uncoverings 1984*, it began: "Until recently, comparatively little had been written about women's quiltmaking activities that made money either for themselves or for charitable causes." Fundraisers, which I am defining as those quilts made specifically for the purpose of soliciting money for individuals or groups, were virtually ignored in quilt histories before 1970. *Quilts in America*, published in 1974, pictures two quilts that probably were fundraisers, and identifies one as such in the caption beneath the photo.[1] *America's Quilts and Coverlets* also pictures two fundraisers and identifies them as such.[2] *Three Hundred Years of Canada's Quilts* pictures and describes one fundraiser in some detail and also indicates that many more have been made in Canada.[3] *A People and Their Quilts* not only gives a typical description of the method used in making and raising money on a quilt, it also mentions several instances in which individuals and groups in Tennessee made and sold quilts, or did quilting, then gave the money to churches.[4] Quilt catalogs have identified and pictured several fundraisers, and *Kentucky Quilts 1800–1900, Quilts and Carousels*, and *Nova Scotia Workbasket* contain brief discussion of fundraising quilts.[5] Nancy J. Rowley's paper in *Uncoverings 1982* dealt with fundraising quilts made for a specific purpose, "Red Cross Quilts for the Great War."[6]

It is apparent from this introduction that as quilt scholarship began focusing on regional quilt history, more fundraising quilts were discovered.

Dorothy Cozart *taught at Phillips University, Enid, Oklahoma, prior to her retirement. She has continued her research of signature fundraisers since writing the first article in* Uncoverings, 1984. *The Oklahoma connection to a Maryland quiltmaker and an examination of the letters and handwork of members of her husband's family appeared in* Uncoverings 1986, *and* Uncoverings 1992, *respectively. Route 1, Box 93, Waukomis, OK 73773.*

Since 1984, most of the states have conducted documentation projects, and many of them have published some of their discoveries, which include fundraising quilts. The publication of this *Uncoverings* retrospective has given me the opportunity to update my findings, which discussed what I chose to call "group fundraisers," those made by a group of people, rather than by individuals, as were some of the Red Cross quilts, which both Nancy Rowley and I had located in the 1980s. Because almost all of the quilts found in my research have been *signature* fundraisers, I will limit this chapter to those quilts.

The following is from "The History of Olive Hill Church," published in the *Holton (KS) Recorder* in July 1927.[7] This excerpt, about the fundraising activity of a small Methodist church, is what sparked my interest in fundraising quilts.

From the files of the *Holton Recorder*, W. E. Beighter has secured these items. In the issue of July 23, 1883, "The good people of Olive Hill have raised $1,600 in funds to build a church edifice."

June 4, 1884: "Olive Hill will have an ice cream supper June 16. They will sell the wheel quilt at that time, the proceeds will be used to finish the church."

If memory serves us right, this same wheel quilt was a design of a wheel in red on foundation of white for which names were solicited with 10 cents for placing the name on the tire, 25 cents on a spoke, and 50 cents on the hub. Much money was raised in this way, different ladies vieing with each other in securing the most names and money on their block. . . . Mr. Stauffer was the auctioneer who disposed of the wheel quilt, which sold for twenty-five dollars to John Dix.

Unfortunately, the quilt itself has not been located, but this writing is representative of the written and oral accounts of the signature fundraisers that I have subsequently discovered. This account is also typical in that the quilt was made as a fundraiser by a group of church women. My research indicates that most fundraising quilts

were made to benefit churches, most often Methodist churches, with the funds being used in various ways, including the building of a new church.

In the context of this chapter, the word "fundraiser" can be taken to mean "signature fundraiser." Other names for signature fundraisers do occur, and, in fact, *The Needleworker's Dictionary*, a British publication with an American contributing editor, defines signature quilts thus: "Type of American album quilt often worked to raise money for good causes. The quilt was designed to accommodate as many names as possible, each person paying a fee for the privilege. One example, worked in 1893 in Terre Haute, Indiana, has over a thousand names on it."[8] Other names for signature fundraisers include "charity quilts," "subscription quilts,"[9] "tithing quilts,"[10] and "beddelman quilts."[11] Incidentally, some fundraisers are truly "signature" quilts: that is, the people who donated money actually signed their names to fabric used in the quilt. In other cases, the signatures were all written by one or more people who had good "hands" (handwriting).

Although fundraising quilts have been documented from every decade during the period studied, 1860 through 1960, the majority were made from 1880 through World War I. Before 1890, most of the fundraisers were pieced, the most popular patterns being the Single and Double Irish Chains. Fundraisers of the crazy quilt type were made periodically from the 1880s until about 1915, and some Log Cabin fundraisers were made throughout the period surveyed. During the World War I era, from 1916 until after the war, Red Cross quilts were very popular, and many of them were fundraisers.

Probably because they are more recent, the majority of the quilts located were made using a circular design, which became popular at about the turn of the twentieth century. Most resemble wheels, having a "hub" in

the center in which names are written, with more names radiating like "spokes" out from the center. While most of the wheels were embroidered, some were appliquéd, with the names appearing between the spokes and/or outside the rim, and even a few crazy quilt types contain the wheel design. Other circular designs include a circle that is a pieced Sunburst; the names being embroidered in the center and on each of the diamonds in the "burst."[12] On later quilts, some of the circles are sunflowers or other flowers, and some are Dresden Plate or Friendship Ring. On one quilt the circular design was created by picturing a series of cards, each containing one name, strung on a ribbon. The ribbon was tied in a bow, and the cards lay in a circle.[13] The circular design quilts date from about 1890 to the end of the period surveyed.

Red on white was the most common color combination used on the wheel signature quilts, and many of them were embroidered. The use of red is to be expected, because red was considered "color fast" when most of them were made. Later wheel quilts are orange, blue, old rose, and gold on a white background. Only one quilt's description noted the significance of the colors: a 1911 quilt in Montgomery County, New York, which was settled by people from the Netherlands. It used orange, blue, and white, the colors of the Netherlands' flag.[14]

Beginning about 1890, the names, addresses, and even slogans of businesses in the community began to appear on fundraisers. A quilt owned by the Sloan Museum in Flint, Michigan, was made about 1888. It is eight feet square and "provides a partial directory of the city of Flint" at that time.[15] The women of the Ladies' Aid Society of Garland Street Methodist Episcopal Church made etchings to accompany business advertisements, one being of "a hearse with raised driver's seat and elegantly tasseled curtains." In addition, about 1,000

names appear on it. The group raised around $2,000.

The Monroeville (OH) Town Hall quilt, also made in 1888, contains names of Monroeville merchants and has a central painted velvet block picturing the town hall.[16] A number of other quilts of the same vintage, and also later, have pictures of churches or other buildings as a central motif, and Mary Conroy states in *300 Years of Canada's Quilts* that she has seen several Canadian quilts that have a central panel of an embroidered church, school, or other building.[17]

During the 1880s, it became popular to write to famous people asking for pieces of their clothing to be used in crazy quilts. Some church women also asked for fabric scraps and/or signatures, and in some cases groups made records of their fundraising efforts, which have been preserved with the quilts.[18] It is quite possible that other extant quilts containing names of well-known people may have been fundraisers.

Very few quilts have the individual makers of the quilt identified as such. However, stories that accompany the quilts often do identify makers. Sometimes the names were embroidered by one person, and her name may be remembered. Some quilts have the names of the women who quilted them quilted into the border. In some cases, the woman who was responsible for the signatures on a certain block may have her name in the hub, but that information is not often noted on the quilt. A quilt made by Circle Number 3 of the First Methodist Episcopal of Wichita, Kansas, was made in 1915 and 1916. The central block is identified as the "history block." It contains the names of the officers of the circle, the woman who put it together, how much was charged for each name, the proceeds, what the money was to be used for (building a new church), the pastor's name, the name of the president of the General Aid Society, and the name of the woman who suggested

Detail of Irish Chain of white and print cottons, 83" x 75", made by women of the Salem Evangelical United Brethren Church, Adams County, Pennsylvania, inscribed in ink with names and date, "November 18, 1888." Collection of Annette Gero. Courtesy of the Oral Traditions Project.

Most of the inscriptions were made after the top was completed, which is an unusual feature, as most fundraisers were inscribed one block at a time. Note the amounts of money donated below each name, of which 921 appear on the quilt. The $300 raised was used—as noted for posterity in indelible ink—to furnish the new church.

Detail of embroidered spoked wheel fundraiser, made by Circle Number 3, First Methodist Episcopal Church, Wichita, Kansas. Collection of the Wichita/Sedgwick County Historical Museum. Courtesy of Cuesta Benberry.

Fundraiser of white cotton with embroidered red thread, 98" x 80", made by the Ladies of the Methodist Episcopal Church of Amboy, Astabula County, Ohio, 1891. Collection of Mrs. Robert Bossley. Courtesy of Ohio Historical Society.

Detail of quilt made in Snyder County, Pennsylvania, of pieced white and appliqué red cottons, 83" x 82", between August 1918 and April 1919. White wholecloth back, applied binding, and quilted with white thread 8–10 stitches per inch. Collection of Jean W. Haines. Courtesy of the Oral Traditions Project.

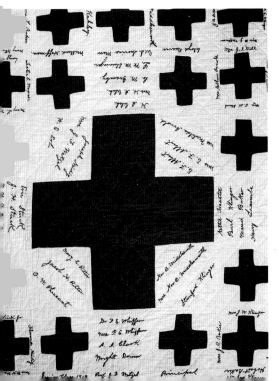

that the quilt be made.[19] This much information, however, is an exception.

An indication of how hard these mostly anonymous women worked obtaining signatures is given in the Linden, Iowa, Methodist Church *Centennial, 1882–1982.* This was sent to me by Mary Barton, whose grandmother, Allie Lisle, is mentioned. "Names cost 10 cents to be embroidered by the women and Allie Lisle twisted most of the arms in town. When Martha Bilmore had the quilt, she listed all the names and put in some not there until all blocks were filled."[20] There are 169 names on the quilt.

The number of names on a quilt may indicate that it was a fundraiser. Many quilts found have at least 150 names on them, and some have more than 400. A few quilts contain more than 1,000 signatures. One of the quilts containing the most signatures is the one called the "Refrigerator quilt."

The Refrigerator quilt was made by the Trinity Evangelical Church in Kansas City in 1935 and 1937.[21] The purpose was to collect money to buy a kerosene refrigerator for Juanita and Wilbur Harr, who were leaving to serve as missionaries to Nigeria. All the churches in the Kansas Conference of the Evangelical Church were contacted, and, as a result, there are approximately 1,860 signatures on the Sunflower quilt. Enough money was raised to buy the refrigerator, cover freight costs, and buy some kerosene. The quilt was then given to the Harrs, and they used it while in Africa and for many years after they returned. It now belongs to the daughter of Mrs. Arthur J. Brunner, the instigator and moving force behind this money-making project.

A few quilts, all made in the 1930s, contain a minimal number of signatures, and only the provenance of the quilts reveal that they were fundraisers, rather than friendship quilts. Funds were raised in identical ways for all the quilts in this small group, and all were made at about the same time by Methodist women's groups in Kansas or Oklahoma. Each woman pieced a block, choosing her own pattern, and she paid a penny for each pattern piece. The woman whose block contained the most pieces won the quilt. At about the same time that these quilts were made, "The Piece Bag" column in *Home Arts-Needlecraft* for July 1936 told about "A church society in Kansas" that raised funds in the same way.[22] More of these quilts are surely still in existence, but no one remembers that they were fundraisers.

Funds were usually raised in two ways: first, individuals donated money so that their signatures would be on the quilt, and second, the finished quilt was sold or raffled. As was described in the account of the Olive Hill quilt above, the placement on the wheel, or in the center of the block, sometimes determined the amount paid for a signature. In central designs, the center was usually the highest, with twenty-five cents and fifty cents being common amounts paid for that space. Otherwise, ten cents was the amount most often mentioned, and two cents was the smallest amount found. Usually from twenty-five to fifty dollars were collected for the signatures. Prices began to inflate by the 1940s and 1950s, and spaces sold for fifty cents to five dollars. An exception was the Baptist Orphans' Home quilt. Kentucky Sunday School classes, church organizations, and a few individual members of Baptist churches were asked to buy blocks, for a minimum of eighteen dollars, with their names then appearing on the blocks. The eighty-one blocks sold for a minimum of eighteen dollars each, and, as a result, about $5,000 was raised on that quilt in 1882.[23]

Some quilts have amounts of money written on the quilt. The earliest one found is the "tithing quilt," made about 1860. Each member of the congregation inscribed his or her name around the Oak Leaf appliqué, and

after each name is the sum of money that the individual gave to the minister, ten, fifteen, or twenty-five cents.[24] On other quilts, each block contains the name of the person who collected the money for that block and the amount of money collected. Still others have the amount raised and the donors listed on the back of the quilt.[25]

Many of the quilts were sold at auctions, which might have been held after an ice cream social or a box or pie supper, or sometimes in connection with a bazaar. Clemmie Pugh of Monterey, Tennessee, gave ten dollars at an auction for the Dresden Plate she helped make, probably in the 1930s, and she said later: "Why, I wouldn't take anything for this quilt. They's so many of them that's dead and gone."[26] Several times I have heard or read remarks similar to Pugh's, made by other informants.

Some quilts were raffled. However, this method of fundraising was opposed by some churches and some ministers. In the centennial history of the church in Linden, Iowa, cited earlier, the author, Ruth Ketelson, commented: "In 1928 in Redfield [another church on the minister's circuit], Rev. Nightengale 'helped the board decide that the church would not allow any quilt to be raffled off in the name of any department of the church. Since he was also our minister I doubt if any 'raffling' was done here either.'"[27] Bonnie Carden recalls the women's experience with a raffle at the Andersonville (TN) church. "We began to get criticism from other members that this was a form of gambling. That was the first and last time we ever raffled a quilt."[28]

Of course there were ways of eluding such criticism. One was to give something like a stick of gum in return for the money; if they bought something they wouldn't be gambling. A more common way was to call the money a "donation." Usually tickets were given in return for a donation, and one such occurrence,

Detail of crazy quilt pieced of colored silks, 84" x 62", made by the women of the Virginia Presbyterian Church, Virginia, Illinois, 1886–1991. Shown here with the subscription book, which recorded the names of donors that correspond to the numbers used instead of names on the quilt. Collection of The State Museum, Lincoln, Illinois. Courtesy of Dorothy Cozart.

Detail of brick comfort or hap pieced of solid-color wools by members of the Mazeppa Evangelical Church, Mazeppa, Union County, Pennsylvania, 1926. Knotted and with names in colored embroidery floss. Courtesy of the Oral Traditions Project.

Although most signature fundraisers were made of cottons—usually white with red thread embroidered names—occasionally one is seen in fancy fabric like silk. Less often seen are wool examples or those that have been knotted (tied).

Little Dutch Girl fundraiser quilt of pieced and appliqué cottons, 86" x 72", made by the Woman's Society of Christian Service of the Turkey (NC) United Methodist Church in 1950. Collection of Mary Ann Hester. Courtesy of North Carolina Quilt Documentation Project.

Everyone whose name is sewn on the quilt paid 25¢. The quilt raised an additional $125 when it was auctioned.

during World War II, resulted in a wonderful fundraising quilt story. The Women's Missionary Union of a Baptist church in Clark County, Missouri, made a quilt, putting the names of each woman and man then in the Armed Forces in the center of each album block. The only one killed during the war whose name appeared on the quilt was Raymond S. Grinstead. In 1946, it was decided to raffle the quilt. During the meeting at which the quilt was raffled, several people announced that they had purchased tickets in Ray's honor. They had put Ray's father's name on the tickets, and perhaps others did the same. At any rate, when the drawing took place, Ray's father's name was on the winning ticket. This quilt, and the story, are still cherished by the Grinstead family.[29]

What happened to the quilts after the money was raised? Of those not auctioned or raffled, at least two were given to bishops, one Methodist, and one Church of the Latter-day Saints.[30] Many were given to the ministers of the churches in which the quilts were made, or to their wives. A

letter in *American Woman* (December 1911) told of a "Sewing Circle Quilt-block." "This block was so named because it was originally intended for an album-quilt, which our circle made for a church fair. In each white strip or bar was written the name of a friend who contributed a dime to the purpose in view; and the quilt, when completed, was presented to our minister's wife."[31] Some quilts were given to the women who collected the most names. Sometimes the church bought the quilt and presented it to the president of the sponsoring organization because she had done so much work on it.

No doubt many women regretted that the quilts their groups had made

had been raffled or auctioned. One woman told me that the woman who won such a quilt had only one ticket, and then she didn't take care of the quilt, and it was worn out long ago.[32] At least one group could not give up its quilt and kept it instead. A circular crazy quilt type fundraiser was documented by the Kansas Quilt Project. It was made by the Ladies' Aid Society of the Liberal, Kansas, Methodist Episcopal Church in 1910. The organization's minutes revealed that the group had intended to auction it; however, when the time came, they couldn't part with it, and decided to pass it around among the members so that all could enjoy it. When documented, it was still owned by the daughter-in-law of the woman who was secretary of the group at the time it was made.[33] The daughter-in-law later gave the quilt to the church, and it is displayed as a part of the church's history. Other signature fundraisers have also been given to the churches whose members' names are displayed on the quilts.

Almost ten years after first writing about fundraisers in *Uncoverings*, I can report that the signature fundraisers have been quite well documented. Every state quilt project has uncovered examples of fundraiser quilts, and they have also been recorded as being made in Great Britain, Ireland, Australia, and New Zealand.

Although most fundraisers made in the nineteenth century were made by church groups,[34] early in the twentieth century other organizations such as the Women's Christian Temperance Union, auxiliaries of the Grand Army of the Republic, and the Suffragettes borrowed the idea. During World War I, the Red Cross raised more money with quilts than any other secular group. However, by World War II, very few signature quilts were being made, and by 1960 there were practically none.

It was inevitable that, in the 1970s, with the revival of interest in quiltmaking, there would come a rediscovery of the revenue-producing capabilities of fundraising quilts. And it is ironic that many emerging quilt guilds and other groups, still haunted by earlier beliefs, or state laws, about gambling, found it necessary to label their creations "opportunity," but never "raffle" quilts. Perhaps because the historical significance of signature fundraisers became recognized in the 1980s, more groups produced quilts featuring names of individuals. And it is appropriate to conclude with information about a fundraiser for the American Quilt Study Group (AQSG), called "Sally's Quilt," a memorial to the late Sally Garoutte, who was editor of *Uncoverings* when this

chapter was first published. Each strip-pieced block contains a signature of an AQSG member, surrounded by printed 1970s fabric strips from Sally Garoutte's collection. The income generated by this 1993 project will be used to support the AQSG Research Library, which was Sally Garoutte's ultimate dream.

Notes and References

[1]Patsy and Myron Orlofsky, *Quilts in America* (New York: McGraw Hill, 1974), 241.

[2]Carleton Safford and Robert Bishop, *America's Quilts and Coverlets* (New York: Weathervane Books, 1974), 161, 193.

[3]Mary Conroy, *300 Years of Canada's Quilts* (Toronto: Griffin House, 1976), 60–61, 77, 84, 95.

[4]John Rice Irwin, *A People and Their Quilts* (Exton, PA: Schiffer, 1983), 13–16, 82, 95, 142, 193.

[5]John Finley and Jonathan Holstein, *Kentucky Quilts, 1800–1900* (Louisville: Kentucky Quilt Project, 1982), 60–63; Ricky Clark, *Quilts and Carousels: Folk Art in the Firelands* (Oberlin, OH: FAVA, 1983), 22; Marlene Davis, *Nova Scotia Workbasket*, (Nova Scotia Museum, 1976), 68.

[6]Nancy J. Rowley, "Red Cross Quilts for the Great War," *Uncoverings 1982*, ed. Sally Garoutte (Mill Valley, CA: American Quilt Study Group, 1983), 43–51.

[7]*Holton (KS) Recorder*, July 1927, page unknown.

[8]Pamela Clabburn and Helene Von Rosenstiel, *The Needleworker's Dictionary* (New York: Morrow, 1976), 243.

[9]Joyce Ice and Linda Norris, *Quilted Together: Women, Quilts, and Communities* (Delhi, NY: Delaware County Historical Association, 1989), 6; Marsha MacDonald and Ruth D. Fitzgerald, eds., *Michigan Quilts* (East Lansing, MI: Michigan State University Museum, 1987), 8.

[10]Safford and Bishop, 161.

[11]Nancy Roan, "Quilting in Goshenhoppen," *In the Heart of Pennsylvania: Symposium Papers*, ed. Jeannette Lasansky (Lewisburg, PA: Oral Traditions Project, 1986), 52.

[12]Pieced quilt, Sunburst, made by members of Mason Methodist Society, Bethel, ME, in 1880; Nancy Halpern, letter to author, Sept. 12, 1983.

[13]Embroidered Missionary quilt, made by women of Zion Methodist Church, Brownsville Circuit, Brownsville, TN, 1927; Merikay Waldvogel, letter to the author, Sept. 9, 1988.

[14]*Quilts from Montgomery County, New York* (Fort Jackson, NY: Montgomery County Historical Society, 1981), quilt no. 37.

[15]*Flint (MI) Journal*, Feb. 18, 1968.

[16]Clark, 22.

[17]Conroy, 77.

[18]Dorothy Cozart, "The Role and Look of Fundraising Quilts, 1850 to 1930," *Pieced by Mother: Symposium Papers*, ed. Jeanette Lasansky (Lewisburg, PA: Oral Traditions Project, 1988), 86–95; Pat Flynn Kyser, "Pieces and Patches," *Quilt World*: July-August 1985: 46–49.

[19]Embroidered quilt, wheel design, made by Circle Number 3, First Methodist Episcopal Church, Wichita, KS, 1915–16.

[20]Ruth Ketelson, *Centennial 1882–1982*, unpublished manuscript, (Linden, IA: 1982), 8.

[21]Appliqué quilt, Refrigerator quilt, made by women of Trinity Evangelical Church, Kansas City, KS, in 1935 and 1936. Lois Brunner, letter to author, Dec. 19, 1983.

[22]Amy V. Edwards, "The Piece Bag," *Home Arts-Needlecraft* (July 1936): 26.

[23]Finley and Holstein, 61.

[24]Safford and Bishop, p. 161.

[25]Ricky Clark, George W. Knepper, and Ellice Ronshein, *Quilts in Community* (Nashville, TN: Rutledge Hill Press, 1991), 136–37.

[26]Irwin, 95.

[27]Ketelson, 8.

[28]Irwin, 82.

[29]Pieced quilt, album block, made by the Women's Missionary Union of a Baptist church in Clark County, MO, ca. 1944. Rosie Grinstead, letter to author, Sept. 14, 1984.

[30]Log Cabin, Straight Furrows, made for a Methodist Episcopal church bazaar in Missouri in 1866. Missouri Historical Society, St. Louis; Embroidered quilt, Beehive and Seagull, made for Bishop Earl. W. Walker by members of a ward of the Church of Latter-day Saints. *Utah Folk Art* (Provo, UT: Brigham Young Univ. Press, n.d.).

[31]Mrs. H. F. Cole, letter to *American Woman*, December 1911.

[32]Pattern unknown, made by Golden Circle Club, Ashley Community, Grant County, OK, ca. 1943. Interview with one of the club members by author.

[33]Crazy quilt type, made by the Ladies' Aid Society of the Liberal, KS, Methodist Episcopal Church, 1910. Minutes of meetings for Feb. 10 and Dec. 2, 1910.

[34]For an excellent discussion on the "change in the nature of church-made quilts," see Clark, Knepper, and Ronsheim, 136–37.

Four Twentieth-Century Quiltmakers

Joyce R. Gross

Although a number of the nation's art museums have quilts in their collections made by nationally known quiltmakers, information about the quiltmakers was almost totally lacking when this study was undertaken in the early 1970s. In some instances, not even significant dates of the artists were known by the museums. The author found this to be highly frustrating, so she began to research and collect items and quilts pertaining to twentieth-century quiltmakers. Her collection includes Bertha Stenge's *Tiger Lily*, Dr. Jeannette Throckmorton's *Modernistic Star* and a doll's quilt made of "materials of her childhood," and a partially completed quilt top made by Florence Peto, as well as a sizeable collection of ephemera about these artists. The collection has now expanded to fill file cabinets and bookshelves with materials not only related to these quiltmakers and their quilts, but also correspondence, scrapbooks, and related national and local periodical articles about exhibitions, shops, quilting groups, companies, museums, quilt collectors, etc., from the beginning of the twentieth century. This archival material has, and will continue, to contribute and document a more complete history of twentieth-century quiltmaking.

Four of these master quiltmakers are presented here. Better known than many of their colleagues because their work is in museums and has been photographed for catalogs and other publications, they are not the only master quiltmakers of their period. Many other master quiltmakers are now being discovered.

Joyce Gross is a quilt historian whose broad research interests include the biographies of twentieth-century quiltmakers, designers, and researchers. She edited the Quilter's Journal *from 1977–1987, and maintains an extensive research archive. 853 D Street, Petaluma, CA 94952.*

Modernistic Star

Submitted by

Miss Rose Marie Lowery, Davenport, Nebraska

made one.
atto time

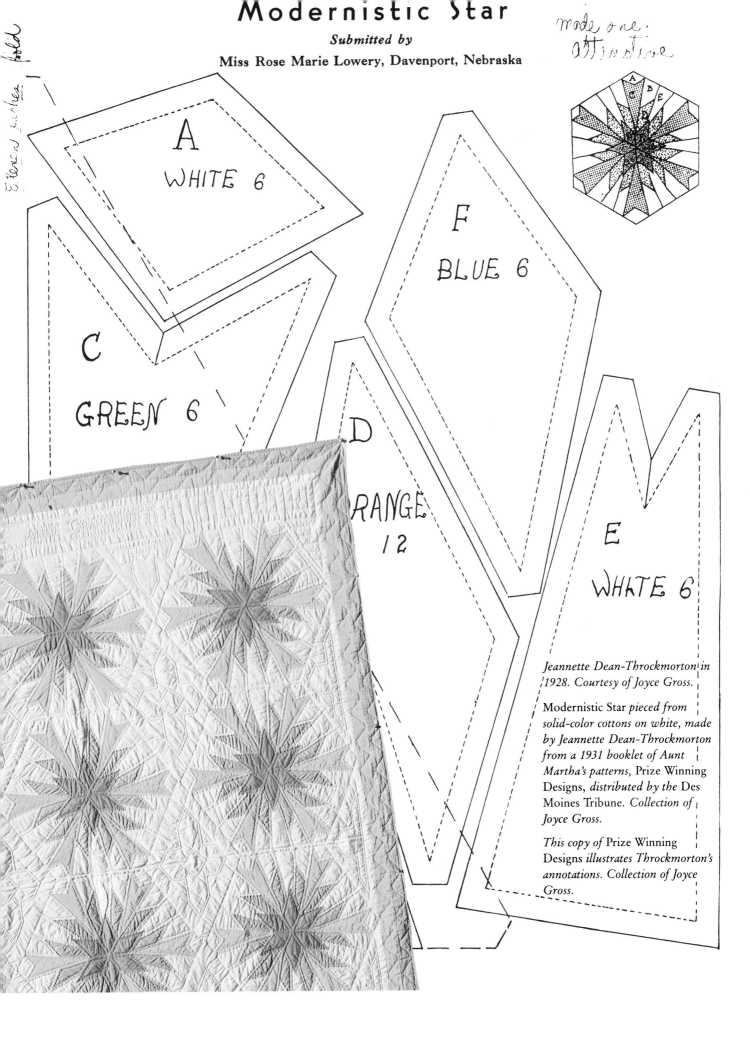

Eleven inches fold

A

WHITE 6

F

BLUE 6

C

GREEN 6

D

RANGE
12

E

WHITE 6

Jeannette Dean-Throckmorton in 1928. Courtesy of Joyce Gross.

Modernistic Star pieced from solid-color cottons on white, made by Jeannette Dean-Throckmorton from a 1931 booklet of Aunt Martha's patterns, Prize Winning Designs, *distributed by the Des Moines Tribune. Collection of Joyce Gross.*

This copy of Prize Winning Designs *illustrates Throckmorton's annotations. Collection of Joyce Gross.*

Matterhorn *quilt, pieced of 9,135 one-inch squares of print and solid-color cottons, 102" x 84", made by Myrtle Mae Fortner (1880–1966) of Llano, California, in-scribed in quilting on the back "Myrtle M. Fortner, July, 1934." Collection of the Denver Art Museum (#1967.89). Courtesy of the Denver Art Museum.*

Material for these biographies comes from diaries, letters, periodical articles now in the author's collection, and interviews with families and friends over a period of years.

Myrtle May Fortner
(12/13/1880–5/6/1966)

The author has a copy of Myrtle Fortner's diary of 1955, which is the only diary of hers known to exist. All of the quotes are from the 1955 diary unless otherwise noted.

Myrtle Mae Fortner is known for a single quilt, the *Matterhorn,* in the collections of the Denver Art Museum. It has been shown in major exhibitions at the museum, at the Hallmark Gallery in New York, in the American Pavilion at Expo '70 in Osaka, Japan, in the San Francisco area at two "Patch in Time" quilt exhibits, and at the Bank of America World Headquarters Gallery in San Francisco.

Born Myrtle Mae Melvin in Camden, Illinois, December 13, 1880, the artist was the ninth of ten children. When Mertie (as she was called by her family) was small, her older sister died, leaving two daughters. Those two little girls, Flora and Myrtle, came to live with the Melvin family, and Flora was to become a favorite of her aunt's. In the diary she kept in 1955, her seventy-fifth year, Mertie wrote on April 7: "This is Flora's birthday. I did not send her a card or a gift but insisted on paying for our lunch when we were in Lancaster on Saturday. No one can ever know how very much I have loved that precious baby. I myself was still playing with dolls when she was brought to our home at two-and-one-half months. This one was far more loveable and interesting than any doll. I hope I have never failed her when I could be of help to her."

In 1901, Mertie married her first cousin, Linneous Fortner, despite parental objection. Two years later she left, alone, for Los Angeles. On October 22, 1955, she wrote in her diary, "I married in Denver, Colorado, fifty-four years ago today. It doesn't seem that it can be so long ago. There is neither pleasure nor regret in the memory. It now seems that it was just an experience, which was part of my education, and no one was to blame—just two people with ideas and ideals so different that there could be no adjustment, and I am glad it happened so soon."

In Los Angeles she became successful building and managing apartment houses. During the Depression, she lost everything and was forced to start a new life in the small desert town of Llano, California. With her own hands, she built a small cabin. She had neither running water nor electricity but she managed a pleasant life. On August 14, 1955, she wrote, "I am glad to be left to my own quiet way except when some of my real friends or relatives come." On December 13, "I have spent the day alone but not lonely." Her life was made up of many everyday tasks. On January 22, she wrote, "Emptied ashes this A.M. That is a major operation . . . always three buckets full and a mess on the floor to be cleaned up. Melted some more snow. Carried in several loads of wood." February 1, she noted, "Cold and windy today. I have carried in six loads of wood and two of water. Looks like another storm in a day or two." On February 5, she wrote, "Just a quiet morning washing dishes. Hoped the man would be here to adjust the gas but he did not come." On August 16, she wrote, "Went to the store this afternoon and now have more variety to eat."

Mertie loved Scrabble games, which she played by herself and with her niece Flora who was a frequent visitor. On January 30, the diary reads, "I read aloud awhile this evening, and then she beat me at Scrabble. I am sure I don't know why I never win games of any kind but that seems to be the case. Well, I enjoyed the game—and we'll try it again. We always learn a few new words, but I wish they were longer ones instead of three to five letters as most of them are."

On March 29, she wrote, "Played a game of Scrabble this evening with R and L representing two players—R won as usual though I favor neither—that one usually has letters that fit better." On Sunday, May 15, she noted, "I played a solo game of Scrabble this evening, and for the first time I got all of my seven letters moved to the board at one time. The word was 'smeared' so I got fifty points for that but my score was still only 576. John May says his highest score was 665 out of a possible 1,000 so I'm not satisfied yet."

Myrtle frequently mentioned her Christian Science faith in her diary. On May 13, she wrote "I am so very thankful that Christian Science came to me (or I to it) a long time ago, 1908." On February 7, she wrote, "Our C[hristian] S[cience] Lesson for this week is on Soul and I enjoyed my reading this A.M. more than usual." On October 4, 1955, her entry read, "I found a C.S. Lecture in the *(Christian Science) Monitor* I was reading this A.M. so read that instead of the Sunday Lesson. It was very good and I have had a happy day."

Quiltmaking is not mentioned in this diary, but several references are made to the *Matterhorn* and a large braided rug, which she had made. The first reference was on January 2, "This has been a good day. Four people came to see my quilt and braided rug. The quilt pieced in small squares—9,135 of them and is a picture of the Matterhorn—mountains, stream, trees, and rocks all in place—with two cabins." Her family believes that the two cabins represent her own and one belonging to Flora that she could see from her window. On June 5, she wrote, "They admired my quilt and rug."

Flora and her husband did a great deal of traveling, and it is probable that they visited the Matterhorn in Switzerland. They may have brought a picture postcard but Mertie made it her own with the addition of redwood

Flora's Quilt of pieced and appliqué crêpe de Chine, 100" x 98", for Flora Mann by Myrtle Mae Fortner, circa 1930. Private collection. Courtesy of Joyce Gross.

Myrtle Mae Fortner (at right) in front of her cabin in Llano, California, with Flora Mann, her niece, circa 1950. Collection of Joyce Gross.

trees, stream, and cabins. She painted a watercolor of the scene with only one cabin, which she evidently painted before she made the quilt.

Flora's Quilt, the only other quilt we know to have been made by Myrtle Fortner, remains in the family. It is both pieced and appliqué. Mertie also painted china and did watercolors.

Toward the end of the year 1955, Mrs. Fortner began to mention that a change in her lifestyle would occur. On Sunday October 2, she noted, "We attended church at Victorville today. Went to the Desert Inn for lunch, bought the *Sunday Times* [from Los Angeles] and read it while listening to soft music being broadcast from the station in the morning. Had dinner here and have been looking at house plans again. I guess it is decided that I will put the house on the market and have a cottage built near Victorville so

I will have electricity and no longer carry water, chop wood, and put up with my crudities in my manner of living—I am sure it is time to quit— so I will be happy to make the change soon."

One of the last entries of the year was Tuesday, December 27, "Flora and I went downtown (to Los Angeles) today and looked at furniture. They are using more handpainted than for several years so I am going to try my skill on some pieces I have. Want to get them ready for the new home."

She moved to her new home near Victorville soon after 1955, and there are no more diaries. According to her nephew, she became ill, and he lost track of her until her attorney notified him of his inheritance. She died October 6, 1966, in San Bernadino, California.

Her nephew, Melvin Dorsett, wrote to the author on July 30, 1973: "We had been thrilled in her desert home when she pulled back the protective drapes and showed us her textile masterpiece. She did another quilt but this was the one she created with the hope that 'it would someday be judged worthy of exhibition in a museum.'"

Today, the *Matterhorn* is part of the Denver Art Museum quilt collection, a gift of her nephew. He also gave them a copy of her poem:

> I quilt with stitches small
> and know a century hence
> Posterity will gasp and say
> "how neat."

Jeannette Franc Dean-Throckmorton
(1/26/1883–7/24/1963)
Dr. Jeannette Dean-Throckmorton presented five of her quilts to the Art Institute of Chicago for their collection. One of the quilts, the *Feather Edged Star* (1947), was lost and there are now only four in the collection: *Goldfinch and Flowers,* inscribed "1947," *Blue Iris,* inscribed "1945," *Rosebreasted Grosbeaks,* inscribed "1951," and *State Birds and Flowers,* 1950. They are described and pictured in *American Quilts of The Art Institute of Chicago* (1966).

Jeannette Franc Throckmorton was born at 8 A.M. on Friday, January 26, 1883, in Derby, Iowa. She was third in a family of seven children. Her father, Dr. Thomas Throckmorton, and her mother, Mary Ann Bentley Throckmorton, were both from large families, so many cousins lived nearby. Large family gatherings were frequent and much visiting between families occurred. It is probable that much of the social life of that small Midwestern community was family oriented. For Jeannette, her family remained an integral part of her life.

Jeannette was a good student and received excellent grades from the public schools in Chariton, Iowa. She performed prodigious feats of memory such as memorizing the Declaration of Independence at the age of twelve and the entire Constitution at the age of fourteen. Her father rewarded her with twenty-five cents for the first accomplishment and two dollars for the second. Both events were duly noted in the hometown paper and appeared later in her genealogy book.

The Chariton High School Commencement Program of 1900 lists Jeannette and her cousin Maude Bentley as graduates. Jeannette played in a quartet and was a speaker at the graduating ceremonies. Her thesis was "The Wisdom of Mother Goose." Unfortunately no copy of that document has survived.

She was most anxious to go to college and was obviously a bright student, but her father opposed her plans. Some family members feel that her father only allowed her to go to college after she had promised to go to medical school, enter her father's medical practice, and remain single.

She attended the Simpson College of Liberal Arts and received her Ph.B. in June 1904 before attending the Keokuck Medical School where she completed the four-year course in three years. She was graduated on May 14, 1907. It was also the year she began quilting.

When Jeannette took the State

Board of Medicine's Examination for a certificate to practice, she received the highest grades of all 140 doctors who were examined by the board. She received a 94% average and 100% in some subjects. These facts were also duly noted in the hometown newspaper and clipped for her genealogy book.

Dr. Jeannette joined her father's medical practice in 1907 and continued with him until 1919 when her loss of hearing became too much of a problem.

In 1914 she completed an extensive genealogy of her family, tracing the Throckmorton family back to John Throckmorton, who came to this country in 1630. She presented six-inch-thick books to the members of the six branches of the family. The inscription in each of the books reads, "It has been said, the best possessions of a family are its common memories. To honor and preserve the memory of those who have passed to the Great Beyond, to foster a proper family feeling and pride, to keep for the future generations the record of their ancestry, these pages are placed in the hands of the six branches of the family and entrusted to their keeping." Each book was filled with letters, snippets of wedding dresses, photographs, drawings, locks of hair, etc.

In 1916, Dr. Jeannette received a letter from her brother, Dr. Tom Bentley Throckmorton, which announced that she had been passed over for office as a member of the State Board of Health. According to "Dr. Tom," the appointment had almost been "air tight," but at the last moment the governor had changed his interpretation of the rules of appointment. Tom wrote, "I almost shed tears today, but I am glad to know I have a sister who at least is known to be better qualified than *any man in the state*, but the failure for Suffrage to carry, and hence your inability to declare yourself a member of a political party, defeated you."

After leaving her father's medical practice in 1919, she went into the

U.S. Public Health Service, and for the next six years lectured throughout Iowa and nearby states. Her lectures included "A Study of the Heredity of Feeblemindedness," "Blood Examinations," and "A Preliminary Report on the Health of Women Students in the College of the State." In 1920, she was sent to Belgium as a representative of the U.S. Public Health Service and was entertained by the Queen, who was herself an M.D.

On March 1, 1929 (after the death of her father), Dr. Jeannette married Dr. Charles N. Dean, a former classmate from Keokuck with whom she had remained friends since graduation. Now age 46, her photograph in her wedding dress shows the dress to be short and quite elaborate. She wore a head piece and dress-length veil, which was finished with fringe. Unfortunately the bridegroom suffered a rupture of the pulmonary artery only a few hours after the ceremony and died ten days later. He was survived by his daughter Jeannette, a child from his first marriage.

On the inside cover of her copy of Marie Webster's book, *Quilts: Their Story and How To Make Them*, is the inscription in her handwriting, "Dr. Jeannette Throckmorton-Dean, Sumner, March 11, 1929," the day of her husband's death. She was extremely proud of her names—both Christian and maiden names. For some time after her husband's death, she signed her name "Throckmorton-Dean," but eventually reversed the names and used "Dean-Throckmorton." She loved to have children named "Jeannette" or "Jean" and was not above applying pressure on family members to do so.

The P.E.O. Record (a periodical of a sisterhood that originated in Iowa) noted that Dr. Jeannette was listed in the 1938 edition of *Who's Who Among Physicians and Surgeons*. After Dr. Dean's death, she took the position of Medical Librarian with the Iowa State Medical Library, and continued to serve in that capacity until her death on July 24, 1963. She enjoyed her position and the young people with whom she associated. She died holding a manuscript by one of the students.

In 1947 *Blue Iris* won a prize at the eighth annual American Medical Association (AMA) convention in San Francisco. In 1948, *Goldfinches and Flowers* was awarded first prize at the tenth annual AMA convention in Chicago. *State Birds and Flowers* was awarded first prize at the 1953 Iowa State Fair.

Dr. Jeannette entered her *Dogwood* quilt in the 1944 American Physicians Art Association. They had no "quilt" classification so she entered it in the "tapestry" class. In another competition in 1953, a letter from F. H. Rediwill, M.D., Secretary, American Physicians Art Association, congratulated her for the "piece" being voted the most popular by the judges and the finest piece of artwork in the whole show. He asked, "Would you mind accepting this cup express collect? Our treasury as you probably know is not too flush."

In writing to the curator at the University of Kansas Museum of Art (now known as the Spencer Museum of Art) in 1947, Dr. Jeannette mentions she has only three books on quilts (Hall & Kretsinger, Webster, and Finley). In addition she owned many of the current pattern catalogs. Both books and pattern catalogs were underlined, annotated, and sometimes even contained sketches of her own designs. She wrote names of the recipients of her quilts beside the quilt names, and it was not unusual to have four or five names beside a single quilt. Under the picture of the Drunkard's Path in Carrie Hall's and Rose Kretsinger's *The Romance of the Patchwork Quilt in America*, she wrote, "I made one for Cousin Merva, Cousin Willa, Clarice Bargor, myself 1950." She wrote, "This is a mistake" beside another picture of a Drunkard's Path, which showed many errors in piecing.

Sometime in the 1950s, relatives sent her a booklet from the Victoria and Albert Museum (London, England), which showed pictures of quilts donated to the museum by an American, Mrs. Foster Stearns. According to Evans Foster Stearns, Chairman of the Board, Stearns & Foster, and a member of the Stearns family, she was a distant relative. Dr. Throckmorton immediately wrote to the museum asking them if they would be interested in receiving some of her quilts. They replied with a suggestion that she contact the Smithsonian Institution. The then-current Smithsonian policy of not accepting recent works led her to the Art Institute of Chicago, which was closer to home.

Five of her quilts were finally accepted by the museum, two of them in 1958, one in 1959, and two in 1963. In a letter dated November 26, 1963, on stationery of the Art Institute of Chicago, Mildred Davison, Curator of Textiles, wrote Dr. Throckmorton that the Board of Trustees had accepted her gift of two quilts. The notification came two months after Dr. Jeannette's death.

In the catalog of the Art Institute of Chicago dated 1959 for an exhibition of their collection titled "American Quilts 1819–1948," *Feather Edged Star* is listed as #37. It is listed as a gift of Dr. Jeannette Dean-Throckmorton (accession #58.513). *The Des Moines Tribune* of September 6, 1965, published an article, "Quilts by Iowan in Exhibit at Chicago Art Institute," with a picture of Dr. Throckmorton holding her *Rose-breasted Grosbeak and Iris* and another picture of a portion of her *Goldfinch and Flowers*, which were part of the quilt exhibit on display at the Art Institute of Chicago for the entire month. The article lists the five quilts made by Dr. Throckmorton that were exhibited. The *Feather Edged Star* was included. The 1966 catalog titled *American Quilts* has pictures and text about the other four quilts, but no mention is made of the *Feather Edged Star*.

In response to the author's query about the whereabouts of the *Feather Edged Star* quilt, Christa C. M. Thurman, curator, Department of Textiles, the Art Institute of Chicago, dated March 10, 1980, "It is true that Dr. Throckmorton made a Feather Star quilt. She gave it to the collection in 1958. In 1966, a year before I came to Chicago, this quilt was sent out of the building to New York to be used in a magazine and at that time was lost. It was stolen, and was, therefore, never returned to the Art Institute of Chicago."

According to her own notes, Dr. Jeannette made many pieced quilts, but she became known for her elaborate appliqué quilts with stuffed and corded work. Most of them are inscribed with a date and signature and many with the recipient's name. She also used kits, especially for the appliqué quilts. She didn't use a frame for quilting but preferred to work on her lap with large sections in a quilt-as-you-go method. In her later years, she quilted with her good friend "Aunt Fanny Crist." In the summer they quilted at Aunt Fanny's, where they could enjoy the garden and birds, but in winter they returned to Dr. Jeannette's, where they had electricity and a warmer house.

It isn't known how many quilts she made in her lifetime. Sixteen years before she died, however, she estimated that she had made between fifty-five and sixty. She lost track because she had given so many away.

In a tribute published in *Nimble Needle Treasures* (Vol. 7, No. 2, 1975), Maxine Teele wrote, "Long before the phrase had been coined, Dr. Jeannette Franc Dean-Throckmorton was a woman's libber in the very best sense. In spite of tragedy and handicaps (deafness plagued her most of her life, and her eyesight was greatly impaired in later years), she faced life with zest, optimism, and a complete lack of bitterness. Her accomplishments are remarkable today. When we take into consideration the era in which she was born, they are monumental."

Bertha Stenge (2/8/1891–6/18/1957)
In the 1940s and 1950s, Bertha Stenge was a name well-known to quilters and quilt lovers. She won first prize at the 1939 New York World's Fair and the Grand National Prize at the 1942 *Woman's Day* National Needlework Exhibition. Her quilts appeared in one-woman shows on both sides of the nation; she had been interviewed on radio and in newspapers. She won scores of blue ribbons in county and state fairs, and her designs and patterns were carried in leading magazines such as *Woman's Day* and *Ladies' Home Journal*.

Bertha Stenge was born Bertha Sheramsky on February 8, 1891, in Alameda, California, across the Bay from San Francisco. Her father later changed the family name to Sheram. She attended Longfellow Grammar School and Alameda High School. It is not clear whether she attended the University of California at Berkeley, but she was a student—possibly a private student—of Eugen Neuhaus, head of the Art Department at the University of California.

In 1912, she married Bernard Stenge, an attorney who lived in Chicago. They had three daughters, Frances, Ruth, and Prudence. All three married, but only Ruth had children. On Mrs. Stenge's death, her quilts were divided among her three daughters.

Bertha carefully filed her personal correspondence by the correspondent's city and state. There were many letters from quilters asking for work or replying to Bertha's request for information regarding their fees for quilting and the type of material they would use. The daughters remember their mother quilting at her frame in the early mornings, so it is likely that she used professional quilters only later in life when she became pressed for time. Mrs. Maud Sielbeck of Karnack, Illinois, quilted the *Persian Garden*, the *Victory* quilt, and the *Quilt Show*.

Although Bertha did not begin quiltmaking until her daughters were grown, she won many prizes in state fairs and contests. In the 1939 New York World's Fair contest, she entered her *Palm Leaf* quilt. It won the National Prize ($500), First Prize in Class III (Embroidery, Appliqué, and Patchwork), and tied with Mrs. Charles Glasgow in the voting for the popular award, bringing her total earnings for that one show on that one quilt to $725. The quilt was later shown in *The American Home* magazine of September 1947 as an advertisement for the pattern.

At the *Woman's Day* National

Needlework Exhibition in 1942, Mrs. Stenge won the $1,000 Grand Award for her *Victory* quilt, a first prize in the Appliqué Division, and a third prize in the Quilting Division, for a total of $125 in additional prizes. After the contest, the entries were shown at a large exhibition held at Madison Square Garden with Mary Margaret McBride, a radio celebrity, officiating at the ceremony. It was broadcast over NBC. Mrs. Stenge was invited to the ceremonies as a guest of *Woman's Day*. In the March 1943 issue of *Woman's Day*, the *Victory* quilt was pictured in full color. The caption under the picture assured the readers that they could reproduce the quilt in cotton materials for about $6.

Thirteen of Bertha Stenge's quilts were hung for a one-woman show at the University of California Art Gallery from November 9 to December 1, 1941. The exhibition was arranged by Eugen Neuhaus, head of the Art Department. In the summer of 1943, seventeen of her quilts were exhibited at the Art Institute of Chicago. *Newsweek* for August 2, 1943, carried a review of the show titled, "Quilts as Art." Mrs. Stenge apparently objected to the review and wrote *Newsweek* that she was offended by the inaccuracies. Hilda Loveman, the magazine's art editor, wrote to Mrs. Stenge on August 6, explaining the difficulties she had in obtaining the correct information about the exhibit. Nevertheless, it was a review by a major news publication. It was considered a success, and Mrs. Stenge received a great deal of publicity.

As a result of the publicity, she received letters from friends and strangers asking to come to her home to see her quilts. She was extremely generous with them, and her personal correspondence is full of letters from visitors thanking her for her hospitality and the opportunity to see her wonderful quilts. They frequently

Quilting Show *of pieced and appliqué print and solid-color cottons, 93" x 78", made by Bertha Stenge, 1943. Collection of Frances Stenge Traynor. Courtesy of Merikay Waldvogel.*

Thirteen patterns are hand held in blocks approximately 6" x 6" and fifty-two pieced blocks form the quilt's border.

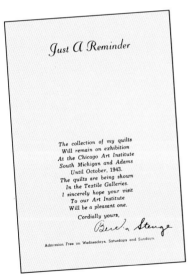

Just A Reminder

The collection of my quilts
Will remain on exhibition
At the Chicago Art Institute
South Michigan and Adams
Until October, 1943.
The quilts are being shown
In the Textile Galleries.
I sincerely hope your visit
To our Art Institute
Will be a pleasant one.
Cordially yours,
Bertha Stenge

Admission Free on Wednesdays, Saturdays and Sundays.

Stenge's invitation to her one-woman quilt exhibition at the Art Institute of Chicago in October 1943. Collection of Joyce Gross.

Opposite: Florence Peto's quilt booth at the Nutley (NJ) Antiques Show (1950) featuring antique appliqué quilts she had for sale as well as her book American Quilts and Coverlets. *Mrs. Peto set up the booth but became ill and her daughter-in-law, Dorothy, and her daughter, Marjorie, staffed it. Courtesy of Joyce Gross.*

Bertha Stenge's appliqué quilt Victory, *winner of* Woman's Day National Needlework Exhibition *held in 1942 and shown in the March 1943 issue. The copy claimed that readers could "reproduce the double-size quilt in cotton materials for about $6.00." Collection of Merikay Waldvogel.*

mention Bertha's husband and her daughters, so it is obvious that "show time" was a family affair.

In November 1954, thirty of her quilts were shown at the annual Women's International Exposition of Arts and Industries at the New York Armory as a featured attraction, according to the *St. Cloud (MN) Daily Times.* Mrs. Stenge was in New York for the week of the show.

According to a letter from Florence Peto to Emma Andres dated December 6, 1954, "Bertha Stenge was in New York for the duration. Thirty of her quilts were shown. . . . I'm not sure that was the best place for Bertha to receive the recognition she deserves. I asked her when I wrote what results she had had from the exhibition. She said—exasperation, for her quilts came home with nail holes in them where they had been hung."

Upon Mrs. Stenge's death her quilts were divided among her three daughters, Ruth, Frances, and Prudence. When Ruth died, her quilts were divided among her three daughters.

In 1971, Mrs. Stenge's daughter Prudence Fuchsman offered some of her quilts for sale. The *Chicago Tribune* (April 5, 1971) numbered the quilts for sale as eleven, and the *Quilter's Newsletter* (no. 24, 1971) as nine. Two-thirds of Bertha Stenge's quilts remain in the family. The Art Institute of Chicago has the *Toby Lil* in its collections, and the Chicago Historical Society has *Chicago Fair.* The Quilt Conservancy owns the *Lotus* and the author owns *Tiger Lily.* Prudence kept *American Holiday, Victory,* and *Life's Flower Basket.* Unfortunately no records of the sale were kept so the present whereabouts of some of the quilts are unknown.

In 1979, seven of Mrs. Stenge's quilts were exhibited at the "Patch in Time IV" show in San Francisco. The show was curated by the author and the quilts included *Iva's Pincushion,* the *Quilt Show,* the *Quilting Bee, Holidays,* and *Victory,* through the courtesy of her daughters, Frances Traynor and Prudence Fuchsman.

Bertha Stenge died in Chicago after a brief illness on June 18, 1957. Florence Peto, a personal friend, wrote to her daughter: "The world has lost a magnificent needlewoman; there isn't another with the skill and ingenuity she displayed."

Florence Cowdin Peto
(11/25/1881–8/29/1970)

Florence Peto's influence, more than that of the other three women profiled here, extended far beyond the world of quilting. As testament to her excellence as a quiltmaker, one of her quilts is in the Henry Ford Museum and another in the collection of Shelburne Museum. She wrote extensively for such periodicals as *Antiques, American Home, Woman's Day, McCall's Needlework & Crafts Annual*, and *Hobbies*. She was the author of two books, and she researched and drafted three pattern books for the Spool Cotton Company that were distributed nationwide. She lectured to hundreds of groups and influenced museums to appreciate quilts as historical documents, encouraging them to exhibit and purchase them for part of their permanent collections. She researched the history of some of our best-known museum quilts, such as Mary Totten's *Rising Sun* in the Smithsonian Institution, Sophonisba Peale's *Star Medallion* in the Philadelphia Museum of Art, and the *Demarest Medley* quilt in the Newark Museum.

She was born Florence Cowdin, one of four children, on November 25, 1881, in New York State. She married Joseph Peto and had two children, John and Marjorie. John and his wife had two sons, but Marjorie did not marry and lived at home with her parents. Marjorie went to Europe during World War II as a lieutenant in the army nurse corps. She later became a captain, and was retired from the corps as a lieutenant-colonel. After the war, Marjorie returned as Director of Babies Hospital at the Medical Center and lived at home with her parents.

Following are excerpts from Florence Peto's letters to Emma Andres between 1939 and 1957, copies of which are in the author's collection. Miss Andres and Mrs. Peto met only once, after many years of corresponding, when Miss Andres was visiting

relatives on the East Coast and discovered that her "pen pal" lived nearby in New Jersey.

In the years 1939–43, there were many letters. As the years went by and Mrs. Peto became busier, the letters were less frequent and shorter. But Florence always remembered Emma at birthdays, Easter, and other holidays. She sent copies of all of her writings and many newspaper clippings. Most of the letters are typewritten about everyday life, but frequently she wrote at length about an antique show or her latest find— descriptions that are invaluable to those of us interested in quilt research.

Her first letter to Miss Andres, dated April 1, 1939, began, "It was courteous of *McCall's* to send you my address for I enjoyed receiving your letter and am pleased to hear about your hobby. All this began as a hobby with me, too, only I feel now that, after giving thirty-five lectures this winter to Women's Clubs and for the Board of Education to their textile arts groups—well, it has outgrown the hobby stage.

"My photographs of American-made quilts, spreads and woven

coverlets number over three hundred—all have authentic histories verified by family records and papers. . . . What I desire to do in gathering this material [is to]preserve the memory and identity of the quiltmaker as well as her needlework."

On May 24, 1940, Mrs. Peto wrote, "Well I lived through another broadcast experience—the subject was 'Friendship and Album Quilts.' An announcer asked all the questions and I had all the answers. The Index of American Design, for whom I gave the broadcast, has given me a lot of photographs of quilts, some of them most unusual. Now I have a lot of research to do for there were no histories for them."

On August 13, a letter stated, "Am to repeat my lecture at the World's Fair; the Index of American Design considered it so successful they want to throw another 'Quilting Bee.'"

March 21, 1941: "You are right; they keep me talking and talking. It is a wonder someone hasn't popped me into the U.S. Senate—the only place where there is more talking than I do! Next week, I give two more lectures and again one on the 26th. So when you do not hear from me, picture me with my mouth open."

June 3, 1941: "For two days before Memorial Day, I gave out and lay flat on my back in bed; suppose I was overdoing it with all that work in such awful hot weather. . . . Was enough better yesterday to hobble over to town and get my hair done—because I had decided that even if I was going to die, I could not die with hair in such a mess as mine was! I felt very sorry for myself. Got a new permanent—a short haircut and now have curls all over my pate and look as nearly like Shirley Temple as I ever will!"

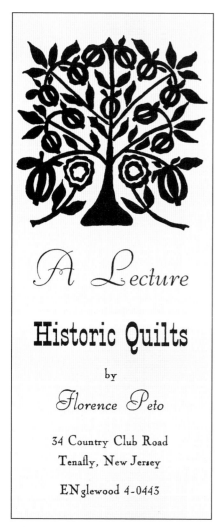

A Lecture

Historic Quilts

by

Florence Peto

34 Country Club Road
Tenafly, New Jersey

ENglewood 4-0443

Flyer for Peto lecture, The Joyce Gross Collection.

June 6, 1941: "Maybe it was to pay me back for the Shirley Temple hairdo that I have been ill in bed most of the time since."

June 13, 1941: "My husband is funny: he can cook fairly well and clean up pretty well but there won't be a dish left if I don't get around soon! He comes upstairs like a small boy after I've heard a crash and tries to say that he didn't do it—it slips from some place or bounces without anyone being near it—so help him."

December 8, 1941: "The fun of Christmas is halted with the awful news over the radio last night; we were visiting friends in Brooklyn and we all sat as if stunned when we heard the news and realized the perfidy of Japan. Who knows what may be ahead. Must go and make a pudding now—we have to eat no matter how sad and worried. Maybe I'll get out my Nine-Patch quilt and try to finish it—practice what I preach. Good to keep busy when you are in trouble or worried."

August 10, 1944: "I finished my Nine-Patch quilt and sent it out to Ohio to be quilted—certainly I couldn't do it. It looked very pretty."

February 13, 1945: "My friend in Ohio, who gave my Nine-Patch out to be quilted, writes that it is done, all but the binding!"

February 26, 1942: "After I put my aunt on her train yesterday in New York, I wandered into the stores; it was fatal for I bought two new dresses and a red, red hat! I was feeling rather 'down' and thought it might cheer me up to have some new clothes. I'm usually very conservative about what I wear on the platform but the next group listening to me is going to have to look at a red bonnet! I hope there will be no bulls among them."

February 6, 1942: "Well the lightning has struck; daughter Marjorie goes away next Tuesday. I cannot imagine my life without her gay and loving personality about. She has been such a good child; how I hope she can be of service to her country and yet not have to undergo too many cruel hardships herself."

February 15, 1942: "More dead than alive after a week of the most emotional upset; my daughter finally

got away this morning. I did not go over to New York to say 'Goodbye' for I felt one more Goodbye would finish me. Well, that's that; I simply cannot cry anymore. My heart is so leaden you could make bullets out of it. We didn't cry when we parted with her though—we laughed—she is the grandest girl to have laughs with!"

September 11, 1945: "We have had such thrilling news: Marjorie is on her way home! She is to sail from Marseilles on September 15. The house is being scrubbed until the paint comes off!"

December 2, 1945: "Since Marjorie came home this house has been in such a whirl. I've had no time for my own affairs and, indeed, owe everyone I know a letter."

Miss Andres (left) and Mrs. Peto (right). Collection of Joyce Gross.

January 4, 1955: "Guess what Marjorie gave me? Sure, a quilt! A beautiful Cockscomb and Currants, exquisitely quilted! It was fun to see the children of the family on Christmas afternoon when we rode over to my son's."

The last letter from Mrs. Peto to Emma Andres is dated December 1957, in which she enclosed a "hankie" with the brief note, "This month has been so busy! Talks, quilt judging at E. Orange, the Thanksgiving with the whole family here."

Mrs. Peto liked to enter her quilts in contests and state fairs. Evidently she sometimes entered the same contests as Bertha Stenge, though in different classifications. She sent a quilt to the contest at the Eastern States Exposition as late as 1967, three years before her death. She wrote a friend on November 28, 1967, "The work on some of the antique pieces will never be duplicated but it is far from a 'lost art.' 'Lost art of quilting'—indeed—there is excellent work being done commercially and privately even by myself, and I've a bureau drawer full of ribbons to prove it."

Quilts from her antique collection were frequently on display. In 1948, the New York Historical Society had an exhibition of quilts. A newspaper article states that it included Mrs. Peto's "entire collection of fifty quilts." In 1955 the Henry Ford Museum had an exhibit of her quilts. On December 12, 1967, she wrote to a friend, "Now I am getting ready for the big exhibition of my whole quilt collection in the Suffolk County Museum in Stony Brook, Long Island. It will go from January 23 to April 23. This will be the last time I will show quilts as a collection for, after the show, I mean to offer many of them for sale. I have already sold some. I need the storage space."

On February 17, 1968, she wrote the same friend, "I . . . have taken apart my lecture chart, which I used to illustrate my Quilt Talk. There were forty-five quilt blocks—handmade by me, of course, and in colors that would project from the platform. Now I am having pillows made of several, and our local Woman's Exchange sells them as fast as I get them made. They are attractive and different. But I feel as if I were betraying old friends."

In the 1960s, Florence Peto launched another career. She began giving classes, writing articles, and designing kits for crewel embroidery. She didn't forsake her interest in quilts and historical textiles; she just

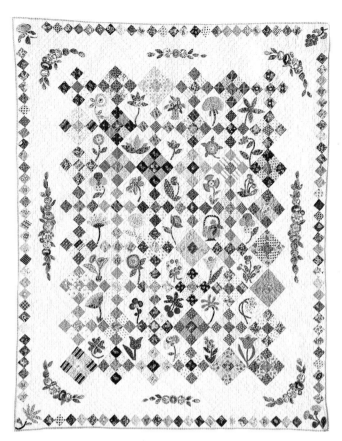

added another full-time interest. She frequently complained about being tired, but she loved the activity and complained just as bitterly if she had to give up something because of ill health.

Mrs. Peto had always been very close to her daughter. When Marjorie died following surgery in 1969, Mrs. Peto took to her bed and never got up again. She died about a year later at the age of 88.

A note from John Peto (Florence's son) dated September 30, 1970, told Emma Andres the sad news, "Dear Friend of my Mother's, who passed away August 29, 1970. Marjorie died a year ago today and I am still trying to settle her estate while starting on my mother's—so you can see that my neglect in not notifying you before this is excusable—I hope. I know Mother always looked forward to your letters and hope you will understand my problem."

What a full life Florence Peto led, and what a wonderful heritage she left us! There are many historical quilts in museums from her collection. Four of the most famous of her antique quilts are the *Emeline Dean* quilt and the

Calico Garden *pieced and appliqué quilt of hand-blocked and copperplate prints, chintzes, and French and English calicoes, 49" x 39", made by Florence Peto, circa 1950.* Woman's Day *(December 1951) described the quilt: "Familiar nine-patch blocks blend with imaginative posies and fruit, no two alike. Sprays consisting of flowers and leaves cut from chintz contrast with the border of tiny appliquéd squares." Collection of the Shelburne Museum, gift of Florence Peto (accession #52-548). Courtesy of Shelburne Museum.*

Demarest Medley in the Newark Museum, Mary Totten's *Rising Sun* in the Smithsonian Institution, and Sophonisba Peale's *Star Medallion* in the Philadelphia Museum of Art.

Conclusion

Myrtle Mae Fortner, Jeannette Franc Dean-Throckmorton, Bertha Stenge, and Florence Cowdin Peto are but four of the large number of "fine" quiltmakers of the 1940s and 1950s. Their names are well-known to most of us, not necessarily because they were the best but because their quilts were placed in museum collections. There are many more who deserve the same honor.

Uncle Eli's Quilting Party

Erma H. Kirkpatrick

E li Whitney is widely recognized as the father of the cotton gin. In the southern part of Alamance County, North Carolina, he is equally well known as the "uncle" of a quilting party.

"Uncle Eli's Quilting Party" has been a tradition in the Eli Whitney community since 1931. This all-day event takes place every year on the first Thursday in April when the countryside is bursting with bloom. White dogwood blossoms stand out against the green pine trees, and the deciduous trees are budding or leafing just enough to soften and color the outline of their bare branches. The many shades of green contrast with the reds and browns of the newly plowed fields. Masses of yellow daffodils and lavender thrift bloom along the banks at the edge of the road. Neither rain nor a cloudy sky can spoil the brightness of the landscape, which appears even brighter on a dark day. The spring morning journey to the quilting party sets the stage for pleasures to come.

The day begins early. By 8:00 A.M., the first cars have parked outside the big old brick gymnasium, which is the Eli Whitney Community Center. Nannie McBane, quilter, quilting instructor, and coordinator of the quilting party, unlocks the door.

Inside, the gym seems huge, cavernous, and bare. One or two quilts have been "put in" the previous day so the quilters can get an early start. Otherwise the gym is empty, with bleachers folded against the wall and tables stretched out along one end, ready to receive food.

Gradually the room comes to life. A table is placed by the door so that everyone can sign the register and make a nametag to wear.

Erma Kirkpatrick is a quiltmaker who since 1977 has opened her home on Tuesday mornings to women from other countries who want to learn to quilt. She was a regional coordinator for the North Carolina Quilt Project and wrote part of North Carolina Quilts. *She has presented three research papers to the annual seminar of the American Quilt Study Group. 503 Whitehead Road, Chapel Hill, NC 27514–4832.*

In 1982, Nannie McBane (center, holding quilt) received a quilt commemorating the fiftieth anniversary of Uncle Eli's Quilting Party. Courtesy of Erma Kirkpatrick.

The Burlington (NC) Times-News *and the* Alamance News *(Graham, NC) faithfully cover Uncle Eli's Quilting Party every April; other area papers feature it occasionally. These 1980s clippings are from the collection of Erma Kirkpatrick. Photo by Terry Wild Studio.*

Early arrivals unfold chairs brought from the storage room and begin to wipe off the bleachers. As women bring in quilted items for display, willing hands help drape the quilts over the now-dusted bleachers or hang them on clotheslines that are stretched around the walls. Suddenly there is a quilt show!

Mildred Guthrie, who has been attending these quiltings since 1958, arranges her display of quilts in one corner and begins to demonstrate quilting on her oval hoop. Mildred is famous for her beautifully quilted white-on-white quilts that commemorate happenings such as Tricia Nixon's wedding in the White House rose garden, the astronauts' landing on the moon, Watergate, and the Iranian hostage crisis. Often one of these is on exhibit.

By now, more quilting frames have been set up and quilters settle down to work. Visitors drift through, observing the quilters and the quilts on display. The tradition is that everyone who attends must put in at least one stitch. The gentle murmur of voices becomes a loud hum as acquaintances from previous years are renewed and new quilting friends are made. Quilting techniques and designs are discussed and patterns are exchanged. Uncle Eli's party is in full swing.

Nannie McBane moves around the room, cheerful and unassuming, answering questions, available to help. She appears more like a favorite quilting friend than an event coordinator. She says that Uncle Eli's "just happens" each year. Most events of this magnitude would "just happen" by means of a steering committee, plus three subcommittees, each of which would meet several times and be urged to file a written report to assist next year's committees. In fact, Uncle Eli's "just happens" because the members of the community have lived and worked together for so many years and also because Nannie has checked ahead of time to make sure that enough quilts will be available to

work on, enough people will bring tea, and that the chairs from the volunteer fire department down the road have been delivered. In her low-key way she manages the many details of the day.

The day and the quilting progress. Around noon the covered dishes are uncovered, the line forms, a blessing is asked, and a serious attack is made on the heavily loaded tables. Quantities of deviled eggs, fried chicken, ham biscuits, sausage biscuits, homemade rolls, chicken salad, potato salad, molded salad, green salad, pasta salad, three-bean salad, and slaw are available. There are assorted casseroles. Desserts include pies (pecan, apple, chess, lemon chess, lemon, chocolate, coconut, and cherry) and cakes (chocolate, coconut, and pound). There are also chocolate and butterscotch brownies, lemon squares, and an assortment of cookies. The quilters take pride in their cooking as well as in their quilting.

Quilting resumes briefly after "dinner," but by three o'clock the day begins to wind down. Children will be coming home from school, the evening meal must be prepared and the evening chores accomplished. Quilting frames are dismantled and unfinished quilts folded carefully to be taken home and worked on. Gradually the quilt show disappears and the gym returns to its empty state as chairs are put away, trash disposed of, and people leave. Few, if any, quilts have been completed, but the day has been rewarding nonetheless.

This is a description of Uncle Eli's Quilting Party in the 1980s. Its founder, Ernest Dixon, might be surprised at how it has changed over the years. Mr. Dixon was the first principal of Eli Whitney High School, which was formed in 1921 by combining the schools from five small neighborhoods. The first classes were held in an abandoned cotton gin, hence the name. (The school song was "There Were Five Little Schools," and

Views of the 1982 Uncle Eli's Quilting Party capture the activities at the annual event: the set up, spontaneous sharing, quilting, viewing, and eating. Courtesy of Erma Kirkpatrick.

the teams were known as the "Ginners.")

Ernest Dixon, a Quaker who came from a heritage of people who were trained to act on their beliefs, was the leader in the formation of the school. He believed that one high school of ninety students could better educate students than five smaller neighborhood schools. He also believed that schools should be community gathering places. Acting on these principles, he helped establish the school in 1921, became its first principal and, in 1931, proposed and engineered the first of Uncle Eli's quilting parties.

Eighty women gathered in April 1931 at that first quilting. Thirteen quilts were put in and thirteen were completed. A lunch of sandwiches and coffee was served by the freshman home economics students. In the eve-

ning, families came to eat supper and admire the completed quilts. A prize was given for the first quilt finished that day. After supper there was music: fiddling, performances by local bands and two glee clubs, and then everyone joined together to sing old-time songs. The evening ended with a candy pull. That day was such a success that it became the "first annual."

By the end of the 1930s, the quilting was a well-established tradition. At that time there was a school building and the quilting was held in the auditorium from which seats had been removed. Teachers marched the classes of younger children through to observe the quilters. High school students and their teachers dropped by when they had free time. Quilts were put on the frames in the morning and completed by the end of the day. A woman or a group from a church or other organization arrived with a quilt

and quilters committed to working on that quilt. Sometimes the quilt owner would provide a picnic lunch for her quilters. There was spirited competition among the groups to be the first to finish a quilt. Families joined in for supper and evening activities.

In 1935, a quilt in the scarlet-and-black Whitney School colors was made in the Lone Star pattern for Vice President John Nance Garner, a Texas native. North Carolina representative John Umstead presented the quilt to the Vice President. A Little Red Schoolhouse quilt, also in the school colors, was quilted at the 1937 party and given to Mr. Dixon, by that time retired.

By 1940, the PTA had scheduled a meeting on the evening of the quilting. Quilts worked on in the daytime were exhibited at the meeting and prizes were awarded for the prettiest and for the first one completed. PTA committees were in charge of hospitality, exhibits, and judging. After-meeting activities might include oratory, a performance by the community choir, square dancing, or a taffy pull.

In the early 1950s, Robert Hutchison, retired agriculture teacher from the Whitney School and official host at the party, designed a quilt that was a map of Alamance County. Women in the community made the quilt, quilted it at the party, and presented it to Kerr Scott, governor of North Carolina and a native of Alamance County. Today that quilt is a prized possession of the Scott family.

During the 1960s, attendance decreased. A comment in a 1962 newspaper account was that the day is not to be measured by the number attending.[1] Even so, it is obvious that there was less interest in the party that year when only thirty-one women attended and two quilts were completed. Compare that with the record, set earlier, of twenty-two quilts quilted and two tied. During this period it became the custom to bring recipes, plants, and cuttings to ex-

change. Another popular tradition evolved in the 1960s when Mildred Guthrie began bringing quilts to exhibit as well as to work on. Since that time bringing "bragging quilts" to show off has become a well-established feature of the quilting party.

In 1974, students at Eli Whitney were absorbed into a larger school. Just as consolidation had created the school, further consolidation closed it. Some in the community were concerned lest the party cease to exist. Others believed that the quilting should end when the school closed. Through the strong efforts of a few persons such as Nannie McBane, Pat Bailey, and others, the party weathered the crisis of the school's closing and continued without interruption. In 1971, when the building was empty and had been vandalized, the quilting was moved to the firehouse. By the following year, although the school building had been taken down, the big brick gymnasium that remained had become a facility of the county recreation department, so the quilting party returned to its original site.

Curiously, during this period, the party picked up in terms of the number of persons attending. In 1974, 150 persons came and seven quilts were completed. In 1976, there were 180 persons and four quilts. In 1977, the April 10 issue of the *Burlington Times-News* pictured University of North Carolina folklore student Laurel Horton quilting on her Attic Windows quilt, one of six worked on that day.

In 1979, 220 persons registered, including a number of women from other countries who brought and worked on a quilt they had made as a gift to the hostess of an English conversation class in Chapel Hill. In 1980, there were four quilts in frames and 218 persons registered. Another quilt was brought by the same international group.

The next year marked the fiftieth anniversary of the quilting party and there was a big celebration attended by 366 people, including the North Carolina Commissioner of Agriculture and local notables. A play was presented. Special efforts were made to bring back quilts that had been quilted at Uncle Eli's parties. These included Mr. Dixon's Little Red Schoolhouse and Governor Scott's map of Alamance County. John Nance Garner's quilt could not be located. Nannie McBane designed an anniversary quilt (which was later presented to her). Each block represented a quilt that had been quilted at an earlier party: a red-and-black Little Red Schoolhouse, a map of the county, a Lone Star, and so on. The central medallion proclaimed in embroidery:

THE COMMON THREAD
50 YEARS
UNCLE ELI'S QUILTING PARTY
1931–1981.

That year, one longtime participant was quoted in a newspaper as saying: "All the old hands—they're gone. These are all newcomers from Chapel Hill and the home demonstration clubs."[2] (Chapel Hill is fifteen miles away.) All who attended, including the "newcomers," were warmly welcomed.

Since the celebration of the fiftieth anniversary, attendance has very gradually decreased and the focus of the day has changed. In the beginning, the purpose of the quilting was to use the school as a gathering place, to bring together parents and other members of the community, and to complete as many quilts as possible in one day. Only active participants attended and the audience consisted of teachers and school children with an occasional husband dropping by. Some longtime residents suggest that Mr. Dixon also had in mind the fact that early in the history of the school, when children were bused in from small neighborhoods, parents felt some threat of a loss of their community identity. This seems natural. All but one of the neighborhoods were

farm communities that centered on a church (Baptist, Methodist, and Friends Meeting), while the largest, Saxapahaw, was a mill town. Although the children did well together in school, Mr. Dixon recognized that the parents needed to be brought together. As Dorothy McBane put it, "Some of the neighborhoods just didn't gee-haw together."[3]

Today the quilting party is a social gathering for which the Eli Whitney community is well known. People attend from as far away as fifty miles. It is no longer a family community event. There is less dedication to putting in and completing a quilt. In fact, seldom is a single quilt completed by the end of the day. The number of quilts in frames has gone down and

Little Red Schoolhouse quilt, pieced solid-color cottons, 83" x 66". Applied binding, red quilting thread, 5 stitches per inch. Presented to Ernest P. Dixon at the 1937 Quilting Party in recognition of his role as founder of the quilting party and longtime principal of the Eli Whitney School. Collection of the Ernest Dixon family. Photo by Terry Wild Studio.

Ernest P. Dixon, a moving force in the establishment of the Eli Whitney School in 1921 and principal 1921–36. He introduced the quilting party in 1931 as a means of bringing parents together and making the school a center for community activities. Picture taken in the mid-1930s. Courtesy of the Ernest Dixon family.

the number of visitors has increased. It has become a spectator sport. Dorothy McBane says, "It's more of a Show and See than a real quilting."[4] Groups of senior citizens are bused in to view the quilts and the quilters. Quilters themselves are more interested in the social aspects of the day than they are in a day of hard work at the quilting frame. Few would say today as Nannie McBane's mother-in-law did some years ago on the evening of the quilting, "I feel as if I've been working like fighting fire all day."[5] Edith Mogle, a former teacher at Whitney, sums it up, "It has become a celebration of quilting rather than a quilting."[6]

There is some concern expressed about the future of the quilting. Mildred Guthrie says it is left up to the young people whether it continues,[7] and others tend to agree. Nannie McBane says, "I hope it will continue, but I just don't know."[8] She wonders if changes would be helpful, such as a return to a business meeting during the course of the day. She regrets that people now leave so early in the day because when people leave they take their quilts, and so the quilt show disappears.

No matter what the future holds, it is clear that Uncle Eli's Quilting Party has been and is presently a source of pride to this small rural community. For example, in 1948, when the county celebrated its centennial, each community was invited to participate in the parade and Eli Whitney chose Uncle Eli's Quilting Party as the theme for its entry. The float had on it a quilting frame with quilters around it. The Little Red Schoolhouse quilt, which was displayed on the float, bears scars from that occasion because it rained on the parade, causing the dye from the crepe paper streamers to run onto the quilt.

Furthermore, there is evidence that residents have given high priority to their attendance at the party. Miss Sallie Jane Braxton for many years was known for being the first to arrive and one of the oldest quilters present. In 1973, just before her 90th birthday, she died. The newspaper account of her death reported that she had quilted until a week before her death and that she had missed only one of Uncle Eli's quilting parties (and that, the newspaper explained, was because

she was expecting a shipment of baby chicks momentarily).[9]

Dorothy McBane, who worked in five different local mills, told each employer when she was hired that she needed to have the day off on the first Thursday in April. She was never turned down. Dorothy is still a regular attender, and has missed only five of the parties (all because of illness).[10]

In 1972, Mrs. Addie Richardson explained that she had missed only one quilting and that was in 1936 when she was in the hospital. Dorothy McBane tells that one year when Mrs. Richardson was all ready to go to the quilting she discovered that her car would not start. She was so confident that she would be missed that she simply sat on her front porch waiting for someone to come for her. And someone did!

James and Donna Patterson, packed and ready to move to Georgia, delayed driving to their new home so that Donna could attend the quilting.[11] Margaret Elkins, in 1979, took the day off from her job as a secretary at Wachovia Bank to attend the quilting. Also in 1979, Barbara James took her three daughters out of school and brought them to the quilting, explaining that she believed that this was an important part of their heritage.

Newspaper coverage has been extensive. Every year the *Alamance News* and the *Burlington Times-News* have covered Uncle Eli's party in great detail. Other newspapers have run occasional feature stories. Several area residents have better clipping files than the newspapers.

From time to time a political candidate has considered this gathering worthy of his presence and has dropped by and allowed himself to be photographed with a needle in his hand.

One remarkable fact is that it has never been a fundraising event. There is no admission charge, there has never been a quilt raffled. There is not even a donation basket to defray the cost of paper plates, utensils, napkins,

or ice for the tea. Members of the community, the recreation department, and the local technical college quietly underwrite the costs.

The Common Thread was the name of the quilt made for the fiftieth anniversary celebration in 1981. In some ways today's party has very little resemblance to the ones of earlier years, but there is a common thread. The common thread is that quiltmaking, through all the changes in the nature of Uncle Eli's Quilting Party, has been the means of bringing people together, once more demonstrating that the process of quiltmaking often has a value greater than that of the quilted product.

Notes and References

[1]Unidentified clipping, Aretta Barrett scrapbook, Eli Whitney, NC, July 16, 1986.

[2]Wendy McBane, "Y'all Sit Down, Quilt a Spell at Uncle Eli's," *The News and Observer* (Raleigh, NC), April 4, 1981, 7.

[3]Dorothy McBane, interview with author, Eli Whitney, NC, July 16, 1986.

[4]Dorothy McBane, interview with author, Eli Whitney, NC, July 16, 1986.

[5]Nannie McBane, interview with author, Eli Whitney, NC, July 22, 1986.

[6]Edith Mogle, conversation with author, July 24, 1986.

[7]James and Mildred Guthrie, interview with author, Snow Camp, NC, July 31, 1986.

[8]Nannie McBane, interview with author, Eli Whitney, NC, July 22, 1986.

[9]Unidentified clipping, Pat Bailey file, Graham, NC, July 1986.

[10]Dorothy McBane, interview with author, Eli Whitney, NC, July 16, 1986.

[11]Dorothy McBane, interview by author, tape recording, July 16, 1986.

Sources used in writing this chapter include these newspapers: *The Daily Times-News*, Burlington, NC; *Alamance News*, Graham, NC; *Winston-Salem Journal*, Winston-Salem, NC; *News and Observer*, Raleigh, NC. (Most of these newspaper clippings were from scrapbooks and clipping files belonging to members of the community. Some had no identification as to date or specific newspaper. Files and scrapbooks belonged to Aretta Barrett, Daphne Newlin, Pat Bailey, and Nannie McBane). In addition, the author relied on personal recollections of nine of Uncle Eli's parties in the 1970s and 1980s.

The Land of Cotton

Quiltmaking by African-American Women in Three Southern States

Bets Ramsey

"**I** learned to quilt from my grandmother," said Sam Ella Gilmore.

"We lived in the country, near Rogersville, Alabama, and we raised cotton and everything we needed to eat. We had to chop cotton and pick it and take care of sheep, hogs, ducks, and chickens. My first job at making quilts was ironing the pieces of cloth for my grandmother. Us kids would whip the cotton with a switch to make it fluffy when she needed filler. The women went from house to house in winter to quilt and have prayer meeting. I'd play under the quilt frame when they came to our house. They liked to show off new patterns and trade with each other.

When I got older, I made four quilts for my hope chest. I sewed them on the sewing machine and we quilted them. You know, I never did use them quilts 'cause I ran off to get married and left them behind. I stopped making quilts until I quit work and joined a senior citizens' group. Now I've made four more quilts. I just love to cover up in bed and enjoy the handwork my friends have put in my quilt."[1]

Interviews with thirty-five black women, quiltmakers from Alabama, Georgia, and Tennessee, reveal a variety of backgrounds and circumstances that have shaped their lives. Many of them grew up in rural settings, ranging from sharecroppers' farms to extensive plantations, and a few have lived only in the city. They are joined together by the common bond of quilting and share their knowledge with each other the same way their mothers and grandmothers did.

Lillian Beattie at 101 years old. Courtesy of Mike O'Neal.

Appliqué wall hanging of print and solid-color cotton and poly/cottons, 70" x 55", made in 1981 by Lillian Beattie (born in Athens, Tennessee, 1879–1988). Poly/cotton back turned to front as edge treatment with no quilting. Collection of Mr. and Mrs. John Majors. Courtesy of Hunter Museum of Art, Chattanooga.

Bets Ramsey is an exhibiting fiber artist who has specialized in quilts and quilt research of the southeastern United States since 1971. She has curated numerous exhibitions and is the co-author of The Quilts of Tennessee *and* Southern Quilts: A New View, *among other publications. 322 Pine Ridge Road, Chattanooga, TN 37405.*

My study was directed toward determining any existing characteristics and differences between the quilts made in the country and those made later by the same women after they had moved to the city. I wished to see how ready access to fabric, better income, social interaction, and urban styles affected their products and whether certain qualities set them apart as African-American quilters.

Herbert G. Gutman, in *The Black Family in Slavery and Freedom 1750–1925*, states that during the period of slavery, despite harsh conditions, the family unit was strongly maintained whenever possible, not without maternal and paternal sacrifice and determination, and sometimes with the assistance of an extended family. Providing meager household necessities was a challenge requiring ingenuity and hours of work.[2]

This view is confirmed by Ozella Angel, who grew up in Heflin, Alabama. Her paternal grandmother bore sixteen children, eight in slavery, and was able to maintain the family intact during that period. Then, as a free woman, she was employed on the plantation of Lena Blake, who taught her to sew. Some years later she acquired a farm and became self-sufficient. Even later, instead of resting from long labor, she assumed the responsibility for nurturing the four motherless children of her son.[3]

The major importation of slaves from Africa to the United States occurred in the seventeenth and eighteenth centuries when they were brought to New England and the Eastern and upper Southern states for various labors. After the invention of the cotton gin and an increased production of cotton, black people made a major migration to the lower South. Planters from Virginia, the Carolinas, and other regions envisioned possibilities for vast financial gain and quickly purchased extensive holdings in Georgia, Alabama, and Mississippi.

Joseph Gee, for example, a planter from Halifax, North Carolina, established a vast plantation in central Alabama in 1816. Through the years it prospered until Gee's descendants sold 4,000 acres in 1895.[4]

The removal of the landowners' households, including slaves, to new territory was a cumbersome ordeal. After Gee's death and those of his two nephews who inherited his estate, the land went to another relative, Mark H. Pettway, in 1846. It took weeks for Pettway and his family to prepare and move a caravan of a hundred or more slaves and their household goods. Except for one cook, the slaves literally walked from North Carolina to Alabama.[5]

Large and small plantations and farms used the services of black people who were considered the property of their owners. Their treatment varied from humane to extremely cruel. Many diaries, letters, and later interviews with former slaves supply vivid descriptions of mistreatment and suffering.[6]

Families were separated for financial gain. Alice Stovall, of Stevenson, in northeast Alabama, never knew her mother's relatives. Her mother was sold at the age of twelve and never saw her family again. Shortly thereafter, the Civil War ended and she was freed. She came to live in north Alabama where she married and remained the rest of her life.[7]

Unlike Alice Stovall's mother, her son-in-law's family had experienced better relationships with their owners, the Johnsons, in nearby Hollywood, Alabama. After Emancipation, having been in the household for several generations, the black Johnsons were given their freedom and a choice of some property. Both Johnson families, black and white, held each other in high regard, acknowledged kinship, and remained close to one another. All members of the black Johnson family became successful landowners themselves by the twentieth century.[8]

Perhaps less dramatic are the eighteenth- and early nineteenth-century account books from several large plantations in the South, which demonstrate the continuity of family groups maintained there for generations. One can see a fairly stable community working together to maintain itself with food and clothing and to make a profit for the landowner.[9]

Plantation tasks were many and those with special skills became valued for their work. Domestic duties went along with agricultural production and some women were trained in spinning, weaving, sewing, and quilting. Thomas Chaplin, in his plantation journal, complained of the number of mouths he had to feed— thirty besides his family—and only ten of those were put in the field for profitable employment. The others included a cook, seamstress, washer, nurse, housemaid, hog-tender, and "Old Sam, who can't do anything." Chaplin had already lost thirty or forty slaves in payment for bad debts.[10]

Helen Moore has described the loom house and production of goods, including blankets and quilts, accomplished by the slaves of her ancestors near Murfreesboro, Tennessee, in the mid-1800s.[11] Examples made by other black women attest to their skills and can be seen in a Plume quilt in the Tennessee State Museum,[12] a floral appliqué quilt,[13] and a stuffed Rose quilt,[14] all made by household slaves.

The grandfather of Luella Jones was sold when he was a young boy because he was not large enough to do field work. He went to the home of a landowner near Rome, Georgia, where he was taught various processes of textile production. His primary task was to prepare cotton for weaving, for his mistress had to clothe an extensive household. In addition to spinning thread and warping looms, he learned to knit cotton thread into sturdy socks that were long-lasting, a skill he retained all his life. He was accomplished at his work and was regarded with affection. When his master went off to war, he accompanied him, "to polish his boots," said Luella, and had many tales of adventure to tell his grandchildren in later years.[15]

Reconstruction brought about immediate or gradual relocations. Some chose to stay close to their former owners, as employees or sharecroppers, and others acquired land by gift or purchase for establishing their own farms.[16] Some individuals moved into Northern or Southern urban areas seeking employment. Jacqueline Jones, in *Labor of Love, Labor of Sorrow*, points out that many of those moving to the cities were widows, with families, who were unable to continue living on the land. With few employment opportunities other than laundress, cook, or maid, they faced a continual struggle for existence. Men, too, had little choice but to accept low-paying jobs with negligible security. During slavery it had been necessary to improvise and make-do and the lesson continued for those who were free but of little means.[17]

The majority of the women I interviewed grew up in the country, for the most part on self-sufficient farms where their families raised cotton, sugar cane, fruit and vegetable gardens, and livestock. Cotton was the main cash crop. "My father was a wonderful farmer," said Ruby Beard, who lived near Athens, Georgia. "He raised everything we used. We all helped with the crops and the animals, but my main job was looking after the younger children. We were a big family and everyone had a share in the work."[18] Sarah Belle Douglas said her father worked for a white family and only grew a garden for his family's use, and, with the cow given him by his employer, they needed little else.[19]

Elizabeth Hudson's family lived in middle Georgia and she described them as sharecroppers, that is, her father rented land that he paid for with a share of his produce. He had a prosperous farm where he raised peaches, cotton, sugar cane for sorghum, and a kitchen garden. His wife worked for the Walker family where she learned to cook, sew, and keep house. Hattie Clark, Mrs. Hudson's grandmother, passed down a meticulously made Double Irish Chain quilt, which is evidence that she was well trained in sewing arts. Dating from about 1880 or 1890, new material was purchased for its making. Pieces for the blocks when seamed were 1¼" square. The thin cotton batt and even stitches are exceedingly fine. It is obvious that much time and expense went into the making of this quilt.[20]

Growing up on a farm near Huntsville, Alabama, meant that Rose Grimmett was well acquainted with hard work. She plowed, chopped and picked cotton, and could manage almost any other required task. She began to make quilts when she was six years old and has never put them aside.[21] Mattie Porter, from the same area, did not have to perform such physical labor. Her father was a nursery-man and she was not expected to do field work. She did sometimes have to pick leftover cotton scraps from neighbors' fields for use in making quilt filler.[22]

Another viewpoint is found in the story of Hattie Bryant's life in Commerce, near Athens, Georgia. Her grandmother was a slave whose oldest daughter was three years old when their freedom was granted. The grandmother had acquired fine needlework skills, which, in turn, she passed on to her daughter, Mathilda. Mathilda, Hattie's mother, was reared in the home of the Wards, a highly respected white family in the community. They were able to provide her with advantageous educational opportunities. (During the interviews, I found this practice of placing a young black girl in a white home for the purpose of educating her repeated a number of times.)[23] She married

Star quilt pieced of print and solid-color cottons, 81" x 73", made circa 1930 by Estella Daniel of Emerson, Georgia (?–1955). Muslin back with applied binding of two fabrics and filler of hand-carded homegrown cotton. Collection of Bets Ramsey. Courtesy of Bets Ramsey.

Autumn Leaves quilt of appliqué print and solid-color cottons made by Hattie Bryant (born in Commerce, Georgia, 1903) and quilted by Eastside Senior Neighbors, Chattanooga, Tennessee, 1980. Cotton back turned to front as edge treatment with filler of polyester. Private collection. Courtesy of Bets Ramsey.

James Wood, a prosperous cotton farmer, reared a family, had careers as lawyer, nurse, and businesswoman, and all the while made beautiful quilts.[24]

Hattie remembers the years, after she reached the age of nine, when the annual fall Cotton Fair was held following sales at the cotton market. Her father was likely to sell eight or ten bales of cotton, at $1,000 a bale, and cotton seed, also at a good price. The fair was a time to celebrate. He gave each of his children $100 to spend in any way they chose. Sometimes they bought magic tricks and theatrical props for future home performances for which they charged 1¢ admission.

With similarities and differences, these families share their identities as being black and Southern, with rural backgrounds. Most of them raised cotton, produced quilts, and had contact with white people to greater or lesser extent. Several common practices occurred in their quiltmaking. Almost all the women interviewed stated that quiltmaking was largely a matter of necessity and economy. The string quilt, narrow strips stitched on paper that was later removed, was the most ordinary type of utility quilt. String quilts were made in squares that were simply joined together, or diamonds that could form stars, or triangles for spider webs. Young girls had their first lessons making the blocks and, when a sufficient number had been completed and they were tall enough to sit at the quilting frame, they learned to quilt.[25]

Ozella Angel described a utility quilt she helped make for her brothers' use. She called it Cocklebur and it was made from all kinds of scraps and worn-out clothing, including overalls. "It was plenty heavy enough to keep them warm on the coldest nights," she said. She took a square of fabric, folded it in half and the half in thirds to make a point (a contemporary name for this technique is Prairie Points). Starting in the center of the quilt, she sewed overlapping units in concentric circles to cover the entire surface. The result was a heavy bedcover that did not require batting but was given a backing.[26]

These everyday quilts were made from the smallest scraps and odd-shaped pieces, easily assembled, and required little or no preplanning. Because most of the households were engaged in the production of cotton, filler was readily available. Some women hand-carded the cotton into batts, a few beat and fluffed the cotton with slender branches, and they occasionally used recycled quilts or blankets as filler.

Feed and flour sacks were widely used for backing. Preparation of the sacks was assigned to the younger girls. "We'uns would have to take the stitching out of the sacks," said Vacie Thomas.

Then we'd wash and bleach them in a black washpot out back, using homemade lye soap and well water.[27] We had an old broom handle to stir with and punch down the sacks. After they had boiled a while we lifted them out with the stick and rinsed them in a tub of water. When they had dried we had to iron them so's they'd be smooth for sewing. Sometimes the letters didn't come out but the sack was used anyway. It was a lot of hard work but we were taught to use what we had and not waste anything.[28]

Some women dyed the sacks with walnut, oak, or red mud to give color and show less soil. Even small sugar and tobacco sacks were unravelled and dyed for quiltmaking. Sometimes the thread was saved for later sewing or quilting. Inexpensive domestic (unbleached muslin) was often purchased for the back, or, less often, a coarse gingham called cotton checks.

Better quilts were made from a variety of patterns with the use of all-new material or combined with scraps. Gentleman's Bowtie, Trip Around the World, Flower Garden, Bear Paw, Sweet Gum Leaf, Basket, Fan, Star, Love Triangle, Nine Diamond (Nine Patch), Yo-Yo, Spool, Wedding Ring, Dutch Doll, Dresden Plate, Brick

Layer, and Log Cabin were mentioned as being favorites of mothers and grandmothers. Several women were noted for their ability to cut and make original designs, including intricate appliqué, and to execute fancy embroidery on wool and silk crazy quilts.

Hattie Bryant talked about her mother.

My mother was very talented. She could cut out anything and make her own patterns for appliqué, anything she wanted. I try to follow her example today. She was always thinking of other people, too. By the time I was nine years old I had pieced five tops for my hope chest. When the local teacher was burned out my mother had a quilting party to quilt my tops for her. She told me I'd have time to make more but the same thing kept happening, and I never did have any quilts to take when I got married. I've made quilts all my life, starting when I was five years old, in 1908.[29]

Two major factors contributed to the twentieth-century move in the South from country to city. The first occurred just before and during the 1920s when successful cotton farmers lost a series of annual profits due to the infestation of the boll weevil.[30] Without money to plant the next year's crop and recover losses, farmers were forced to sell or give up farms and seek employment elsewhere. The movement in the 1920s, according to those interviewed, was made by whole families—father, mother, children, and perhaps other relatives attached to the household. When local employment was found, it was usually low-paying jobs requiring physical labor. The woman who went to work was limited almost entirely to domestic or laundry service.

The second motivation was the opportunity for employment arising with industrialization. Most of the survey participants came to the city as young wives whose husbands were offered jobs in factories, foundries, or industrial plants. Aware of the precarious existence and hard work connected with farming, they sought a better life. Women, and some men, were anxious for more educational advantages for their children than could be obtained in the country.[31]

The Drummond children attended a country school that offered six grades of education. They were unable to attend high school in the nearest sizeable town because of the expense of room and board. Even so, their education went further than many children who were required to give more time to farm labor.[32]

Luella Jones did not live near enough to a school for black children to allow her to attend so she had to pay to go to school in Dalton, Georgia. Then she went to a boarding high school in Knoxville and college in Rogersville, Tennessee. Her family had to pay for her entire education, and it was a great sacrifice.[33]

The move to the city presented more occasions for social interaction than had occurred in the country. Associates in the workplace, neighbors, and acquaintances made through church and club memberships became a part of urban life.[34] There was a much wider circle of influence than before. Women who had traded quilt patterns among half-a-dozen members of their quilting parties began to have access to quilt patterns in magazines and newspapers and had a broader base of exchange.

"Mrs. Hobday, the woman I worked for, used to buy patterns and material for quilts and she let me copy her patterns," said Ruby Beard.

The pattern for the Umbrella Girl I made in 1960 was given to me by a friend. I still like to read quilt magazines and get patterns from them but I don't make as many quilts as I used to. I love to quilt, even when it is for someone else. I've done a lot of quilting for people who have made cross-stitch tops or inherited quilt tops. They are always pleased and I am too, because I make a little money that way.[35]

Lillie Johnson is a talented quiltmaker who did not become serious about quiltmaking until she broke her arm and was forced, temporarily, to leave her job in a textile mill. She had rejected her mother's efforts to

Tree of Life pieced of print cottons made circa 1900 by Lizzie Harris (born in Fayetteville, Tennessee, and died circa 1960). Woven cotton plaid back with filler of hand-carded homegrown cotton. Collection of Sarah Belle Harris Douglas. Courtesy of Hunter Museum of Art, Chattanooga.

H quilt of pieced print and solid-color cottons made in 1968 by Vacie Thomas (born in Selmer, Tennessee, 1908–84) and quilted in 1974. Cotton print back turned to front as edge treatment with cotton blanket filler. Private collection. Courtesy of Hunter Museum of Art, Chattanooga.

teach her to make quilts at a younger age. She recalls that her grandmother had made quilts, but she was not interested at that time. Having moved from south Georgia to a small farm on the outskirts of Chattanooga and, "not working out," the grandmother apparently tried every pattern that came her way. Years after her death several dozen unquilted tops were discovered. The grandmother's work was imaginative and well constructed. She made quilts with evident pride and personal fulfillment.[36]

Mrs. Johnson began quiltmaking in the 1970s by making several appliqué quilts from kits, then by using a 1940s set of patterns to make the Bible

Verses quilt. Before long she was doing appliqué work of her own design, making several stunning medallion quilts. After retirement she was able to spend most of her spare time making quilts and, like her grandmother, wanted to try patterns new to her and experiment with her own ideas. She exchanges patterns with her friends, both black and white, and always has future quilts in mind. Although her late grandmother and mother failed to teach her to quilt, she has since gained a strong emotional bond with them through her own recent work.[37]

Ella McCoy was born in Chattanooga and, although her mother and grandmother were quilters, she waited until her retirement to make her first quilt, the Lone Star. As a young married woman she did dressmaking at home. When she was able to go to work she became a skilled machine operator working in a hosiery mill, a shirt factory, and a blue jeans factory. She was assigned as "utility girl" because she could work any of the machines in the plant. Her quiltmaking reflects her training. It is highly original, somewhat unorthodox, and is pieced and quilted by machine.[38]

Another quiltmaker, rebellious in youth, was Lillian Beattie, who learned to piece quilts as a girl living in the household of a white family in Athens, Tennessee. It was not until she visited the New York World's Fair in 1939 and saw appliqué work that she had any interest in quiltmaking. Using newspaper and magazine illustrations as pattern sources, she selected appropriate material for the interpretation of her designs. Her daughter, Helen Spurgeon, with whom she lived, says some days her mother got so carried away with her work that she forgot her noon meal. At the age of 108, Mrs. Beattie had to give up her sewing due to failing eyesight. Her work is included in several private collections and she has received considerable acclaim.[39] Mrs. Beattie died in 1988 at age 108.

In comparing the family quiltmaking of the women interviewed here with studies done by Roland Freeman, Laurel Horton, and Maude Wahlman, several points come to mind. These writers did their research in predominantly black communities having little interaction with white people. This may account for their finding a greater continuity of tradi-

tional African concepts. Or it may mean the people there have less regard for conformity of pattern in quiltmaking.[40]

African-American quilts have been characterized by Maude Wahlman as having strips, bold colors, large designs, asymmetry, multiple patterns, and improvisation. She calls this a "creolization" derived from African textile ideas and religious symbolism in combination with American technical and functional ideas.[41] The quilts she selected, primarily from Alabama and Mississippi, support her thesis. The fallacy here, as Cuesta Benberry often reiterates, is that the black experience is as long and varied as the white experience. Many samplings of work by black quiltmakers in varied locations and economic levels are necessary to give a valid interpretation of the nature of African-American quilts.

While the five previously stated characteristics are found in many quilts made by black women, the same can be found in the work of white women. For example, at the Cleveland Museum's fine exhibition,

Umbrella Girl of pieced and appliqué print and solid-color cottons, 83" x 74", made circa 1960 by Ruby Beard (born in Athens, Georgia, and living in Chattanooga, Tennessee). Cotton batiste back with back turned to front as edge treatment and with thin cotton filler. Collection of Ruby Beard. Courtesy of Hunter Museum of Art, Chattanooga.

The Afro-American Tradition in Decorative Arts, curator John Vlach included a quilt made in Triune, Tennessee, about 1910. A variety of blocks were arranged in strips and joined together, with a larger, more dominant block placed near the center. He maintains that the quilt shows elements of African design in the strip arrangement, multiplicity of pattern, improvisation, and off-center placement.[42] Another Tennessee quilt, made about 1870 or a little later by Iora Almina Philo Pool, shows great similarity. She lived in Sunbright, in Morgan County, and she was white.[43]

Roland Freeman, on the other hand, has not found it necessary to interpret the work of the women he interviewed. As a photographer, he presents his findings as he sees them

Shoo-Fly of pieced print and solid-color cottons made by Rose Grimmett (born in Huntsville, Alabama) and quilted by the Senior Neighbors' Friday Quilters, 1987. Muslin back turned to front as edge treatment with polyester filler. Collection of Rose Grimmett. Courtesy of Hunter Museum of Art, Chattanooga.

and does not attempt to equate them with African concepts. Thus, he sees worth in the work for its own sake. He meets the quiltmaker where she is, with her own values, experience, and training. He sees her attitudes and imagination reflected in the quilts she produces. He sees the work as an extension of that person and accepts it for what it is without looking for a hidden and unintentional meaning.

In a lecture presented at the Southern Quilt Symposium, Laurel Horton expressed concern for the categorizing of black and white quiltmakers.

As often happens with cultural matters that are not fully understood, the existence of African retentions in American quilts is now sometimes misused as a way of stereotyping black quiltmakers and exaggerating black and white differences. A

set of aesthetic guidelines is being applied to African-American quilts, and those which do not match the criteria risk being regarded as "impure" examples. . . . In an effort to recognize African-American design traditions as a viable part of American culture, we are moving toward a polarization. I think this is a dangerous situation because it emphasizes the differences rather than the similarities among black and white quiltmakers.[44]

It is true that Rose Grimmett still makes quilts from the patterns her mother taught her—Nine Diamond, Shoo-Fly, Monkey Wrench. She has less regard for the alignment of blocks and correct placement of pieces than her friends. When she joins the blocks in rows to put together with vertical stripping, the horizontal strips don't always match, but this is not a concern. As a farm laborer, she was used to putting quilts together as rapidly as possible, and she retains that habit. Her carefree attitude and good nature are expressed in her work. Her more particular friends shrug and say, "That's Rose!" when they stitch on one of her quilts.

On the other hand, Rose's friends

who have attended quilt workshops and taken classes at their senior centers have benefitted more noticeably. Some still follow long established routines, but they have acquired new ideas and gained greater assurance in their own abilities. Even though they are now able to purchase fabric for quiltmaking, many still like to use leftover scraps mixed with a variety of new material for a "scrap look." Color selection is often bold and bright, reflecting the choice of an individual's clothing, but the use of strong color is not an inherent characteristic. Some black women prefer muted and pastel colors. These women blend the past and the present in their quilts by whatever choices they make.

The move from country to city has been personified by the two sisters, Maggie and Dee, in Alice Walker's brilliant story, "Everyday Use." Their mother awards the family heirloom quilts to Maggie, who will remain in the country, use the quilts, and remember their makers. Dee, her liberated sister who has affected urban styles, sees the quilts as momentarily fashionable elements of interior decoration. She fails to recognize and value their sentimental meaning.[45]

Although my findings are less extreme than the attitudes expressed in the Walker story, there have been noticeable changes occurring in the lives of the women I interviewed. The majority of them grew up in the country and learned domestic skills in the home at an early age. Frugality was impressed upon them and they learned the art of making-do with whatever was available. Many of their families had been closely associated with white people where instructional opportunities were possible. Most of them had moved to the city between the ages of fifteen and twenty-five.

For fifty or sixty years they have resided in an urban area offering experiences and situations quite different from those of their early homes. They have, generally, enjoyed a higher standard of living, better job offerings, educational advantages for their children, a wider circle of acquaintances through church, social, and civic organizations, and have been exposed to trends in fashion and culture.[46]

The most significant change in the work done by these quiltmakers is in purpose. Sixty years ago most of their quilts were made out of need. Today they are made for pleasure. Leisure time provides a chance to try new patterns gleaned from quilt books and magazines or traded with friends. New ideas come from attending quilt shows and seeing the work of others. One can see pride and a sense of worth increase when a quilt is exhibited or admired. These women are not concerned with the monetary value of their work, even though they are aware of the present popularity and market value of patchwork. They are making quilts for personal satisfaction and the pleasure of working in an excellent support group of friends. Most of their quilts will be given as gifts to a family member, a minister, or a dear friend, for they know that a gift of a quilt is a gift of oneself and establishes a loving bond between giver and receiver. There may be differences in their quilts and those of their grandmothers, but the transition has been merely an extension of a long tradition enduring through many generations.

Notes and References

[1]Sam Ella Gilmore, interview with author. All interviews were conducted in Chattanooga, TN, during 1986–88.

[2]Herbert G. Gutman, *The Black Family in Slavery and Freedom, 1720–1925* (New York: Pantheon, 1976), 213.

[3]Ozella Angel, interviews with author.

[4]Nancy Callahan, *The Freedom Quilting Bee* (Tuscaloosa, AL: Univ. of Alabama Press, 1987), 32–34.

[5]Ibid.

[6]Jacqueline Jones, *Labor of Love, Labor of Sorrow: Black Women, Work, and the Family from Slavery to the Present* (New York: Basic Books, 1985). The subject is dealt with extensively throughout the book.

[7]Ethel Daniel, interviews with author. (Daniel is the daughter of Alice Stovall.)

[8]Daniel interview.

[9]Gutman, appendices.

[10]Theodore Rosengarten, *Tombee, Portrait of a Cotton Planter* (New York: Morrow, 1986), 152–53.

[11]Helen Moore, interview with author. The blankets and a Pieced Rose quilt are in the collection of the Tennessee State Museum.

[12]Plume and Star quilt made by an unknown slave, ca. 1860, for Emma Florida Lispscomb McFall. In collection of the Tennessee State Museum.

[13]Bets Ramsey and Merikay Waldvogel, *The Quilts of Tennessee: Images of Domestic Life Prior to 1930* (Nashville, TN: Rutledge Hill Press, 1986), 2–3; quilt made by Eliza McKenzie, slave in the family of Tennie Marler, ca. 1860. Private collection.

[14]Stuffed Rose quilt made by a member of the Hughes family and her slaves, 1848–49, Calhoun, GA. Private collection.

[15]Luella Jones, interviews with author. When she was a child her grandfather taught her to knit a small sock, still in her possession, using saved string and broom straws for knitting needles.

[16]The will of Matthew Ramsey (1792–1867) of Amite County, MS, left $7,000 to Jackson Ramsey, "a freedman who formerly belonged to me and who has been a faithful servant, to be invested and annual income paid to him until his youngest child is of age and educated, after which the sum will be withdrawn and divided among Jackson Ramsey and his children, share and share alike."

[17]Jones, *Labor of Love*, 73–76.

[18]Ruby Beard, interview with author.

[19]Sarah Belle Douglas, interview with author.

[20]Elizabeth Hudson, interview with author.

[21]Rose Grimmett, interview with author.

[22]Mattie Porter, interview with author.

[23]Jones, in *Labor of Love*, attributes the practice to a desire to lessen overcrowding at home and bring in extra money. My interviews did not substantiate that theory.

[24]Hattie Bryant, interview with author.

[25]Ramsey and Waldvogel, 77.

[26]Ibid., 78. Another name is Pine Burr, a pattern not made exclusively by blacks as some have claimed.

[27]The phrase "strong lye soap" is probably used by someone who is unacquainted with homemade soap. Lye is, indeed, strong, but when it is combined with household grease or renderings, it is chemically changed to make a mild soap of excellent cleaning quality.

[28]Vacie Thomas, interview with author.

[29]Bryant interview.

[30]Roger L. Ransom and Richard Sutch, *One Kind of Freedom: The Economic Consequences of Emancipation* (Cambridge, England: Cambridge University Press, 1977), 171–72.

[31]Jones, *Labor of Love*, 75.

[32]Ramsey and Waldvogel, 78.

[33]Jones interview.

[34]Jones, *Labor of Love*, 75–76.

[35]Beard interview.

[36]Lillie Johnson, interview with author.

[37]Ibid.

[38]Ella McCoy, interview with author.

[39]Lillian Beattie, interviews with author. Her work has been shown at the Hunter Museum of Art, Chattanooga; the St. Louis Art Museum; the Arvada Art Center in Colorado; the American Museum of Quilts and Textiles, San Jose; and elsewhere.

[40]Roland Freeman, *Something to Keep You Warm* (Jackson, MS: Mississippi Department of Archives and History, 1981); Laurel Horton, "Quilts Like My Mama Did," slide/sound documentary (Columbia, SC: McKissick Museum, 1986); Maude Wahlman, "The Art of Afro-American Quiltmaking: Origins, Development, and Significance" (Doctoral diss., Yale University, 1980).

[41]Wahlman, "Aesthetic Principles," *Afro-American Folk Art and Crafts*, ed. William Ferris (Jackson, MS: University Press of Mississippi, 1983), 86–92.

[42]John Vlach, *The Afro-American Tradition in Decorative Arts* (Cleveland: Cleveland Museum of Art, 1978), 74.

[43]Ramsey and Waldvogel, 12, 108.

[44]Horton lecture, "Perspectives on African-American Quilts," Southern Quilt Symposium, Hunter Museum of Art, Chattanooga, TN, March 22, 1988.

[45]Alice Walker, "Everyday Use," in *In Love and Trouble: Stories of Black Women* (New York: Harcourt Brace Jovanovich, 1973), 47–59.

[46]Those interviewed and their children have been employed as cook, dietician, practical nurse, surgical nurse, custodian, teacher, beautician, insurance agent, noncommissioned officer in the United States Army, fire department captain, and Tennessee Valley Authority executive, to name but a few of their occupations.

Index